MENTAL HEALTH AND OFFENDING

This book explores the controversial relationship between mental health and offending and looks at the ways in which offenders with mental health problems are cared for, coerced and controlled by the criminal justice and mental health systems. It provides a much-needed criminological approach to the field of forensic mental health.

Beginning with an exploration into why the relationship between mental health and offending is so complex, readers will be introduced to a range of perspectives through which mental health and its relationship to offending behaviour can be understood. The book considers the politics surrounding mental health and offending, focusing particularly on the changing policy response to mentally disordered offenders since the mid-1990s. With dedicated chapters concerning the police, courts, secure services and the community, this book explores a range of issues including:

- The tensions between the care, coercion and control of mentally disordered offenders
- The increasingly blurred boundaries between mental health and criminal justice
- Rights, responsibilities, accountability and blame
- Risk, public protection and precaution
- Challenges involved with treatment, recovery and rehabilitation
- Staffing challenges surrounding multi-agency working
- Funding, privatisation and challenges surrounding service commissioning
- Methodological challenges in the field.

Providing an accessible and concise overview of the field and its key perspectives, this book is essential reading for undergraduate and post-graduate courses in mental health offered by criminology, criminal justice, sociology, social work, nursing and public policy departments. It will also be of interest to a wide range of mental health and criminal justice practitioners.

Dr Julie D. Trebilcock is a Senior Lecturer in Criminology at Middlesex University. Her research has been primarily concerned with the management of violent and sexual offenders with personality disorders under the Dangerous and Severe Personality Disorder (DSPD) Programme, and the more recent Offender Personality Disorder (OPD) pathway. Her particular expertise is with the institutional pathways and legal authority by which high-risk offenders are detained, Parole Board and Mental Health Tribunal decision-making, and the staffing challenges involved with working with offenders with personality disorders.

Dr Samantha K. Weston is a Senior Lecturer in Criminology at Keele University. Much of her research has focused on how risk prevention measures have been applied to vulnerable and marginalised populations including those who use substances, (potential) victims and (potential) perpetrators of child sexual exploitation and those experiencing mental ill health. This focus has enabled her to explore in more detail how certain, marginalised and vulnerable populations and their behaviour are understood, 'managed', 'controlled' and responded to.

'The field of mental disorder and crime is so all-encompassing as to put off many authors, but not criminologists Trebilcock and Weston. Their *Mental Health and Offending: Care, Coercion and Control* makes accessible a wealth of material. The book deftly takes the reader through the complex intersection of socio-legal issues pertaining across the criminal justice process as they affect those with mental disorder. Their analysis alone of the recent political landscape makes the book an outstanding contribution'.

—Jill Peay, *Professor of Law, The London School of Economics and Political Science, UK*

'This book provides an authoritative and accessible exploration of some of the key dilemmas in offender mental health care. Combining academic rigour and a clear understanding of the issues faced in everyday practice, the authors address the core theme of care *vs.* control in a wide range of criminal justice settings, from initial contact with police, through custody, to rehabilitation in the community. This book is essential reading for criminal justice students but is also an invaluable resource for mental health professionals who want to better understand some of the core dilemmas in this complex field'.

—Dr. Colin Campbell, *Consultant Forensic Psychiatrist, King's College London and South London and Maudsley NHS Foundation Trust, UK*

'The relationship between mental health and criminal justice has been the source of much contemporary penal policy debate. This clear and comprehensive book allows the reader to grapple with issues ranging from health ethics to the care of those with mental disorders in secure settings. It should be a must read for anyone wanting to understand the complex range of theories, issues and public policy responses to the challenges posed to the seemingly intractable dilemma of how to best serve the needs of those with mental health needs and to ensure that the needs of justice are met'.

—Anita Dockley, *Research Director, The Howard League for Penal Reform, UK*

MENTAL HEALTH AND OFFENDING

Care, Coercion and Control

Julie D. Trebilcock and Samantha K. Weston

Routledge
Taylor & Francis Group

LONDON AND NEW YORK

First published 2020
by Routledge
2 Park Square, Milton Park, Abingdon, Oxon OX14 4RN

and by Routledge
52 Vanderbilt Avenue, New York, NY 10017

Routledge is an imprint of the Taylor & Francis Group, an informa business

British Library Cataloguing-in-Publication Data
A catalogue record for this book is available from the British Library

Library of Congress Cataloging-in-Publication Data
A catalog record has been requested for this book

ISBN: 978-1-138-69792-8 (hbk)
ISBN: 978-1-138-69793-5 (pbk)
ISBN: 978-1-315-52037-7 (ebk)

Typeset in Bembo
by codeMantra
Printed and bound by CPI Group (UK) Ltd, Croydon, CR0 4YY

JDT: For Ben, Dylan and Keira
SKW: For Eden and Oscar

CONTENTS

BOXES

TABLES

ABBREVIATIONS

A&E	Accident and Emergency
AA	Appropriate Adult
AC	Approved Clinician
ADHD	Attention-Deficit Hyperactivity Disorder
AMHP	Approved Mental Health Professional
AOT	Assertive Outreach Team
AP	Approved Premises
ASW	Approved Social Worker
ATR	Alcohol Treatment Requirement
BAME	Black, Asian and Minority Ethnic
CARATS	Counselling Assessment and Throughcare Services
CBT	Cognitive Behavioural Therapy
CCG	Clinical Commissioning Group
CCRC	Criminal Cases Review Commission
CDA 1998	Crime and Disorder Act 1998
CIT	Crisis Intervention Team
CJA 2003	Criminal Justice Act 2003
CJCSA 2000	Criminal Justice and Courts Services Act 2000
CJS	Criminal Justice System
CMHT	Community Mental Health Team
CPA	Care Programme Approach
CPIA 1964	Criminal Procedures (Insanity) Act 1964
CPN	Community Psychiatric Nurse
CPS	Crown Prosecution Service
CQC	Care Quality Commission
CRC	Community Rehabilitation Company
CRHT	Crisis Resolution and Home Treatment
CRT	Crisis Resolution Team
C(S)A 1997	Crime (Sentences) Act 1997
CSAP	Correctional Services Accreditation Panel
CTO	Community Treatment Order
CTP	Care and Treatment Planning

DBT	Dialectical Behavioural Therapy
DoH	Department of Health
DHS	Directorate of High Security
DRR	Drug Rehabilitation Requirement
DSM-5	Diagnostic and Statistical Manual 5
DSPD	Dangerous and Severe Personality Disorder
DVCVA 2004	Domestic Violence, Crime and Victims Act 2004
ECHR	European Convention on Human Rights
ECtHR	European Court of Human Rights
FME	Forensic Medical Examiner
GLM	Good Lives Model
GMC	General Medical Council
GP	General Practitioner
IAPT	Improving Access to Psychological Therapies
ICD-11	International Classification of Diseases 11
IOPC	Independent Office for Police Conduct
IPCC	Independent Police Complaints Commission
IPDE	International Personality Disorder Examination
IPP	Imprisonment for Public Protection
IRC	Immigration Removal Centre
HBPOS	Health-based place of safety
HCP	Health Care Professional
HCR-20	Historical – Clinical – Risk 20
HO	Home Office
HM	Her Majesty's
HMIC	Her Majesty's Inspectorate of Constabulary
HMICFRS	Her Majesty's Inspectorate of Constabulary and Fire & Rescue Services
HMIP	Her Majesty's Inspectorate of Prisons
HMIP	Her Majesty's Inspectorate of Probation
HMPPS	Her Majesty's Prison and Probation Service
L&D	Liaison and Diversion
LASPO 2012	Legal Aid, Sentencing and Punishment of Offenders Act 2012
LHB	Local Health Board
MAPPA	Multi-Agency Public Protection Arrangements
MAPPP	Multi-Agency Public Protection Panel
MHA	Mental Health Act
MHAC	Mental Health Act Commission
MHIT	Mental Health In-Reach Team
MHRT	Mental Health Review Tribunal
MHTR	Mental Health Treatment Requirement
MOJ	Ministry of Justice

MSU	Medium Secure Unit
NAAN	National Appropriate Adult Network
NCISH	National Confidential Inquiry into Suicide and Safety in Mental Health
NHS	National Health Service
NHSE	National Health Service England
NICE	National Institute for Health and Care Excellence
NIMH	National Institute of Mental Health
NIMHE	National Institute for Mental Health in England
NMHDU	National Mental Health Development Unit
NOMS	National Offender Management Service
NPCC	National Police Chiefs' Council
NPIA	National Policing Improvement Agency
NPS	National Probation Service
OASys	Offender Assessment System
OCD	Obsessive-Compulsive Disorder
OGRS	Offender Group Reconviction Scale
OPD	Offender Personality Disorder
ORA 2014	Offender Rehabilitation Act 2014
PACE 1984	Police and Criminal Evidence Act 1984
PB	Parole Board
PbR	Payment by Results
PCA 2017	Policing and Crime Act 2017
PCC	Police and Crime Commissioner
PCL-R	Psychopathy Checklist – Revised
PD	Personality Disorder
PHE	Public Health England
PICU	Psychiatric Intensive Care Unit
PIPE	Psychologically Informed Planned Environment
PSO	Prison Service Order
PTSD	Post-Traumatic Stress Disorder
RAR	Rehabilitation Activity Requirement
RC	Responsible Clinician
RM2000	Risk Matrix 2000
RMA	Risk Management Authority
RMO	Responsible Medical Officer
RNR	Risk Need Responsivity
ROTL	Release on Temporary License
RSHO	Risk of Sexual Harm Orders
RSU	Regional Secure Unit
SARN	Structured Assessment of Risk and Need
SOPO	Sex Offender Prevention Order
SOSO	Sex Offender Supervision Order

SOTP   Sex Offender Treatment Programme
TC   Therapeutic Community
VRS   Violence Risk Scale
VRAG   Violence Risk Appraisal Guide
YOT   Youth Offending Team

CHAPTER 1

The controversial relationship between mental health and offending

INTRODUCTION

Despite having a one in ten million chance of being killed by a stranger with schizophrenia (about the same chance of being hit by lightening) (Szmulker, 2000), we live in a society that appears to be preoccupied by the dangerousness of those with mental health problems. The stigma surrounding mental disorder can be acute and one reason for this is that mental disorder and crime, particularly violent crime, are often thought to be closely linked. While this may sometimes be true, the links are often overstated by the media, with academic research suggesting that people with mental health problems do not pose the level of risk that some assume. Moreover, people with mental disorder are consistently shown to be more at risk of violence from others (Brekke et al., 2001). However, the relationship between mental disorder and violence is an 'ideologically charged issue' (Markowitz, 2011:39) and despite common agreement that the violence committed by those with mental disorder is low, punitive and risk-orientated policies that unfairly target those with mental illness often prevail (see Chapter 3).

We begin this chapter by discussing the challenges involved with defining what we mean by key concepts like 'mental disorder', 'mental illness' and 'mentally disordered offenders'. The chapter introduces readers to clinical definitions of mental disorder, as defined by diagnostic classification systems like the American Psychiatric Association's (APA) *Diagnostic and Statistical Manual of Mental Disorders*, fifth edition (DSM-5; APA, 2013) and the World Health Organization's (WHO) *International Classification of Diseases*, 11th edition (ICD-11; WHO, 2018), along with the legal framework under the Mental Health Act (MHA) 1983 (as amended by the MHA 2007) in England and Wales. After considering a range of definitional issues we turn our attention towards the relationship between mental health and offending. This is followed by a discussion of the challenges involved with assessing the risk posed by mentally disordered offenders and consideration of some of the key methodological limitations in the field of forensic mental health. The chapter concludes by discussing the implications of these issues for policy and practice.

MENTAL DISORDER, MENTAL ILLNESS AND MENTALLY DISORDERED OFFENDERS

Below we briefly consider some of the main ways in which mental disorders are defined. Reflecting the lack of consensus about key concepts in the mental health field (Winstone, 2016), this discussion is split into 'clinical', 'legal' and 'social/political' definitions of mental disorder. Indeed, the lead editor of the DSM-4, Allen Frances, is quoted as having said: '[t]here is no definition of a mental disorder. It's bullshit. I mean, you just can't define it' (Walvisch, 2017:7). The limited agreement about key concepts in forensic mental health generates many challenges, since a range of different actors must make important decisions on the basis of these concepts. While differences in terminology and understanding are most evident between those with different professional backgrounds and training, the very nature of mental disorder means that even similar experts will contest meanings.

'Mental disorder' is a common and broad term that usually refers to a very wide range of mental health problems. It is also our preferred term throughout the book, in part because key disorders that we discuss, such as 'personality disorder' are captured by this term, but not by 'mental illness'. 'Mental illness' is a more specific term that tends to focus on those mental disorders that can be thought of in terms of an *illness*, such as schizophrenia. According to the National Institute for Health and Care Excellence (NICE) (2011), depression, anxiety disorders, obsessive-compulsive disorders (OCD) and post-traumatic stress disorder (PTSD) are the most common mental health problems in the UK, affecting up to 15% of the population at any one time. However, lifetime prevalence of mental disorder will be much higher, with one US study estimating that 50% of the population will experience a mental disorder by their 75th birthday (Kessler et al., 2005). In the UK, the largest single cause of disabilities is reported to be mental ill health, with a cost of £105 billion a year to the economy (Mental Health Taskforce, 2016). In addition to the high economic cost, mental disorders such as depression can be lifelong conditions with periods of relapse and remission, and are associated with higher mortality rates (NICE, 2011). This reminds us of the close links between mental and physical health, and that people with long-term and severe mental illness die on average 15–20 years earlier than people without (Mental Health Taskforce, 2016).

In line with common parlance, official documents (such as those authored by the Ministry of Justice and Department of Health) and other academics in the field, we commonly use phrases such as 'mentally disordered offenders' or 'offenders with mental disorder' throughout the book to refer to *people* who have a mental health problem and have also come into contact with the criminal justice system. While this should mean the terminology we use is familiar to those working and studying in the field, it is important to acknowledge there are many problems with these phrases (see Peay (2017) for a discussion). One obvious problem follows from the lack of consensus about what mental disorders are or what we mean by 'offenders', a discussion we come to below. Phrases such as 'mentally disordered offenders' are problematic because they reduce people to their worst behaviour as offenders, and it is essential to recognise 'first and above all – offenders are human beings' (Vandevelde et al., 2017:72). Peay (2017:641) also argues against treating offenders with mental health problems as an isolated category, not least because this would presuppose the existence of another group of 'mentally ordered offenders' and 'such a clear-cut division is problematic'.

CLINICAL CLASSIFICATIONS OF MENTAL DISORDER

One of the most established classification tools used to diagnose mental disorders is the DSM-5, with the most recent edition published in 2013. First published in 1952 by the APA, it has been described as 'one of the most influential and controversial terminological standards ever produced' (Pickersgill, 2012:544).[1] Another well-known classification system, available in 43 languages and used by more than 100 countries across the globe, is the WHO's ICD-11. The latest and 11th revision of the ICD was released in June 2018,[2] although the WHO has been responsible for the ICD since 1948 following publication of the ICD-6.[3] In contrast to the DSM-5, the ICD-11 covers all diseases, disorders and related health problems, with only one part relating to behavioural and mental disorders.

The development of these classification tools is closely linked to the growth of psychiatry (and other 'psy' disciplines such as psychology and psychoanalysis) and the 'systematic control' of mental disorder that began in the nineteenth century (Rogers and Pilgrim, 2014). An extended critique about these clinical classification systems, and the medical model on which they are based, is provided in Chapter 2. However, it is worth noting here, that mental disorders are often extremely difficult to define, and our understandings of mental disorder are culturally and historically specific. Duggan (2008:505) argues that questioning the 'very existence' of a disorder is common within the mental health field, in a way that it is not in other more traditional areas of medicine. Most mental disorders do not have a clear and specific aetiology (in the way that other medical problems do) and most mental health problems can only be diagnosed by self-reported behaviours and clinical observation (rather than specific tests like those found in general medicine) (Anckarsäter et al., 2009).

LEGAL DEFINITIONS AND FRAMEWORK

The main legislation that governs the detention and community management of people with mental disorder in England and Wales[4] is the MHA 1983 (as amended by the MHA 2007), although offenders with mental health problems may also be governed by other legislation including the Mental Capacity Act 2005, the Criminal Procedure (Insanity) Act 1964 (as amended by the Criminal Procedure (Insanity and Unfitness to Plead) Act 1991 and the Domestic Violence, Crime and Victims Act 2004). While we explore the MHA 1983 (as amended by the MHA 2007) throughout the book, a full discussion of these other legislative powers is beyond the scope of this text and readers are directed to Beswick and Gunn (2017) and Bartlett and Sandland (2014) for further information.

At this early stage it is important to highlight how powerful mental health law is. Pilgrim and Ramon (2009:274) help illuminate this point when they note that 'the power to constrain, without trial, those posing a putative future risk is only found in mental health services and in statutes to pre-empt terrorism'. Similarly, Simon Wessely, chair of the recent independent review of the MHA in England and Wales, along with his colleagues, reminds us that

> The MHA confers powers on the state that do not exist across the rest of health care. These powers are usually exercised when people are at their most vulnerable. Where people are anxious, quite reasonably, that their rights and personal dignity may suffer through the use of those powers, *the state is under a heavy obligation both to ensure that they are no greater than necessary and to oversee and regulate their use.*
>
> (Department of Health and Social Care, 2018b:5, our emphasis)

Following an independent review of the MHA 1983, which concluded in December 2018, reform of mental health law in England and Wales is now anticipated (Department of Health and Social Care, 2018a). Prior to this, the last substantial changes to the MHA in England and Wales were made by the MHA 2007, which amended (rather than replaced) the earlier MHA 1983. During the process of review Peay (2002:747) observed that mental health policy in England and Wales was 'permeated by perceptions and attributes of risk' rather than humanitarian concerns. Controversially, the MHA 2007 did away with previous categories of mental disorder that were set out under the MHA 1983, in favour of a single definition of mental disorder, defined as 'any disorder or disability of the mind' (s1(2), MHA 2007). In practice, those detained under the legislation have a variety of mental disorders including: schizophrenia, depression and/or bipolar disorder, personality disorders, eating disorders and autistic spectrum disorders. Those with learning disabilities can be detained under the Act but only if their disability is associated with 'abnormally aggressive or seriously irresponsible conduct' (s2, MHA 2007). While both the DSM-5 and ICD-11 include substance use disorders, dependence on drugs and alcohol is excluded from the definition of mental disorder under the MHA 2007. Promiscuity and sexual orientation are also excluded; however, changes to the MHA 2007 mean that deviant sexual conduct no longer is (see Harrison (2011) for a brief discussion).

Part Two of the MHA 1983 sets out the main provisions for compulsory admission to hospital under the Act for 'civil' patients, that is, people not involved with criminal proceedings (i.e. non-offenders). It is important to remember that only a small minority of people with mental health problems are actually detained in hospital for treatment, with approximately 5.6% of adults in contact of mental health or learning disability services admitted to hospital during 2015/16 (National Health Service (NHS) Digital, 2016b). Individuals can be admitted for 28 days for assessment under section 2 of the Act, initially for six months for treatment under section 3 or for up to 72 hours in an emergency under section 4. Because people are detained in hospital under different sections of the MHA you may sometimes hear colloquial references to 'sectioning' or someone being 'sectioned'.

Those involved with criminal proceedings are dealt with under Part Three of the MHA 1983. Cummins (2016:49) reminds us that the 'most important differences between these and civil powers are that they follow on from conviction and form part of a criminal record'. There are many provisions under the Act that allow for detention in hospital and diversion away from the criminal justice system, and these are described in more detail throughout the book. Chapter 4 outlines the key powers available to the police to take people with suspected mental health problems to a 'place of safety', before Chapter 5 sets out some of the ways mental disorder may impact on court proceedings and the sentencing options available to the court. Chapter 6 considers the legal framework for the transfer of prisoners to secure mental health facilities, while Chapter 7 outlines the legal mechanisms by which mentally disordered offenders may be discharged to the community and then subject to supervision and monitoring.

The MHA 2007 was a controversial piece of legislation and one that took ten years from conception (Department of Health, 1998) to implementation (November 2008). We discuss the key reforms and controversies in Chapter 3, along with its current review, but it is worth noting here that since the MHA 2007 was implemented, detentions under mental health legislation have risen considerably. In 2015/16, 63,622 detentions under the MHA were recorded, a rise of 9% from the previous year and a staggering 47% rise in the ten years from 2005/6 (n=43,361) (NHS Digital, 2016a). Substantial changes have been made to the way mental health data are collated and analysed so the analysis of more recent trends is difficult to make. However, NHS Digital (2018) indicates that detentions under mental health legislation are continuing to rise, with an estimated increase of 2.4% in 2017–2018.

SOCIAL AND POLITICAL UNDERSTANDINGS OF MENTAL DISORDER

Because diagnoses of mental disorder change over time, some argue that they are little more than moral judgements (Blackburn, 1998). A good illustration of this is the case of homosexuality. Until 1973 homosexuality was listed as a mental disorder in the DSM, and it was not until the Sexual Offences Act 1967 that homosexual acts (in private and between adults aged 21 and above) were decriminalised in England and Wales. This highlights how particular types of behaviour can be criminalised and medicalised in different historical periods. This point is further illustrated by recent calls to include *homophobia* within diagnostic tools such as the DSM (Harrington, 2015).

Other more recent examples of what might be termed 'social' or 'political' definitions of mental disorder can also be found. In Chapter 3 we will learn more about the 'Dangerous and Severe Personality Disorder' (DSPD) programme, a political initiative designed to quell public anxieties about the perceived dangerousness and 'untreatability' of those with severe personality disorder. Controversially, when the reforms were first introduced, professionals were at a loss as to where the term of DSPD had come from, complaining that it was a political term that did not correspond to existing clinical or legal categories of understanding (Eastman, 2002; Farnham and James, 2001).

MEDIA AND PUBLIC ATTITUDES TOWARDS MENTAL DISORDER

While Mullins (2014) argues that some progress has been made regarding the media's presentation of mental disorder, especially among broadsheet newspapers, it is well established that the media's portrayal of people with mental health problems tends to be negative. The media appear to be particularly fascinated with the violence and murder committed by those with mental health problems (Busfield, 2002) and commonly depict those with mental health problems as violent (Cummins, 2011). Newspapers tend to focus on negative events, such as murders by those known to psychiatric services, while films and TV dramas continue to use 'mental illness as an excuse for depicting violence and horrific crimes' (Anderson, 2003:304). In a review, Shift (2010) found that in 45% of TV programmes with storylines involving mental illness, the characters with mental health problems were portrayed as dangerous.

Cummins (2016:49) argues that the high level of media interest in mentally disordered offenders follows from the common belief that they have 'escaped punishment'. Another reason for the media's apparent fascination, along with the public's apparent happiness to consume, is that many high-profile murders committed by those with mental disorder involve 'double unpredictability: not only is the death unpredictable, but so too is the killer' (Busfield, 2002:69). Importantly, these observations highlight that mentally disordered offenders are often framed in contradictory ways by the media, simultaneously presented as both rational and irrational (Cross, 2014; Olstead, 2002).

While the media can influence public opinion, 'people are not simply blank slates on which its messages are written' (Philo, 1996:103). It is therefore difficult to establish what the public know or understand about mental disorder, or the impact that media reporting may have on their views. However, public attitudes are generally thought to be negative, and those with mental disorder are commonly viewed as dangerous and unpredictable (Morrall, 2000). While the public's understanding of mental illness is thought to have broadened in the second half of the twentieth century, the perception that people with mental illness are violent and dangerous is thought to have substantially increased (Markowitz, 2011; Phelan et al., 2000). A considerable stigma surrounding mental illness continues to prevail and this has important implications for those who are unwell, especially if they are also in contact with the criminal justice system.

While it is difficult to establish the impact that media reporting has on public attitudes, one reason it is thought to be dangerous follows from its tendency to frame an issue in very black and white terms 'which sees perpetrators and victims as inhabiting entirely different worlds' (Mullen, 2002a:xiv). This process ignores the fact that mentally disordered offenders are highly likely to also be victims and that people with mental disorder experience more victimisation than those without. This also highlights the media's power to generate and 'champion' issues for political attention, validate existing ones, and popularise fears of particular 'others' or issues (Kemshall, 2008). Sadly, the media often fails to raise important issues for mental health professionals or highlight when things in mental health services are working well.

While the impact of both media and public concerns about those with mental disorder is difficult to establish, political responses to those with mental disorder often appear to be structured by anxieties about public protection (see Chapter 3). Some social policy responses (such as homicide inquiries where the perpetrator is known to mental health services) help generate problematic associations between mental disorder and dangerousness. Yet paradoxically, political reactions to quell public and media concerns may distract policy-makers and direct resources at the wrong targets (Kitzinger, 2004). On the ground, this may lead to more restrictive approaches which can generate unforeseen risks because of the subsequent difficulties involved with aftercare and resettlement (Carroll, Lyall and Forrester, 2004).

THE RELATIONSHIP BETWEEN MENTAL DISORDER AND OFFENDING

Concepts such as mental disorder and offending become even more troublesome when we try to consider their relationship to one another. But, as Harris (1999) reminds us, we have little choice but to explore the relationship between 'offenders' and 'mental disorder' because the law requires the defence to demonstrate a causal link between the crime and a defendant's mental disorder if the insanity defence or diminished responsibility are to be used in court. Mentally disordered offenders (as well as those with mental health problems who have not offended) are often subject to a range of restrictive measures. Given that many of these may be justified on the basis of their potential for dangerousness, we also have an ethical obligation to interrogate the relationship between their mental health and propensity to offend.

While many uncertainties continue to characterise the field, Duggan (2008) notes that there has been something of a radical shift in thinking over the last 40 years, with academic psychiatry having moved from a firmly held view that crime and mental disorder are not linked, to a consensus that the opposite may be true. Some areas of consensus have now emerged and many now claim there is 'undoubtedly a link' between mental disorder and offending (Holloway and Davies, 2017:307; see also Peay, 2011), with severe mental illness correlating with an increased risk of behaving violently (Hodgins, 2008). However, psychiatrists warn that we should not 'exaggerate the significance of this link' (Duggan, 2008:507) since mental disorder is likely to make a 'trivial contribution' to levels of violence (Monahan, 2007:144). This is because the relationship appears to be 'modest' (Pilgrim and Rogers, 2003) and there are a number of methodological challenges with trying to understand the relationship between mental disorder and offending.

One key problem involved with making sense of the vast literature available is that the majority of research studies tend to focus on only one type of disorder (e.g. schizophrenia or personality disorder) and one type of offence (e.g. murder) or type of offending (e.g. violent crime) (Vinkers et al., 2011). There is a wide variation in study findings about the link between mental disorder and offending and this reflects the range of different diagnoses, definitions of crime/violence and methodologies used (ranging from self-report to conviction data) (Hodgins, 2008). The use of treatment samples, which may include disproportionate numbers of patients 'inclined towards disruptive behaviour' (Markowitz, 2011:39), also represents a common limitation across studies. While it is clear that offenders have a high prevalence of mental disorder, one fundamental challenge is that the mental health problems experienced by these offenders may have little to do with their offending behaviour. While correlations between mental disorder and offending certainly exist, associations between mental disorder and offending do not explain the nature of the relationship (Vinkers et al., 2011) and 'any causal basis for the association between mental illness and offending has yet to be established' (Peay, 2009:491). Moreover, the precise nature of the relationship is not only unclear; it is impossible to define (Peay, 2011).

Notwithstanding these challenges, in the pages that follow we attempt to outline some of the key areas of consensus. We pay specific attention to the academic literature surrounding schizophrenia and personality disorder and also consider the role that drug and alcohol use may play along with other key criminogenic factors. We also consider the levels of victimisation experienced by people with mental disorder revealing that contrary to popular anxieties they are, in fact, far more at risk from 'us' than we are from 'them'.

TYPES OF OFFENDING BY THOSE WITH MENTAL DISORDER

Hiday (1999) hypothesises that mentally disordered offenders most often fall into one of three groups. The first group is involved with minor survival crimes or misdemeanours, such as shoplifting and loitering. The second group are those who, in addition to severe mental health problems, also have substance misuse issues which may increase their involvement with the criminal justice system. The final group is the smallest group and the one most commonly assumed by stereotypical presentations of those with mental disorder. This group is comprised of a small number of very ill people who also engage with violent and dangerous behaviour as a result of their delusionary behaviour. What is particularly revealing is that 'all three of these groups tend to live in impoverished communities and within social environments that have substantially deteriorated in the last twentieth century' (Hiday, 1999:525).

Serious violence committed by the mentally ill is usually committed in very similar ways as that committed by those without mental illness and is most commonly directed towards family members or people close to them, rather than strangers (National Confidential Inquiry into Suicide and Safety in Mental Health (NCISH), 2018; Pilgrim and Rogers, 2003). Given that people with mental health problems tend to offend in the same ways that people without mental health problems do, it is very difficult to establish what role, if any, the mental disorder may have played in their offence (Canton, 2016). This reminds us that mentally disordered offenders are a heterogeneous population and just as 'crime amongst the ordered is diverse, opportunistic and diverse ... so it is amongst the mentally disordered' (Peay, 2011:97).

SCHIZOPHRENIA AND LINKS TO VIOLENT OFFENDING

There has long been a lack of empirical evidence to link mental illness and violence (Pilgrim and Rogers, 2003). However, this began to change in the 1990s with a number of well-designed studies. For example, in a community-based study, Swanson et al. (1990) found that patients with psychosis alone were more likely to be violent. Additionally, those who had psychosis and comorbid problems with alcohol or drugs were significantly more likely to be violent. Research conducted by Steadman et al. (1998) almost a decade later, found that patients with psychosis alone were not more likely to be violent (Steadman et al., 1998). However, in support of the earlier study by Swanson et al. (1990), violence was found to more likely among those with mental illness and substance misuse issues (Monahan et al., 2001). A later study by Swanson and colleagues (2006) involving community-based patients with schizophrenia, found that 19% reported having behaved violently in the last six months, a far higher level than would be expected within the wider community.

Studies such as these have overturned a long-held belief that there is no relationship between schizophrenia and violent offending. Rather, a consensus that those with schizophrenia are more likely to be violent than those without is now more common (Hodgins, 2008; McMurran, Khalifa and Gibbon, 2009). In a review, Hodgins (2008:400) notes that this is a robust finding that has been confirmed in a number of different countries, using a variety of methods and sampling strategies. The studies reviewed by Hodgins (2008) confirm four further points. The first is that while severe mental illness appears to increase the risk of violence at a similar level across different studies, the proportion of people with severe mental illness who commit violent offences is different in different time periods and countries. Second, the proportion of offenders with mental illness also differs in different locations and time periods. Third, serious mental illness leads to a higher risk of violence in women, even though many more men with severe mental illness commit violent crime. And finally, only small numbers of people with severe mental illness have murdered someone. However, a significant minority of people with mental illnesses such as schizophrenia do present with persistently aggressive behaviour (Hodgins, 2008).

A consensus now generally exists that patients with schizophrenia who do not take their medication (Fazel et al., 2009), especially those experiencing delusions (Taylor and Estroff, 2003) or other positive symptoms (Hodgins, Hiscoke and Freese, 2003) along with those misusing substances (Fazel et al., 2009), are more likely to behave violently. However, the majority of people with schizophrenia are not violent and most do not abuse alcohol and drugs (Pilgrim and Rogers, 2003). Moreover, some research has found that people with schizophrenia may actually be less likely to offend because they are more socially withdrawn and consequently have less potential contact with victims (Markowitz, 2011; Pilgrim and Rogers, 2003). We should also be mindful that those suffering with schizophrenia and experiencing paranoid symptoms may be less likely to consent to take part in research, and consequently this may skew estimates of violence among this group (Torrey et al., 2008). In any case, it is important to take note of Peay's (2011:95) reminder that the context and meaning of violence (or any other offending behaviour) is paramount because 'violence occurs in a context; it is rarely a unilateral event'.

PERSONALITY DISORDER AND LINKS TO VIOLENT OFFENDING

In contrast to the debate surrounding the relationship between mental illnesses like schizophrenia and violence, a strong empirical link has long been established between personality disorder and serious crimes such as homicide and sexual offending (Vinkers et al., 2011). In particular, Cluster B personality disorders (anti-social, borderline, histrionic and narcissistic personality disorders) are particularly common among offenders charged with violent crime (Vinkers et al., 2011). Woodworth and Porter (2002:442) found that offenders with psychopathy and a score of 30 and above on the PCL-R (see Box 1.1) were more likely than other offenders to commit 'instrumental and cold-blooded homicides'. Offenders with personality disorder are also considered to be 'responsible for a disproportionate amount of serious repetitive crime and violence' (Hare and Hart, 1993:106). When compared to offenders without personality disorder, they are more likely to be violent in prison (Hare and Hart, 1993), and more likely to be reconvicted at a higher and faster rate following release (Jamieson and Taylor, 2004). Indeed, one UK study found those with personality disorder were seven times more likely than those with mental illness to be convicted of a serious offence after discharge from a secure hospital (Jamieson and Taylor, 2004).

While there is a strong relationship between personality disorder (especially anti-social personality disorder) and offending, it is important to remember that this is 'logically inevitable, because the diagnosis is derived tautologically from anti-social actions' (Pilgrim and Rogers, 2003:8). Of all psychiatric diagnoses, personality disorder is considered as one of the most problematic because of its lack of specificity and validity (Robles et al., 2014).[5] This has led some to question the extent to which personality disorder is a legitimate medical diagnosis and whether it can be effectively treated. As we will learn in Chapter 3, these uncertainties have played out through a number of legislative and policy changes concerning personality disorder in England and Wales.

THE ROLE OF SUBSTANCE MISUSE

Many studies suggest that substance misuse may have a greater explanatory value than mental disorder for patients who act violently (see e.g. Fazel et al., 2009; Monahan et al., 2001; Silver, Mulvey and Monahan, 1999). In a review of all homicides committed by those known to mental health services since 1997, the NCISH (2018) reports that the majority of perpetrators with mental health problems also had comorbid substance misuse issues. Importantly, the combination of mental disorder and substance misuse may increase the likelihood of violent crime because anti-social traits such as impulsivity and aggression are exacerbated by substance misuse (McMurran, 2008). Substance misuse may also serve to work against effective treatment and this may elevate a person's risk of being violent (McMurran, 2008). But, while the empirical relationship between substance misuse, mental disorder and offending appears strong, it is important to remember that the relationship between substance use and offending is, like the relationship between mental disorder and offending, also inherently problematic (Seddon, 2000; Stevens, 2007). While there are clear correlations, there are also many challenges involved with understanding the nature and direction of the relationship (Anckarsäter et al., 2009). Given that substance 'misuse' can involve many different things, including intoxication, dependence and harmful use (McMurran, 2008), establishing a clear understanding of the relationship between mental disorder, substance use and offending is far from straightforward.

THE ROLE OF CRIMINOGENIC FACTORS

General theories of crime can usually be applied to crime committed by those with mental disorder (Markowitz, 2011) and when compared to other factors such as gender, age, social class and employment, mental illness appears to be a weak predictor of dangerousness (Pilgrim and Rogers, 2003). This reminds us of the importance of criminogenic factors for offending. Moreover, it reminds us that the risk factors linked to offending are often the same for offenders with and without mental disorder (Bonta, Law and Hanson, 1998). Peay (2011:93) asserts that

> it is important to remember that mentally disordered people are, first and foremost, people; which means all of the factors that bear on people in terms of their preponderance for offending will also bear on the mentally disordered.

Risk factors, such as the environment in which people reside, increase the risk of offending for people with and without mental health problems (Walsh et al., 2003). For example, research suggests that the relationship between violence and schizophrenia is influenced by the living circumstances of the patient (Hodgins, 2008). This is significant because people with mental illness are more likely to reside in 'socially disorganised' neighbourhoods, characterised by greater levels of deprivation, fragmented families and greater racial diversity (Markowitz, 2011). Moreover, people who reside in such localities are more likely to break the law (Silver, Mulvey and Monahan, 1999).

VICTIMISATION, SOCIAL DEPRIVATION AND SOCIAL EXCLUSION

The victimisation of people with mental disorder is disproportionately high and despite common perceptions that those with mental disorder are dangerous, the evidence suggests that they are more likely to be a victim of crime than to harm others (see Chapter 4 for a discussion). People with mental health problems are also more likely to have been exposed to a range and higher incidence of traumatic events (Georgiadis et al., 2016) with forensic patients found to have a higher prevalence of PTSD when compared to the general population (Sarkar et al., 2005; Spitzer et al., 2006). Research also suggests that people with mental health problems are more likely to die as a result of both suicide and murder (Hiroeh et al., 2001).

While the relationship between mental health, social deprivation and poverty is complex (Payne, 2012), studies have found a higher prevalence of mental health (and substance misuse) problems in countries with greater economic and social inequalities (Pickett and Wilkinson, 2010). In the UK, there has been recognition that people with mental health problems are more likely to experience social deprivation (Department of Health, 2009; Social Exclusion Unit, 2002). Along with rising levels of substance abuse, the living standards experienced by psychiatric patients are thought to be in decline (Pilgrim and Rogers, 2003). Poverty may lead to homelessness, and this has been identified as a risk factor for the mentally ill (McNiel, Binder and Robinson, 2005). Poverty and deprivation may contribute to hopelessness and poorer mental well-being, as well as lower physical well-being because of the impact of poor diet and drug and alcohol use (Pilgrim and Rogers, 2003). People with severe mental illness, such as schizophrenia, are disproportionately over-represented in homelessness, imprisonment and migration statistics (Kelly, 2005). For Kelly (2005:721), the 'adverse effects of these social, economic and societal factors, along with the social stigma of mental illness, constitute a form of "structural violence"' that restricts access to services and results in the mentally ill being 'systematically excluded from full participation in civic and social life'.

Experiences of social exclusion among offenders with mental disorder are considerable (Winstone, 2016) and it is likely that this is related to the stigma that surrounds mental disorder. Mentally disordered offenders may experience additional stigma as a result of being diagnosed with mental illness and detained in hospital (Ferrito et al., 2012). In addition, mental health policy and practice have the potential to further stigmatise service users (Link, Castille and Stuber, 2008). Sadly, negative political rhetoric and ill-informed media reporting about mental health can be 'self-defeating' because it may increase the social exclusion and vulnerability of those with mental health problems. This, in turn, can increase their likelihood of becoming unwell and involvement with crime (Winstone, 2016:7). Involvement with the criminal justice system can also lead to higher levels of mental health problems (Peay, 2011), while the stigma attached to being a 'mentally disordered offender' can deter people from seeking help (Clement et al., 2014), result in people not being give meaningful support (Canton, 2016), negatively impact on their relationships with others (Mezey et al., 2016) and thereby negatively impact on reintegration efforts (Livingston, Rossiter and Verdun-Jones, 2011).

TREATING OFFENDERS WITH MENTAL DISORDER

Regardless of the relationship between mental disorder and crime, diagnosing and treating mental health problems remain important tasks for psychiatry (Anckarsäter et al., 2009). The wide range of offences committed by mentally disordered offenders, along with their broad range of psychiatric diagnoses, means that treatment needs can vary considerably (Knabb, Welsh and Graham-Howard, 2011). While there continues to be a reliance on the medication of psychiatric problems (Spandler and Calton, 2009), research suggests that mentally disordered offenders are likely to benefit from treatment that tackles a broad range of problems, providing it is multidisciplinary, psychologically informed, structured, supports the acquisition of skills, and focuses on the treatment of both mental illness and risk (Robertson, Barnao and Ward, 2011:482).

Since the early 1990s there has been an 'unprecedented and exceptional rate of development' of treatment programmes to address offending behaviour in prison and probation services (McMurran, Khalifa and Gibbon, 2009:136). Barnao and Ward (2015) identity three approaches that structure interventions with mentally disordered offenders: treatments targeting mental health or psychological issues, treatments based on Risk-Need-Responsivity (RNR) principles or strengths-based approaches such as the Good Lives Model (GLM). Many of these are accredited and therefore supported by some evidence of effectiveness. However, research suggests that their effectiveness is only modest (Duggan, 2008:510).

While a 'meagre, although expanding' evidence base concerning treatments for mentally disordered offenders is beginning to emerge (Barnao and Ward, 2015:77), research about the effectiveness of rehabilitation or different treatment models *specifically* with mentally disordered offenders has historically been limited. As a result, many interventions are based on general guidelines or research that has been undertaken with general populations (either offenders or people with mental disorder) (Barnao and Ward, 2015; Robertson, Barnao and Ward, 2011). While some practitioners have made a number of adaptations to offending behaviour programmes to help support mentally disordered offenders (such as enhanced motivational work and slower delivery), little is known about the desirability or effectiveness of these changes (Duggan, 2008:512). As a result, many treatments lack empirical validation especially with specific (or more complex) mentally disordered offenders (Knabb, Welsh and Graham-Howard, 2011). While treatments such as cognitive behavioural therapy (CBT) have been shown to be effective with some offenders with mental disorder, they have also been criticised for failing to address the heterogeneity of mentally disordered offenders and their wide range of offending and psychiatric disorders (Knabb, Welsh and Graham-Howard, 2011). Future offender behaviour programmes need to be developed with more attention towards mentally disordered offenders, as well as being more sensitive to Black, Asian and Minority Ethnic (BAME) people, women, those with learning disabilities, and young offenders (McMurran, Khalifa and Gibbon, 2009).

Duggan (2008) reminds us that the context in which treatment is delivered and its over-riding purpose are important considerations when working with mentally disordered offenders. Indeed, he asks, is 'the focus of the intervention merely to reduce the likelihood of reoffending (largely, though not exclusively, a societal good) or should it also address the psychological ill health of the individual being treated?' (Duggan, 2008:505). In addition to exploring the purpose of treatment, Duggan (2008) encourages us to think further about the context in which treatment is delivered, and the extent to which mentally disordered offenders may be coerced into treatment. By virtue of being detained or subject to community supervision, many mentally disordered offenders may feel they are coerced into treatment and this has implications for how they view and engage with the treatment on offer.

Therefore, before treatment can start, an offender's motivation to change must be addressed (McMurran, 2012). Mentally disordered offenders are sometimes seen as difficult to treat because 'they may be viewed as hostile, acutely unwell, traumatized by their index offence, mistrustful of forensic services and unwilling to cooperate with attempts at rehabilitation' (Robertson, Barnao and Ward, 2011:482). Chaotic lifestyles, belief that treatment is unhelpful, refusal to seek help and inaccurate mental health diagnoses are all reasons for why offenders may have not received treatment in the past (Caulfield, 2016). In addition, features of their mental disorder may make treatment engagement more challenging. For example, some mentally disordered offenders, like those with personality disorder, have been identified as particularly difficult to engage with treatment (Howells and Day, 2007; McMurran, 2012).

There are also a number of important issues surrounding the timing of treatment. It is difficult to assess when people, especially those serving long sentences in prison or likely to be detained for a long period in hospital, should start treatment. Sometimes people are not ready and have not come to terms with their offence. For those who have begun and engaged with treatment, it is also very difficult to know when treatment has concluded satisfactorily. Indeed, 'resolution of active symptoms does not represent the completion of the therapeutic task' (Carroll, Lyall and Forrester, 2004:415). Therefore, one of the real challenges involved with treatment is relapse prevention, enabling people to maintain change over time and after their treatment has ended (McMurran, Khalifa and Gibbon, 2009).

RISK ASSESSMENT, PREVENTION AND MANAGEMENT

In addition to trying to understand the relationship between offending and mental disorder, another fundamental challenge follows from trying to assess the risk posed by those with mental disorder and their potential for future offending (Kemshall, 2008; Peay, 2011). Assessing and managing the risk people present to others is no longer an exclusive activity performed by specialised clinicians (Mullen, 2002b) and now represents a core function of mental health services (Holloway and Davies, 2017). The ever-expanding list of risk assessment tools for use with offenders in criminal justice and mental health services reflects this. Risk assessment tools are now found at most stages of the criminal justice system, including sentencing, sentence planning, decisions about release and community supervision, and can therefore significantly impact on the ways in which offenders are punished and treated (Douglas et al., 2017). The use of risk assessment tools at these different stages of the criminal justice system inevitably raises important ethical dilemmas, particularly in terms an offender's right not to be unnecessarily detained (or monitored) versus the rights of the public to protection from those who may pose a harm.

Risk assessment tools are often described, and critiqued, in terms of different generations. First generation assessment tools refer to unstructured clinical risk assessments that are undertaken without the support of structured actuarial risk assessment tools. Clinical risk assessment involves collecting detailed information (through self-report and documentation) about a service user's clinical and social history in order to make an assessment about their potential risk. Historically, this is the most common approach to risk assessment (Doyle and Dolan, 2008) and while such forms of risk assessment are celebrated for being individualised (British Psychological Society, 2006), they are commonly criticised for being unstructured, unreliable (Andrews, Bonta and Wormith, 2006), biased (Carroll, Lyall and Forrester, 2004) and for having little supporting evidence (Ægisdóttir et al., 2006).

To address concerns about the unreliability of unstructured clinical risk assessments, and in the context of renewed efforts to find out 'what works' in offender management, a second generation of standardised actuarial risk assessments began to emerge during the 1980s and early

1990s. While actuarial assessments of risk (when compared to clinical judgement alone) are considered to be superior in terms of their predictive accuracy, many problems still surround their use (Duggan, 2008) and some still question their predictive validity (Fazel et al., 2012). Actuarial tools are also criticised for being time-consuming (Viljoen, McLachlan and Vincent, 2010), expensive (Fazel et al., 2012), being overly reliant on static factors (that an individual cannot change), and for overlooking individual risk factors that lack an evidence base (Duggan, 2008).

In an attempt to address the problems inherent with clinical and actuarial assessments of risk, a third generation of 'structured professional judgement' emerged (see Douglas, Ogloff and Hart, 2003). This approach combines structured risk assessment tools with clinical interviews and has been judged as the most effective risk assessment practice (Scott and Resnick, 2006). The emphasis, according to Duggan (2008:248), is to develop evidence-based frameworks for assessing risk which are systematic and consistent as well as 'flexible enough to account for case-specific influences and the contexts in which assessments are conducted'.

A common criticism of the risk assessment approaches described above is that they are not particularly useful for devising a suitable risk management or prevention plan. This has led some to observe the emergence of a fourth generation of risk assessment that aims to move beyond 'assessment' and provide a structure to support the supervision and case management of offenders (Andrews, Bonta and Wormith, 2006:8). Risk assessments are also increasingly structured by strengths-based approaches that attempt to explore offender goals and aspirations as well as their problems and risks (Vandevelde et al., 2017).[6]

Assessments of risk, whether clinical or actuarial, often focus on an offender's static and dynamic risk factors. Static risk factors are historical and fixed factors in an offender's life that cannot be changed. They might include histories of violence, the nature of an offender's index offence or previous experiences of abuse. In contrast, dynamic risk factors are changeable and include the use of drugs and alcohol or active symptoms of mental illness. Therefore, the risks associated with these types of factors may be reduced through targeted intervention and management. In the context of risk assessment, static risk factors are sometimes thought to be problematic because they focus on features of an offender's life that cannot be changed. This can be stigmatising and detract attention away from the changing nature of people's dynamic risk to others (Mullen, 2002b). However, static risk factors are also usually thought to represent good predictors of behaviour like future violence, leading Carroll, Lyall and Forrester (2004:412) to observe that 'ethically, it is consistent with the notion of proportionality for a higher degree of caution to be applied where there is a very serious index offence'.

With more than 200 structured risk assessment tools now in use across forensic and criminal justice settings (Singh et al., 2014), we do not have space to permit a thorough review. However, some of the most common risk assessment tools used with violent, sexual and/ or mentally disordered offenders in England and Wales are listed in Box 1.1, and in the pages that follow, we briefly outline some of the key challenges involved with the risk assessment and management of mentally disordered offenders.

BOX 1.1 COMMON RISK ASSESSMENT TOOLS USED IN ENGLAND AND WALES

- The **Offender Assessment System (OASys)** is a structured risk assessment tool used with adult offenders across England and Wales. OASys is used throughout an offender's sentence to help probation staff assess offending related needs, assess an offenders risk of serious harm and likelihood of reoffending, and to help inform sentence planning (NOMS, 2016).
- The **Offender Group Reconviction Scale (OGRS)** (Howard et al., 2009) is a risk assessment tool based on static factors and has been routinely used by the probation service in England and Wales since the 1990s (Francis, Soothill and Humphreys, 2007). The most recent version (OGRS-III) is based on a large sample of offenders (n=71,519) and can generate reconviction probabilities for 12- and 24-month periods (Francis, Soothill and Humphreys, 2007).
- The **Risk Matrix 2000 (RM2000)** (Thornton et al., 2003) is used with men convicted of a sexual offence. The violence version, the RM2000/V, is used in respect of non-sexual violence. Each uses verified historical information (i.e. static factors) to place the assessed person into one of four risk categories (low, medium, high or very high).
- The **HCR-20** (Webster et al., 1997) is a structured clinical risk assessment tool with 20 items – ten historical (H), five clinical (C) and five risk management (R). Scoring is based on a 0–2 scale (0 = not present, 1 = possibly present and 2 = item present), yielding a maximum score of 40. The HCR-20 has been used in civil and forensic settings and has been found to have good predictive validity (Douglas et al., 2005).
- The **Violence Risk Scale (VRS)** (Wong and Gordon, 2000) was designed to assess the risk presented by forensic patients. Version 2 of the VRS is

based on 6 static and 20 dynamic risk factors, each rated between 0 and 3. Over a two-year period, Duggan (2008) reports that the VRS has a strong predictive validity.

- The **Violence Risk Appraisal Guide (VRAG)** (Webster et al., 1994) is based on 12 items. Duggan (2008) suggests that given 3 of the 12 items rely on previous convictions, it is a tool best suited to those in custodial or secure forensic settings. One of the reasons for this is that it does not take drug and alcohol use into account and its validity in community samples may therefore be limited (Murray and Thomson, 2010).

- The **Psychopathy Checklist-Revised (PCL-R)** (Hare, 1991) is an assessment tool that is used to assess psychopathy. The tool is based on a 20-item scale. Each item is scored 0-2 with a maximum score of 40. The cut-off score for psychopathy varies in different services and countries but is often set at 25 or 30. While the PCL-R was originally developed to diagnose psychopathy, its association with criminality has led to it also being commonly used for assessing offender risk (Leistico et al., 2008).

PROBLEMS WITH ACCURACY AND BIAS

Despite common perceptions that psychiatrists are good at predicting future risk, the empirical evidence suggests they are not (see Kemshall (2003) for a review). Some have even suggested that psychiatric judgements about dangerousness are usually no better than lay judgements (Gardner et al., 1996). One problem follows from the 'actuarial fallacy'. The problem here is that while individuals may belong to groups statistically more likely to commit a crime or pose a threat, risk assessment tools are unable to identify which specific individuals in those groups will go on to commit such acts (Fitzgibbon 2007b; Mullen, 2006). This can lead to a high number of 'false positives', people incorrectly judged by risk assessment tools as likely to offend but who do not go on to offend (Fazel el al., 2012). Given many of these people may be subject to longer periods of detention or extra-stringent community supervision, this raises a number of ethical challenges. Risk assessments are also thought to be problematic because they tend to stereotype vulnerable groups, including those with mental illness (Fitzgibbon, 2007a). This reminds us that risk assessments are not neutral and can involve problematic cultural assumptions (Maurutto and Hannah-Moffat, 2006; Shepherd and Anthony, 2018).

ETHICALLY PROBLEMATIC

There are significant ethical issues involved with assessing the risk of people with mental disorder (Buchanan and Grounds, 2011; Eastman, 2002; Mullen, 2000b; Roychowdhury and Adshead, 2014). Ethical challenges are raised by the presence of competing values involved with risk assessment and are made worse by their poor predictive accuracy (Douglas et al., 2017). Because individual factors are given greater weight in risk assessment practices larger structural factors are often overlooked (Langan, 2010) and, given the significant disadvantage experienced by many mentally disordered offenders, this can leave them 'doubly disadvantaged'. In practice, Gergel and Szmulker (2017:226) note that 'despite hopes that coercive measures in psychiatry should reflect the patient's best interests, all too often it appears that inaccurate and unsubstantiated estimation of risk becomes the over-riding motivation'.

While risk assessments can infringe patient freedoms, there are also clear benefits to the patient including more in-depth risk assessment, closer supervision and proactive interventions (Duggan, 2008). Even when a risk assessment leads to an offender being detained in secure services for longer, this may still be seen in the 'best interests' of this person, since detention may prevent a relapse of their symptoms, re-offending and future periods of hospitalisation (Douglas et al., 2017). Moreover, 'the view that medical professionals ought never to act against a patient's best interests can be contested' since there may be circumstances when it is just and appropriate for a clinician to act in a way that protects others (Douglas et al., 2017:135).

AN ATTEMPT TO KNOW THE UNKNOWABLE

The accuracy of a risk assessment is inevitably dependent on the quality of information available (Carroll, Lyall and Forrester, 2004). However, assessing the risk of harm to others is a difficult and uncertain enterprise (McAlinden, 2001; McSherry, 2004). Essentially, risk assessment tools are characterised by an attempt to predict events that are unpredictable (Kemshall, 2003). Yet, despite the 'significant issues in "knowing" the risk of dangerous offenders, risk assessment practice (along with policy and legislation) are all conducted *as if* we can know them' (Kemshall, 2008:13, emphasis in original). While we can estimate the likelihood of 'new stressful life events … their actual occurrence is "unknowable"' (Carroll, Lyall and Forrester, 2004:414). Problematically, risk assessment tools are most limited in their ability to accurately predict rare events (Crawford, 2000; Szmulker, 2000; von Hirsch, 1998). The difficulty of course is that rare events, such as murder and serious sexual violence, are the types of event that we want to prevent most (Kemshall, 2008).

INDUCTIVE PREVENTION PARADOX AND STAFF-OFFENDER RESPONSES

A further problem is presented by the 'inductive prevention paradox' (see Davison, Frankel and Smith, 1992 cited in Markham, 2018). This occurs when professionals in secure settings are required to make assessments of how likely a patient is to offend in the very environment (i.e. a ward or prison wing) that is designed to prevent such events from happening (Markham, 2018). This reflects how risk assessments lack ecological validity because they are 'unclear how the skills which service users develop in order to cope with highly structured institutionalised environments will equip them to cope with greater freedom' (Heyman et al., 2007:5). The consequences of this can be problematic, since patients may respond by 'faking' good behaviour and, in turn, clinicians 'may engage in deception in the hope of seeing through the camouflage of self-presentation' (Heyman et al., 2007:8). Compliance, therefore, becomes a 'game' and a 'tactical resource' (Davies et al., 2006:1104) as forensic patients aim to 'actively manage their own risk status' in order to secure greater autonomy and freedom (Reynolds et al., 2014:199).

RISK ASSESSMENT MAY UNDERMINE TREATMENT AND RESETTLEMENT

One problem that follows from offenders (and staff) 'playing a game' when it comes to risk assessment is that such reactions have the potential to undermine the therapeutic relationship, which is thought to be key to reducing an offender's risk. Yet, many criminal justice practices, such as probation supervision, are constructed in such a way that offenders are encouraged to 'play the system' (Durnescu, 2011). In addition, some exhibit concern that risk assessment is a process *done* to offenders and that this may lead to poor engagement or trust in the process (Crewe, 2011). Crewe (2011:516) also highlights that 'many prisoners regard psychological discourse as a form of normative imperialism' that fails to properly take offender perspectives and values into account. A preoccupation with risk assessment may also distract practitioners from providing good care and treatment (Holloway and Davies, 2017) as well as resettlement and aftercare (Trebilcock and Worrall, 2018).

DESISTANCE AND OFFENDERS WITH MENTAL DISORDER

Compared to research about the risk factors for future reoffending and the mentally ill, research concerning protective factors has been sparse (Göbbels, Thakker and Ward, 2016) (although see de Ruiter and Nicholls (2011) for an exception). However, there is increasing evidence that focusing on protective factors is an important part of encouraging effective recovery and should be an essential part of risk management (Rennie and Dolan, 2010). An essential part of recovery for forensic patients also involves developing a sense of self that is separate from the 'offender' identity that they may also have (Simpson and Penney, 2018). However, mentally disordered offenders have often been marginalised by overly medicalised understandings of their behaviour and this has meant that the desistance perspective is less apparent in the academic and policy discussions that surround them (Canton, 2016). While the desistance literature highlights the importance of individual narratives (see e.g. Maruna, 2001), detention in secure mental health services, and the loss of individuality that may follow, can work against service users developing a sense of self (Simpson and Penney, 2018). Similarly, in the community, stringent risk management may undermine a service user's attempt to construct a new identity and reintegrate themselves (Coffey, 2011). For example, in his research about aftercare monitoring, Coffey (2011:757) observes that 'while patients constructed deviant labels as historical, workers orientated towards these as current, thereby challenging emergent identity work'. However, research suggests that an essential part of recovery for forensic patients involves developing a sense of self that is separate from the 'offender' identity that they may also have (Simpson and Penney, 2018).

METHODOLOGICAL CHALLENGES IN THE FORENSIC MENTAL HEALTH FIELD

The methodological challenges in this field extend far beyond the difficult question about the nature of the relationship between mental disorder and offending. At all stages of the criminal justice system substantial gaps, along with variation in research design and quality, make it difficult to not only establish the prevalence of mental health problems but also the effectiveness of interventions that are used with mentally disordered offenders. In the following pages, we summarise some of the key challenges, but readers are directed to Peay (2011) for a thorough overview of the methodological difficulties that permeate this field.

GAPS IN KNOWLEDGE AND UNDERSTANDING

Undertaking research with mentally disordered offenders is a far from straightforward task. Mental health services are often described as the Cinderella of NHS services, with considerably more funding allocated to other more 'worthy' health problems. Unfortunately, this discrepancy is also replicated in the money that is allocated to mental health research, with mental disorders receiving far less research attention than physical disorders (McManus et al., 2009). Studies about probation and mental health (Brooker et al., 2012; Sirdifield, 2012) and the effectiveness of public protection measures in the community are also sparse (Kemshall, 2008). In addition, there are a number of challenges involved with reviewing the evidence surrounding the 'policing of mental health' (Cummins, 2012; Young et al., 2013) and evaluating the impact of liaison and diversion schemes because of their considerable variation (Dyer, 2013). Research in this field can also be limited because of the challenges involved with gaining access to suitable samples of participants. These challenges mean that many gaps in the literature remain.

ESTABLISHING PREVALENCE

There are numerous problems with data concerning the prevalence of mental disorders. In fact, the diverse prevalence rates found across different research studies may tell us more about the methodological variation between these studies than actual prevalence (Lindsay, Hastings and Beech, 2011). As a result, the reported findings of many studies may be significant under-representations. Many mental disorders go undiagnosed because patients do not seek treatment or because GPs are poor at identifying milder cases of mental disorder (NICE, 2011). Moreover, many offenders are not registered with a GP (Department of Health, 2007), or do not receive treatment, and this may mean they are overlooked by official statistics (Caulfield, 2016). As we will learn throughout the book, there are many problems involved with identifying people with mental health needs, and this has implications for service delivery as well for the reliability of research.

ESTABLISHING EFFECTIVENESS

A recent review by Völlm and colleagues (2018:69) concludes that 'overall, the evidence base for forensic psychiatry is weak and future high quality trials are urgently needed in this complex and doubly stigmatised patient group'. However, while psychiatric research strives to adopt a 'scientific approach', in practice, psychiatry has a poor empirical basis because it is 'virtually impossible' to design an adequate experimental study in this field (Anckarsäter et al., 2009). Many treatment studies in this field are poorly controlled. Therefore, many argue that more research with adequate control groups is needed to validate the range of treatments that are available to, and used with, offenders with mental health problems (Knabb, Welsh and Graham-Howard, 2011). However, there are several ethical and methodological challenges involved with using control groups with high-risk offenders (Ferriter and Huband, 2005; Kemshall, 2008). Consequently, many treatment studies concerning mentally disordered offenders tend to rely on case studies or theoretical conceptualisations (Knabb, Welsh and Graham-Howard, 2011). In addition to methodological problems surrounding treatment populations and the use of satisfactory controls, some studies are limited as a result of the interventions being poorly defined (Knabb, Welsh and Graham-Howard, 2011).

DISCUSSION

This first chapter has illuminated some of the many complexities that surround people who have a mental disorder and who have also come to the attention of the criminal justice system. In the closing pages, we seek to outline some of the key implications that follow from the issues we have described. While a relationship between mental health and offending can definitely be observed, we have highlighted that too many factors are at play to say with any certainty that one leads to the other. Thornicroft (2006:13) clearly articulates this when he observes:

> whether or not there is any additional risk depends upon the type of diagnosis, the nature and severity of the symptoms present,

whether the person is receiving treatment and care, if there is a past history of violence by the individual, the co-occurrence of antisocial personality disorder and substance misuse and the social, economic and cultural context in which an individual lives.

The problematic (and ultimately, unknown) relationship between mental health and offending raises significant issues for law and policy, as well as for practice. Every year the criminal justice and mental health systems must deal with large numbers of people who come under their care and who may pose a very real risk of harm to themselves and others. This reminds us that the mental health of offenders is a critical public health issue (Seymour, 2010). Questions about whether someone's mental disorder led them to commit a crime may be difficult to answer, but the views formed will impact on what happens to a defendant at court (Buchanan and Zonana, 2009). This means that the 'mental health of an individual is a factor that *can, and should*, be a consideration in decision making at all points of the criminal justice system' (Cummins, 2016:20, our emphasis). However, policy commonly fails to recognise the diversity of what is meant by mental disorder and the experiences that may follow (Canton, 2016), while challenges with the lack of adequate data mean that it is difficult to plan services as well as monitor outcomes (National Audit Office, 2017). Once involved in services, a lack of shared meanings can lead to misunderstandings between different professionals (Durcan, 2016).

These final observations remind us that mentally disordered offenders present 'problems of organisational responsibility' (Harris, 1999:13), in part, because of the plurality of perspectives that surround them (Davies et al., 2006). As a result, the extent to which offenders with mental health problems fall under the criminal justice or forensic mental health system, is serendipitous (Prins, 2016:102). As we will see in the remainder of the book, criminal justice and mental health services must manage a difficult balance between the ethical care of the patient along with adequate protection of the public (Carroll, Lyall and Forrester, 2004). Unfortunately, this can leave mentally disordered offenders in 'no-man's-land' where they risk being rejected by health practitioners because of their offending behaviour and by criminal justice practitioners because they have mental health problems (Duggan, 2008:508; see also Howells, Day and Thomas-Peter, 2004). Alternatively, professional anxieties about the risk posed by those with mental health problems and a lack of clarity about who should be responsible, may lead to responses that are disproportionate and overly-controlling.

FURTHER READING

For a considered discussion about the challenges involved with both psychiatric and legal classification and understandings of mental disorder see Walvisch (2017). For the case for abolishing psychiatric diagnoses see Timimi (2014). For a discussion about the value of the medical model (as well as a critique) see Bartlett (2010). For a comprehensive overview of the relationship between mental health and crime see Peay (2011, 2017) and Silver (2006). For a recent review of the assessment and treatment of offenders with mental disorder see Völlm et al. (2018), although see also Duggan (2008). For a discussion about the problems involved with risk assessment in criminal justice and forensic psychiatry see Douglas et al. (2017). For an overview of different theoretical models used in the treatment and rehabilitation of mentally disordered offenders see Robertson, Barnao and Ward (2011) along with Howells, Day and Thomas-Peter (2004). Finally, for an extended discussion about desistance, mental disorder and offending see Göbbels, Thakker and Ward (2016).

REFERENCES

Ægisdóttir, S., White, M.J., Spengler, P.M., Maugherman, A.S., Anderson, L.A., Cook, R.S., Nichols, C.N., Lampropoulos, G.K. and Walker, B.S. (2006) 'The meta-analysis of clinical judgement project: Fifty-six years of accumulated research on clinical versus statistical prediction', *Counselling Psychologist*, 34(3): 341–382.

American Psychiatric Association (APA) (2013) *Diagnostic and statistical manual of mental disorders (Fifth edition)*, Arlington, VA: American Psychiatric Publishing.

Anckarsäter, H. (2010) 'Beyond categorical diagnostics in psychiatry: Scientific and medicolegal implications', *International Journal of Law and Psychiatry*, 33(2): 59–65.

Anckarsäter, H., Radovic, S., Svennerlind, C., Höglund, P. and Radovic, F. (2009) 'Mental disorder is a cause of crime: The cornerstone of forensic psychiatry', *International Journal of Law and Psychiatry*, 32(6): 342–347.

Anderson, M. (2003) '"One flew over the psychiatric unit": Mental illness and the media', *Journal of Psychiatric and Mental Health Nursing*, 10(3): 297–306.

Andrews, D., Bonta, J. and Wormith, S. (2006) 'The recent past and near future of risk and/or need assessment in crime and delinquency', *Crime and Delinquency*, 52(1): 7–27.

Barnao, M. and Ward, T. (2015) 'Sailing uncharted seas without a compass: A review of interventions in forensic mental health', *Aggression and Violent Behavior*, 22: 77–86.

Bartlett, A. (2010) 'Medical models of mental disorder' in Bartlett, A. and McGauley, G. (eds.) *Forensic mental health: Concepts, systems and practice*, Oxford: Oxford University Press.

Bartlett, P. and Sandland, R. (2014) *Mental health law: Policy and practice (Fourth edition)*, Oxford: Oxford University Press.

Beswick, J. and Gunn, M. (2017) 'The law in England and Wales on mental health treatment in the community' in Buchanan, A. and Wootton, L. (eds.) *Care of the mentally disordered offender in the community (Second edition)*, Oxford: Oxford University Press.

Blackburn, R. (1998) 'Criminality and the interpersonal circle in mentally disordered offenders', *Criminal Justice and Behaviour*, 25(2): 155–176.

Blashfield, R.K., Keeley, J.W., Flanagan, E.H. and Miles, S.R. (2014) 'The cycle of classification: DSM-I through DSM-5', *Annual Review of Clinical Psychology*, 10(1): 25–51.

Bonta, J., Law, M. and Hanson, K. (1998) 'The prediction of criminal and violent recidivism among mentally disordered offenders: A meta-analysis', *Psychological Bulletin*, 123(2): 123–142.

Brekke, J.S., Prindle, C., Woo Bae, S. and Long, J.D. (2001) 'Risks for individuals with schizophrenia who are living in the community', *Psychiatric Services*, 52(10): 1358–1366.

British Psychological Society (2006) *Occasional briefing paper no. 4: Risk assessment and management*, Leicester: British Psychological Society.

Brooker, C., Sirdifield, C., Blizard, R., Denney, D. and Pluck, G. (2012) 'Probation and mental illness', *Journal of Forensic Psychiatry and Psychology*, 23(4): 522–537.

Buchanan, A. and Grounds, A. (2011) 'Forensic psychiatry and public protection', *British Journal of Psychiatry*, 198(6): 420–423.

Buchanan, A. and Zonana, H. (2009) 'Mental disorder as the cause of a crime', *International Journal of Law and Psychiatry*, 32(3): 142–146.

Busfield, J. (2002) 'Psychiatric discourse and individual violence: Imagined death, risk and mental health policy' in Buchanan, A. (ed.) *Care of the mentally disordered offender in the community*, Oxford: Oxford University Press.

Canton, R. (2016) 'Troublesome offenders, undeserving patients? The precarious rights of mentally disordered offenders' in Winstone, J. (ed.) *Mental health, crime and criminal justice*, Basingstoke: Palgrave Macmillan.

Carroll, A., Lyall, M. and Forrester, A. (2004) 'Clinical hopes and public fears in forensic mental health', *Journal of Forensic Psychiatry and Psychology*, 15(3): 407–425.

Caulfield, L.S. (2016) 'Counterintuitive findings from a qualitative study of mental health in English women's prison', *International Journal of Prisoner Health*, 12(4): 216–229.

Clement, S., Schauman, O., Graham, T., Maggioni, F., Evans-Lacko, S., Bezborodovs, N., Morgan, C., Rüsch, N., Brown, J.S. and Thornicroft, G. (2014) 'What is the impact of mental health-related stigma on help-seeking? A systematic review of quantitative and qualitative studies', *Psychological Medicine*, 45(1): 11–27.

Coffey, M. (2011) 'Resistance and challenge: Competing accounts in aftercare monitoring', *Sociology of Health and Illness*, 33(5): 748–760.

Crawford, M.J. (2000) 'Homicide is impossible to predict', *Psychiatric Bulletin*, 24(4): 152.

Crewe, B. (2011) 'Depth, weight, tightness: Revisiting the pains of imprisonment', *Punishment and Society*, 13(5): 509–529.

Cross, S. (2014) 'Mad and bad media: Populism and pathology in the British tabloids', *European Journal of Communication*, 29(2): 204–217.

Cummins, I. (2012) 'Policing and mental illness in England and Wales post Bradley', *Policing*, 6(4): 365–376.

Cummins, I. (2016) *Mental health and the criminal justice system: A social work perspective*, Northwich: Critical Publishing Ltd.

Cummins, I. (2011) 'Distant voices still lives: Reflections on the impact of media reporting of the cases of Christopher Clunis and Ben Silcock', *Ethnicity and Inequalities in Health and Social Care Journal*, 3(4): 18–29.

Davies, J.P., Heyman, B., Godin, P.M., Shaw, M.P. and Reynolds, L. (2006) 'The problems of offenders with mental disorders: A plurality of perspectives within a single mental health care organization', *Social Science and Medicine*, 63(4): 1097–1108.

de Ruiter, C. and Nicholls, T.L. (2011) 'Protective factors in forensic mental health: A new frontier', *International Journal of Forensic Mental Health*, 10(3): 160–170.

Department of Health (1998) *Modernising mental health services: Safe sound and supportive*, London: The Stationery Office.

Department of Health (2007) *Improving health, supporting justice: A consultation document. A strategy for improving health and social care services for people subject to the criminal justice system*, London: Department of Health.

Department of Health (2009) *The Bradley report. Lord Bradley's review of people with mental health problems or learning disabilities in the criminal justice system*, London: Department of Health.

Department of Health and Social Care (2018a) 'Government commits to reform the Mental Health Act' [Press release] 6 December 2018. London: Department of Health and Social Care.

Department of Health and Social Care (2018b) *The independent review of the Mental Health Act. Interim report*, London: Department of Health and Social Care.

Douglas, K.S., Guy, L.S., Reeves, K.A. and Weir, J. (2005) 'HCR-20 violence risk assessment scheme: Overview and annotated bibliography', *Systems and Psychosocial Advances Research Center Publications and Presentations*, 335: 1–90.

Douglas, K.S., Ogloff, J.R. and Hart, S.D. (2003) 'Evaluation of a model of violence risk assessment among forensic psychiatric patients', *Psychiatric Services*, 54(10): 1372–1379.

Douglas, T., Pugh, J., Singh, I., Savulescu, J. and Fazel, S. (2017) 'Risk assessment tools in criminal justice and forensic psychiatry: The need for better data', *European Psychiatry*, 42: 134–137.

Doyle, M. and Dolan, M. (2008) 'Understanding and managing risk' in Soothill, K., Rogers, P. and Dolan, M. (eds.) *Handbook of forensic mental health*, Cullompton: Willan Publishing.

Duggan, C. (2008) 'Focusing on treatment: The main interventions and their implications' in Soothill, K., Rogers, P. and Dolan, M. (eds.) *Handbook of forensic mental health*, Cullompton: Willan Publishing.

Durcan, G. (2016) *Mental health and criminal justice: Views from consultations across England and Wales*, London: Centre for Mental Health.

Durnescu, I. (2011) 'Pains of probation: Effective practice and human rights', *International Journal of Offender Therapy and Comparative Criminology*, 55(4): 530–545.

Dyer, W. (2013) 'Criminal justice diversion and liaison services: A path to success?' *Social Policy and Society*, 12(1): 31–45.

Eastman, N. (2002) 'The ethics of clinical risk assessment and management' in Gray, N., Laing, J. and Noaks, L. (eds.) *Criminal justice, mental health and the politics of risk*, Abingdon: Routledge.

Farnham, F.R. and James, D.V. (2001) '"Dangerousness" and dangerous law', *The Lancet*, 358(9297): 1926.

Fazel, S., Gulati, G., Linsell, L., Geddes, J.R. and Grann, M. (2009) 'Schizophrenia and violence: Systematic review and meta-analysis', *PLoS Medicine*, 6(8): e1000120.

Fazel, S., Singh, J.P., Doll, H. and Grann, M. (2012) 'Use of risk assessment instruments to predict violence and antisocial behaviour in 73 samples involving 24,827 people: Systematic review and meta-analysis', *British Medical Journal*, 345: e4692.

Ferriter, E.H. and Huband, D. (2005) 'Does the non-randomized controlled study have a place in the systematic review? A pilot study', *Criminal Behaviour and Mental Health*, 15(2): 111–120.

Ferrito, M., Vetere, A., Adshead, G. and Moore, E. (2012) 'Life after homicide: accounts and redemption of offender patients in a high security hospital – a qualitative study', *Journal of Forensic Psychiatry and Psychology*, 23(3): 327–344.

Fitzgibbon, D.W. (2007a) 'Institutional racism, pre-emptive criminalisation and risk analysis'. *Howard Journal of Criminal Justice*, 46(2): 128–144.

Fitzgibbon, D.W. (2007b) 'Risk analysis and the new practitioner: Myth or reality?', *Punishment and Society*, 9(1): 87–97.

Francis, B., Soothill, K. and Humphreys, L. (2007) *Development of a reoffending measure using the Police National Computer database*, Lancaster: Lancaster University.

Gardner, W., Lidz, C.W., Mulvey, E.P. and Shaw, E.C. (1996) 'Clinical versus actuarial predictions of violence in patients with mental illness', *Journal of Consulting and Clinical Psychology*, 64(3): 602–609.

Georgiadis, A., Byng, R., Coomber, R. and Quinn, C. (2016) 'The social, relational and mental health characteristics of justice-involved men in the south-west England', *Journal of Forensic Psychiatry and Psychology*, 27(6): 835–852.

Gergel, T. and Szmulker, G. (2017) 'The ethics of coercion in community mental health care' in Buchanan, A. and Wootton, L. (eds.) *Care of the mentally disordered offender in the community (Second edition)*, Oxford: Oxford University Press.

Göbbels, S., Thakker, J. and Ward, T. (2016) 'Desistance in offenders with mental illness' in Winstone, J. (ed.) *Mental health, crime and criminal justice*, Basingstoke: Palgrave Macmillan.

Hare, R.D. (1991) *The Hare Psychopathy Checklist – Revised*, Toronto, Ontario: Multi-Health Systems.

Hare, R.D. and Hart, S.D. (1993) 'Psychopathy, mental disorder and crime' in Hodgins, S. (ed.) *Mental disorder and crime*, Newbury Park, CA: Sage.

Harrington, R. (2015) 'One scientist has a very controversial idea about homophobia', *Business Insider UK*, 10 September 2015. Available from: http://uk.businessinsider.com/is-homophobia-a-disease-2015-9?r=US&IR=T [Last accessed 10 June 2017].

Harris, R. (1999) 'Mental disorder and social order: Underlying themes in crime management' in Webb, D. and Harris, R. (eds.) *Mentally disordered offenders: Managing people nobody owns*, London: Routledge.

Harrison, K. (2011) *Dangerousness, risk and the governance of serious sexual and violent offenders*, Abingdon: Routledge.

Heyman, B., Davies, J., Reynolds, L., Godin, P. and Shaw, M. (2007) 'How do you measure a virtual object? Assessing the risk of releasing offenders with mental health problems', *Risk and Rationalities Conference, Cambridge 29–31st March 2007*, Cambridge, 1–21.

Hiday, V.A. (1999) 'Mental illness and the criminal justice system' in Horwitz, A.V. and Scheid, T.L. (eds.) *A handbook for the study of mental health: Social contexts, theories, and systems*, Cambridge: Cambridge University Press.

Hiroeh, U., Appleby, L., Mortensen, P.B. and Dunn, G. (2001) 'Death by homicide, suicide and other unnatural causes in people with mental illness', *Lancet*, 358(9299): 2110–2112.

Hodgins, S. (2008) 'Criminality among persons with severe mental illness' in Soothill, K., Rogers, P. and Dolan, M. (eds.) *Handbook of forensic mental health*, Cullompton: Willan Publishing.

Hodgins, S., Hiscoke, U.L. and Freese, R. (2003) 'The antecedents of aggressive behavior among men with schizophrenia: A prospective investigation of patients in community treatment', *Behavioral Sciences and the Law*, 21(4): 523–546.

Holloway, F. and Davies, T. (2017) 'The Community Mental Health Team and the mentally disordered offender' in Buchanan, A. and Wootton, L. (eds.) *Care of the mentally disordered offender in the community (Second edition)*, Oxford: Oxford University Press.

Howard, P., Francis, B., Soothill, K. and Humphreys, L. (2009) *OGRS 3: The revised Offender Group Reconviction Scale. Ministry of Justice research summary 7/09*, London: Ministry of Justice.

Howells, K. and Day, A. (2007) 'Readiness for treatment in high risk offenders with personality disorders', *Psychology, Crime and Law*, 13(1): 47–56.

Howells, K., Day, A. and Thomas-Peter, B. (2004) 'Changing violent behaviour: Forensic mental health and criminological models compared', *Journal of Forensic Psychiatry and Psychology*, 15(3): 391–406.

Jamieson, L. and Taylor, P.J. (2004) 'A re-conviction study of special (high security) hospital patients', *British Journal of Criminology*, 44(5): 783–802.

Kelly, B.D. (2005) 'Structural violence and schizophrenia', *Social Science and Medicine*, 61(3): 721–730.

Kemshall, H. (2003) *Understanding risk in criminal justice*, Maidenhead: Open University Press.

Kemshall, H. (2008) *Understanding the community management of high risk offenders*, Maidenhead: Open University Press.

Kessler, R.C., Berglund, P., Demler, O., Jin, R., Merikangas, K.R. and Walters, E.E. (2005) 'Lifetime prevalence and age-of-onset distributions of DSM-IV disorders in the National Comorbidity Survey replication', *Archives of General Psychiatry*, 62(6): 593–602.

Kitzinger, J. (2004) *Framing abuse: Media influence and public understanding of sexual violence against children*, London: Pluto Press.

Knabb, J.J., Welsh, R.K. and Graham-Howard, M.L. (2011) 'Treatment alternatives for mentally disordered offenders: A literature review', *Psychology*, 2(2): 122–131.

Langan, J. (2010) 'Challenging assumptions about risk factors and the role of screening for violence risk assessment in the field of mental health', *Health, Risk and Society*, 12(2): 85–100.

Leistico, A., Salekin, R., DeCoster, J. and Rogers, R. (2008) 'A large-scale meta-analysis relating the Hare measures of psychopathy to antisocial conduct', *Law and Human Behaviour*, 32(1): 28–45.

Lindsay, W.R., Hastings, R.P. and Beech, A.R. (2011) 'Forensic research in offenders with intellectual and developmental disabilities 1: Prevalence and risk assessment', *Psychology, Crime and Law*, 17(1): 3–7.

Link, B., Castille, D.M. and Stuber, J. (2008) 'Stigma and coercion in the context of outpatient treatment for people with mental illness', *Social Science and Medicine*, 67(3): 409–419.

Livingston, J.D., Rossiter, K.R. and Verdun-Jones, S.N. (2011) '"Forensic" labelling: An empirical assessment of its effects on self-stigma for people with severe mental illness', *Psychiatry Research*, 188(1): 115–122.

Markham, S. (2018) 'Red-teaming the panopticon (mobilising adaptive change in secure and forensic settings)', *Journal of Forensic Psychiatry and Psychology*, 29(1): 16–36.

Markowitz, F.E. (2011) 'Mental illness, crime, and violence: Risk, context, and social control', *Aggression and Violent Behavior*, 16(1): 36–44.

Maruna, S. (2001) *Making good: How ex-convicts reform and rebuild their lives*, Washington, DC: American Psychological Association Books.

Maurutto, P. and Hannah-Moffat, K. (2006) 'Assembling risk and the restructuring of penal control', *British Journal of Criminology*, 46(3): 438–454.

McAlinden, A. (2001) 'Indeterminate sentences for the severely personality disordered', *Criminal Law Review*, Feb: 108–123.

McManus, S., Meltzer, H., Brugha, T.S., Bebbington, P.E. and Jenkins, R. (2009) *Adult psychiatric morbidity in England, 2007: Results of a household survey*, Leeds: The NHS Information Centre for Health and Social Care.

McMurran, M. (2008) 'Substance abuse' in Soothill, K., Rogers, P. and Dolan, M. (eds.) *Handbook of forensic mental health*, Cullompton: Willan Publishing.

McMurran, M. (2012) 'Readiness to engage in treatments for personality disorder', *International Journal of Forensic Mental Health*, 11(4): 289–298.

McMurran, M., Khalifa, N. and Gibbon, S. (2009) *Forensic mental health*, Cullompton: Willan Publishing.

McNiel, D.E., Binder, R.L. and Robinson, J.L. (2005) 'Incarceration associated with homelessness, mental disorder, and co-occurring substance abuse', *Psychiatric Services*, 56(7): 840–846.

McSherry, B. (2004) 'Risk assessment by mental health professionals and the prevention of future violent behaviour', *Trends and Issues in Crime and Criminal Justice*, no.281, Canberra: Australian Institute of Criminology.

Mental Health Taskforce (2016) *The five year forward view for mental health*, London: Mental Health Taskforce.

Mezey, G., Youngman, H., Kretzschmar, I. and White, S. (2016) 'Stigma and discrimination in mentally disordered offender patients – a comparison with a non-forensic population', *Journal of Forensic Psychiatry and Psychology*, 27(4): 517–529.

Monahan, J. (2007) 'Clinical and actuarial predictions of violence. II Scientific status' in Faigman, D., Kaye, D., Saks, M., Sanders, J. and Cheng, E. (eds.) *Modern scientific evidence: The law and science of expert testimony*, St Paul, MN: West Publishing Company.

Monahan, J., Steadman, H.J., Silver, E., Appelbaum, P.S., Robbins, P.C., Mulvey, E.P., Roth, L.H., Grisso, T. and Banks, S. (2001) *Rethinking risk assessment: The MacArthur study of mental disorder and violence*, Oxford: Oxford University Press.

Morrall, P. (2000) *Madness and murder*, London: Whurr.

Mullen, P. (2002a) 'Introduction' in Buchanan, A. (ed.) *Care of the mentally disordered offender in the community*, Oxford: Oxford University Press.

Mullen, P. (2002b) 'Serious mental disorder and offending behaviours' in McGuire, J. (ed.) *Offender rehabilitation and treatment: Effective programmes and policies to reduce re-offending*, Chichester: John Wiley and Sons.

Mullen, P. (2006) 'Schizophrenia and violence: From correlations to preventive strategies', *Advances in Psychiatric Treatment*, 12(4): 239–248.

Mullins, J. (2014) 'The power of the media to shape perceptions of mental illness', *Mental Health Practice*, 17(8): 34–35.

Murray, J. and Thomson, M.E. (2010) 'Clinical judgement in violence risk assessment', *Europe's Journal of Psychology*, 6(1): 128–149.

National Audit Office (2017) *Mental health in prisons*, London: National Audit Office.

National Confidential Inquiry into Suicide and Safety in Mental Health (NCISH) (2018) *National confidential inquiry into suicide and safety in mental health annual report 2018*, Manchester: NCISH.

National Health Service (NHS) Digital (2016a) *Inpatients formally detained in hospital under the Mental Health Act 1983, and patients subject to supervised community treatment. Uses of the Mental Health Act: Annual statistics 2015/16*, London: NHS Digital.

National Health Service (NHS) Digital (2016b) *Mental health bulletin 2015–16. Annual report*, London: NHS Digital.

National Health Service (NHS) Digital (2018) *Mental Health Act statistics. Annual figures England, 2017–18*, London: NHS Digital.

National Institute for Health and Care Excellence (NICE) (2011) *Common mental health problems: Identification and pathways to care. NICE guidelines CG123*, Manchester: NICE.

National Offender Management Service (NOMS) (2016) *Public protection manual, 2016 edition*, London: NOMS.

Olstead, R. (2002) 'Contesting the text: Canadian media depictions of the con-flation of mental illness and criminality', *Sociology of Health and Illness*, 24(5): 621–643.

Payne, S. (2012) *Mental health, poverty and social exclusion*, Bristol: University of Bristol.

Peay, J. (2002) 'Mentally disordered offenders, mental health, and crime' in Maguire, M., Morgan, R. and Reiner, R. (eds.) *The Oxford handbook of criminology (Third edition)*, Oxford: Oxford University Press.

Peay, J. (2009) 'Mental illness, dangerousness and protecting society', *Psychiatry*, 8(12): 490–492.

Peay, J. (2011) *Mental health and crime*, Abingdon: Routledge.

Peay, J. (2017) 'Mental health, mental disabilities and crime', in Liebling, A., Maruna, S. and McAra, L. (eds.) *The Oxford handbook of criminology (Sixth edition)*, Oxford: Oxford University Press.

Phelan, J.C., Link, B.G., Steuve, A. and Pescosolido, B.A. (2000) 'Public concep-tions of mental illness in 1950 and 1996: What is mental illness and is it to be feared?', *Journal of Health and Social Behavior*, 41(2): 188–207.

Philo, G. (1996) 'The media and public belief' in Philo, G. (ed.) *Media and mental distress*, Harlow: Addison Wesley Longman Limited.

Pickersgill, M. (2012) 'Standardising antisocial personality disorder: The social shaping of a psychiatric terminology', *Sociology of Health and Illness*, 34(4): 544–559.

Pickett, K.E. and Wilkinson, R.G. (2010) 'Inequality: An underacknowledged source of mental illness and distress', *British Journal of Psychiatry*, 197(6): 426–428.

Pilgrim, D. and Ramon, S. (2009) 'English mental health policy under New Labour', *Policy and Politics*, 37(2): 273–288.

Pilgrim, D. and Rogers, A. (2003) 'Mental disorder and violence: An empirical picture in context', *Journal of Mental Health*, 12(1): 7–18.

Prins, H. (2016) *Offenders, deviants and patients: An introduction to clinical criminology (Fifth edition)*, Hove: Routledge.

Rennie, C.E. and Dolan, M.C. (2010) 'The significance of protective factors in the assessment of risk', *Criminal Behaviour and Mental Health*, 20(1): 8–22.

Reynolds, L.M., Jones, J.C., Davies, J.P., Freeth, D. and Heyman, B. (2014) 'Playing the game: Service users' management of risk status in a UK medium secure forensic mental health service', *Health, Risk and Society*, 16(3): 199–209.

Robertson, P., Barnao, M. and Ward, T. (2011) 'Rehabilitation frameworks in forensic mental health', *Aggression and Violent Behaviour*, 16(6): 472–484.

Robles, R., Fresán, A., Evans, S.C., Lovell, A.M., Medina-Mora, M.E., Maj, M. and Reed, G.M. (2014) 'Problematic, absent and stigmatizing diagnoses in cur-rent mental disorders classifications: Results from the WHO-WPA and WHO-IUPsyS global surveys', *International Journal of Clinical and Health Psychology*, 14(3): 165–177.

Rogers, A. and Pilgrim, D. (2014) *A sociology of mental health and illness (Fifth edition)*, Maidenhead: Open University Press.

Roychowdhury, A. and Adshead, G. (2014) 'Violence risk assessment as a medical intervention: Ethical tensions', *The Psychiatric Bulletin*, 38(2): 75–82.

Sarkar, J., Mezey, G., Cohen, A., Singh, S.P. and Olumoroti, O. (2005) 'Comorbidity of post-traumatic stress disorder and paranoid schizophrenia: A comparison of offender and non-offender patients', *Journal of Forensic Psychiatry and Psychology*, 16(4): 660–670.

Scott, C.L. and Resnick, P.J. (2006) 'Violence risk assessment in persons with mental illness', *Aggression and Violent Behaviour*, 11(6): 598–611.

Seddon, T. (2000) 'Explaining the drug-crime link: Theoretical, policy and research issues', *Journal of Social Policy*, 29(1): 95–107.

Seymour, L. (2010) *Public health and criminal justice*, London: Centre for Mental Health.

Shepherd, S.M. and Anthony, T. (2018) 'Popping the cultural bubble of violence risk assessment tools', *Journal of Forensic Psychiatry and Psychology*, 29(2): 211–220.

Shift (2010) *Making a drama out of a crisis*, London: Shift.

Silver, E., (2006) 'Understanding the relationship between mental disorder and violence: The need for a criminological perspective' *Law and Human Behavior*, 30(6): 685–706.

Silver, E., Mulvey, E.P. and Monahan, J. (1999) 'Assessing violence risk among discharged psychiatric patients: Toward an ecological approach', *Law and Human Behaviour*, 23(2): 237–255.

Simpson, A.I.F. and Penney, S.R. (2018) 'Recovery and forensic care: Recent advances and future directions', *Criminal Behaviour and Mental Health*, 28(5): 383–389.

Singh, J.P., Desmarais, S.L., Hurducas, C., Arbach-Lucioni, K., Condemarin, C., Dean, K., Doyle, M., Folino, J.O., Godoy-Cervera, V., Grann, M., Ho, R.M.Y., Large, M.M., Nielsen, L.H., Pham, T.H., Rebocho, M.F., Reeves, K.A., Rettenberger, M., de Ruiter, C., Seewald, K. and Otto, R.K. (2014) 'International perspectives on the practical application of violence risk assessment: A global survey of 44 countries', *International Journal of Forensic Mental Health*, 13(3): 193–206.

Sirdifield, C. (2012) 'The prevalence of mental health disorders amongst offenders on probation: A literature review', *Journal of Mental Health*, 21(5): 485–498.

Social Exclusion Unit (2002) *Reducing re-offending by ex-prisoners*, London: Social Exclusion Unit.

Spandler, H. and Calton, T. (2009) 'Psychosis and human rights: Conflicts in mental health policy and practice', *Social Policy and Society*, 8(2): 245–256.

Spitzer, C., Chevalier, C., Gillner, M., Freyberger, H. and Barnow, S. (2006) 'Complex post-traumatic stress disorder and child maltreatment in forensic inpatients', *Journal of Forensic Psychiatry and Psychology*, 17(2): 204–216.

Steadman, H.J., Mulvey, E.P., Monahan, J., Robbins, P.C., Appelbaum, P.S. and Grisso, T. (1998) 'Violence by people discharged from acute psychiatric inpatient facilities and by others in the same neighborhoods', *Archives of General Psychiatry*, 55(5): 393–401.

Stevens, A. (2007) 'When two dark figures collide: Evidence and discourse on drug-related crime' *Critical Social Policy*, 27(1): 77–99.

Swanson, J.W., Holzer, C.E., Ganju, V.K. and Jono, R.T. (1990) 'Violence and psychiatric disorders in the community: Evidence from the epidemiologic catchment area surveys', *Hospital and Community Psychiatry*, 41(7): 761–770.

Swanson, J.W., Swartz, M.S., Van Dorn, R.A., Elbogen, E.B., Wagner, H.R., Rosenheck, R.A., Stroup, T.S., McEvoy, J.P. and Lieberman, J.A. (2006) 'National study of violent behaviour in persons with schizophrenia', *Archives of General Psychiatry*, 63: 490–499.

Szmulker, G. (2000) 'Homicide inquiries: What sense do they make?', *Psychiatric Bulletin*, 24(1): 6–10.

Taylor, P.J. and Estroff, S.E. (2003) 'Schizophrenia and violence' in Hirsch, S.R. and Weinberger, D.R. (eds.) *Schizophrenia*, Oxford: Blackwell.

Thornicroft, G. (2006) *Shunned: Discrimination against people with mental illness*, Oxford: Oxford University Press.

Thornton, D., Mann, R., Webster, S., Blud, L., Travers, R., Friendship, C. and Erikson, M. (2003) 'Distinguishing and combining risks for sexual and violent recidivism', *Annals of New York Academy of Sciences*, 989(1): 225–235.

Timimi, S. (2014) 'No more psychiatric labels: Why formal psychiatric systems should be abolished', *International Journal of Clinical and Health Psychology*, 14(3): 208–215.

Torrey, E.F., Stanley, J., Monahan, J. and Steadman, H.J. (2008) 'The MacArthur violence risk assessment study revisited: Two views ten years after its initial publication', *Psychiatric Services*, 59(2): 147–152.

Trebilcock, J. and Worrall, A. (2018) 'The importance of throughcare and resettlement for working with violent and sexual offenders' in Ireland, J.L., Ireland, C.A. and Birch, P. (eds.) *Violent and sexual offenders: Assessment, treatment and management (Second edition)*, London: Routledge.

Vandevelde, S., Vander Laenen, F., Van Damme, L., Vanderplasschen, W., Audenaert, K., Broekaert, E. and Vander Beken, T. (2017) 'Dilemmas in applying strengths-based approaches in working with offenders with mental illness: A critical multidisciplinary review', *Aggression and Behavior*, 32: 71–79.

Viljoen, J.L., McLachlan, K. and Vincent, G.M. (2010) 'Assessing violence risk and psychopathy in juvenile and adult offenders: A survey of clinical practices', *Assessment*, 17(3): 377–395.

Vinkers, D.J., de Beurs, E., Barendregt, M., Rinne, T. and Hoek, H.W. (2011) 'The relationship between mental disorders and different types of crime', *Criminal Behaviour and Mental Health*, 21(5): 307–320.

Völlm, B.A., Clarke, M., Herrando, V.T., Seppänen, A.O., Gosek, P. Heitzman, J. and Bulten, E. (2018) 'European Psychiatric Association (EPA) guidance on forensic psychiatry: Evidence based assessment and treatment of mentally disordered offenders', *European Psychiatry*, 51: 58–73.

von Hirsch, A. (1998) 'The problem of false positives' in von Hirsch, A. and Ashworth, A. (eds.) *Principled sentencing: Readings on theory and policy*, Oxford: Hart Publishing.

Walsh, E., Moran, P., Scott, C., McKenzie, K., Burns, T., Creed, F., Tyrer, P., Murray, R.M. and Fahy, T. (2003) 'Prevalence of violent victimisation in severe mental illness', *British Journal of Psychiatry*, 183(3): 233–238.

Walvisch, J. (2017) 'Defining "mental disorder" in legal contexts', *International Journal of Law and Psychiatry*, 52: 7–18.

Webster, C.D., Douglas, K., Eaves, D. and Hart, S. (1997) *HCR:20: Assessing risk for violence – Version 2*, Vancouver, BC: Simon Fraser University.

Webster, C.D., Harris, G., Rice, M., Cormier, C. and Quinsey, V. (1994) *The violence prediction scheme: Assessing risk in high risk men*, Toronto: University of Toronto.

Winstone, J. (2016) 'Crime, exclusion and mental health: Current realities and future responses' in Winstone, J. (ed.) *Mental health, crime and criminal justice*, Basingstoke: Palgrave Macmillan.

Woodworth, M. and Porter, S. (2002) 'In cold blood: Characteristics of criminal homicides as a function of psychopathy', *Journal of Abnormal Psychology*, 111(3): 436–455.

Wong, S. and Gordon, A. (2000) *Violence Risk Scale (VRS): Assessment manual*, Saskatoon: Correctional Service of Canada and University of Saskatchewan.

World Health Organization (WHO) (2018) *ICD-11 International Classification of Diseases for mortality and morbidity statistics. Eleventh revision*, Geneva, Switzerland: WHO.

Young, S., Goodwin, E.J., Sedgwick, O. and Gudjonsson, G.H. (2013) 'The effectiveness of police custody assessments in identifying suspects with intellectual disabilities and attention deficit hyperactivity disorder', *BMC Medicine*, 11: 1–11.

NOTES

1 For a detailed history of the DSM see Blashfield et al. (2014).

2 More information about the ICD is available here: www.who.int/classifications/icd/factsheet/en/

3 The first version of what is now the ICD was published by the International Statistical Institute in 1893 and was called the International List of Causes of Death.

4 While the MHA 1983 (as amended by the MHA 2007) applies in Wales, since the Government of Wales Act 2006, the Welsh Assembly has been able to pass its own laws and make changes to England-Wales laws as they apply in Wales. Therefore, see also the Mental Health (Wales) Measure (2010).

5 For a broader discussion about the validity of psychiatric diagnosis see Anckarsäter (2010).

6 For a discussion about the challenges involved with strengths-based approaches see Vandevelde et al. (2017).

CHAPTER 2

Key perspectives surrounding mental health and offending

▌INTRODUCTION

In this chapter we explore a range of perspectives about mental health and offending. This will enable readers to explore the variety of different ways in which mental health and offending can be understood. Crime and offending behaviour are often associated with deviation from a set of rules or norms. In a similar manner, symptoms and behaviours which may lead to a diagnosable mental health condition, also represent ways in which behaviour is regarded as having deviated from a set of 'normal' or 'healthy' behaviours. To support this discussion, readers will be introduced to the 'medical model' and explore its strengths and weaknesses as applied to mentally disordered offenders. In order to explore its related critique, the chapter will consider a range of sociological perspectives about mental health and offending including the 'anti-psychiatry' movement, literature surrounding medicalisation and other sociological perspectives concerning risk, dangerousness and precaution. This discussion will bring us naturally to the somewhat controversial role of forensic mental health professionals and the challenges they confront when tasked with balancing the rights and confidentiality of their client with the rights of the public to protection.

THE ORIGINS AND EARLY DEVELOPMENT OF FORENSIC PSYCHIATRY

HISTORICAL UNDERSTANDINGS OF MENTAL DISORDER

Mental disorder is neither a new nor modern phenomenon. Abnormal behaviour seems to have existed as far back as the means to detect it can determine, yet ways of understanding it have changed dramatically. Skeletal remains thousands of years old that show signs of trephination – circular holes of about two inches in diameter that have been drilled into the skulls of living individuals – suggest the existence of primitive medical procedures (Campillo, 1984; Zimmerman et al., 1981). While some have suggested that these procedures were carried out to relieve pressure following a head injury, others have shown that in the absence of scientific knowledge about mental disorder, trephination was used on disturbed individuals to release the 'evil demon' believed to have caused their behaviour (Faria, 2013). By 1300, fear of the Devil and a belief in witchcraft were widespread and those suffering from mental disorders were often portrayed as witches, providing scapegoats for the ills of society (Zilboorg, 1935). Symptoms such as being withdrawn or eccentric, hearing voices or holding strange beliefs, could be seen to characterise possession by the Devil.

Not all disordered individuals were accused of witchcraft during this period. Many were left to wander as beggars, though a few were taken into early asylums. One of the first purpose-built hospitals was the Priory of St Mary of Bethlehem, which was founded in 1243 and came to house a handful of mentally ill individuals over the following two centuries. It was used exclusively for the mentally ill from 1547 and managed by the London authority to clear some of the disordered individuals from their streets. Care in these institutions fell far short of clinical. Many became tourist attractions for the paying public, who gave one or two pennies to watch chained inmates strewn with their excrement. One of the most famous early institutions came to be known as 'Bedlam', which in current parlance means a place of chaos.

Described now as the period of the 'Great Confinement' (Foucault, 1961), from the 1660s private madhouses for the mentally insane began to grow (McDonald, 1981 cited in Seddon, 2007). Yet, these were not medical institutions and physicians played a very small role in confinement and providing 'treatment'. In England, it was not until 1774 that a physician's certificate was required for commitment to a madhouse (Wright, 1998). Until that point, the judgement of a magistrate was sufficient. Neither was it apparent that a physician might have any expert knowledge about mental illness as most of the therapies used by them during this period were ancient ones including bloodletting. Inducing fear, restraint, castration and starvation were also popular 'treatments'. The physician's ability to cure was certainly limited.

EARLY FOUNDATIONS OF PSYCHIATRY

By the end of the eighteenth century, the humanitarian movement developed and produced a number of reformers with an interest in the treatment of both incarcerated prisoners and the mentally ill. Philippe Pinel and his ordering of the removal of chains from patients in France came to illustrate the movement symbolically (Levine, 1996). As Levine documents, as well as being a defender of liberalism and the poor, Pinel embraced medicine and was considered the 'father of scientific psychiatry'. Pinel viewed the insane as suffering human beings rather than depraved animals. Contrary to his historical image, Pinel did not strike the chains from inmates, but progressively had his employees implement humane conditions.

In England, it was William Tuke who independently led the development of a radical new type of institution in the north of England. In 1796 he founded the York Retreat, where eventually about 30 patients lived as part of a small community in a quiet country house and engaged in a combination of rest, talk and manual work. The efforts of the York Retreat centred around minimising restraints and cultivating rationality and moral strength. The entire Tuke family became known as some of the founders of 'moral treatment'. They created a family-style ethos and patients performed chores to give them a sense of contribution.

Moral treatment, however, failed to cope with seriously disordered individuals for whom institutionalisation was the only intervention. Open conditions with few beds could not cater for the increase in mentally ill individuals as science advanced. Thus, conditions in many large institutions built in the wake of this period were less than ideal, having to house large numbers. At the same time, prejudice against the mentally ill rose among the public, who became less sympathetic to the suffering of those who were unwell (Peay, 2011).

During the nineteenth century major structural and ideological changes occurred (Forrester, 2002) as the systematic control of madness began (Rogers and Pilgrim, 2014). Drawing on the work of Scull (1993), Seddon (2007) describes two particularly significant developments. The first was the substantial expansion of the public asylum system, which began with the County Asylum Act 1808. This piece of legislation allowed local authorities to build state-run asylums and was consolidated by the Lunacy and County Asylum Act of 1845, which made the provision of asylum care a statutory responsibility (Seddon, 2007). Alongside the expansion of state-funded asylums, the establishment of separate facilities for 'criminal lunatics', such as Broadmoor Hospital, represented another significant development (Seddon, 2007). As Seddon (2007) notes, in the first half of the nineteenth century, asylums were intended to be curative and humanitarian but by the end of the same century they had become increasingly custodial. Asylums became dumping grounds for the troublesome and inadequate who may have previously been cared for by their families (Seddon, 2007). Along with prison doctors, asylum doctors were criticised as exercising disciplinary functions under the cloak of medical treatment (Scull, 1993).

The increasing numbers of people being locked up by the state in asylums led to a proliferation of legislation. As more and more asylums emerged, so too did a legal framework with which to regulate the detention of the insane. This sought to offer protections to citizens from unnecessary detention. The emerging legal framework also tried to address key issues surrounding culpability and responsibility (e.g. the McNaughten rules, see Chapter 4 for a discussion). While substantial changes were made to the law during the nineteenth century, most early mental health legislation directed legislative power to the courts rather than to medical experts. In many respects this reflects the infancy of psychiatry at the time. But as the number of people detained in public asylums grew, and new attempts to classify mental health problems and direct treatment emerged, the 'birth of psychiatry' began.

THE BIRTH OF PSYCHIATRY AND THE MEDICAL MODEL OF MENTAL DISORDER

Ignorance about the aetiology of abnormal behaviour limited treatment to physical forms of calming and restraint. These procedures mostly kept order, paralleling the restraint of offenders, but as the asylum system expanded so too did the need for new treatments. During the mid-nineteenth century the term of psychiatry first emerged and along with the 'birth of psychiatry' came an increasing focus on the development of diagnostic classifications and the study of madness. Anckarsäter et al. (2009:342) claim that 'psychiatry was developed with the core ambition to describe, explain and treat states of insanity by applying the modern medical model'.

Emil Kraepelin, a key founder of modern psychiatry, produced one of the first biologically based coherent classificatory systems: *A Textbook of Psychiatry*. He pioneered drug effects and surgical procedures as clinical investigations, which due to the clinical authority of Kraepelin's work led to their somewhat premature and rapid adoption. Kraepelin suggested two broad syndromes in mental disorder, 'dementia praecox' (later labelled as schizophrenia by Eugen Bleuler) and 'manic depressive disorders'. It was Kraepelin's work that formed the foundation for the *Diagnostic and Statistical Manual of Mental Disorders* (DSM), which is now considered the 'holy book' of psychiatric disease classification (van Bergen, 2015) (see Chapter 1).

The emergence and growth of the medical model for mental disorders is, according to Miller (1986, cited in Bartlett, 2010), inextricably linked to changes in the care of mad during the nineteenth century. The County Asylums Act 1808 gave local authorities the permission to build large asylums. This, alongside the implementation of the Lunacy and County Asylum Act 1845, which made it an obligation to provide adequate provision for the mentally ill, meant that there was a substantial expansion of the public asylum system (Scull, 1993). This system provided more opportunities to study phenomena and provide concentrated treatments. As the asylum population continued to expand there was increasing enthusiasm for the medical model of mental disorder.

Although there is no complete consensus on what constitutes the medical model, Bartlett (2010) suggests that several components can be identified: aetiology (causes), symptoms and signs, investigations, diagnosis, treatment plans and prognosis. The common use of these terms (or terms similar to them) illustrates the need for practitioners to be able to communicate effectively about the patients they see within a structured framework.

THE MEDICAL MODEL AND ITS VALUE

Spitzer and Wilson (1975) have argued that there is an absence of physiological dysfunction in many mental disorders. For most psychiatric disorders, they suggest, there is no understanding of specific aetiology. Rather, causal determinants are multi-factorial and hard to identify. Moreover, the features of psychiatric disorder are not always dissimilar to some aspects of normal functioning. In other words, coughs and heart pain are not part of the ordinary experience, whereas feeling anxious before an exam may well be. Spitzer and Wilson (1975) also suggest that for there to be a physiological disorder there must be a measurable change in the person. Elsewhere in medicine, this can be evidenced by something like an X-ray, but in psychiatry, the presence of biological variation and its significance is debateable. Mercer and Mason (1998:15) also criticise the medical model for being 'based on a tenuous relationship between the ideas that unhealthy individuals can be returned to a state of health, or that normal individuals can be created from abnormal ones'. These issues are further amplified when trying to understand the mentally disordered offender (Harris, 1999).

The medical model has also been criticised for ignoring the patient's subjective understandings of their own state of mind. The patient's own experiences, which will not necessarily be expressed within the language of symptoms and signs, are sometimes ignored in the search of a diagnosis (Bartlett, 2010). Some patients see diagnosis and treatment as a form of power and complain that staff are 'prone to apply overly reductive medial models that [do] not take account of their individual circumstances' (Dixon, 2015:1307). The medical model is certainly powerful, and as Beresford (2002:582) reminds us, 'on the basis of diagnostic categories … people may be locked up, subjected to compulsory (and health damaging) "treatment" and have their rights restricted'.

The 'medical model' has its strengths in some other areas of medicine, particularly those where there is substantial consensus as to what constitutes and causes a 'problem', and where such problems involve fairly simple cause-effect relationships. For example, smoking might lead to lung cancer, a poor diet might lead to heart disease and so on. However, in the mental health arena, the 'medical model' has clear limitations. Among these are an over-reliance on 'categories', 'ideals' and 'objectivity' and a failure to appreciate the significance of internal experiences (Bartlett, 2010). The medical model has also been criticised for its lack of appreciation for diversity, and the essential role played by individuals, their culture and the wider environment, in mental health (Bartlett, 2010).

The medical model provides legitimacy for medical interventions because it is based on scientific evidence about the disease process. However, suggestions have been made that the medical model prevails as a consequence of research bias. Often funded by the pharmaceutical industry, there has been considerable research into the biological basis of psychological disorders, despite biology often being the 'end-point for more complex causation' (Bartlett, 2010:8). While classification tools like the DSM-5 and ICD-11 are praised for offering a common language to mental health practitioners by which they can communicate effectively about their clients, many powerful critiques also exist. Thornton (1992), for example, highlights that the DSM represents a way by which psychiatry tries to legitimise itself and extend its legitimacy. In *Making us Crazy*, Kutchins and Kirk (1997:x) highlight that the DSM is not an objective scientific tool, but rather a 'repository of a strange mix of social values, political compromise, scientific evidence and material for insurance claim forms'.

The medical model has been described, however, as the least 'bad' option (Spitzer and Wilson, 1975). As indicated above, previous responses have included the persecution of witches, the incarceration of people in prisons and workhouses and the construction as the mad person as evil. The medical model, therefore, has the advantage of being more humanitarian than the alternatives. However, other forms of critique have emerged from disciplines external to psychiatry, most notably sociology to which we turn our attention in the following section.

THE DEVELOPMENT OF THE ANTI-PSYCHIATRY MOVEMENT

MEDICINE AS AN INSTITUTION OF SOCIAL CONTROL

Interest in issues of power, authority and social control within the sociology of health and illness can be traced back to the work of Talcott Parsons (1951) who was the first to conceptualise medicine as an agent of social control in his seminal essay on the 'sick role'. In contrast to the biomedical model, which constructs illness as a mechanical malfunction or a microbiological invasion, Parsons described the sick role as a temporary, medically sanctioned form of deviant behaviour. Using ideas from Freud's psychoanalytical theories as well as from functionalism and Max Weber's work on authority, Parsons created an 'ideal type' that could be used to shed light on the social forces involved in episodes of sickness. Sickness, according to Parsons (1951:112), is a form of deviance and involves a recognition of the 'impairment of the individual's capacity for effective performance of social roles and of those tasks which are organised subject to role expectations'. Moreover, according to Parsons (1951:113), the 'traditional' sick role has certain characteristics. First, the 'sick role' is a 'partially and conditionally legitimated state in which others are expected to treat the sick person with compassion, support and help'. Second, it forms 'the basis of a series of legitimised exemptions from the fulfilment of normal expectations' in relation to everyday social obligations and relationships (e.g. an inability to work, an inability to maintain a good relationship with others). Third, by reason of incapacity, 'the individual is not held responsible for his state, in the sense that he could be expected to become well through "pulling himself together" by an act of will'. Finally, the sick role has 'a definitely ascribed goal of action … namely to "get well"' through active cooperation within a therapeutic regime (Parsons, 1951:112). Thus, a person who is sick cannot be expected to fulfil normal social obligations and is not held responsible for their illness. In turn, however, the sick role assumes that the sick person should want to get well, and to this end, must seek and cooperate with medical help in order to resume expectations of everyday roles. Therefore, the physician in this relationship becomes an agent of social control.

The creep of medicalisation in the early twentieth century was initially observed by Menninger (1928:373) who suggested that 'the time will come, when stealing or murder will be thought of as a symptom, indicating the presence of a disease'. Many more examples can also be seen within the world of forensic mental health. Mechanisms of social control can be found across legislation, policy and practice. For example, the inclusion of 'psychopathic disorder' in the Mental Health Act (MHA) 1959 and the emergence of 'Dangerous and Severe Personality Disorder' (DSPD) 40 years later, are commonly seen as mechanisms of socially controlling deviant populations (Manning, 2002). Similarly, Timimi, as part of a written debate in the *British Journal of Psychiatry*, argues that the diagnosis of 'Attention-Deficit Hyperactivity Disorder' (ADHD) is hugely problematic and serves to generate profit for the pharmaceutical industry while taking power (and responsibility) away from young people and their parents (Timimi and Taylor, 2004). Indeed, Timimi argues that

> ADHD scripts a potentially life-long story of disability and deficit, resulting in an attitude of a 'pill for life's problems'. We create unnecessary dependence on doctors, discouraging children and their families from engaging their own abilities to solve problems. ADHD is de-skilling for us as a profession.
>
> (Timimi and Taylor, 2004:8–9)

While social control has remained a solid theme within criminological inquiry, most conventional criminologists have remained firmly focused on the traditional variables of criminology and have not properly considered conformity and deviance in regards to medicine (Timmermans and Gabe, 2003). Radical and critical criminologists (i.e. Cohen, 1989 and Young, 1992 cited in Timmermans and Gabe, 2003) have sought to highlight how the main purpose of crime control initiatives is social control and to keep minority groups socially excluded. Medical tools such as drugs and medical records are important, particularly when they are used in court, since they make 'criminological actions and conclusions possible' (Timmermans and Gabe, 2003:8). However, the implications of such medical tools remain underdeveloped.

MICHEL FOUCAULT: THE ASYLUM AS A MODE OF SOCIAL REGULATION

As functionalism began to lose its appeal, key themes of social control in regard to mental health emerged in social constructivist perspectives (Timmermans and Gabe, 2003). Arguing that all knowledge is constituted and socially constructed under conditions of power, Michel Foucault explored how the development of modern institutions such as prisons and psychiatric hospitals also represented modern modes of social regulation. In one of his most influential works, *Madness and Civilisation*, Foucault (1961) identifies historical shifts in approaches to mental illness, arguing that exclusionary measures began to emerge during the 'Great Confinement' of the nineteenth century. During this period, Foucault identifies that the mad were no longer left wandering throughout society and were instead confined in designated places such as the asylum. The geography and architecture of the asylums reflected notions of exclusion. They were physically separated from wider society and this allowed for the surveillance and daily management of the patients. Foucault used the phrase 'dividing practices' to capture the way that new forms of knowledge – in this case psychiatry – are used by new groups of professionals to identify, classify and ultimately separate groups. This term has particular relevance in today's treatment of the mentally ill as different forensic services set about to define 'their' patients (Wootton et al., 2017).

Unlike the view of some historians, Foucault believed that the introduction of so-called 'moral treatment' was not driven by humanitarian concerns but was done because it provided a different, if not better, means of control. The development of psychiatry, he suggests, became a 'monologue of reason about madness'; in other words, psychiatry and psychiatrists legitimately debated madness within the confines of the profession. As a consequence, the mad become subject to the disciplinary gaze of the emerging psychiatric profession.

However, with the exception of penal reform, criminology is criticised by Timmermans and Gabe (2003) for not ranking Foucault more prominently. They complain that this has led to 'conceptual impoverishment and … disregard for the multiple intersections between criminal justice and medicine' (Timmermans and Gabe, 2003:6). In contrast, the sociology of health and illness has more properly integrated the work of Foucault, which may be explained by 'the fact that public health symbolised the manifestation of new power replacing the older repressive power of the justice system' (Timmermans and Gabe, 2003:6). Foucault's (1991) later ideas about 'governmentality' are also thought to have been influential in the development of mental health practice (Busfield, 2003).

ERVING GOFFMAN: THE ASYLUM AS A TOTAL INSTITUTION

In his ethnographic account of the asylum, Goffman (1961), as an athletics director, was able to document life at St Elizabeth's hospital. Central to Goffman's observations were the power and control that the psychiatrist had in society, and that the institution (asylum) was a means to maintain that power. Drawing on the work of his mentor, Everett Hughes, Goffman (1961:5–6) identifies the asylum as a 'total institution', whereby the basic social arrangement in modern society of individuals tending to 'sleep, play and work in different places, with different co-participants, under different authorities, and without an overall rational plan' is broken down. Those living in total institutions are separated from wider society because they are seen as a threat to society or in need of support or management. In total institutions, the barriers that exist between sleep, play and work are broken down or disappear completely. All aspects of life are conducted in the same physical and psychological space which is controlled by a single authority. The total institution means that individuals carry out each aspect of their daily lives alongside a large group of others who follow a tightly scheduled regime. Like other scholars, Goffman argues that the aim of the regime is to control the havoc that led to the patient's admission but also to ensure that they can re-enter mainstream society. Goffman's legacy is one of highlighting that large institutions produce a culture that is dehumanising and potentially abusive, an argument that is counterweight to the one that abuse in such settings is the result of individual staff. This is one of the key messages that led to the deinstitutionalisation in the years that followed the publication of *Asylums*.

In *Asylums*, Goffman (1961) describes how the institutionalisation process socialises people into the role of a good patient, someone 'dull, harmless and inconspicuous', which, in turn, reinforces notions of chronicity in severe mental illness. This state of compliance has been observed in more recent research by Dixon (2015:1306), who argued that the supervision of psychiatric patients in the community was a form of disciplinary control that aimed to 'instil and maintain in them certain types of thinking that were not related to treatment'. Prior to their conditional discharge, elements of their detention, such as hospital routines, were also seen as ways of socialising service users to think and act in particular ways. As a result of the power of the institution and its practitioners, service users quickly learn that it is in their interests to comply and indeed, 'conformity was seen as a means through which trust between service users and staff might be established' (Dixon, 2015:1309).

THOMAS SZASZ: THE MYTH OF MENTAL ILLNESS

Unlike his contemporaries, Szasz was a libertarian, believing that the role of the state is to be limited as it involves restricting the liberty of some individuals. Very much like his contemporaries, however, Szasz (1960, 1962) viewed psychiatry as a form of social control. He argued that mental illness should not be regarded as a disease but rather a metaphor for a series of personal and social problems. Conversely, a genuine disease must be found in an autopsy or by other medical tests and must be physically present in the organs of the body. None of these can be applied to the field of mental health and psychiatry. Therefore, he suggested that the term mental illness is used for a range of behaviours that society has deemed unacceptable.

Szasz notes that psychiatry is the only medical discipline where diseases are said to no longer exist and where changes in social attitudes have led to changes in diagnosis. Reflecting the changing attitudes of the 1970s, for example, homosexuality was removed from the DSM. The treatment of gay people in the period leading up to this illustrates one of Szasz's key arguments, that a psychiatric diagnosis can act as a powerful but often unacknowledged form of rejection and stigmatisation.

Defining mental illness as a disease, Szasz suggests, has a series of unwanted consequences including the use of compulsory treatment and allowing individuals to escape full responsibility for their actions. This highlights that one of the dangers of medical involvement with deviance is the removal of personal responsibility (Conrad and Schneider, 1992). The expansion of psychiatry into broader aspects of social life means that doctors can create new and increasingly opaque categories of 'sick people'. The constant revision of the DSM is an example of this process. In each edition, new psychiatric conditions are added while old ones are removed. Szasz is not only concerned with the scientific basis for these decisions but also the power that diagnosis and categorisation gives to doctors as representatives of the state.

Where Szasz separates himself from his contemporaries is when talking about the identity attached to those defined as being mentally ill. These identities, he suggests, allow for individuals to behave in a way that is anti-social or criminal and the categorisation of mental illness allows them to deny or escape full responsibility for their actions. Szasz's work has been very influential for service user movements and activism. The notions that psychiatric interventions are coercive, abusive and stigmatising, the lack of scientific basis for psychiatric diagnosis and concerns with human rights for mental health patients all echo Szasz's major preoccupations.

Szasz, however, has also been heavily criticised. For example, Clare (1980) argues that there was no empirical basis for Szasz's assertions and that it is unfair to deny the reality of the suffering of those with mental illness.

THOMAS SCHEFF: ON BEING MENTALLY ILL

Thomas Scheff's (1966) book, *On Being Mentally Ill*, argues that diagnostic formulations neglect the accompanying social processes. Like Szasz, Scheff argues that mental illness, and the symptoms that accompany it, should be regarded as metaphors for deviant behaviours that violate accepted social norms. Scheff, therefore, added the concept of 'residual rule breaking' to the labelling view of mental illness. Residual rule breaking is based upon the idea that most social conventions or norms are fairly clear and understood, yet there is a residual area of social convention that is assumed to be so natural that it is part of 'human nature'. These residual conventions include such behaviours as looking at the person you are talking to or responding to someone who calls your name. To violate these residual conventions goes beyond just violating norms, it involves acting contrary to human nature. Such 'unnatural behaviour' may be regarded by others as mental illness.

While some labelling theorists like Scheff (1966) believed that those labelled as mentally ill may engage with secondary deviance as they accept the deviant label given to them, more recent research with psychiatric patients asserts that some patients may seek to do the opposite and give the appearance of being compliant by responding with 'secrecy and withdrawal' (Dixon, 2015:1309).

Scheff's theory is now quite dated and, like Szasz's, is undermined by recent advances in our understanding of the organic changes that accompany some major mental health problems.

DAVID ROSENHAN: ON BEING SANE IN INSANE PLACES

By asking the question 'if sanity and insanity exist, how shall we know them?', along with his predecessors, Rosenhan (1973) set out to demonstrate that psychiatric classification is unreliable. Influenced by the work of Becker (1964), Rosenhan's work began with the premise that terms such as normal, abnormal and so on, are culturally generated and specific. In other words, what is regarded in one culture or social setting as normal may be regarded in another as bizarre or strange. The main conclusion drawn from Rosenhan's (1973) study, published under the title of 'On being sane in insane places', was that diagnosis in psychiatry is inherently unreliable.

In this study, Rosenhan and his colleagues, including three women and five men, began by calling different hospitals and making appointments. When they arrived for their appointment they complained of hearing voices. The voices, they said, were unclear but sounded like they were saying empty, hollow and thud. Some of the pseudo-patients also reported hallucinations. The pseudo-patients were admitted to 12 different hospitals in five different US states over the course of the experiment for either schizophrenia or manic depression. When the pseudo-patients were admitted to the wards they stopped simulating any symptoms, began to act 'normally' and told staff that they felt fine and were no longer experiencing hallucinations or hearing voices. The hospital staff misinterpreted their normal behaviour and instead believed that the pseudo-patients were exhibiting ongoing signs of mental illness. All were prescribed medication, although the researchers made sure not to take it. The length of admissions varied between 7 and 52 days, with an average length of 19 days. The pseudo-patients were eventually discharged but most were described as being in remission. This discharge status, according to Rosenhan, is not the same as being 'cured', and in effect means that it is impossible to escape a psychiatric diagnosis.

CONTEMPORARY CRITIQUES OF PSYCHIATRY

Although the likes of Goffman, Szasz, Scheff and Foucault were publishing during the mid-twentieth century their work remains relevant at the time of writing and is considered the foundation of anti-psychiatry, illustrating the enduring power of sociological concepts. For example, the legacy of Parsons' (1951) sick role, Foucault's (1991) governmentality, Goffman's (1961) 'asylums' and Scheff's (1966) labelling theory, can all be found in Dixon's (2015) study of mental health patients subject to supervision in the community following conditional discharge from hospital.

Contemporary critiques of the medical model can be thematically grouped around culture, gender and service user experiences (Bartlett, 2010). While approaching their critique from somewhat differing perspectives, all three dispute the value of the medical model and highlight the value systems implicit in medical judgement. Consistent with the anti-psychiatry movement, contemporary critiques commonly challenge the scientific basis for the medical model. While medicine has played a crucial role in 'making up people', as these critiques show 'some people are more made up than others – women more than men, the wealthy differently from the poor, children more than adults, and, of course, differently in different countries and regions of the world' (Rose, 2007:700).

Those criticising psychiatry from a cultural perspective argue that the classificatory systems – ICD-11 and DSM-5 – were developed in Europe and North America with relatively little input from researchers and practitioners elsewhere across the globe. Anthropologists, in particular, have criticised the medical model's assumption of universality (Kleinman, 1977, 1987), emphasising how different cultures have different concepts of person thus different ideas about appropriate social relations. Moreover, behaviours viewed as 'abnormal' in the West may not be construed indigenously. Indeed, we are reminded by Marsella and White (1982:ix) that 'all behaviour is culturally related and all mental disorders and therapies are culture specific'.

To counter this debate, the UK has tried to involve Black, Asian and Minority Ethnic (BAME) people in the development of psychiatric care, particularly where there are examples of over- and under-representation in patient populations (Davies et al., 1996; Morgan et al., 2004). Explanations for the over-representation of BAME people in psychiatric services have included: racism among practitioners of psychiatry; that the stress of migration gives rise to increasing levels of psychiatric disorders; that the stress of living in a racist society is more likely to induce mental disorder; that people with BAME status may be misdiagnosed due to a lack of understanding and 'cultural congruity' between patient and clinician; and that there may be biological differences among BAME groups (Bartlett, 2010).

While some BAME groups like black men are over-represented at every stage of the mental health system (Department of Health, 2009), many BAME people involved with mental health care also feel marginalised and excluded from mainstream services. In addition to BAME people being over-represented in the criminal justice system, they are also more likely to have disparate access to health care (Primm,

Osher and Gomez, 2005; Rabiee and Smith, 2014). This highlights that BAME people often experience 'negative' care pathways (Morgan et al., 2005) and that the care some BAME offenders receive is lacking in 'cultural competence' (Primm, Osher and Gomez, 2005).

Those criticising psychiatry from a gender perspective emphasise how women, during the nineteenth century, were detained much more frequently than their male counterparts. Historically, women have been construed as irrational, whereas men have been associated with reason, culture and intellectual discourse (Bartlett, 2010). Showalter (1987) highlights that even the most powerful critics of the medical model failed to consider gender and argues that changing diagnostic fashions within psychiatry have disguised a very basic problem, which is that women are still more frequently defined as being unwell. Others have argued that the use of medication, particularly in prisons, is a form of governance that not only acts as a mechanism of social control, but also a punitive and disciplinary enterprise delegitimising women's self-identified needs (Kilty, 2012). While sociologists have explored the links between gender and mental health, the focus has tended to be on women. Rogers and Pilgrim (2014) warn that this approach may neglect the social processes that leave men particularly vulnerable to coercive interventions while also serving to increase the associations made between women and madness.

Service user critiques of psychiatry and the medical model began to grow in the 1970s and 1980s (Wallcraft and Bryant, 2003). A key theme of the service user critique is inequality between patients and experts, made worse by legislation that gives experts power over patients. Recent research by Beresford et al. (2016) found that most service users feel the medical model is too dominant in mental health services, is stigmatising, and can lead to an over-reliance on drug treatment. Despite having expertise resulting from their experience, service users have not traditionally been given a voice (Tait and Lester, 2005). Chamberlin (1988), for example, identifies that an individual's subjective experience is often ignored by the medical account of their condition, and that there is often disagreement around diagnosis and treatment plans. However, there have been growing attempts to involve service users in their mental health care over the last 20 years (Newman et al., 2015). While service users disagree about the value of extending a social model of disability to their experience, the majority feel that a holistic approach which takes account of the individual person and their wider social circumstances would improve their experiences of mental health services (Beresford et al., 2016).

In contrast to more traditional critiques, contemporary critiques have allowed for the development of a discourse that is not only sensitive to the issue of meaning but also promotes a partnership with emerging user movements (Bracken and Thomas, 2010:226). For example, Bracken (2002) has been able to develop detailed cultural critiques of the concept of post-traumatic stress disorder (PTSD) and particularly its use in people from non-Western cultures. Crucially, through a critique of current ideas and practices, this type of research opens the field of psychiatry to different ways of understanding, framing and responding to differing experiences. As Bracken and Thomas (2010:227) suggest:

> by critiquing the status quo, by revealing the constructed nature of psychiatric theory and practice, the aim is not to replace one psychiatric authority with another but to weaken the notion of authority in the field of mental health altogether.

Similarly, Priebe (2016:525) observes that while the social constructionist critique of mental disorders is provocative for many psychiatrists 'because the statement might be seen as questioning the position of psychiatry in medicine, ... recognising mental disorders as social constructs does not render them useless'. Constructs are necessary for enabling action and are necessary to conduct research (Priebe, 2016). Moreover, the medical model, for all its flaws, enables practitioners to communicate effectively about their patients (Bartlett, 2010). Processes of diagnosis, for example, enable practitioners and other professionals to discuss mental health problems, identify need and allocate appropriate treatment.

TOWARDS A CRIMINOLOGY OF MENTAL HEALTH

As we learnt in the last chapter the relationship between mental health and offending is complex, surrounded by many intractable questions. People with mental health problems are commonly seen as dangerous or riskier because of their health problems. Yet, people with mental health problems are actually far more at risk of victimisation than those without (and often as a result of the prejudice directed towards them). Surprisingly, mental health has received less attention than might be expected among criminologists despite its obvious relevance. Problems with defining what we mean by 'mentally disordered offenders' along with the practical challenges of looking after people who can sometimes be challenging, leads Peay (2017:641) to note that 'it is perhaps not surprising that they have been relegated and isolated, both in theory and practice'. But, Peay (2017:641) also argues that 'how we deal conceptually, practically, and in principle with those deemed "mentally disordered offenders" is central to the scope of criminology'. We agree with Peay (2017). The relationship between mental ill health, exclusion, deviance and offending should be of significant interest to criminologists. As should the high levels of victimisation and public discourses of fear and hostility that commonly surround those with mental health problems. Those in contact with the criminal justice system have a high prevalence of mental health problems. Indeed, Peay (2017) reminds us, only 10% of the prison population does not have some form of diagnosable mental health condition. Whatever the reasons for this high prevalence of mental disorder, it should remind us of our responsibility to interrogate the way in which this heterogeneous and changing group of people are governed. Too often, those with mental health problems in contact with the criminal justice system are defined in terms of their potential risks, rather than in terms of their rights or needs (Langan and Lindow, 2004). While managing the risk that some offenders with poor mental health pose is a legitimate aim, we also have a responsibility to provide humane and effective care for those who are unwell.

BACK TO BASICS: CLASSICAL CRIMINOLOGY AND POSITIVISM

The most common starting point of criminology is with classical criminology. Classical criminology, commonly associated with the writings of Cesare Beccaria, assumes that people act with free will and therefore criminal behaviour is understood as the consequence of rational choice. As a result, the legal system should be proportionate with punishments aimed at deterring people from offending.

In contrast, early positivist schools of criminology focused on the factors that may contribute to offending or constrain the choices that offenders have, thereby countering the notion that offenders act rationally and with free will. For positivism, choices are constrained and the causes of offending lie beyond the individual offender. The rise of psychiatry and psychology is closely linked to the positivist view that 'man's body and mind should be studied according to the methods and approaches of the natural sciences' (Oosterhuis and Loughnan, 2014:2).

Conflicts between voluntarism and determinism have also troubled forensic psychiatry, criminology and the legal system for many years (Oosterhuis and Loughnan, 2014). Indeed, Reznek (1997:8) observes that in courts of law, psychiatric and legal conceptual systems lock horns. Psychiatrists talk of manic-depression and schizophrenia, lawyers of insanity and diminished responsibility. Psychiatrists make deterministic assumptions and explain behaviour in terms of serotonin levels and frontal lobe damage, while lawyers assume free will and explain behaviour in terms of desires and beliefs. Psychiatrists analyse the causes of the behaviour, and lawyers look for the reasons.

While the increasing involvement of psychiatric expertise in the judicial system has been 'applauded as a desirable humanization of legal processes', it is also feared for its 'infringement on legal standards of culpability' and for its ability to violate principles of proportionality (Oosterhuis and Longnan, 2014:3). Psychiatric opinion is, in many cases, offered as an expert view on the presence or absence of mental disorder, and legal frameworks have a tendency to accept that mental disorder is what 'experts' say it is. In many ways, the legal framework has to accept and embrace the psychiatric framework and when the latter is lacking has to refer to lay people through the jury system to clarify the presence or absence of mental disorder. The risk is amplified in serious cases of offending such as murder or sexual offending, where lay people may argue, on the one hand, that a person must be 'sick' to commit such an act but, on the other hand, that such acts warrant severe punishment.

While considerable attention has been directed at the growth of forensic psychiatry and criminology in the nineteenth and early twentieth centuries, a notable gap exists when it comes to the later twentieth and earlier twenty-first centuries with few scholars exploring the boundary between medicine, including 'psy' disciplines, and the penal system and its concern with the administration of justice (Oosterhuis and Loughnan, 2014:1). Concepts such as dangerousness, risk and populist punitivism, developed more recently in the disciplines of sociology and criminology, have been used to explain the processes and decisions made at the intersection between health and criminal justice, a discussion that we turn to next.

CONTEMPORARY CRIMINOLOGICAL THINKING

DANGEROUSNESS

The association of the mentally disordered with dangerousness has a long history. Dangerousness was first associated with 'vagrants' but eventually extended to the mentally disordered as early as the sixteenth century (Thomas, 2005, cited in Kemshall, 2008). In contemporary times, media portrayals of mental illness give rise to the belief that the sole condition necessary for violence towards another is the presence of a mental disorder (Stuart, 2006). These types of beliefs are reinforced by sensationalist reporting on occasions where a person with a mental disorder has caused injury to another (Diefenbach, 1997). According to Szasz (2003:227), the very term mental illness implies that people with such illnesses are more likely to be a danger to themselves and others than those without such illnesses.

Dangerousness, however, is often linked to what we fear most rather than what is actually dangerous (Harrison, 2011). Gunn (1982), for example, suggests that dangerousness is made up of 'destructiveness, prediction and fear'. He also observes how 'fear, makes it at least partially subjective, therefore it can never be entirely objective' (Gunn, 1982:7). The mentally disordered offender, therefore, is often wrapped up with notions of fear and danger. One commonly held belief is that community care policies are failing and that there are more people on the streets due to the deinstitutionalisation programme of the 1980s. This has perpetuated the belief that the public are at risk of being harmed by those who were released into the community from mental health asylums. Such perceptions are able to flourish in a climate where understanding about mental disorder and the governance of those with mental disorder is limited. Yet, despite rises in the overall murder rate, the number of murders committed by those with mental illness has continued to fall following the closure of the asylums (Large et al., 2008).

The public's preoccupation with dangerousness has been further amplified by widely reported scandals and it is against this backdrop that the state has taken on increasing responsibility for the management of dangerousness in the late twentieth century (Kemshall, 2008). A range of measures, including homicide inquiries, more stringent community supervision and indeterminate sentences, have been introduced to support the increasing attention given to so-called 'dangerous' offenders (see Chapter 3 for a discussion).

RISK

Debates about the dangerousness of the mentally ill in the early 1980s (Floud, 1982; Floud and Young, 1981) were gradually replaced in the 1990s with discussions about risk assessment and management (Mullen, 2000). In large part because of the problems surrounding dangerousness, risk came to take centre stage. Castel (1991) charts the ways in which criminal justice policy has shifted from dangerousness to risk (see also Steadman et al., 1993). Beginning as a fairly neutral term in the insurance industry, it has come to dominate our way of thinking about the world more generally and this of course, includes the criminal justice and mental health arenas (Harrison, 2011). Today, risk is regarded as a fundamental element of mental health practice, for both offenders and non-offenders (Mullen, 2000).

The rise in risk thinking is well captured by Beck's (1992) 'risk society' (see also Giddens, 1991). Risk, and our preoccupation with its assessment and management have become pervasive in late modernity. Moreover, risk is at the heart of the public protection agenda (Solomon, 2008) and subsequently the governance of mentally disordered offenders (Peay, 2007; Rose, 1998a). In late modernity, risks have become more incalculable (Beck, 1992) and unknown, while becoming ever more omnipresent (Giddens, 1991). 'Calculating and managing risks which nobody really knows has become one of our main preoccupations' (Beck, 1998:12; see also Hacking, 1990) with the management of dangerous offenders now requiring us to think the 'unthinkable' and ask the 'unaskable' (Prins, 1988:604).

One consequence of this shift is that major institutions (i.e. police, health services, education etc.) have become organised around acquiring 'risk knowledge' (Ericson and Haggerty, 1997). Key actors, such as the police, or in forensic mental health, psychiatrists, become 'risk knowledge workers' where risk 'is not just a language of communication. Risk becomes the means by which professionals think, act and justify their actions' (Rose, 2017:7). Kemshall (2008) argues that criminological and legal perspectives have focused on a technical understanding of risk alongside attempts to develop reliable risk assessment tools. The development of risk assessment tools has helped support the revival of the 'psy' disciplines (Rose, 1998b), and risk management has consequently become central to the role of mental health practitioners (Fennell and Yeates, 2002).

High-profile murders in the community following the closure of large psychiatric hospitals (see Chapter 3) have helped expose the perceived failures of deinstitutionalisation and served to heighten the public's feeling of broken trust. Such tragedies are no longer understood as the result of fate but as an unintended consequence of modernity (Giddens, 1991) and the failure of professional expertise for which someone must be responsible and accountable (Rose, 1998a). 'Whose fault? Is the first question' often asked (Douglas, 1992:16) highlighting that our trust in experts (Beck, 1992; Garland, 2001; Giddens, 1991) and their methods for assessing and managing risk

(Kemshall and Maguire, 2001; Power, 2007; Solomon, 2008) are diminishing. Moreover, it highlights that public and political interest in penology is heightened when things go wrong (Kemshall, 2008; Sparks, 2000) and that a key feature of modernity 'is the necessity of establishing "the facts" in situations where something has gone wrong and taking rational and systematic steps to rectify the situation' (Webb and Harris, 1999:2).

Many strategies have been developed to find out what has gone wrong, including the introduction of inquiries into homicides committed by those known to mental health services, supervision registers and guidance on discharge (see the next chapter for a discussion). A number of inquiries have exposed some of the problems involved with managing the risk of 'dangerous' and/or 'mentally disordered' offenders. However, one paradox of these inquiries is that rather than making us feel safer, they serve to perpetuate and add to our fear of the mentally disordered. Unfortunately, our attempts to control risk around us have not left us feeling more secure and in control, but rather fear and anxiety have come to dominate as we become increasingly concerned about menace and 'dangerization' (Lianos and Douglas, 2000).

The notion of 'risk society' 'obscures as much as it reveals' given that it is doubtful that society is any 'more risky' than societies in the past (Rose, 2017:6). Nevertheless, Rose (2017:7) advocates thinking of the risk society as '*a style of thought* that seeks to bring the future into the present and make it calculable' (emphasis added). In his discussion of modernity as a 'risk culture', Giddens (1991:3) makes the same point when he asserts that society is no more risky than it used to be; 'rather, the concept of risk becomes fundamental to the way both lay actors and technical specialists organise the social world'.

POPULIST PUNITIVISM AND PUBLIC PROTECTION

The developments discussed under the concepts of 'dangerousness' and 'risk' suggest that we have moved from an elitist model of penal policy to a more populist model (Johnstone, 2000; Ryan, 1999) where the government are now 'more keen to engage the public than to exclude it' (Johnstone, 2000:161). This has led some to observe the rise of 'populist punitiveness' (Bottoms, 1995) and a 'new punitiveness' (Pratt, 2000). While the mental health field has come under increasing pressure of populist punitivism and concerns for victims (Fennell and Yeates, 2002), it is important to remember that the public are often painted as more punitive than they actually are (Hough, 1996), and

> there is a division between those who see this surge in punitiveness as being driven from "below" by an anxious and angry general public and those who see it as an essentially "top down" process in which ambitious and manipulative politicians play on public fears and anxieties in order to get tough on crime and to increase their electoral support.
>
> (Matthews, 2005:176)

This highlights that policies can be shaped by what the government believes concerns the wider public (Edgar, 2010). Markham (2018) reminds us that we do not really know what the public think about mental illness and the criminal justice system. Moreover, public understandings about mental illness change over time (Phelan et al., 2000). Many political responses to high-profile events are done with reference to public safety, but it is important to remember that public anxiety and/or demands for tougher policies regarding those with mental health problems may be assumed, rather than actual. This may well reflect Carroll, Lyall and Forrester's (2004:409) observation that 'whereas increased spending on mental health is unlikely to gain votes, a perceived weak approach to "dangerous patients" may well lose them'. Similarly, Pilgrim and Rogers (2003:12) observe that 'psychiatric patients are powerless, cast relatively few votes and their episodic loss of reasons makes it easy for politicians to target a group, which lacks social credibility in the eyes of others'.

Whether it is public or politically led, ethical and civil liberty concerns have had a decreasing influence on legislators (Kemshall and Maguire, 2001) and mental health policy now has an 'increasingly coercive appearance' (Cutcliffe and Hannigan, 2001:315). Such risk thinking has consequences for the 'small fish' who may not otherwise have come to state attention and therefore control, as well as the 'big fish', that is, those considered to be monstrous (Rose, 2002:10). The media, politicians and corresponding 'moral panics' often centre around particularly 'monstrous' individuals who are felt to pose an unacceptable threat, helping to justify the most punitive of responses (Rose, 2002).

Given this, it is unsurprising that practitioners involved with mental health clients face multiple ethical challenges in their work (Szmulker, 2009). Many of these manifest from ethical concerns that patient confidentiality may be undermined by the duty to try and avoid harm to others (see Chapter 8 for an extended discussion).

ACTUARIALISM AND THE NEW PENOLOGY

Explanations and descriptions of risk in criminology have often centred around Feeley and Simon's (1992) claim that a 'new penology' has emerged based on actuarial techniques for identifying and managing groups arranged by dangerousness. Actuarial justice is concerned with the probabilistic calculation of risk and the statistical distribution of different populations rather than individual characteristics. This penology, in contrast to earlier forms, has a managerial rather than transformative task. Indeed,

> [t]he new penology is markedly less concerned with responsibility, fault, moral sensibility, diagnosis, or intervention and treatment of the individual offender. Rather it is concerned with techniques to identify, classify, and manage groupings of sorted dangerousness.
>
> (Feeley and Simon, 1992:452)

The extent to which actuarial justice has displaced other traditional penological practices has been subject to much debate (Pratt, 2000; O'Malley, 2004; Robinson, 2002; Sparks, 2000). Risk is a heterogeneous array of practices that can have varying effects and may take several forms, including treatment and the identification of offender needs (O'Malley, 2004). Furthermore, risk discourse is not as static as actuarial justice suggests but ever shifting and criminologists have a 'responsibility to consider the promise, as well as the problems of risk' (O'Malley, 2008:453). 'There is no obvious reason why risk cannot be inclusive and reformist rather than exclusionary and merely incapacitating' (O'Malley, 2008:453). Moreover, statistical probabilities are only one method of estimating the probability of harm, and clinical judgements still inform many assessments in the criminal justice system (O'Malley, 2000).

COMBINING RISK AND REHABILITATION: THE TRANSFORMATIVE RISK SUBJECT

Rose (2002) highlights that while the new penology theory holds value, it is misleading in the field of mental health where risk thinking is actuarial but also requires practitioners to identify and manage risky individuals. Busfield (2002:80) makes a similar point, asserting that risk assessment in psychiatry still focuses on the individual in an attempt to predict the risk of that specific individual being violent, rather than simply aggregating risks across forensic populations. This reflects that 'psy' disciplines, such as psychiatry and psychology, tend to adopt a hybrid approach to risk, using both actuarial and clinical approaches in tandem (Kemshall, 2008). Moreover, psychological approaches to dangerousness and risk, have tended to look at individual traits in order to answer questions about culpability and treatability (Kemshall, 2008). Such approaches have also led to the implementation of accredited treatment programmes often based on cognitive behavioural therapy (CBT) and administered by prison and probation staff (Kemshall, 2008).

This reflects that while the new penology argues that rehabilitation is sidestepped in the interests of categorising and managing risk, others highlight that strategies of risk and rehabilitation are often combined. For example, Armstrong (2003), in her analysis of the juvenile justice system in Massachusetts, argues that the use of mental health language and techniques by staff to legitimise diagnosis and treatment reflects an attempt by the juvenile justice system to simultaneously achieve rehabilitation and retribution.

Hannah-Moffat (2005:29) highlights the emergence of a '*transformative risk subject* who unlike the "*fixed or static risk subject*" is amenable to targeted therapeutic intervention' (emphasis in original). While risk thinking has certainly permeated social policy with dangerous offenders, there has also been a focus on therapeutic aims (McBride, 2017) and a 'renaissance in the quest to find "what works"' (Brooker, Denney and Sirdifield, 2014:485). Prison spaces have been redefined as new therapeutic resources and staff are now required to be increasingly 'psychologically-aware' (McBride, 2017). This is a significant development because 'the remoulding of prisons into therapeutic spaces legitimates them as sites of detention for those who occupy the border lands of madness and criminality' (McBride, 2017:1268). 'Psy' developments continue to represent advances of social control. Indeterminate detention in the criminal justice system and involuntary detention in the mental health system can be justified on the basis of there being a therapeutic provision. Increasing assessment and therapeutic resources serve to justify the advancement of therapeutic penality as more and more offenders come to be identified as mentally disordered and in need of treatment (McBride, 2017).

THE EMERGENCE OF A PRECAUTIONARY LOGIC

The 'turn' towards risk has been well documented in the social sciences and continues to represent a pervasive framework in which to understand attempts by the state to govern those whose behaviour has been or is thought to be potentially undesirable. In recent years, scholars have begun to document a new turn, where risk becomes obsolete because of the need to remove it completely. Indeed, many have documented the emergence of an increasingly 'precautionary' (Ericson, 2007; Hebenton and Seddon, 2009) or 'pre-emptive' (Zedner, 2009) logic which has developed in response to a 'zero-risk problematic' (Ewald, 2000:378). The management of high-risk offenders now involves the identification of prevention of risks to the public, 'with zero risk an unstated but implicit aim' (Kemshall, 2008:85). Hebenton and Seddon (2009:4–10) argue that 'uncertainty is no longer an excuse [and] false "negatives" (incorrectly rating a person as "safe") cannot be tolerated'. In this context, professionals come under increasing 'obligation' to '[act] in the present in order to manage the future' (Rose, 2002:212). This moves our focus beyond traditional concerns for probabilistic risk, towards possibilistic concerns about the 'worst case scenario' (Clarke, 2006; Furedi, 2009). One of the main consequences of this turn is that punishment is now 'required to fit the potential risk as well as fit the crime' (Kemshall, 2008:29).

MANAGING OR ELIMINATING RISK: A PARADOX UNVEILED

Several paradoxes are created by the increasing preoccupation with public protection and the desire to eliminate risk. Greater demands for protection have generated greater anxiety among the public and increased the media's preoccupation with the dangerousness of strangers. Consequently, public protection efforts often come to focus on the rare types of offender, thereby ignoring those closest, and most risky to us (Kitzinger, 2004). Paradoxically, this increases the likelihood of harm (Kitzinger, 2004).

Of course, political promises to secure public protection can be limited by obstacles on the ground. These obstacles may include the judiciary who may resist new waves of dangerousness legislation and resources, thereby restricting the extent to which a public protection agenda can be pursued (Kemshall, 2008).

RECONCILING THE ROLE OF FORENSIC PSYCHIATRY

It is important to explore the role of forensic psychiatry in its changing context and increasing social obligations to assess, manage and control risk (Rose, 2002:6). Forensic psychiatry as a specialist branch of medicine, first emerged in the late eighteenth and early nineteenth centuries as mental asylums began to grow in number and began to adopt a more therapeutic approach (Oosterhuis and Loughnan, 2014). During these times psychiatrists were almost exclusively concerned with a small group of mentally disordered offenders in hospital. In contemporary times, however, 'forensic' issues are encountered in a range of settings including police custody, the courts, prisons and the community (Rose, 2002).

The somewhat necessary relationship between psychiatry and the criminal justice system has, however, as always been controversial. The increased focus during the 1990s on high-risk offenders (of which many have some form of mental disorder) led to the development of numerous offending behaviour programmes. These included a renewed commitment around 'what works' and increasing confidence in CBT to treat offenders. Despite this shift, however, psychiatric pessimism continued. Risk management during this period became more of an urgent political priority. Consequently, many initiatives to try and rehabilitate (mentally disordered) offenders came second to attempts to manage, and ultimately prevent, the risk of violent, sexual and sometimes mentally disordered, offenders from committing offences (see Chapter 3).

While there has been a proliferation of accredited programmes available to offenders serving custodial and community sentences, thus embracing the 'what works' model and placing therapy high on the agenda, McAlinden (2012:172) reminds us that in practice 'contemporary therapeutic strategies have become embedded and subsumed within a broader penal rhetoric of risk management and public protection'. Offenders convicted of violent or sexual offences, many of whom will be serving indeterminate sentences, may find that they have little choice but to engage with these therapeutic programmes if they wish to make progress with their sentence and ultimately return to the community. This is all the more difficult for those with mental disorder, who may find themselves excluded from these programmes because of their symptoms.

In recent years, the Good Lives Model (GLM), a strengths-based theory of offender rehabilitation, has emerged. This focuses on an individual offender's goals, the pursuit of basic goods and attempts to equip offenders with the resources to legitimately achieve these. In the GLM, offending is seen as an attempt to obtain these basic goods in the context of the offender's individual and wider social disadvantage (i.e. poor education, social support, poverty). By focusing on these criminogenic factors, the model aims to equip offenders with the ability to obtain basic goods through legitimate means, thereby reducing offender risk.

The GLM is thought to offer considerable promise with mentally disordered offenders for its ability to integrate risk and rehabilitation in a comprehensive theory (Robertson, Barnao and Ward, 2011). The developers also assert that the model 'bypasses the tensions inherent in balancing the roles of treatment and duty to protect society' that are present in other rehabilitation models, because of its focus on addressing offending, mental disorder and an offender's individual goals and aspirations (Robertson, Barnao and Ward, 2011:483). The GLM can also encourage engagement with treatment and support better therapeutic relationships (Robertson, Barnao and Ward, 2011). However, statistical evidence in support of the GLM, especially with mentally disordered offenders, is still limited (Barnao and Ward, 2015).

Over the years several different paradigms in forensic psychology for thinking about the rehabilitation of mentally disordered offenders have developed. These include the risk paradigm (a criminal justice approach focusing on the risk of reoffending), the psychopathology paradigm (a mental health approach focusing on treatment) and a combination (or blurring) of the two (including the GLM). Whatever paradigm is used, the forensic mental health system is confronted with the challenge of having to try and reconcile the two different, and often competing, perspectives of public protection and patient welfare. As Rose (2002:23) emphasises, it is 'clear that contemporary psychiatric dilemmas about control are not so much medical and scientific as ethical and political'.

DISCUSSION

We began this chapter by tracing the origins and early development of forensic mental health. We started by charting, albeit briefly, the growth of the public asylum system from the seventeenth to nineteenth centuries. This discussion has enabled us to consider the historical governance of people with mental disorder and a number of associated developments including the growth of (forensic) psychiatry (and psychology) and developments in the treatment and understanding of mental disorder. A number of transformations in the policy and practice associated with mental disorder have been observed, but this history has also illustrated that a number of continuities and 'echoes from the past' remain.

It has been the growth of psychiatry, however, that has come under much criticism, particularly the use of the medical model to understand behaviour that is now associated with mental disorder. The medical model provides a useful framework for practitioners to communicate between themselves about symptoms, diagnosis and the identification of treatment, but it is not a model that always extends beyond the medical profession. As we have illustrated in this chapter, the medical model has served to legitimise medical understandings of mental disorder and made the medical expert an agent of social control. In turn, the patient's subjective experiences of their state of mind are sometimes neglected.

As we highlighted in Chapter 1, despite the lack of consensus about the relationship between mental disorder and crime, there is an inevitable intersection between the criminal justice and mental health systems. Irrespective of the validity and accuracy of various definitions and/or understandings of mental health and crime, these systems must still deal with large numbers of people who come under their care each year and who may pose a very real risk of harm to themselves and others.

Yet, criminology has remained relatively mute on the subject of forensic mental health. Accordingly, in this chapter, we have tried to encourage our readers towards understanding mental disorder within criminological frameworks. The public's preoccupation with dangerousness and risk have led to a fundamental shift in the way in which psychiatrists and other mental health specialists work whereby risk management has become central to their roles. Alongside this shift has been a move towards more populist approaches to deal with so-called 'dangerous' patients. Whether this shift has been publicly or politically led remains unknown (Markham, 2018), but mental health policy, as we will see in the next chapter, has often had an increasingly coercive feel.

FURTHER READING

For an extended discussion about medicine as an institution of social control see Conrad and Schneider (1992). For a very accessible overview of the different perspective surrounding forensic mental health see Oosterhuis and Loughnan (2014). For a critical discussion about the history of insanity see Foucault (1961) and Seddon (2007). For extended discussions from those involved in the anti-psychiatry movement see Parsons (1951), Goffman (1961), Szasz (1960, 1962), Scheff (1966) and Rosenhan (1973). For a critique of the DSM in particular see Thornton (1992) and Kutchins and Kurt (1997).

REFERENCES

Anckarsäter, H., Radovic, S., Svennerlind, C., Hoglund, P. and Radovic, F. (2009) 'Mental disorder is a cause of crime: The cornerstone of forensic psychiatry', *International Journal of Law and Psychiatry*, 32(6): 342–347.

Armstrong, S. (2003) 'The emergence and implications of a mental health ethos in juvenile justice' in Timmermans, S. and Gabe, J. (eds.) *Partners in health, partners in crime*, Oxford: Blackwell Publishing.

Barnao, M. and Ward, T. (2015) 'Sailing unchartered seas without a compass: A review of interventions in forensic mental health', *Aggression and Violent Behavior*, 22: 77–86.

Bartlett, A. (2010) 'Medical models of mental disorder' in Bartlett, A. and McGauley, G. (eds.) *Forensic mental health: Concepts, systems and practice*, Oxford: Oxford University Press.

Beck, U. (1992) *Risk society*, London: Sage.

Beck, U. (1998) 'Politics in risk society' in Franklin, J. (ed.) *The politics of risk society*, Cambridge: Polity Press.

Becker, H. (1964) *The other side: Perspectives on deviance*, New York: The Free Press.

Beresford, P. (2002) 'Thinking about "mental health": Towards a social model', *Journal of Mental Health*, 11(6): 581–584.

Beresford, P., Perring, R., Nettle, M. and Wallcraft, J. (2016) *From mental illness to a social model of madness and distress*, London: Shaping Our Lives.

Bottoms, A. (1995) 'The politics of sentencing reform' in Clarkson, C. and Morgan, R. (eds.) *The philosophy and politics of punishment and sentencing*, Oxford: Oxford University Press.

Bracken, P. (2002) *Trauma: Culture, meaning and philosophy*, Philadelphia: Whurr Publishers.

Bracken, P. and Thomas, P. (2010) 'From Szasz to Foucault: On the role of critical psychiatry', *Philosophy, Psychiatry and Psychology*, 17(3): 219–228.

Brooker, C., Denney, D. and Sirdifield, C. (2014) 'Mental disorder and probation policy and practice: A view from the UK', *International Journal of Law and Psychiatry*, 37(5): 484–489.

Busfield, J. (2002) 'Psychiatric discourse and individual violence: Imagined death, risk and mental health policy' in Buchanan, A. (ed.) *Care of the mentally disordered offender in the community*, Oxford: Oxford University Press.

Busfield, J. (2003) 'Introduction: Rethinking the sociology of mental health', *Sociology of Health and Illness*, 22(5): 543–558.

Campillo, D. (1984) 'Neurological pathology in prehistory', *Acta Neurochirurgica*, 70(3–4): 275–290.

Carroll, A., Lyall, M. and Forrester, A. (2004) 'Clinical hopes and public fears in forensic mental health', *Journal of Forensic Psychiatry and Psychology*, 15(3): 407–425.

Castel, R. (1991) 'From dangerousness to risk' in Burchell, G., Gordon, C. and Miller, P. (eds.) *The Foucault effect: Studies in governmentality*, Hemel Hempstead: Harvester Wheatsheaf.

Chamberlin, J. (1988) *On our own: Patient controlled alternatives to the mental health system*, London: Mind.

Clare, A. (1980) *Psychiatry in dissent*, London: Routledge.

Clarke, L. (2006) *Worst cases: Terror and catastrophe in the popular imagination*, Chicago: University of Chicago Press.

Conrad, P. and Schneider, J.W. (1992) *Deviance and medicalization: From badness to sickness*, Philadelphia: Temple University Press.

Cutcliffe, J.R. and Hannigan, B. (2001) 'Mass media, "monsters" and mental health clients: The need for increased lobbying', *Journal of Psychiatric and Mental Health Nursing*, 8(4): 315–321.

Davies, S., Thorncroft, G., Leese, M., Higginbotham, A. and Phelan, M. (1996) 'Ethnic differences in risk of compulsory psychiatric admission among representative cases of psychosis in London', *British Medical Journal*, 312(7030): 533–537.

Department of Health (2009) *The Bradley Report. Lord Bradley's review of people with mental health problems or learning disabilities in the criminal justice system*, London: Department of Health.

Diefenbach, D. (1997) 'The portrayal of mental illness on prime-time television', *Journal of Community Psychology*, 25(3): 289–302.

Dixon, J. (2015) 'Treatment, deterrence or labelling: Mentally disordered offenders' perspectives on social control', *Sociology of Health and Illness*, 37(8): 1299–1313.

Douglas, M. (1992) *Risk and blame: Essays in cultural theory*, London: Routledge.

Edgar, K. (2010) 'Recognising mental health: Balancing risk and care' in Royal College of Nursing (ed.) *Prison mental health: Vision and reality*, London: Royal College of Nursing.

Ericson, R. (2007) *Crime in an insecure world*, Cambridge: Polity Press.

Ericson, R. and Haggerty, K. (1997) *Policing the risk society*, Toronto: University of Toronto Press.

Ewald, F. (2000) 'Risk in contemporary society', *Connecticut Insurance Law Journal*, 6: 365–379.

Faria, M.A. (2013) 'Violence, mental illness, and the brain – A brief history of psychosurgery: Part 1 – From trephination to lobotomy', *Surgical Neurology International*, 4: 49.

Feeley, M. and Simon, J. (1992) 'The new penology: Notes on the emerging strategy of correction and its implications', *Criminology*, 30(4): 449–475.

Fennell, P. and Yeates, V. (2002) '"To serve which master?" – Criminal justice policy, community care and the mentally disordered offender' in Buchanan, A. (ed.) *Care of the mentally disordered offender in the community*, Oxford: Oxford University Press.

Floud, J. (1982) 'Dangerousness and criminal justice', *British Journal of Criminology*, 22(3): 213–228.

Floud, J. and Young, W. (1981) *Dangerousness and criminal justice*, Cambridge: Cambridge University Press.

Forrester, A. (2002) 'Preventive detention, public protection and mental health', *Journal of Forensic Psychiatry*, 13(2): 329–344.

Foucault, M. (1961) *Madness and civilisation: A history of insanity in the age of reason*, Paris: Labrairie Pron.

Foucault, M. (1991) 'Governmentality' in Burchell, G. and Miller, P. (eds.) *The Foucault effect*, Chicago: University of Chicago Press.

Furedi, F. (2009) 'Fear and security: A vulnerability-led policy response' in Denney, D. (ed.) *Living in dangerous times: Fear, insecurity, risk and social policy*, Chichester: John Wiley and Sons Ltd.

Garland, D. (2001) *The culture of control: Crime and social order in contemporary society*, Oxford: Open University Press.

Giddens, A. (1991) *Modernity and self-identity: Self and society in the late modern age*, Cambridge: Polity Press.

Goffman, E. (1961) *Asylums: Essays on the social situation of mental patients and other inmates*, Harmonsworth: Penguin Books Ltd.

Gunn, J. (1982) 'Defining the terms' in Hamilton, J. and Freeman, H. (eds.) *Dangerousness: Psychiatric assessment and management*, London: Gaskell.

Hacking, I. (1990) *The taming of chance*, Cambridge: Cambridge University Press.

Hannah-Moffat, K. (2005) 'Criminogenic need and the transformative risk subject: Hybridizations of risk/need in penality', *Punishment and Society*, 7(1): 29–51.

Harris, R. (1999) 'Mental disorder and social order: Underlying themes in crime management' in Webb, D. and Harris, R. (eds.) *Mentally disordered offenders: Managing people nobody owns*, London: Routledge.

Harrison, K. (2011) *Dangerousness, risk and the governance of serious sexual and violent offenders*, Abingdon: Routledge.

Hebenton, B. and Seddon, T. (2009) 'From dangerousness to precaution: Managing sexual and violent offenders in an insecure and uncertain age', *British Journal of Criminology*, 42(2): 371–394.

Hough, M. (1996) 'People talking about punishment', *Howard Journal of Criminal Justice*, 35(3): 191–214.

Johnstone, G. (2000) 'Penal policy making: Elitist, populist or participatory?, *Punishment and Society*, 2(2): 161–180.

Kemshall, H. (2008) *Understanding the community management of high risk offenders*, Maidenhead: Open University Press.

Kemshall, H. and Maguire, M. (2001) 'Public protection, partnership and risk penality: The multi-agency risk management of sexual and violent offenders', *Punishment and Society*, 3(2): 237–264.

Kilty, J. (2012) '"It's like they don't want you to get better": Psy control of women in the carceral context', *Feminism and Psychology*, 22(2): 162–182.

Kitzinger, J. (2004) *Framing abuse: Media influence and public understanding of sexual violence against children*, London: Pluto Press.

Kleinman, A. (1977) 'Culture, depression and the "new" cross-cultural psychiatry', *Social Science and Medicine*, 11: 3–11.

Kleinman, A. (1987) 'Anthropology and psychiatry: The role of culture in cross-cultural research on illness', *The British Journal of Psychiatry*, 151(4): 447–454.

Kutchins, H. and Kirk, S.A. (1997) *Making us crazy: DSM: The psychiatric bible and the creation of mental disorders*, New York: Free Press.

Langan, J. and Lindow, V. (2004) *Living with risk: Mental health service user involvement in risk assessment and management*, Bristol: The Policy Press.

Large, M., Smith, G., Swinson, N., Shaw, J. and Nielssen, O. (2008) 'Homicide due to mental disorder in England and Wales over 50 years', *British Journal of Psychiatry*, 193(2): 130–133.

Levine, J.M. (1996) 'Historical notes on restraint reduction: The legacy of Dr. Philippe Pinel', *Journal of the American Geriatrics Society*, 44(9): 1130–1133.

Lianos, M. and Douglas, M. (2000) 'Dangerization and the end of deviance: The institutional environment', *British Journal of Criminology*, 40(2): 261–278.

Manning, N. (2002) 'Actor networks, policy networks and personality disorder', *Sociology of Health and Illness*, 24: 644–666.

Markham, S. (2018) 'Red-teaming the panopticon (mobilising adaptive change in secure and forensic settings)', *Journal of Forensic Psychiatry and Psychology*, 29(1): 16–36.

Marsella, A.J. and White, G.M. (1982) 'Preface' in Marsella, A.J. and White, G.M. (eds.) *Cultural conceptions of mental health and therapy*, London: D. Reidel Publishing Company.

Matthews, R. (2005) 'The myth of punitiveness', *Theoretical Criminology*, 9(2): 175–201.

McAlinden, A. (2012) 'The governance of sexual offending across Europe: Penal policies, political economies and the institutionalization of risk', *Punishment and Society*, 14(2): 166–192.

McBride, R. (2017) 'On the advancement of therapeutic penality: Therapeutic authority, personality science and the therapeutic community', *Sociology of Health and Illness*, 39(7): 1258–1272.

Menninger, K. (1928) 'Medicolegal proposals of the American Psychiatric Association', *Journal of Criminal Law and Criminology*, 19(3): 367–373.

Mercer, D. and Mason, T. (1998) 'From devilry to diagnosis: The painful birth of forensic psychiatry' in Mason, T. and Mercer, D. (ed.) *Critical perspectives in forensic care: Inside out*, London: Macmillan Press Ltd.

Morgan, C., Mallett, R., Hutchinson, G., Bagalkote, H., Morgan, K., Fearon, P., Dazzan, P., Boydell, J., Mckenzie, K., Harrison, G., Murray, R., Jones, P., Craig, T. and Leff, J. (2005) 'Pathways to care and ethnicity. 2: Source of referral and help-seeking: Report from the AeSOP study', *British Journal of Psychiatry*, 186(4): 290–296.

Morgan, C., Mallett, R., Hutchinson, G. and Leff, J. (2004) 'Negative pathways to psychiatric care and ethnicity: The bridge between social science and psychiatry', *Social Science and Medicine*, 58(4): 739–752.

Mullen, P. (2000) 'Dangerousness, risk and the prediction of probability' in Gelder, M.G. Lopez-Ibor, J.J. and Andreason, N. (eds.) *New Oxford textbook of psychiatry*, London: Oxford University Press.

Newman, D., O'Reilly, P., Lee, S. and Kennedy, C. (2015) 'Mental health service users experiences of mental health care: An integrative literature review', *Psychiatric and Mental Health Nursing*, 22(3): 171–182.

O'Malley, P. (2000) 'Risk societies and the government of crime' in Brown, M. and Pratt, J. (eds.) *Dangerous offenders: Punishment and social order*, London: Routledge.

O'Malley, P. (2004) *Risk, uncertainty and government*, London: Glasshouse Press.

O'Malley, P. (2008) 'Experiments in risk and criminal justice', *Theoretical Criminology*, 12(4): 451–469.

Oosterhuis, H. and Loughnan, A. (2014) 'Madness and crime: Historical perspectives on forensic psychiatry', *International Journal of Law and Psychiatry*, 37(1): 1–16.

Parsons, T. (1951) *The social system*, Glencoe, IL: The Free Press.

Peay, J. (2007) 'Mentally disordered offenders, mental health and crime' in Maguire, M., Morgan, R. and Reiner, R. (eds.) *The Oxford handbook of criminology (Fourth edition)*, Oxford: Oxford University Press.

Peay, J. (2011) *Mental health and crime*, Abingdon: Routledge.

Peay, J. (2017) 'Mental health, mental disabilities and crime' in Liebling, A., Maruna, S. and McAra, L. (eds.) *The Oxford handbook of criminology (Sixth edition)*, Oxford: Oxford University Press.

Phelan, J.C., Link, B.G., Steuve, A. and Pescosolido, B.A. (2000) 'Public conceptions of mental illness in 1950 and 1996: What is mental illness and is it to be feared?', *Journal of Health and Social Behavior*, 41(2): 188–207.

Pilgrim, D. and Rogers, A. (2003) 'Mental disorder and violence: An empirical picture in context', *Journal of Mental Health*, 12(1): 7–18.

Power, M. (2007) *Organized uncertainty: Designing a world of risk management*, Oxford: Oxford University Press.

Pratt, J. (2000) 'Emotive and ostentatious punishment: Its decline and resurgence in modern society', *Punishment and Society*, 2(4): 417–440.

Priebe, S. (2016) 'A social paradigm in psychiatry – themes and perspectives', *Epidemiology and Psychiatric Sciences*, 25(6): 521–527.

Primm, A.B., Osher, F.C. and Gomez, M.B. (2005) 'Race and ethnicity, mental health services and cultural competence in the criminal justice system: Are we ready to change?', *Community Mental Health Journal*, 41(5): 557–569.

Prins, H. (1988) 'Dangerous clients: Further observations on the limitation of mayhem', *British Journal of Social Work*, 18(6): 593–609.

Rabiee, F. and Smith, P. (2014) 'Understanding mental health and experience of accessing services in African and African Caribbean users and carers in Birmingham, UK', *Journal of Diversity and Ethnicity in Health and Care*, 11: 125–134.

Reznek, L. (1997) *Evil or ill? Justifying the insanity defence*, London: Routledge.

Robertson, P., Barnao, M. and Ward, T. (2011) 'Rehabilitation frameworks in forensic mental health', *Aggression and Violent Behaviour*, 16(6): 472–484.

Robinson, G. (2002) 'Exploring risk management in the probation service: Contemporary developments in the probation service: Contemporary developments in England and Wales', *Punishment and Society*, 4(1): 5–25.

Rogers, A. and Pilgrim, D. (2014) *A sociology of mental health and illness (Fifth edition)*, Maidenhead: Open University Press.

Rose, N. (1998a) 'Governing risky individuals: The role of psychiatry in new regimes of control', *Psychiatry, Psychology and Law*, 5(2): 177–195.

Rose, N. (1998b) *Inventing ourselves: Psychology, power and personhood*, Cambridge: Cambridge University Press.

Rose, N. (2002) 'Society, madness and control' in Buchanan, A. (ed.) *Care of the mentally disordered offender in the community*, Oxford: Oxford University Press.

Rose, N. (2007) 'Beyond medicalisation', *The Lancet*, 369(9562): 700–702.

Rose, N. (2017) 'Society, madness and control' in Buchanan, A. and Wootton, L. (eds.) *Care of the mentally disordered offender in the community*, Oxford: Oxford University Press.

Rosenhan, D. (1973) 'On being sane in insane places', *Science*, 179(4070): 250–258.

Ryan, M. (1999) 'Penal policy making towards the millennium: Elites and populists; New Labour and the new criminology', *International Journal of the Sociology of the Law*, 27(1): 1–22.

Scheff, T.J. (1966) *Being mentally ill*, London: Weidenfeld and Nicolson.

Scull, A. (1993) *The most solitary of afflictions*, New Haven: Yale University Press.

Seddon, T. (2007) *Punishment and madness: Governing prisoners with mental health problems*, Abingdon: Routledge-Cavendish.

Showalter, E. (1987) *The female malady: Women, madness and English culture, 1839–1980*, London: Virago.

Solomon, E. (2008) 'Dangerousness and society. Perrie lectures 2007', *Prison Service Journal*, 175: 28–33.

Sparks, R. (2000) 'Perspectives on risk and penal politics' in Hope, T. and Sparks, R. (eds.) *Crime, risk and insecurity*, London: Routledge.

Spitzer, R. and Wilson, P. (1975) 'Nosology and the official psychiatric nomenclature' in Freedman, A. and Kaplan, H. (eds.) *Comprehensive textbook of psychiatry*, New York: Williams and Wilkins.

Steadman, H.J., Monahan, J., Robbins, P.C., Appelbaum, P.S., Grisso, T., Klassen, D., Mulvey, E.P. and Roth, L.H. (1993) 'From dangerousness to risk assessment: Implications for appropriate risk strategies' in Hodgins, S. (ed.) *Crime and mental disorder*, Newbury Park, California: Sage Publications.

Stuart, H. (2006) 'Media portrayal of mental illness and its treatments: What effect does it have on people with mental illness', *CNS Drugs*, 20(2): 99–106.

Szasz, T.S. (1960) 'The myth of mental illness', *American Psychologist*, 15(2): 113–118.

Szasz, T.S. (1962) *The myth of mental illness: Foundations of a theory of personal conduct*, New York: Harper and Row.

Szasz, T.S. (2003) 'The psychiatric protection order for the "battered mental patient"', *British Medical Journal*, 327(7429): 1449–1451.

Szmulker, G. (2009) 'Ethics in community psychiatry' in Bloch, S., Chodoff, P. and Green, S.A. (eds.) *Psychiatric ethics*, Oxford: Oxford University Press.

Tait, L. and Lester, H. (2005) 'Encouraging user involvement in mental health services', *Advances in Psychiatric Treatment*, 11(3): 168–175.

Timimi, S. and Taylor, E. (2004) 'ADHD is best understood as a cultural construct', *British Journal of Psychiatry*, 184(1): 8–9.

Timmermans, S. and Gabe, J. (2003) 'Introduction: Connecting criminology and the sociology of health and illness' in Timmermans, S. and Gabe, J. (eds.) *Partners in health, partners in crime*, Oxford: Blackwell Publishing.

Thornton, P. (1992) 'Psychiatric diagnosis as sign and symbol: Nomenclature as an organising and legitimising strategy', *Perspectives on Social Problems*, 4: 155–176.

van Bergen, L. (2015) 'Emil Kraeplin: Grandfather of the DSM'. *Medicine, Conflict and Survival*, 31(3–4): 158–161.

Wallcraft, J. and Bryant, M. (2003) *The mental health service user movement in England*, London: Sainsbury Centre for Mental Health.

Webb, D. and Harris, R. (1999) 'Introduction' in Webb, D. and Harris, R. (eds.) *Mentally disordered offenders: Managing people nobody owns*, London: Routledge.

Wootton, L., Fahy, T., Wilson, S. and Buchanan, A. (2017) 'The interface of general psychiatric and forensic psychiatric services' in Buchanan, A. and Wootton, L. (eds.) *Care of the mentally disordered offender in the community*, Oxford: Oxford University Press.

Wright, D. (1998) 'The certification of insanity in nineteenth-century England and Wales', *History of Psychiatry*, ix: 267–290.

Zedner, L. (2009) 'Fixing the future: The pre-emptive turn in criminal justice' in McSherry, B., Norrie, A. and Bronitt, S. (eds.) *Regulating deviance: The redirection of criminalisation and the futures of criminal law*, Oxford: Hart Publishing.

Zilboorg, G. (1935) *The medical man and the witch during the renaissance*, Baltimore: John Hopkins Press.

Zimmerman, M., Trinkaus, E., Lemay, M., Aufderheide, A., Reyman, T., Marrocco, G., Shultes, R. and Coughlin, E. (1981) 'Trauma and trephination in a Peruvian mummy', *American Journal of Physical Anthropology*, 55(4): 497–501.

CHAPTER 3

Exploring the politics of care, coercion and control

INTRODUCTION

This chapter aims to provide an overview of recent mental health policy and legislation in England and Wales. We begin by exploring the deinstitutionalisation of the mentally ill and move towards 'care in the community' in the second part of the twentieth century and the subsequent political and public responses to a small number of high-profile offences by those with a mental disorder in the 1990s. The chapter then considers recent policy under the New Labour (1997–2010), Conservative-Liberal Democrats coalition (2010–2015) and current Conservative (2015–) governments. We end the chapter by considering some key and current developments relating to mentally disordered offenders, paying particular attention to the progress that has been made since the Bradley report (Department of Health, 2009b), the impact of austerity on the ambition to create a parity of esteem between mental and physical health care, and recent Conservative government proposals to reform the Mental Health Act (MHA) 1983 (as amended by the MHA 2007). For more information about current policy and practice in relation to policing, courts, prisons, secure mental health services and the community, the reader is advised to consult Chapters 4–7.

FROM THE ASYLUMS TO CARE IN THE COMMUNITY

Many explanations for deinstitutionalisation and the closure of the asylums have been put forward. As explored in the anti-psychiatry literature in Chapter 2, the critique from inside and outside of psychiatry, along with the rise and influence of user and civil liberty groups in the 1970s and 1980s, helped reinforce concerns about the asylum system (Bartlett, 2010). Changes in mental health law, along with changes to the structure of mental health services in the second half of the twentieth century also helped facilitate the emergence of new systems of community psychiatric care. Importantly, the financial savings to be made by offering care in the community rather than in large asylums helped further support the move towards deinstitutionalisation (Rugkåsa, Molodynski and Burns, 2016). In addition, the development of anti-psychotic and anti-depressant drugs have 'rightly been credited' with the move towards care in the community (Burns, 2014:337).

THE MENTAL HEALTH ACT 1959

Concerns about the number of people in the asylum system, and the poor outcomes that they had, began to gain momentum in the 1950s. In 1954 a Private Member's Bill highlighted a number of issues including overcrowding, staffing challenges and the stagnation of longer term patients within the asylums (Bartlett, 2010). There was also growing recognition during this period that the majority of people in the asylums were not actually dangerous (Jewesbury and McCulloch, 2002), along with emerging concerns that the asylums were being used as 'receptacles for all manner of failed or anti-citizens unable or unwilling to accept the obligations of civility' (Rose, 2002:11).

Significant changes were brought about by the MHA 1959, leading some to claim that the Act represented part of a foundation for community care (Dixon, 2015). The Act allowed for wider use of voluntary admission (Tighe, Henderson and Thornicroft, 2002) while the power of admission to hospital was transferred from magistrates to doctors (McMurran, Khalifa and Gibbon, 2009). Importantly the MHA 1959 also led to a number of changes in service structure and this enabled more community-based services to emerge (Bartlett, 2010). Following the recommendations of the Percy Commission (1957) the MHA 1959 also introduced a new legal category of 'psychopathic disorder' under s4(4), which was defined as 'a persistent disorder or disability of mind (whether or not including subnormality of intelligence) which results in abnormally aggressive or seriously irresponsible conduct on the part of the patient concerned and requires or is susceptible to treatment'. 'Psychopathic disorder' is the closest legal term to the clinical term of 'personality disorder', and was one of four legal categories of mental disorder under the MHA 1959.

GLANCY AND BUTLER REPORTS

While the MHA 1959 paved the way for changes in service structure such as the introduction of day hospitals, it was only following the recommendations of the Glancy (Department of Health and Social Security (DHSS), 1974) and Butler (Home Office and DHSS, 1975) reports that regional secure units (RSUs, now more commonly known as medium secure units (MSUs)) were set up in each health authority to help assist with the progression of those in the asylums. While these reforms were put forward in the mid-1970s, in practice, the emergence of RSUs was slow, with the 1,000 RSU beds recommended by Glancy not materialising until 1996 (Jewesbury and McCulloch, 2002). Closure of the asylums also took some time, and although the psychiatric population halved between the 1950s and 1980s, it was not until 1986 that the first psychiatric hospital closed (Gilburt et al., 2014).

THE MENTAL HEALTH ACT 1983

The MHA 1983 represented a shift away from a paternalist view of patients to a rights-based approach (Gostin, 2007 cited in Cummins, 2012). The Act introduced stricter controls of treatment and the Mental Health Act Commission (MHAC) to ensure that patients were treated in accordance with their rights (Tighe, Henderson and Thornicroft, 2002). Additionally, some 'due process' rights were given to mental health users (Carpenter, 2009) and this meant that patients were able to have more regular tribunals and given greater powers of discharge (Fennell, 1996 cited in Carpenter, 2009). Importantly, the legal category of 'psychopathic disorder' was retained, but a new 'treatability test' for these patients was introduced, which set out that detention in hospital was only legal if treatment was 'likely to alleviate or prevent deterioration of his condition' (Section 3(2)b).

NATIONAL HEALTH SERVICE AND COMMUNITY CARE ACT 1990 AND THE CARE PROGRAMME APPROACH

The National Health Service (NHS) and Community Care Act 1990 placed responsibility for the care of psychiatric patients (and coordination of this care) on the local authority (Tighe, Henderson and Thornicroft, 2002). This meant that local authorities, along with local health services, became responsible for identifying local health needs, designing appropriate packages of care, and then ensuring their effective delivery. The Act also emphasised that institutional care should only be used when options in the community had been exhausted (Cummins, 2016).

In 1990 a Department of Health circular – HC(90)23/LASSL(90)11 – required local authorities to implement the Care Programme Approach (CPA) by April 1991 (Department of Health, 1990).[1] The CPA emphasised the need for assessment and care plans for patients. Case management underpins the approach and the regular review of each case by a key worker is fundamental. While the CPA has been praised for helping services to maintain more regular contact with users, Simpson, Miller and Bowers (2009:489) have also argued that it has 'failed to provide comprehensive, coordinated care and is associated with increased bed use'.

SOME CONSEQUENCES OF DEINSTITUTIONALISATION

Some argue that the emergence of the community as a new place for treatment and care has led to the reconfiguration (Moon, 2000; Rose, 1998), dispersal, and therefore widening, of state control (Austin and Krisberg, 1981; Cohen, 1985). Despite any libertarian ambitions that the move towards care in the community would facilitate greater liberty, there is evidence from many countries that the use of coercion in the community has increased (Gergel and Szmulker, 2017). Drawing on the work of Stanley Cohen, Nikolas Rose (2002:8) argues that deinstitutionalisation

blurred the boundaries between the 'inside' and the 'outside' of the system of social control. It widened the net of control, bringing individuals into the field of formalized control mechanisms who would previously have been dealt with informally. It thinned the mesh, so that the 'net' of control caught smaller and smaller fish.

Control is thought to have been reconfigured in many ways. For example, McCann (1998:48) asserts that the move from the asylums 'resulted in a switch from the physical security afforded by buildings and hospital regimes, to the security afforded by increased legislative powers', while Coffey (2011:757) argues that patients who had once been detained in the asylums now found themselves 'locked into risk management regimes which are every bit as difficult to negotiate'. This reflects that social control in the community can be 'pervasive and subtly applied' (Coffey, 2012:479).

It is not only control that has been dispersed. Care is also thought to have been fragmented because of the move towards care in the community. Gilburt (2015), for example, asserts that the move from long-term inpatient care towards the development of diverse services in the community has contributed to a fragmentation of mental health services. This means that while people may find themselves subject to more supervision and control in the community, they also risk 'falling through the net' because of the disjointed provision of mental health care.

Perhaps unsurprisingly then, many assert that the closure of secure mental health facilities placed many unwell people at serious risk, with those previously held in the asylums ending up homeless (Timmermans and Gabe, 2003). While the closure of the asylums was 'indelibly linked in the public consciousness with mentally disordered street people' (Burns, 2014:338), Leff (2001) asserts that there is no sufficient evidence to demonstrate that asylum closures led to an increase in homelessness. Another suggested consequence of deinstitutionalisation is that the criminal justice system has become the de facto mental health care provider (Cummins, 2006:28). This has led many to debate the impact and consequences of what has been termed 'transinstitutionalization' or Penrose's Law (see Penrose, 1939), where a relationship between the number of mental health beds and other institutional beds, such as those in prisons, can be observed (see Prins (2011) and Trieman, Leff and Glover (1999) for a review; for a discussion in the US see Ben-Moshe, 2017). While some argue that the available data is not sufficient to draw firm conclusions (Hiday, 1999), Cummins (2010) argues that the expansion of the prison system in the UK reached its height when the number of inpatient mental health beds began to significantly reduce.

While there is some debate about the extent to which the asylum closures led to increasing homelessness and criminalisation of those with mental illness, there is evidence that the perceived failures of care in the community have led to the 're-institutionalisation' of those with mental illness (Priebe et al., 2005) and a 'return to containment' (Moon, 2000). For example, Henderson, Bindmann and Thornicroft (1998) argue that the closure of the asylums created a new population of 'long-stay' patients in acute psychiatric wards, while Priebe et al. (2005) have observed a rise in inpatient forensic services. Despite numerous concerns about the safety and standards of care for patients, particularly for women and Black, Asian and Minority Ethnic (BAME) patients, by the millennium, inpatient admissions under the MHA had been continuing to rise (Pilgrim and Ramon, 2009). Mental health detentions have continued to increase since this time, with the current rate of mental health detention in England and Wales, now more than three times higher than it was before the MHA 1983 (Keown et al., 2018).

Alongside increases in mental health detentions, it is important to note the significant growth of the prison population in the 1990s and 2000s (see Ministry of Justice, 2016b for a discussion). Between 1993 and 2012 the prison population roughly doubled (Ministry of Justice, 2013a). In an era of 'mass incarceration' (Simon, 2012) there has not only been an unprecedented rise in the number of prisoners, many of whom have mental health problems, but also increases in negative forms of institutional control including segregation, overcrowding, and understaffing (Haney, 2017). This is particularly concerning given prisoners with mental illness are more likely to be segregated than those without (Clark, 2018).

CONSERVATIVE GOVERNMENT RESPONSES TO THE PERCEIVED FAILURE OF COMMUNITY CARE

Although there were concerns about the provision of care in the community in the 1980s (see e.g. DHSS, 1988), care in the community underwent a 'crisis of legitimacy' during the early 1990s (Pilgrim and Ramon, 2009). This crisis largely followed from the media attention surrounding a number of high-profile cases (Cummins, 2011), which some argue resulted in a moral panic about the mentally ill (Cummins, 2015; Holloway, 2002). Two of the most well-known cases include the murder of Jonathan Zito in 1992 by Christopher Clunis, a man with a long history of mental health problems (see Box 3.1), along with the 1996 Michael Stone case (see Box 3.2). Such high-profile cases have served to heighten public anxieties and the political impetus to strengthen mental health policy and legislation. Anxieties about care in the community were largely structured around patients in the community (commonly diagnosed with schizophrenia) who were not taking their medication (like Clunis), along with patients with personality disorder who were not considered treatable under mental health law at the time (like Stone).

BOX 3.1 THE CHRISTOPHER CLUNIS CASE

In December 1992, as Jonathan Zito waited for a train at Finsbury Park underground station, he was approached by Christopher Clunis, a man unknown to him, and fatally stabbed three times in the face. The case received considerable media attention and was described by the subsequent inquiry team as having followed from a 'catalogue of failure and missed opportunity' (Ritchie, Dick and Lingham, 1994:105). The Ritchie inquiry revealed that Clunis had a long history of psychiatric illness and in the weeks leading up to the attack had been exhibiting behaviour of concern. Just eight days before Zito was murdered, Clunis had been found wondering the streets with a screwdriver. A range of failures were identified including: problems with multiagency communication and liaison, failure to properly assess (and then act on) Clunis' previous history of violence, and failure to properly follow Clunis up in the community following discharge from hospital.

At his trial, Clunis was convicted of manslaughter on the grounds of diminished responsibility and given a restricted hospital order (s37/41) under the MHA 1983.

While a number of reforms were made following the Clunis case (including compulsory homicide inquiries and greater powers to supervise patients in the community), it is apparent that many issues highlighted by the Clunis case continue to be raised by subsequent independent investigations into murders committed by those known to mental health services.

Several policy responses, including introduction of the CPA, enhanced risk assessment, supervision registers and supervised discharge, formed part of the Conservative government's response to alleviate public concerns (Busfield, 2002). Politically, re-building the asylums would have been unacceptable so calls for action led to new forms of surveillance and control (Cummins, 2016). In 1994, independent inquiries into homicides committed by mental health patients (Department of Health, 1994a) and supervision registers were introduced (Department of Health, 1994b). Supervised discharge was then introduced in 1996 under the Mental Health (Patients in the Community) Act 1995, requiring patients to adhere to an agreed care plan following their discharge from hospital to the community. Policies such as these increased the community surveillance of those with mental disorder and were structured by managerialist concerns for risk and audit (Cummins, 2012). Ultimately these changes meant that 'care' in the community became inextricably linked to the notion of risk (Rose, 2002:18).

Since the introduction of homicide inquiries (Department of Health, 1994a), many common key failings have been identified, including: failures of multiagency communication (between agencies as well as between staff in the same agency), high caseloads, minimal support and supervision, and inexperienced staff without adequate skills (Holloway and Davies, 2017). While inquiries are important for reviewing what may have gone wrong, many commentators point to their more damaging side (Peay, 1996, 1997; Petch and Bradley, 1997; Prins, 1999). Aside from their considerable expense (Busfield, 2002), they have been criticised for their potential to lead to scapegoating (rather than meaningful organisational scrutiny and change) along with 'inquiry fatigue' (where findings can be dismissed because of the belief that all inquiries 'say the same things') (Cummins, 2015). Cummins (2016) argues that rather than consider the lack of funding and problematic conditions which have led to high-profile failings in mental health services, successive governments have sought to undertake a series of inquiries and legislative reform. However, 'such demands seldom address the fundamental issues, only the symptom, seemingly as part of some collective psychological search for meaning out of tragedy' (Harris, 1999:20). This has meant that the high levels of need, along with underfunded and poorly organised services in the community, continue to be overlooked (Cummins, 2016).

BOX 3.2 THE MICHAEL STONE CASE

In July 1996 Lin Russell, along with her two children (Megan, 6 and Josie, 9) and the family dog, were subjected to a brutal hammer attack while walking home from a swimming gala. Only Josie survived the attack, although she was left with severe head injuries.

Understandably the tragedy provoked public outrage, which was heightened when media reports emerged that the suspected perpetrator, Michael Stone, was not only known to psychiatric services as suffering from a personality disorder, but had been refused a secure hospital bed in the weeks leading up to the attack, on the basis that he was 'untreatable'.

In October 1998, Michael Stone was convicted of the murders of Lin and Megan Russell and sentenced to life imprisonment. In some quarters, his conviction continues to be held as questionable, and although the evidence on which he was convicted was weak, Stone was nevertheless presented as the 'sort of person who would have committed such crimes' (Hudson, 2001:107), emphasis in original.

Following Stone's conviction, a significant period of legislative, policy and service reform followed, most notably with the reform of the MHA 1983 (under the MHA 2007) and the introduction of high-security Dangerous and Severe Personality (DSPD) services. Seddon (2007:144) argues that 'being seen to respond quickly and robustly to the apparent legal anomalies revealed by the Michael Stone case was critical', and in practice, the 'announcement of the policy was as important as its actualisation'. Others, such as Nash (2006:74), argue that the DSPD proposals were a 'clear example of policy flying in the face of expert opinion'. This move in the absence of evidence and professional consensus suggests a tendency for politicians to pay greater attention to the perceived feelings of the electorate rather than experts (Sparks, 2000), and highlights that the eruption of scandals via the media 'have consistently proved catalysts for changing policies' (Downes and Morgan, 2002:287).

At the time of writing Stone is still serving his prison sentence and continues to maintain his innocence. After a retrial in 2001 and an unsuccessful appeal in 2005, the Criminal Cases Review Commission (CCRC) reviewed the Stone case but concluded in 2010 that there was no basis on which they could refer the case for appeal. Following an application from Stone's legal representatives in August 2017, the CCRC are currently investigating his case again (CCRC, 2017).

For more details regarding the Michael Stone case see the original inquiry report published by the South East Coast Strategic Health Authority (2006).

DID CARE IN THE COMMUNITY FAIL?

Hannigan and Coffey (2011:223) note that 'having emerged as a solution to the problems of institutions community care has, in some assessments, itself become "the problem"'. However, it is important to remember that there are many challenges involved with assessing (or making) claims that care in the community has failed. Community mental health services represent a scarce resource (Griffiths, 2001) and ultimately, the closure of the asylums was not met with an effective community care system (Harris, 1999). In addition, some have argued that there was a lack of emotional or professional investment in community care, with a corresponding 'reluctance' to work with 'a seriously disadvantaged and often unattractive group of people' (Prins, 2016:105). These points highlight that some of the 'problems' with community mental health care include service failure, under-funded services, deficient guidelines and standards and 'over-burdened and conflicted' staff (Hannigan and Coffey, 2011:223).

Another challenge with making any assessment of failure comes from the ongoing confusion about the meaning of community care and 'a lack of clarity over the ultimate goals of such a policy' (Rogers and Pilgrim, 2010:200). This has led Burns and Priebe (1999:191) to argue that 'in the absence of objective criteria for success or failure of community health care ... [there is] ... no justification for the sweeping statement that it [care in the community] has failed'. Given most psychiatric patients now live their lives in the community rather than in a secure setting, and many people with mental illness now reside in urban areas with minimal supervision and support (Markowitz, 2011), Burns (2014) argues that the closure of the asylums has been positive. Many service users were positive about their resettlement in the community (Trieman, Leff and Glover, 1999) and patients in the community are now happier and less stigmatised than they were in the asylums (Burns, 2014). The movement of psychiatric treatment to the community has also led 'richer, more holistic understanding and a more equal relationship between patients and clinicians' and 'an undoubted achievement of community psychiatry has been to re-energise interest in non-pharmacological treatments' (Burns, 2014:339). Research also suggests that the number of homicides committed by those in contact with psychiatric services has been falling (Large et al., 2008). However, 'for a small minority, community care exposes their suffering and personal failure in the most painful manner' (Burns, 2014:342).

Some argue that one of the key reasons why care in the community is perceived to have failed in the 1990s is the increased 'visibility' of service users and increasing 'invisibility' of services (Leff, 2001; Moon, 2000). Leff (2001:381) argues that anxieties and assessments of failure increased because 'the dramatic architectural presence of the asylum has been replaced by an apparent absence'. By their very nature, community services comprise a complex network of interlinked facilities and multiagency professionals while the asylum represented a centralised and visible form of social control (Leff, 2001). This means that psychiatric confinement has become increasingly invisible (Mason and Mercer, 1998). The 'absence of control' is further exacerbated by the increasing visibility of people with mental health problems as a direct consequence of asylum closures and inadequate community funding (Moon, 2000). The increasing visibility of those with mental illness may also mean that they are more likely to come to the attention of the police. Moon (2000:241) captures the problem well when he observes

[f]or the most part, community care has been outstandingly successful and humane in meeting the challenge and satisfying the diverse constituencies of users, the public, mental health professionals,

politicians and others. In essence however, what deinstitutionalisation accomplished was the replacement of 'concealed others' with 'visible others'. The confinement of potential violence was exchanged for a visible (perceived) threat to safety.

NEW LABOUR, PERSONALITY DISORDER AND REFORM OF MENTAL HEALTH LEGISLATION

After 18 years of Conservative rule, the Labour government returned to Downing Street in 1997. A preoccupation with public protection was clear under this administration and the emphasis quickly shifted from the diversion of the mentally ill (as set out in an earlier Home Office (1990) circular) to risk management (Fennell and Yeates, 2002; Rose, 2017). Less than a year after taking office, in January 1998, a government report entitled *Modernising Mental Health Services: Safe, Sound and Supportive* declared that 'care in the community has failed' (Department of Health, 1998b: Foreword). The 'problem' was formulated as a lack of effective control in the community, with little said about the problematic quality of secure care at the time (Pilgrim and Ramon, 2009). Moreover, the report title and contents clearly put 'safety first and supportive last' (Pilgrim and Ramon, 2009:275). This was illustrated by proposals to ensure that patients are 'no longer allowed to refuse to comply with the treatment they need' and, significantly, that

> we will also be changing the law to permit the detention of a small group of people who have not committed a crime but whose untreatable psychiatric disorder makes them dangerous ... For those people with a severe personality disorder who are considered to pose a grave risk to the public ... admission to the new regime will not be dependent upon the person having committed an offence, nor whether they are treatable under the terms of the Mental Health Act.
>
> (Department of Health, 1998b:
> Foreword – para. 4.33)

It was evident that the government sought to close the perceived 'loophole' within the MHA 1983 regarding the detention of people with personality disorder in hospital. Following the introduction of the 'treatability test' concerns had emerged about the unwillingness of psychiatrists to admit patients with personality disorder to hospital (Pickersgill, 2012). Proposing that a 'third way' was needed in mental health care, an expert committee was set up in September

1998 to review the MHA 1983 (Department of Health, 1998a). But by February 1999, and before this review of the MHA 1983 was complete, Jack Straw, the Home Secretary at the time, announced the intention of the Home Office and the Department of Health to introduce measures to deal with

> a group of dangerous and severe personality disordered individuals from whom the public at present are not properly protected, and who are restrained effectively neither by the criminal law nor by the provisions of the Mental Health Act.
>
> (House of Commons debate,Vol 325, Col 601, 15 Feb 1999)

The proposals sparked considerable debate especially because the term 'Dangerous and Severe Personality Disorder' (DSPD) was unknown to clinicians, criminal justice practitioners and lawyers alike. While the Home Secretary accused psychiatrists of adopting a narrow interpretation of the law in order to wash their hands of 'dangerous psychopaths' (Steele, 2001), psychiatrists complained that they were being forced towards the role of 'society's jailer' (Laurance, 2003:xv). At the time, the then President of the Royal College of Psychiatrists was reported to have said that 'the Home Secretary can't expect psychiatrists to do his dirty work when it's at present excluded by the law' (Dr Kendall quoted in Warden, 1998:1270).

Irrespective of the arguments that ensued and the opposition that was mounting, it was apparent that the 'DSPD problem' was one that needed urgent remedy. A few months later, a joint Home Office and Department of Health (1999:3) document explained: 'decisions on the direction of policy development for managing this group cannot be delayed until the outcomes of the research are known'. Further encouragement was probably unnecessary, but the publication of the Fallon Report (Fallon et al., 1999), following an inquiry into a specialist personality disorder ward at Ashworth High Security Hospital in January 1999,[2] and the release of Noel Ruddle from secure psychiatric care in Scotland on the grounds of untreatability in August 1999[3] are likely to have reinforced the government's determination to tackle the issues presented by DSPD.

In November 1999, the Richardson *Review of the Mental Health Act 1983* (Department of Health, 1999b) and the Green Paper *Reform of the Mental Health Act: Proposals for Consultation* (Department of Health, 1999a) were published. Much concern surrounded the dissonance between the two documents (Peay, 2000). While the Richardson Committee favoured MHA reform on the basis of principles of non–discrimination, patient autonomy and capacity, the Green Paper rejected the central tenets of the report. The Richardson Committee's concern with 'capacity' was seen as 'largely irrelevant' and dropped in favour of risk (Peay, 2003).

In December 2000, a White Paper to reform the MHA 1983 was published in two parts (Department of Health, 2000a, 2000b). With a whole part dedicated to 'high-risk patients' (Department of Health, 2000b) and little regard to the principle of reciprocity or patient rights, it was apparent that risk was high on the agenda. The paper proposed to remove the categories of mental disorder in the MHA 1983 in favour of a broad definition so that 'no particular clinical diagnosis will have the effect of limiting the way that the powers are used' and to 'move away from the narrow concept of "treatability"' (Department of Health, 2000a:22). The proposed broad definition of 'mental disorder' and removal of the 'treatabilty test' raised concerns about how widely the new legislation could be applied. In addition, the White Paper explained that in relation to DSPD legislative changes alone were not sufficient and would therefore need to be supported by a programme of service development. To this end, the paper outlined that £126 million had been allocated to the Home Office, Prison Service and Department of Health for the development of special-ist DSPD services over the next three years. Despite 80% of psychi-atrists not supporting the government's DSPD proposals (Crawford et al., 2001), and estimates that six people with DSPD would have to be detained in order to prevent one person from acting violently (Buchanan and Leese, 2001), it was not long before the first DSPD site opened at HMP Whitemoor in early 2001. By 2005, four high-security units for men had opened: two in the high security prison estate and two more within two of England's high security hospitals.

Attempts to reform the MHA 1983 continued and June 2002 saw the publication of the first Mental Health Bill (Department of Health, 2002). The Bill removed the separate category of psychopathic disorder in favour of a broader definition of mental disorder, amended the treatabil-ity test and introduced provisions for compulsory treatment in the com-munity. The Bill, however, was met with some considerable criticism (see e.g. Justice, 2002; NACRO, 2002; Royal College of Psychiatrists, 2002). Two years later, a second Bill was put before parliament (Department of Health, 2004). Similar, and substantial resistance was reignited when this was published in September 2004 (Joint Committee on the Draft Mental Health Bill, 2005a, 2005b, 2005c; Mental Health Alliance, 2005; Revolv-ing Doors Agency, 2004) because many did not feel the government had satisfactorily responded to concerns about the first draft Mental Health Bill. It was described as 'unfit for the twenty-first century' by the Mental

Health Alliance (2004) and in the face of considerable opposition, it was announced in March 2006 that proposals for a new MHA were to be abandoned. However, reform remained on the cards, and it was proposed that instead of a new Act, the existing MHA 1983 would be amended (Department of Health, 2006a).

Despite ongoing criticism about the focus of reform, the MHA 2007, which amends the MHA 1983, received Royal Assent in July 2007 and came into force in November 2008. As a result of the 'energetic and organised opposition' from the Mental Health Alliance (Pilgrim and Ramon, 2009:277) reform of the MHA 1983 by the MHA 2007 took ten years. However, this opposition ultimately failed to prevent some of the most controversial amendments, including: the removal of the category of psychopathic disorder in favour of a general definition of mental disorder, defined as 'any disorder or disability of the mind' (s1(2)); the amendment of the previous requirement that treatment must 'alleviate or prevent deterioration' to 'appropriate treatment is available' (s3(2)d); and the introduction of Community Treatment Orders (CTOs) under s17a. 'Enforcing compliance was a prime motivator' of the revisions (Spandler and Calton, 2009:248) and the fact that many measures, including CTOs, were brought in despite the overwhelming resistance from key stakeholders is evidence of the continuing marginalisation of the mentally ill (Cummins, 2012:325). Ultimately, 'service users and sceptical practitioners alike saw the 2007 Act as a means of social control with little benefit to the welfare of service users' (Turner et al., 2015:612).

Alongside attempts to reform the MHA 1983, the National Institute for Mental Health in England (NIMHE) sought to ensure that people with personality disorder were 'seen as the legitimate business of mental health services' (NIMHE, 2003a) and to ensure that staff were able to respond effectively to the needs of people with personality disorder (NIMHE, 2003b). These sentiments were reinforced by the National Personality Disorder Programme, the Department of Health (2006b), and National Institute for Health and Care Excellence (NICE, 2009a, 2009b) guidelines for personality disorder. Clear attempts were made to make personality disorders 'everybody's business' (Pidd, Benefield and Duggan, 2005) and encourage psychiatrists and the health service to take responsibility for those with personality disorder. However, the main focus appeared to be with the high security DSPD units, with personality disorder services in lower security facilities not only limited but also embraced in 'a low-key fashion' (Peay, 2007:518). This was reflected in the allocation of 128m to the DSPD units for approximately 300 men and only 18m to the community pilots to treat three million people (Haigh and Pearce, 2005 cited in McBride, 2017).

NEW LABOUR AND THE PRIORITY OF PUBLIC PROTECTION

Appeals to public protection were evident through many criminal justice reforms under New Labour. This is reflected by the unprecedented volume of official guidance directed at key criminal justice agencies during this period, which significantly impacted on their work (Kemshall, 2008).[4] These legislative changes also contributed to unprecedented growth in the prison population, which nearly doubled from 41,800 to more than 86,000 between 1993 and 2012 (Ministry of Justice, 2013a, see also 2016b). This reflects that, alongside the reform of the MHA 1983 and policies to deal with 'dangerous' offenders with personality disorder, many legislative changes were primarily concerned with protecting the public from the risk of violent and sexual offenders (Wootton et al., 2017).

One good example, which we discuss more fully in Chapter 7, is the introduction of Multi-Agency Public Protection Arrangements (MAPPA) under the Criminal Justice and Court Services Act (CJCSA) 2000. MAPPA require close working between health, prison, social care, police and probation services to identify and make shared plans to actively manage the risk posed by violent and sexual offenders in the community (Kemshall and Maguire, 2001). Other examples include the plethora of measures that were directed towards sex offenders. Following the introduction of the sex offenders register under the Sex Offenders Act 1997 – which placed a requirement on sex offenders to notify local police of their address within 14 days of leaving prison (or hospital if under detained under MHA 1983) – registration requirements were tightened under the CJCSA 2000 and then replaced under the Sexual Offences Act (SOA) 2003 (Hebenton, 2008). Controversially, Sexual Offences Prevention Orders (SOPOs) and Risk of Sexual Harm Orders (RSHOs) were also introduced under the SOA 2003, while a child sex offender disclosure scheme was piloted in 2008.

SOPOs, RSHOs, along with other Labour policies to deal with 'potentially dangerous persons' (see Rutherford, 2007), anti-social young people and potential terrorists, demonstrated an increasing reliance on civil and pre-emptive measures (Fitzgibbon, 2004; Rutherford, 2000; Walcott and Beck, 2000) and suggest that a 'cornerstone' of New Labour's criminal policy was 'reliance on civil procedures with a criminal sting' (Rutherford, 2000:33). Such developments also lend support to the notion that a 'shadow carceral state' has emerged, whereby penal power is extended as civil and administrative pathways to imprisonment are increased (Beckett and Murakawa, 2012).

In addition to the tighter surveillance and supervision of violent and sexual offenders through a range of criminal and civil measures, another clear strategy to address the 'problem' presented by high risk offenders was to introduce more incapacitative measures (Kemshall, 2008). A good example of this is the introduction of new Indeterminate for Public Protection (IPP) sentences under the Criminal Justice Act (CJA) 2003. Where the court was of the opinion 'that there is a significant risk to members of the public' from an offender who has committed a serious offence as determined by section 224 of the CJA 2003, the court was required to pass an indeterminate sentence. IPP sentences received considerable criticism, were subject to several judicial reviews, and generated numerous problems across the prison estate. Within three years of their operation, 4,170 people were serving an IPP sentence and it was estimated that an average of 140 people were given an IPP sentence by the courts every week (Ministry of Justice, 2008). During the seven years between their introduction in 2005 and their abolition in 2012, a total of 8,711 IPP sentences were made by the courts (HM Inspectorate of Prisons, 2016). As a result of the multiple problems they generated, they were eventually repealed under the Legal Aid, Sentencing and Punishment of Offenders Act 2012. However, their legacy lives on and there are many prisoners who are still held in prison, long after expiry of their IPP tariff date (Annison, 2018). While the Parole Board has worked hard to tackle a back log of IPP prisoner reviews, concerns have now emerged about high recall rates, with the number of IPP offenders being recalled to prison in 2016–2017 reported to have increased by 26% from the year before (Ministry of Justice, 2017).

DIVERSION AND THE BRADLEY REPORT

Although policies to divert people with mental health problems from the criminal justice system have 'a long, if somewhat obscure history' (Prins, 2016:112), Cavadino (1999:53) suggests that concerns about diversion emerged more explicitly in the 1990s for reasons that were 'part fiscal, part genuinely reformist'. Following the main asylum closures a commitment to diversion was emphasised by both the Home Office circulars 66/90 and 12/95 and the Reed report (Department of Health and Home Office, 1992).[5] Circular 66/90, for example, emphasised that 'it is government policy that, wherever possible, mentally disordered persons should receive care and treatment from the health and social services' (Home Office, 1990:2). However, such sentiments were quickly undermined by the increasingly punitive and tough criminal justice climate that emerged in the remainder of the 1990s. In practice, only a very small number of people are diverted to the mental health system for treatment, with the courts preferring to send people to prison if deemed safe to do so and in the absence of very acute mental illness (Bartlett and Sandland, 2014:395). This leads Shah (2010:1107) to observe that despite the 'seemingly sensible principle' set out by Reed that offenders with mental illness should offered treatment rather punished by the criminal justice system, diversion has been 'extremely difficult to achieve'.

Towards the end of Labour's time in Downing Street, Lord Bradley's review of the treatment of people with mental health problems and people with learning difficulties in the criminal justice system in England and Wales was published (Department of Health, 2009b). Bradley found problems with diversion at all stages of the criminal justice system and emphasised the need to consider the criminal justice and mental health systems as pathways, rather than focusing attention on specific decision points. While policy developments across both the health and criminal justice sectors had created a much more receptive background for diversion, Bradley highlighted the implementation of these initiatives had been inconsistent, 'starting out brightly and fizzling out quietly' (de Lacy, 2016:167). In all, Bradley made 82 recommendations, although they were 'depressingly' and 'extraordinarily similar' to those made in the early 1990s by Reed (Winstone, 2016:2). In support of Bradley's recommendations, the government set up a Health and Criminal Justice Programme Board, comprised of representatives across government and the criminal justice system including those in the Ministry of Justice, Home Office, Department of Health, Her Majesty's Courts and Tribunals Service and the Crown Prosecution Service. Together, this coalition of health, social care and criminal justice departments devised a national strategy for delivering the recommendations set out by Bradley; setting out five cross-departmental objectives:

- Improving the efficiency and effectiveness of systems
- Working in partnership
- Improving capacity and capability
- Equity of access to services
- Improving pathways and continuity of care.

(Department of Health, 2009a)

The new diversion services that have emerged post-Bradley take many forms, but commonly aim to identify people who may have mental health problems and refer them to appropriate services, so they can access the support they need. In addition, liaison and diversion schemes aim to collate up to date information about the suspects and defendants in order to provide the police and courts with the information they need to make informed decisions about prosecution and sentencing. We evaluate the extent to which the Bradley report has had an impact on mental health services for those who are involved with the criminal justice system later in the chapter, and elsewhere in the book. However, it is worth noting that a 'spirit of willingness to succeed' among those responsible for diversion services (Winstone, 2016:2) has been observed, with some suggesting that the report may 'represent a watershed in the development of liaison and diversion services' (Birmingham, Awonogun and Ryland, 2017:376).

THE COALITION GOVERNMENT, MENTAL HEALTH AND PARITY OF ESTEEM

In 2010 the Labour government lost the general election and were replaced by a coalition government between the Conservative and Liberal Democrats parties. Asserting that 'mental health is everyone's business' the coalition government published its new mental health strategy *No Health Without Mental Health* in 2011 (Her Majesty's (HM) Government and Department of Health, 2011:5). The cross-government strategy highlighted the cost of poor mental health for the economy, as well as for individuals themselves, and set out a central argument that there should be a parity of esteem between mental and physical health services (HM Government and Department of Health, 2011:2).

The government's commitment to achieving a parity of esteem across mental and physical health care was reiterated in the *Five Year Forward View* published by NHS England in 2014. Later in the year, the government also published its review of the operation of sections 135 and 136 of the MHA 1983 (Department of Health and Home Office, 2014) in response to growing concerns about the use of police powers to detain people suspected of having a mental health problem in a 'place of safety' (see Chapter 4).

In 2014 the Department of Health, along with key agencies including the police, social care, housing and those in the third sector, also signed the Mental Health Crisis Care Concordat. This aims to provide people in mental health crisis with the same level of care from the NHS as they would receive if they had an urgent or emergency physical health need (HM Government, 2014). At the time of writing, 27 signatories had agreed to work together on four key areas (see Box 3.3).

BOX 3.3 FOUR KEY AREAS OF THE MENTAL HEALTH CRISIS CARE CONCORDAT

- Access to support before crisis point – making sure people with mental health problems can get help 24 hours a day and that when they ask for help, they are taken seriously.
- Urgent and emergency access to crisis care – making sure that a mental health crisis is treated with the same urgency as a physical health emergency.
- Quality of treatment and care when in crisis – making sure that people are treated with dignity and respect, in a therapeutic environment.
- Recovery and staying well – preventing future crises by making sure people are referred to appropriate services.

Source: www.crisiscareconcordat.org.uk/about/

Since 2014, the introduction of nearly 100 local Crisis Concordat groups across the country has helped to bring about a substantial reduction in the number of people held in police custody under s136 (Crisis Care Concordat, 2017). The Crisis Care Concordat has also led to the *Beyond Places of Safety* scheme, which involves the provision of crisis cafes, clinics and other community services, with the aim of helping prevent people with mental health problems reaching crisis point (Department of Health and Social Care, 2018a).

THE OFFENDER PERSONALITY DISORDER (OPD) PATHWAY

The coalition government's mental health strategy (HM Government and Department of Health, 2011:5) (along with an earlier Ministry of Justice (2010) Green Paper) also revealed the coalition government's intention to reshape and increase the capacity of services for offenders with personality disorder. Following consultation, ministerial approval was given to a national Offender Personality Disorder (OPD) pathway strategy, to replace the DSPD Programme (Department of Health and National Offender Management Service (NOMS), 2011a, 2011b) in 2011. The OPD pathway strategy proposed to reinvest the money attached to the small number of high security DSPD units into an active *pathway* of 'psychologically informed' services (Department of Health and NOMS, 2011b). The OPD pathway aims to provide a 'community-to-community' pathway for offenders with personality disorder at all stages of the criminal justice system. Pathway services are found in a range of locations including prisons, NHS facilities (both secure and community based) and in local probation services. The OPD pathway is jointly funded by Her Majesty's Prison and Probation Service (HMPPS) (previously NOMS)[6] and NHS England with the aim of achieving the following outcomes:

1. For men, a reduction in repeat serious sexual and/or violent offending; or for women, a reduction in repeat offending of relevant offences
2. Improved psychological health, well-being, pro-social behaviour and relational outcomes
3. Improved competence, confidence and attitudes of staff working with complex offenders who are likely to have severe personality disorder
4. Increased efficiency, cost-effectiveness and quality of OPD pathway services (NOMS and NHS England, 2015).

The Ministry of Justice originally estimated that around 20,000 offenders would be eligible for the pathway (Benefield et al., 2015). However, 36,459 people, more than a third of the National Probation Service (NPS) caseload, were identified as meeting the criteria for the pathway by June 2016 (Skett, Goode and Barton, 2017). For more information about eligibility and how offenders are 'screened-in' to the pathway see Ministry of Justice (2011:15). Case formulation is a core element of the pathway, and if an offender is found to be eligible for the pathway, this should be undertaken to support pathway planning. If appropriate, offenders may be encouraged to access a number of specific pathway services, including specific PD treatment services, along with Psychologically Informed Planned Environments (PIPEs) (services based in prisons or approved premises that are designed to support progression) (NOMS and Department of Health, 2012).

CRIMINAL JUSTICE AND THE COALITION GOVERNMENT

A central feature of many policies under the coalition government was the development of markets to support the operation and delivery of criminal justice services (Garside and Ford, 2015). While cooperation and partnerships had been encouraged by the Labour government (Le Grand, 1999), initiatives under the coalition, and subsequent Conservative government, have given increasing emphasis to competition between different providers and agencies. A range of measures introduced across health and criminal justice services have served to increase competition, decentralise control and structure services according to a Payment by Results (PbR) model (see Brooker, Denney and Sirdifield, 2014).

Perhaps the best example is offered by the coalition government's *Transforming Rehabilitation* (TR) reforms, which most controversially, included the privatisation of 70% of probation services in England and Wales. These began in 2010 with the publication of a Green Paper entitled *Breaking the Cycle: Effective Punishment, Rehabilitation and Sentencing of Offenders* (Ministry of Justice, 2010). This paper proposed to introduce a PbR model to encourage criminal justice providers to reduce reoffending (Ministry of Justice, 2010). Following consultation in the first few months of 2013 (see Ministry of Justice, 2013b) in May 2013 the government published *Transforming Rehabilitation: A Strategy for Reform* (Ministry of Justice, 2013c). Most controversially this revealed that the reforms involved 'opening up the market to a diverse range of new rehabilitation providers' (Ministry of Justice, 2013c:6). As a result, in June 2014 the probation service in England and Wales underwent significant upheaval with the introduction of 21, privately run, Community Rehabilitation Companies (CRC) to manage low and medium risk offenders, with high risk offenders remaining the responsibility of the NPS.

As part of the TR reforms, the prison estate was also reorganised in November 2014, with 89 of the 120 prisons in England and Wales designated as 'resettlement prisons', with the purpose of providing seamless rehabilitative support before a prisoner leaves prison and then 'through the gate' to their release in the community (HM Inspectorate of Probation and HM Inspectorate of Prisons, 2017). The TR reforms also led to the introduction of a statutory 12-month supervision period under the Offender Rehabilitation Act 2014 for all short sentence prisoners serving 12 months and under.

Following the unprecedented growth of imprisonment in England and Wales during the 1990s and 2000s, from 2012 the prison population has largely stabilised (Ministry of Justice, 2017).[7] However, concerns about the rising levels of suicide, self-harm and assaults in prisons have emerged (see Chapter 6) with many arguing that these rises are a direct consequence of the substantial cuts that have been made to public services. Indeed, a recent report reveals that financial cuts were particularly acute between 2009–2010 and 2015–2016 when the prison service experienced a 21% fall in real terms of funding (Institute for Government, 2018).

MENTAL HEALTH AND THE CURRENT CONSERVATIVE GOVERNMENT

Since 2015, when the current Conservative government took office, mental health has continued to feature on the political agenda. In 2016, NHS England (2016b) published its strategic direction for health services in the criminal justice system, which aims to promote better care pre-custody, in custody, and after people are released from prison. Significant changes to police powers to detain someone in a 'place of safety' under s135/6 of the MHA 1983 were also brought about by the Policing and Crime Act 2017. These reforms followed from a 'preoccupation' about the additional demands that those experiencing mental health problems were placing on the police in England and Wales (Garside, Grimshaw and Ford, 2018) and are discussed in full in Chapter 4. Growing attention has also been given to the potential reform of the MHA 1983 (as amended by the MHA 2007), following concerns about the growing number of detentions under the Act and the disproportionate rates of BAME people subject to MHA powers. After outlining the progress that has been made with the diversion and parity of esteem agendas, we consider the recent independent review of mental health law in England and Wales.

PROGRESS WITH THE DIVERSION AGENDA FOLLOWING BRADLEY

A new wave of liaison and diversion schemes followed the publication of Lord Bradley's report in 2009 (Dyer, 2013). Early on, these largely took the form of a series of 'pathfinder' pilot projects that were subject to evaluation before being rolled out nationally (Dyer, 2013). Initially, and despite the Department of Health (2009a) *Improving Health, Supporting Justice* document having set out a national strategy for delivering criminal justice and liaison services (Earl et al., 2017), early pilots often emerged with minimal national oversight or direction. While it is important for individual services to be flexible and respond to local needs (Birmingham, Awonogun and Ryland, 2017), a lack of national direction at this time led Dyer (2013:36) to express concern that 'it is not clear what or where the service or support gaps are'.

Since this time, things appear to have improved. Between 2011 and 2013 the Department of Health developed a national liaison and diversion (L&D) model (see NHS England L&D Programme, 2014 for further details about this national model and its core aims). To support this, in January 2014 the Department of Health announced that £25 million would be made available to support L&D schemes in police stations and the courts. Responsibility for the L&D programme moved to NHS England in April 2014 and in the same month ten pilot L&D schemes were launched (see Disley et al. (2016) for a review). The following April, the national L&D model was rolled out in 13 additional locations (Disley et al., 2016). In July 2016 the Health Minister Alistair Burt indicated that a further £12 million funding would be allocated to L&D services. At the time of writing it is estimated that 75% of the country has access to L&D services, with an ambition to achieve full coverage by 2020 (NHS England, 2016a).

Given the pace of implementation, and the extensive expansion of L&D services, Birmingham, Awonogun and Ryland (2017) remind us of the need for robust evaluations of their effectiveness. Some positive research findings have started to emerge. For example, a recent evaluation of a L&D scheme in the South West of England found significant benefit in terms of both health and crime outcomes (Earl et al., 2017). While research suggests several areas of good practice have emerged,[8] there are numerous barriers to the effective operation of criminal justice L&D schemes (Dyer, 2013). Moreover, establishing the effectiveness of diversion schemes is inherently difficult (Prins, 2016) in part because of the considerable variation in L&D schemes across the country (Dyer, 2013; see also Chapter 5).

PROGRESS WITH ACHIEVING A PARITY OF ESTEEM

While cross-government strategies to address mental health have been welcomed, problems with implementation alongside increasing numbers of people trying to access mental health services, are reported to have led to a deterioration in outcomes in recent times (Mental Health Taskforce, 2016:4). A recent review by the Mental Health Alliance (2017:11) suggests there is still some way to go with achieving a parity of esteem, with 80% of people previously detained in mental health services disagreeing that the rights of people with mental illness are 'protected and enforced as effectively' as they are for people with physical illness. In February 2016 an independent Mental Health Taskforce (2016) noted that while the government's mental health strategy was to be welcomed,

challenges with system wide implementation coupled with an increase in people using mental health services has led to inadequate provision and worsening outcomes in recent years, including a rise in the number of people taking their own lives.

(Mental Health Taskforce, 2016:4)

In their review the Mental Health Taskforce made 58 recommendations about how to improve mental health outcomes, including increasing access to psychological therapies, 24/7 mental health crisis services across England, reducing the practice of sending people long distances to access inpatient care, and to reduce the number of MHA detentions. The government accepted the recommendations of the taskforce (HM Government, 2017) and subsequently committed £1 billion to support implementation by 2020–2021 (Parkin, 2018). In order to meet the targets set out in the *Five Year Forward View*, a new commitment to mental health staff recruitment was made. In July 2017, the Secretary of State for Health announced that an additional 21,000 new posts will be introduced by April 2021, constituting 'one of the biggest expansions of mental health services in Europe' (Department of Health and Social Care, 2017b). These new posts will be made across NHS-funded mental health services, including Improving Access to Psychological Therapy (IAPT) services, liaison psychiatry in acute hospitals and crisis services (Health Education England, 2017).

AUSTERITY AND MENTAL HEALTH

The coalition government, along with the Conservative government that followed it, have been preoccupied with reducing costs. In *No Health Without Mental Health* we are told about the financial implications of poor mental health, claiming that mental health problems in England cost £105 billion each year (HM Government, 2011:2). Later, in the foreword to *Closing the Gap* (Department of Health, 2014:4), we are told that poor mental health can lead to unemployment and premature job loss and that 'this is a waste for individuals and for the economy'. This concern for the economic cost of poor mental health has been observed by others. In a review of changing children and adolescent mental health policy in England, Callaghan, Fellin and Waner-Gale (2017:118) observe that 'the policy landscape is marked by a clear shift from constructing socio-economic difficulties as *producing* mental health issues to a framing of mental health *as a socio-economic problem*' (emphasis in original). This highlights how mental health problems have been reconfigured in the context of austerity.

While mental health problems have been increasingly character-ised as economic problems by the Conservative government, their 2017 manifesto also proudly reveals that 'since 2010 we have increased spending on mental health each year to a record £11.4 billion in 2016/17' (The Conservative and Unionist Party, 2017:57). While a renewed focus on mental health is long overdue and to be welcomed, it is important that we do not forget the contradictions that are inher-ent in the Conservative government's approach to mental health. This has already been noted in relation to the coalition government by Mattheys (2015:475) who observes that the 'commitment to improv-ing mental health provision masks the extent that their policies of austerity have already brought harm to those same services'.

Following the 2008 financial crisis there is evidence to suggest that mental health problems in the UK have increased (Barr, Kinder-man and Whitehead, 2015). Increases in demand have 'contributed to a mental health system that is showing signs of strain; including problems of access, pressures on staffing and unsafe environments on some mental health wards' (Care Quality Commission (CQC), 2018:5). Sadly, at a time when potential demand has increased, aus-terity measures under the coalition and Conservative governments, have often had severe and detrimental impacts on public health, social care, and criminal justice services. In criminal justice, for example, the austerity agenda led to a reduction of expenditure by 18% (Garside and Ford, 2015) leaving many agencies like the police, prisons and probation, struggling to deliver effective and safe services. Austerity is also being felt across community and inpatient mental health services (Simpson et al., 2016) and mental health services are facing a number of challenges including: high levels of demand, a shortage of mental health nursing staff, pressure on beds in acute wards and an undesirable level of out of area placements (CQC, 2017).

According to Mattheys (2015), people who experience mental distress have been especially vulnerable to the harms of the austerity programme. In addition to cuts in key services, austerity measures have damaging social and psychological impacts (Cummins, 2016). Indeed, McGrath, Griffin and Mundy (2016:46) suggest five 'ail-ments' that may be caused by austerity: (1) humiliation and shame, (2) fear and distrust, (3) instability and insecurity, (4) isolation and loneliness and (5) being trapped and powerless.[9] While the Prime Minister Theresa May recently declared in October 2018 that 'aus-terity is over', the extent to which the damage already caused by austerity can be addressed, remains to be seen.

REVIEW OF THE MENTAL HEALTH ACT (MHA) 1983
(AS AMENDED BY THE MHA 2007)

In 2015, towards the end of the coalition government's time in office, there were emerging signs of a political willingness to look at reforming the MHA (Mental Health Alliance, 2017) with the publication of a Green Paper about learning disabilities and mental health (Department of Health, 2015). The prospect of reform was raised again in early 2016 when the Mental Health Taskforce (2016) recommended the MHA be reviewed; a recommendation subsequently accepted by government (HM Government, 2017). In October 2017, terms of reference for a review of the MHA 1983 (as amended by the MHA 2007) were published. The terms of reference reiterated the government's commitment to achieving parity of esteem between mental and physical health and noted that there were particular concerns with the following:

- 'rising rates of detention under the act
- the disproportionate number of people from black and minority ethnicities detained under the act
- stakeholder concerns that some processes relating to the act are out of step with a modern mental health system, including but not limited to:
- the balance of safeguards available to patients, such as tribunals, second opinions and requirements for consent
- the ability of the detained person to determine which family or carers have a say in their care, and of families to find appropriate information about their loved one
- that detention may in some cases be used to detain rather than treat
- questions about the effectiveness of community treatment orders, and the difficulties in getting discharged
- the time required to take decisions and arrange transfers for patients subject to criminal proceedings'.

(Department of Health and Social Care, 2017a)

Chaired by Simon Wessely, President of the Royal Society of Medicine, the final report was published in December 2018. The report recommends that coercion across the system is reduced and that service users are given greater choice and more control over their own care and treatment. To support this, the review recommends that the MHA should be based on the following four principles:

- Choice and autonomy – to ensure the views and choices of service users are respected;
- Least restriction – to ensure that legislative powers are used in the least restrictive way;
- Therapeutic benefit – to ensure patients are properly supported to get better;
- The person as an individual – to insure service users are treated as 'rounded individuals'.

(Department of Health and Social Care, 2018c:20)

At the time of writing, the report is under review by government. However, the government has already accepted the need to modernise mental health law in England and Wales and has indicated that they will introduce a new Mental Health Bill when parliamentary time allows (Department of Health and Social Care, 2018b).

WIDER CRIMINAL JUSTICE DEVELOPMENTS SINCE 2015

The controversial TR reforms brought about by Chris Grayling as Secretary of State for Justice (who served between September 2012 and May 2015) were followed by a lack of coherent or consistent leadership, with four MPs taking the role between May 2015 and the time of writing (December 2018).[10] The TR reforms have presented the probation service with the 'greatest challenge since its inception' (Calder and Goodman, 2013:176) and assessments of their impact have been overwhelmingly negative. While caseloads have increased, financial pressures have led to reductions in CRC staff (Carr, 2018). Concerns have also been raised by HM Inspectorate of Probation (2017) that the TR reforms have created a fragmented and two-tiered service, with many CRCs struggling to deliver and effective service. In addition, the PbR agreement with CRCs is yet to show evidence of success and is considered to have limited value in any case for helping those with complex health needs (Public Health England, 2016:37).

The prison service has continued to experience several challenges under the Conservative government that are likely to be detrimental to the mental health of prisoners (and staff). These challenges (which are discussed more fully in Chapter 6) include problems with staffing and resources, high levels of violence, suicide and self-harm and the rising use of new psychoactive substances. To tackle some of these problems, a White Paper *Prison Safety and Reform* (Ministry of Justice, 2016a) was published in November 2016, which promised to invest

£1.3 billion in new facilities to support an additional 10,000 prison places. The White Paper also included proposals to recruit more prison officers and to give prison governors greater responsibility for commissioning health care for prisoners. Following on from the White Paper and with the promise that it would facilitate the 'biggest overhaul of prisons in a generation' the Prison and Courts Bill was unveiled in February 2017. However, the Bill soon became one of the 'legislative casualties' of an unexpected general election in 2017 (Legal Action Group, 2018).[11]

DISCUSSION

It is clear, from the brief review above, that the volume and pace of interrelated mental health and criminal justice reform has been vast over the last 20–30 years. As Hannigan and Coffey (2011:222) observe, mental health policy is a 'particularly untamed arena' of social policy. This reflects that mental health policy continues to represent 'an ideological battleground' (Carpenter, 2009:220) and that the pace of change in criminal justice and mental health has been 'increasingly rapid' (Prins, 2016:xv). However, 'the past decade and a half has been characterised by a lot of talk and a great deal of political rhetoric, which has not actually resulted in much change for the better' (Birmingham, Awonogun and Ryland, 2017:382). Somewhat paradoxically, 'the zeal with which policymakers have engaged with the mental health field' have created further challenges because of the 'major upheaval' in services that follow from 'a flood of top-down policies' (Hannigan and Coffey, 2011:225). Following the TR reforms and their impact on probation services, it is fair to observe that the same can be said regarding the criminal justice field.

In addition, many changes have been criticised for their prioritisation of the management of potential risk over well-resourced care. This has led mental health policy and legislation to have an increasingly coercive feel. Indeed, Cummins (2016:37) argues that mental health policy in the last 20 years has 'concentrated on essentially bureaucratic responses to the collapse of mental health services' with the main response having involved 'more systematic surveillance of patients and the audit of mental health professionals'. In addition, concerns have been raised that the use of restraint in mental health services is problematic (CQC, 2017). It is apparent that BAME people are disproportionately affected by this, with concerns about the treatment of and outcomes for BAME people in the criminal justice system highlighted by the Lammy (2017) report, and a key driver behind the independent review of mental health legislation. While it is positive that some recognition has been given to the disproportionate rates of detention and use of restraint with some BAME mental health patients, we should also be mindful that concerns about the detention and experiences of such groups have long been expressed (see for example Prins et al., 1993).

While many of the policy developments described in this chapter have clearly placed risk and precautionary concerns at the fore, it is possible for risk strategies to take many forms (O'Malley, 2008). While many have observed a return to containment, some research also observes practices that represent a shift away from containment to active rehabilitation (McDonald, Furtado and Völlm, 2016). Alongside a number of public protection initiatives, a parallel concern for what works, treatment and therapy with 'risky' offenders can also be seen (McBride, 2017). The OPD Pathway along with Bradley's renewed focus on diversion may be recent examples of this shift towards an increasingly therapeutic approach. However, we must remember that diversion to the mental health system involves inevitable coercion and is not exclusively focused on patient needs and desires to keep people out of the criminal justice system (Holloway, 2002). Diversion can take many forms and may be motivated by a range of different agendas.

Looking forwards – it is important that the 'momentum' that followed the Bradley report is maintained and that L&D services are properly supported (Birmingham, Awonogun and Ryland, 2017). There is evidence to suggest that efforts to increase L&D have increased rates of detention under the MHA (CQC, 2018), and while it is desirable that people may be identified earlier and by more informed staff, it is also important that appropriate resources are attached to the increased work that service providers will have been experiencing. In the context of recent austerity measures, this is far from guaranteed.

While the ongoing government interest in mental health is to be welcomed, the extent to which this agenda will be achieved, alongside ongoing negotiations to leave the EU, remains unclear. While the Chancellor of the Exchequer, Philip Hammond, recently announced a £2 billion real-terms increase in mental health spending as part of the UK budget, he also indicated that the proposals were dependent on the government agreeing a deal with the EU as part of 'Brexit'. Should no deal be secured as part of the UK's plan to leave the EU in 2019, a new emergency budget would have to be devised (Sparrow, 2018). In any case, while extra investment is to be welcomed, it is of note that the total spend of £11.9 billion on mental health services in 2017–2018 only represents a 0.4% increase in real terms (Baker, 2018). Given the service costs of mental health care in

2026 are estimated by some to be 47.5 billion (McCrone et al., 2008) it is clear there is still a significant way to go.

With reform of mental health legislation now on the horizon, it is important that proper consideration is given to the necessity, guiding principles and implications of any amendments to the law. However, it is important that we do not rely on the review of the MHA to bring about the change that is required, since legislative change alone will not address the many challenges faced by mental health practitioners and service users. Changes to legislation must coincide with proper funding arrangements so that the services and practitioners involved with the delivery of mental health care can adequately address the demands placed on them. If mental health reform is to have a meaningful impact on those subject to it, the government must also address the reasons why people develop serious mental health problems and ensure greater support is given to those who need it, not just in times of crisis, but earlier on so potential crises can be avoided. This is something that has been recognised by those undertaking the review. Indeed Simon Wessely (2017) has observed that 'reviewing the Act isn't just about changing the legislation. In some ways that might be the easy part. The bigger challenge is changing the way we deliver care so that people do not need to be detained in the first place'. This is especially pertinent for those who may also come into contact with the criminal justice system.

FURTHER READING

For a comprehensive overview of the imprisonment of people with mental health problems since the 1980s see Seddon (2007). For earlier histories see Porter (2002) and Scull (1993). For an overview of criminal justice developments since the UK referendum to leave the EU in June 2016 until the general election in June 2017 see Garside, Grimshaw and Ford (2018). For earlier reviews of criminal justice policy see the other UK Justice Policy Review documents produced by the Centre for Crime and Justice Studies.

REFERENCES

Annison, H. (2018) 'Tracing the Gordian knot: Indeterminate-sentenced prisoners and the pathologies of English penal politics', *The Political Quarterly*, 89(2): 1–9.

Austin, J. and Krisberg, B. (1981) 'Wider, stronger and different nets: The dialectics of criminal justice reform', *Journal of Research in Crime and Delinquency*, 18(1): 165–196.

Baker, C. (2018) *Mental health statistics for England: Prevalence, services and funding. Briefing paper number 6988, 25 April 2018*, London: House of Commons Library.

Barr, B., Kinderman, P. and Whitehead, M. (2015) 'Trends in mental health inequalities in England during a period of recession, austerity and welfare reform 2004 to 2013', *Social Science and Medicine*, 147: 324–331.

Bartlett, A. (2010) 'Medical models of mental disorder' in Bartlett, A. and McGauley, G. (eds.) *Forensic mental health: Concepts, systems and practice*, Oxford: Oxford University Press.

Bartlett, P. and Sandland, R. (2014) *Mental health law: Policy and practice (Fourth edition)*, Oxford: Oxford University Press.

Beckett, K. and Murakawa, N. (2012) 'Mapping the shadow carceral state: Toward an institutionally capacious approach to punishment', *Theoretical Criminology*, 16(2): 221–244.

Ben-Moshe, L. (2017) 'Why prisons are not "the new asylums"', *Punishment and Society*, 19(3): 272–289.

Benefield, N., Joseph, N., Skett, S., Bridgland, S., d'Cruz, L., Goode, I. and Turner, K. (2015) 'The Offender Personality Disorder strategy jointly delivered by NOMS and NHS England', *Prison Service Journal*, 218, 4–9.

Birmingham, L., Awonogun, O. and Ryland, H. (2017) 'Diversion from custody: An update', *BJPsych Advances*, 23(6): 375–384.

Brooker, C., Denney, D. and Sirdifield, C. (2014) 'Mental disorder and probation policy and practice: A view from the UK', *International Journal of Law and Psychiatry*, 37(5): 484–489.

Buchanan, A. and Leese, M. (2001) 'Detention of people with dangerous severe personality disorders: A systematic review', *The Lancet*, 358: 1955–1959.

Burns, T. (2014) 'Community psychiatry's achievements', *Epidemiology and Psychiatric Sciences*, 23(4): 337–344.

Burns, T. and Priebe, S. (1999) 'Mental health care in England: Myth and reality', *British Journal of Psychiatry*, 174(3): 191–192.

Busfield, J. (2002) 'Psychiatric discourse and individual violence: Imagined death, risk and mental health policy' in Buchanan, A. (ed.) *Care of the mentally disordered offender in the community*, Oxford: Oxford University Press.

Calder, S.D. and Goodman, A.H. (2013) 'Transforming rehabilitation, a fiscal motivated approach to offender management', *British Journal of Community Justice*, 11(2–3): 175–188.

Callaghan, J.E.M., Fellin, L.C. and Waner-Gale, F. (2017) 'A critical analysis of child and adolescent mental health services policy in England', *Clinical Child Psychology and Psychiatry*, 22(1): 108–127.

Care Quality Commission (CQC) (2017) *The state of care in mental health services 2014 to 2017. Findings from CQC's programme of comprehensive inspections of specialist mental health services*, Newcastle-Upon-Tyne: Care Quality Commission.

Care Quality Commission (CQC) (2018) *Mental Health Act. The rise in the use of the MHA to detain people in England*, Newcastle-Upon-Tyne: Care Quality Commission.

Carpenter, M. (2009) 'A third wave, not a third way? New Labour, human rights and mental health in historical context', *Social Policy and Society*, 8(2): 215–230.

Carr, N. (2018) 'Transforming rehabilitation? Destination unknown', *Probation Journal*, 65(1): 3–6.

Cavadino, P. (1999) 'Diverting mentally disordered offenders from custody' in Webb, D. and Harris, R. (eds.) *Mentally disordered offenders: Managing people nobody owns*, London: Routledge.

Clark, K. (2018) 'The effect of mental illness on segregation following institutional misconduct', *Criminal Justice and Behavior*, 45(9): 1363–1382.

Coffey, M. (2011) 'Resistance and challenge: Competing accounts in aftercare monitoring', *Sociology of Health and Illness*, 33(5): 748–760.

Coffey, M. (2012) 'A risk worth taking? Value differences and alternative risk constructions in accounts given by patients and their community workers following conditional discharge from forensic mental health services', *Health, Risk and Society*, 14(5): 465–482.

Cohen, S. (1985) *Visions of social control*, Cambridge: Polity Press.

Cooper, V. and Whyte, D. (2017) *The violence of austerity*, London: Pluto Press.

Crawford, M.J., Hopkins, W., Thomas, P., Moncrieff, J., Bindman, J and Gray, J.A. (2001) 'Most psychiatrists oppose plans for a new Mental Health Act', *British Medical Journal*, 322: 72–90.

Criminal Cases Review Commission (CCRC) (2017) *Commission statement on the 2017 application of Michael Stone*, Birmingham: CCRC.

Crisis Care Concordat (2017) *Beyond places of safety grant application guidance final*. Available at: www.crisiscareconcordat.org.uk/wp-content/uploads/2017/10/Beyond-Places-of-Safety-Grant-Application-Guidance-Final.pdf [Last accessed 24 May 2018].

Cummins, I. (2006) 'A path not taken? Mentally disordered offenders and the criminal justice system', *Journal of Social Welfare and Family Law*, 28(3): 267–281.

Cummins, I. (2010) 'The relationship between mental institution beds, prison population and the crime rate' in Royal College of Nursing (eds.) *Prison mental health: Vision and reality*, London: Royal College of Nursing.

Cummins, I. (2011) 'Distant voices still lives: Reflections on the impact of media reporting of the cases of Christopher Clunis and Ben Silcock', *Ethnicity and Inequalities in Health and Social Care Journal*, 3(4): 18–29.

Cummins, I. (2012) 'Using Simon's *Governing through crime* to explore the development of mental health policy in England and Wales since 1983', *Journal of Social Welfare and Family Law*, 34(3): 325–337.

Cummins, I. (2015) 'Discussing race, racism and mental health: Two mental health inquiries reconsidered', *International Journal of Human Rights in Healthcare*, 8(3): 160–172.

Cummins, I. (2016) *Mental health and the criminal justice system: A social work perspective*, Northwich: Critical Publishing Ltd.

de Lacy, C. (2016) 'The role of the mental health clinical nurse specialist in the Crown Court setting: Towards a best practice model' in Winstone, J. (ed.) *Mental health, crime and criminal justice*, Basingstoke: Palgrave Macmillan.

Department of Health (1990) *The Care Programme Approach for people with a mental illness, referred to specialist psychiatric services, HC(90)23/LASSL(90)11*, London: Department of Health.

Department of Health (1994a) *HSG (94)27: Guidance on the discharge of mentally disordered people and their continuing care in the community*, London: Department of Health.

Department of Health (1994b) *Introduction of supervision registers for mentally ill people from 1 April 1994, HSG (94)*, London: Department of Health

Department of Health (1998a) 'Expert advisor appointed to start review of Mental Health Act' [Press release] 22 September 1998. London: Department of Health.

Department of Health (1998b) *Modernising mental health services: Safe, sound and supportive*, London: Department of Health.

Department of Health (1999a) *Reform of the Mental Health Act: Proposals for consultation, Cm 4480*, London: The Stationery Office.

Department of Health (1999b) *Report of the expert committee: Review of the Mental Health Act 1983*, London: The Stationery Office.

Department of Health (2000a) *Reforming the Mental Health Act white paper: Part I: The new legal framework*, London: Department of Health.

Department of Health (2000b) *Reforming the Mental Health Act white paper: Part II: High risk patients*, London: Department of Health.

Department of Health (2002) *Draft Mental Health Bill*, Cm 5538, London: The Stationery Office.

Department of Health (2004) *Draft Mental Health Bill*, Cm 6305 London: The Stationery Office.

Department of Health (2006a) 'Next steps for the Mental Health Bill' [Press release] 23 March 2006. London: Department of Health.

Department of Health (2006b) *Personality disorder capacity plans 2005*, London: Department of Health.

Department of Health (2008) *Refocusing the Care Programme Approach: Policy and positive practical guidance*, London: Department of Health.

Department of Health (2009a) *Improving health, supporting justice: The national delivery plan of the Health and Criminal Justice Programme Board*, London: Department of Health.

Department of Health (2009b) *The Bradley Report. Lord Bradley's review of people with mental health problems or learning disabilities in the criminal justice system*, London: Department of Health.

Department of Health (2014) *Closing the gap: Priorities for essential change in mental health*, London: Department of Health.

Department of Health (2015) *No voice unheard, no right ignored – A consultation for people with learning disabilities, autism and mental health conditions*, London: Department of Health.

Department of Health and Home Office (1992) *Review of health and social services for mentally disordered offenders and others requiring similar services – Final summary report*, London: Her Majesty's Stationery Office.

Department of Health and Home Office (2014) *Review of the operation of sections 135 and 136 of the Mental Health Act 1983: Review report and recommendations*, London: Department of Health and Home Office.

Department of Health and National Offender Management Service (NOMS) (2011a) *Consultation on the Offender Personality Disorder pathway implementation plan*, London: Department of Health.

Department of Health and National Offender Management Service (NOMS) (2011b) *Response to the Offender Personality Disorder consultation*, London: Department of Health.

Department of Health and Social Care (2017a) *Terms of reference – Independent review of the Mental Health Act 1983*, London: Department of Health.

Department of Health and Social Care (2017b) 'Thousands of new roles to be created in mental health workforce plan' [Press release] 31 July 2017. London: Department of Health and Social Care.

Department of Health and Social Care (2018a) '£15 million boost for local mental health crisis services' [Press Release] 25 May 2018, London: Department of Health and Social Care.

Department of Health and Social Care (2018b) 'Government commits to reform the Mental Health Act' [Press release] 6 December 2018. London: Department of Health and Social Care.

Department of Health and Social Care (2018c) *Modernising the Mental Health Act: Increasing choice, reducing compulsion. Final report of the independent review of the Mental Health Act 1983*, London: Department of Health and Social Care.

Department of Health and Social Security (DHSS) (1974) *Revised report of the working party on security in NHS psychiatric hospitals*, London: Her Majesty's Stationery Office.

Department of Health and Social Security (DHSS) (1988) *Report of the committee of inquiry into the care and aftercare of Sharon Campbell*, London: Her Majesty's Stationery Office.

Disley, E., Taylor, C., Kruithof, K., Winpenny, E., Liddle, M., Sutherland, A., Lilford, R., Wright, S., McAteer, L. and Francis, V. (2016) *Evaluation of the offender liaison and diversion trial schemes*, Cambridge: RAND Corporation.

Dixon, J. (2015) 'Treatment, deterrence or labelling: Mentally disordered offenders' perspectives on social control', *Sociology of Health and Illness*, 37(8): 1299–1313.

Downes, D. and Morgan, R. (2002) 'The skeletons in the cupboard: The politics of law and order at the turn of the millennium' in Maguire, M., Morgan, R. and Reiner, R. (eds.) *The Oxford handbook of criminology (Third edition)*, Oxford: Oxford University Press.

Dyer, W. (2013) 'Criminal Justice Diversion and Liaison Services: A path to success?' *Social Policy and Society*, 12(1): 31–45.

Earl, F., Cocksedge, K., Morgan, J. and Bolt, M. (2017) 'Evaluating liaison and diversion schemes: An analysis of health, criminal and economic data', *Journal of Forensic Psychiatry and Psychology*, 28(4): 562–580.

Fallon, P., Bluglass, R., Edwards, B. and Daniels, G. (1999) *Report of the committee of inquiry into the personality disorder unit, Ashworth Special Hospital*, Cm 4195, London: The Stationery Office.

Fennell, P. and Yeates, V. (2002) '"To serve which master?" – Criminal justice policy, community care and the mentally disordered offender' in Buchanan, A. (ed.) *Care of the mentally disordered offender in the community*, Oxford: Oxford University Press.

Fitzgibbon, D.W. (2004) 'Pre-emptive criminalization: Risk control and alternative futures', *Issues in Community and Criminal Justice*, Monograph 4, London: NAPO.

Garside, R. and Ford, M. (2015) *The coalition years: Criminal justice in the United Kingdom: 2010 to 2015*, London: Centre for Crime and Justice Studies.

Garside, R., Grimshaw, R. and Ford, M. (2018) *UK justice policy review: Volume 7. From Brexit referendum to general election 24 June 2016 to 8 June 2017*, London: Centre for Crime and Justice Studies.

Gergel, T. and Szmulker, G. (2017) 'The ethics of coercion in community mental health care' in Buchanan, A. and Wootton, L. (eds.) *Care of the mentally disordered offender in the community (Second edition)*, Oxford: Oxford University Press.

Gilburt, H. (2015) *Mental health under pressure*, London: The King's Fund.

Gilburt, H., Peck, E., Ashton, B., Edwards, N. and Naylor, C. (2014) *Service transformation. Lessons from mental health*, London: The King's Fund.

Griffiths, L. (2001) 'Categorising to exclude: The discursive construction of cases in community mental health teams', *Sociology of Health and Illness*, 23(5): 678–700.

Haney, C. (2017) '"Madness" and penal confinement: Some observations on mental illness and prison pain', *Punishment and Society*, 19(3): 310–326.

Hannigan, B. and Coffey, M. (2011) 'Where the wicked problems are: The case of mental health', *Health Policy*, 101(3): 220–227.

Harris, R. (1999) 'Mental disorder and social order: Underlying themes in crime management' in Webb, D. and Harris, R. (eds.) *Mentally disordered offenders: Managing people nobody owns*, London: Routledge.

Health Education England (2017) *Stepping forward to 2020/21: The mental health workforce plan in England July 2017*, London: Health Education England.

Hebenton, B. (2008) 'Sexual offenders and public protection in an uncertain age' in Letherby, G., Birch, P. Williams, K. and Cain, M. (eds.) *Sex as crime?*, Cullompton: Willan Publishing.

Henderson, C., Bindmann, J. and Thornicroft, G. (1998) 'Can deinstitutionalised care be provided for those at risk of violent offending?', *Epidemiologica e Psichiatria Sociale*, 7(1): 42–51.

Her Majesty's (HM) Government (2011) *No health without mental health: A cross-government mental health outcomes strategy for people of all ages*, London: HM Government and Department of Health.

Her Majesty's (HM) Government (2014) *Mental Health Crisis Care Concordat: Improving outcomes for people experiencing mental health crisis*, London: HM Government.

Her Majesty's (HM) Government (2017) *The government's response to the five year forward view for mental health*, London: HM Government.

Her Majesty's (HM) Inspectorate of Prisons (2016) *Unintended consequences: Finding a way forward for prisoners serving sentences of imprisonment for public protection*, London: HM Inspectorate of Prisons.

Her Majesty's (HM) Inspectorate of Probation (2017) *Annual Report 2017*, Manchester: HM Inspectorate of Probation.

Her Majesty's (HM) Inspectorate of Probation and HM Inspectorate of Prisons (2017) *An inspection of Through the Gate resettlement services for prisoners serving 12 months or more*, London: HM Inspectorate of Probation and HM Inspectorate of Prisons.

Hiday, V.A. (1999) 'Mental illness and the criminal justice system' in Horwitz, A.V. and Scheid, T.L. (eds.) *A handbook for the study of mental health: Social contexts, theories, and systems*, Cambridge: Cambridge University Press.

Holloway, F. (2002) 'Mentally disordered offenders and the community mental health team' in Buchanan, A. (ed.) *Care of the mentally disordered offender in the community*, Oxford: Oxford University Press.

Holloway, F. and Davies, T. (2017) 'The Community Mental Health Team and the mentally disordered offender' in Buchanan, A. and Wootton, L. (eds.) *Care of the mentally disordered offender in the community (Second edition)*, Oxford: Oxford University Press.

Home Office (1990) *Home Office circular no. 66/90. Provision for mentally disordered offenders*, London: Home Office.

Home Office (1995) *Home Office circular no. 12/95. Mentally disordered offenders: Inter-agency working*, London: Home Office.

Home Office and Department of Health (1999) *Managing dangerous people with severe personality disorder*, London: Her Majesty's Stationery Office.

Home Office and Department of Health and Social Security (DHSS) (1975) *Committee on mentally abnormal offenders*, Cmnd 6244. London: Her Majesty's Stationery Office.

House of Commons debate (1999) Vol 325, Col 601, 15 Feb 1999.

Hudson, B. (2001) 'Human rights, public safety and the probation service: Defending justice in the risk society', *Howard Journal*, 40(2): 103–113.

Institute for Government (2018) *Performance tracker 2018*, Available from: www.instituteforgovernment.org.uk/publication/performance-tracker-2018/prisons [Last accessed 01 November 2018].

Jewesbury, I. and McCulloch, A. (2002) 'Public policy and mentally disordered offenders in the UK' in Buchanan, A. (ed.) *Care of the mentally disordered offender in the community*, Oxford: Oxford University Press.

Joint Committee on the Draft Mental Health Bill (2005a) *Draft Mental Health Bill, Volume I: Report*, London: The Stationery Office.

Joint Committee on the Draft Mental Health Bill (2005b) *Draft Mental Health Bill, Volume II: Oral and written evidence*, London: The Stationery Office.

Joint Committee on the Draft Mental Health Bill (2005c) *Draft Mental Health Bill, Volume III: Written evidence*, London: The Stationery Office.

Justice (2002) *Justice response to Draft Mental Health Bill 2002*, London: Justice.

Kemshall, H. (2008) *Understanding the community management of high risk offenders*, Maidenhead: Open University Press.

Kemshall, H. and Maguire, M. (2001) 'Public protection, partnership and risk penality: The multi-agency risk management of sexual and violent offenders', *Punishment and Society*, 3(2): 237–264.

Kemshall, H. and Wood, J. (2008) 'Risk and public protection: Responding to involuntary and "taboo" risk', *Social Policy and Administration*, 42(6): 611–629.

Keown, P., Murphy, H., McKenna, D. and McKinnon, I. (2018) 'Changes in the use of the Mental Health Act 1983 in England 1984/85 to 2015/16', *British Journal of Psychiatry*, 213(4): 295–299.

Lammy, D (2017) *The Lammy review: An independent review into the treatment of, and outcomes for, Black, Asian and Minority Ethnic individuals in the criminal justice system*, London: Lammy Review.

Large, M., Smith, G., Swinson, N., Shaw, J., and Nielssen, O. (2008) 'Homicide due to mental disorder in England and Wales over 50 years', *British Journal of Psychiatry*, 193(2): 130–133.

Laurance, J. (2003) *Pure madness: How fear drives the mental health system*, London: Routledge.

Le Grand, J. (1999) 'Competition, cooperation, or control? Tales from the British National Health Service', *Health Affairs*, 18(3): 27–40.

Leff, J. (2001) 'Why is care in the community perceived as a failure?', *British Journal of Psychiatry*, 179(5): 381–383.

Legal Action Group (2018) 'New courts bill announced', *Legal Action Group*, 24 May 2018. Available from: www.lag.org.uk/article/204968/new-courts-bill-announced [Last accessed 14 July 2017].

Markowitz, F.E. (2011) 'Mental illness, crime, and violence: Risk, context, and social control', *Aggression and Violent Behavior*, 16(1): 36–44.

Mason, T. and Mercer, D. (1998) 'Introduction: The silent scream' in Mason, T. and Mercer, D. (eds.) *Critical perspectives in forensic care: Inside out*, London: Macmillan Press Ltd.

Mattheys, K. (2015) 'The Coalition, austerity and mental health', *Disability and Society*, 30(3): 475–478.

McBride, R. (2017) 'On the advancement of therapeutic penality: Therapeutic authority, personality science and the therapeutic community', *Sociology of Health and Illness*, 39(7): 1258–1272.

McCann, G. (1998) 'Control in the community' in Mason, T. and Mercer, D. (ed.) *Critical perspectives in forensic care: Inside out*, London: Macmillan Press Ltd.

McCrone, P., Dhanasiri, S., Patel, A., Knapp, M., and Lawton-Smith, S. (2008) *Paying the price: The cost of mental health care in England to 2026*, London: King's Fund.

McDonald, R., Furtado, V. and Völlm, B. (2016) 'Managing madness, murderers and paedophiles: Understanding change in the field of English forensic psychiatry', *Social Science and Medicine*, 164: 12–18.

McGrath, L., Griffin, V. and Mundy, E. (2016) 'The psychological impact of austerity: A briefing paper', *Educational Psychology Research and Practice*, 2(2): 46–57.

McMurran, M., Khalifa, N. and Gibbon, S. (2009) *Forensic mental health*, Cullompton: Willan Publishing.

Mental Health Alliance (2004) 'Revised Mental Health Bill is unfit for 21st century' [Press release] 8 September 2014. London: Mental Health Alliance.

Mental Health Alliance (2005) *Towards a better Mental Health Act: The Mental Health Alliance policy agenda*, London: Mental Health Alliance.

Mental Health Alliance (2017) *A Mental Health Act fit for tomorrow: An agenda for reform*, London: Mental Health Alliance.

Mental Health Taskforce (2016) *The five year forward view for mental health*, London: Mental Health Taskforce.

Ministry of Justice (2008) *Prison population projections 2008–2015: Ministry of Justice statistics bulletin*, London: Ministry of Justice.

Ministry of Justice (2010) *Breaking the cycle: Effective punishment, rehabilitation and sentencing of offenders*, London: Ministry of Justice.

Ministry of Justice (2011) *Working with personality disordered offenders: A practitioners guide*, London: Ministry of Justice.

Ministry of Justice (2013a) *Story of the prison population: 1993–2012 England and Wales*, London: Ministry of Justice.

Ministry of Justice (2013b) *Transforming rehabilitation: A revolution in the way we manage offenders*, London: Ministry of Justice.

Ministry of Justice (2013c) *Transforming rehabilitation: A strategy for reform. Response to consultation CP(R) 16/2013*, London: Ministry of Justice.

Ministry of Justice (2016a) *Prison safety and reform*, London: Ministry of Justice.

Ministry of Justice (2016b) *Story of the prison population: 1993–2016 England and Wales*, London: Ministry of Justice.

Ministry of Justice (2017) *Offender management statistics bulletin, England and Wales, Quarterly October to December 2016*, London: Ministry of Justice.

Moon, G. (2000) 'Risk and protection: The discourse of confinement in contemporary mental health policy', *Health and Place*, 6(3): 239–250.

NACRO (2002) *NACRO's response to the Draft Mental Health Bill*, London: NACRO.

Nash, M. (2006) *Public protection and the criminal justice process*, Oxford: Open University Press.

National Health Service (NHS) England (2014) *Five year forward view*, London: NHS England.

National Health Service (NHS) England (2016a) *Implementing the five year forward view for mental health*, London: NHS England.

National Health Service (NHS) England (2016b) *Strategic direction for health services in the justice system 2016–2020*, London: NHS England.

National Health Service (NHS) England Liaison and Diversion (L&D) Programme (2014) *Liaison and diversion operating model 2013/14*, London: NHS England L&D Programme.

National Institute for Health and Care Excellence (NICE) (2009a) *Antisocial personality disorder: Treatment, management and prevention, NICE clinical guidelines 77*, London: NICE.

National Institute for Health and Care Excellence (NICE) (2009b) *Borderline personality disorder: Treatment and management, NICE clinical guidelines 78*, London: NICE.

National Institute for Mental Health in England (NIMHE) (2003a) *Personality disorder – no longer a diagnosis of exclusion. Policy implementation guidance for development of services for people with personality disorder*, London: Department of Health.

National Institute for Mental Health in England (NIMHE) (2003b) *Breaking the cycle of rejection. The personality disorder capabilities framework*, London: Department of Health.

National Offender Management Service (NOMS) and Department of Health (2012) *A guide to Psychologically Informed Planned Environments*, London: NOMS and Department of Health.

National Offender Management Service (NOMS) and National Health Service (NHS) England (2015) *The Offender Personality Disorder pathway strategy 2015*, London: NOMS and NHS England.

O'Malley, P. (2008) 'Experiments in risk and criminal justice', *Theoretical Criminology*, 12(4): 451–469.

Parkin, E. (2018) *Mental health policy in England. Briefing paper number CBP 0754*, London: House of Commons Library.

Peay, J. (1996) (ed.) *Inquiries after homicide*, London: Duckworth.

Peay, J. (1997) 'Clinicians and inquiries: Demons, drones or demigods?', *International Review of Psychiatry*, 9(2–3): 171–177.

Peay, J. (2000) 'Reform of the Mental Health Act 1983: Squandering an opportunity?', *Journal of Mental Health Law*, 9(1): 5–15.

Peay, J. (2003) *Decisions and dilemmas: Working with mental health law*, Oxford: Hart Publishing.

Peay, J. (2007) 'Mentally disordered offenders, mental health, and crime', in Maguire, M., Morgan, R., and Reiner, R. (eds.) *The Oxford handbook of criminology (Fourth edition)*, Oxford: Oxford University Press.

Penrose, L.S. (1939) 'Mental disease and crime: Outline of a comparative study of European statistics', *British Journal of Medical Psychology*, 18(1): 1–15.

Percy Commission (1957) *Report of the royal commission on the law relating to mental illness and mental deficiency 1954–1957*, Cmnd 169, London: Her Majesty's Stationery Office.

Petch, E. and Bradley, C. (1997) 'Learning the lessons from homicide inquiries: Adding insult to injury?', *Journal of Forensic Psychiatry*, 8(1): 161–184.

Pickersgill, M. (2012) 'Standardising antisocial personality disorder: The social shaping of a psychiatric terminology', *Sociology of Health and Illness*, 34(4): 544–559.

Pidd, F., Benefield, N. and Duggan, M. (2005) 'Personality disorder – everybody's business', *Mental Health Review Journal*, 10(3): 8–15.

Pilgrim, D. and Ramon, S. (2009) 'English mental health policy under New Labour', *Policy and Politics*, 37(2): 273–288.

Porter, R. (2002) *Madness: A brief history*, Oxford: Oxford University Press.

Priebe, S., Badesconyi, A., Fioritti, A., Hansson, L., Kilian, R., Torres-Gonzales, F., Turner, T. and Wiersma, D. (2005) 'Reinstitutionaliation in mental health care: Comparison of data on service provision from six European countries', *British Medical Journal*, 330: 123–126.

Prins, H. (1999) *Will they do it again?*, London: Routledge.

Prins, H. (2016) *Offenders, deviants and patients: An introduction to clinical criminology (Fifth edition)*, Hove: Routledge.

Prins, H., Backer-Holst, T., Francis, E. and Keitch, I. (1993) *Report of the committee of inquiry into the death in Broadmoor hospital of Orville Blackwood and a review of the deaths of two other Afro-Caribbean Patients: Big, black and dangerous?*, London: Special Hospitals Service Authority.

Prins, S.J. (2011) 'Does transinstitutionalization explain the overrepresentation of people with serious mental illnesses in the criminal justice system?', *Community Mental Health Journal*, 47(6): 716–722.

Public Health England (PHE) (2016) *Rapid review of evidence of the impact on health outcomes of NHS commissioned health services for people in secure and detained settings to inform future health interventions and prioritisation in England*, London: PHE.

Revolving Doors Agency (2004) *Revolving Doors Agency general comments on Draft Mental Health Bill*, London: Revolving Doors Agency.

Ritchie, J.H., Dick, D. and Lingham, R. (1994) *The report into the inquiry and treatment of Christopher Clunis*, London: Her Majesty's Stationery Office.

Rogers, A. and Pilgrim, D. (2010) *A sociology of mental health and illness (Fourth edition)*, Maidenhead: Open University Press.

Rose, N. (1998) 'Living dangerously: Risky thinking and risk management in mental health care', *Mental Health Care*, 1(8): 263–266.

Rose, N. (2002) 'Society, madness and control' in Buchanan, A. (ed.) *Care of the mentally disordered offender in the community*, Oxford: Oxford University Press.

Rose, N. (2017) 'Society, madness and control' in Buchanan, A. and Wootton, L. (eds.) *Care of the mentally disordered offender in the community*, Oxford: Oxford University Press.

Royal College of Psychiatrists (2002) *Draft Mental Health Bill, Letter from campaign headquarters*, Number 1, October 2002, London: Royal College of Psychiatrists.

Rugkåsa, J., Molodynski, A. and Burns, T. (2016) 'Introduction' in Molodynski, A., Rugkåsa, J. and Burns, T. (eds.) *Coercion in community mental health care*, Oxford: Oxford University Press.

Rutherford, A. (2000) 'An elephant on the doorstop: Criminal policy without crime in New Labour's Britain' in Green, P. and Rutherford, A. (eds.) *Criminal policy in transition*, Oxford: Hart Publishing.

Rutherford, A. (2007) 'Sexual offenders and the path to a purified domain' in Downes, D., Rock, P., Chinkin, C. and Gearty, C. (eds.) *Crime, social control, and human rights: From moral panics to states of denial. Essays in honour of Stanley Cohen*, Cullompton: Willan Publishing.

Scott, D.A., McGilloway, S., Dempster, M., Browne, F. and Donnelly, M. (2013) 'Effectiveness of criminal justice liaison and diversion schemes for offenders with mental disorders: A review', *Psychiatric Services*, 64: 843–849.

Scull, A. (1993) *The most solitary of afflictions: Madness and society in Britain 1700–1900*, London: Yale University Press.

Seddon, T. (2007) *Punishment and madness: Governing prisoners with mental health problems*, Abingdon: Routledge-Cavendish.

Shah, A. (2010) 'Human rights and mentally disordered offenders', *The International Journal of Human Rights*, 14(7): 1107–1116.

Simon, J. (2012) 'Mass incarceration: From social policy to social problem' in Reitz, K. and Petersilia, J. (eds.) *The Oxford handbook of sentencing and corrections*, Oxford: Oxford University Press.

Simpson, A., Hannigan, B., Coffey, M., Barlow, S., Cohen, R., Jones, A., Všetečková, J., Faulkner, A., Thornton, A. and Cartwright, M. (2016) 'Recovery-focused care planning and coordination in England and Wales: A cross-national mixed methods comparative case study', *BMC Psychiatry*, 16(1): 1–18.

Simpson, A., Miller, C. and Bowers, L. (2009) 'The history of the Care Programme Approach in England: Where did it go wrong?', *Journal of Mental Health*, 12(5): 489–504.

Skett, S., Goode, I. and Barton, S. (2017) 'A joint NHS and NOMS offender personality disorder pathway strategy: A perspective from 5 years of operation', *Criminal Behaviour and Mental Health*, 27(3): 214–221.

South East Coast Strategic Health Authority (2006) *Report of the independent inquiry into the care and treatment of Michael Stone*, London: Department of Health.

Spandler, H. and Calton, T. (2009) 'Psychosis and human rights: Conflicts in mental health policy and practice', *Social Policy and Society*, 8(2): 245–256.

Sparks, R. (2000) 'Risk and blame in criminal justice controversies: British press coverage and official discourse on prison security (1993–1996)' in Brown, M. and Pratt, J. (eds.) *Dangerous offenders: Punishment and social order*, London: Routledge.

Sparrow, A. (2018) 'Mental health services to get £2bn funding boost in budget', *The Guardian*, 28 October 2018. Available from: www.theguardian.com/uk-news/2018/oct/28/mental-health-services-to-get-2bn-funding-boost-in-budget [Last accessed 28 October 2018].

Steele, L. (2001) 'Complexities surround treatment of personality disorders', *The Guardian*, 16 February 2001. Available from: www.guardian.co.uk/society/2001/feb/16/health.socialcare [Last accessed 12 January 2018].

The Conservative and Unionist Party (2017) *Forward, together: Our plan for a stronger Britain and a prosperous future*, London: The Conservative and Unionist Party.

Tighe, J., Henderson, C. and Thornicroft, G. (2002) 'Mentally disordered offenders and models of community care provision' in Buchanan, A. (ed.) *Care of the mentally disordered offender in the community*, Oxford: Oxford University Press.

Timmermans, S. and Gabe, J. (2003) 'Introduction: Connecting criminology and the sociology of health and illness' in Timmermans, S. and Gabe, J. (eds.) *Partners in health, partners in crime*, Oxford: Blackwell Publishing.

Trieman, N., Leff, J. and Glover, G. (1999) 'Outcome of long stay psychiatric patients resettled in the community: Prospective cohort study', *British Medical Journal*, 319(7201): 13–16.

Turner, J., Hayward, R., Angel, K., Fulford, B., Hall, J., Millard, C. and Thomson, M. (2015) 'The history of mental health services in modern England: Practitioner memories and the direction of future research', *Medical History*, 59(4): 599–624.

Walcott, C.M. and Beck, J.C. (2000) 'Dangerous severe personality disorder: Extension of the use of civil commitment in the United Kingdom', *Journal of the American Academy of Psychiatry and the Law*, 28(4): 469–475.

Warden, J. (1998) 'Psychiatrists hit back at Home Secretary', *British Medical Journal*, 317: 1270.

Wessely, S. (2017) 'The Prime Minister has asked me to lead a review of the mental health inequality in Britain - Here's why', *Huffington Post*, 6 October 2017. Available from: www.huffingtonpost.co.uk/professor-sir-simon-wessely/mental-health-act_b_18192476.html [Last accessed 13 July 2018].

Winstone, J. (2016) 'Crime, exclusion and mental health: Current realities and future responses' in Winstone, J. (ed.) *Mental health, crime and criminal justice*, Basingstoke: Palgrave Macmillan.

Wootton, L., Fahy, T., Wilson, S. and Buchanan, A. (2017) 'The interface of general psychiatric and forensic psychiatric services' in Buchanan, A. and Wootton, L. (eds.) *Care of the mentally disordered offender in the community (Second edition)*, Oxford: Oxford University Press.

NOTES

1   More information about the Care Programme Approach (CPA) can be found at: www.nhs.uk/Conditions/social-care-and-support-guide/Pages/care-programme-approach.aspx Note that the CPA was revised in 2008 (Department of Health, 2008).

2   This inquiry was commissioned following a former patient's allegations of the misuse of drugs and alcohol, the running of businesses, availability of pornography and paedophilic activity on the unit. The inquiry largely confirmed the allegations, and most worryingly, confirmed that a child was being groomed by patients on the unit. The report recommended the closure of the unit and the introduction of reviewable indeterminate sentences for those with severe personality disorders.

3   On 2 August 1999 Noel Ruddle, a convicted murderer still assessed to present a danger to the public, was released from psychiatric care as his continued detention was judged to be unjustifiable on the basis of him being untreatable (*Ruddle v. Secretary of State for Scotland* (1999). In response, the *Mental Health (Public Safety and Appeals) (Scotland) Act 1999* introduced public safety to the grounds for not discharging patients.

4   Between 1996 and 2008 Kemshall and Wood (2008) observe that seven major criminal justice acts were introduced.

5   It is important to note that diversion was promoted earlier than this, by the Butler Committee (Home Office and DHSS, 1975:266).

6   In 2017 the NOMS was replaced by the newly formed HMPPS. HMPPS retains operational responsibility for prisons, although responsibility for commissioning and policy has been transferred to the Ministry of Justice.

7   Although note that there was an unexpected and sharp rise in the summer of 2017, after which it has fallen.

8   See the reviews by Scott et al. (2013), Disley et al. (2016) and Birmingham, Awonogun and Ryland (2017).

9   For a devastating overview of the violence of austerity see the edited collected by Cooper and Whyte (2017).

10 Michael Gove 09.05.2015–14.07.2016; Liz Truss 14.07.2016–11.06.2017; David Lidington 11.06.2017–08.01.2018; David Gauke 08.01.2018-current.

11 The courts part of the bill re-emerged in May 2018 as the Courts and Tribunals (Judiciary and Functions of Staff) Bill.

CHAPTER 4

Mental health, offending and the police

INTRODUCTION

The police are often the first point of contact for those who are experiencing a mental health crisis and research suggests that the level of contact between the police and those with mental health problems is increasing (Adebowale, 2013; National Policing Improvement Agency (NPIA) 2008; Wells and Schafer, 2006; Weston and Cromar-Hayes, 2017). While some have argued that mental health should be the 'core business of policing' (Adebowale, 2013:6), questions have been raised about the extent to which the police should be called upon as 'the service of first resort' (Her Majesty's Inspectorate of Constabulary (HMIC),[1] 2017:8). In the absence of appropriate training and resources, along with difficulties accessing support from mental health services, the police sometimes struggle to respond appropriately to those with acute mental health problems. In this chapter, we explore the challenges and controversies surrounding police powers to take a person in need to a 'place of safety' under s135 and s136 of the Mental Health Act (MHA) 1983 (as amended by the MHA 2007 and Policing and Crime Act (PCA) 2017). We will also consider some of the provisions set out by the Police and Criminal Evidence Act (PACE) 1984 to help protect the rights of vulnerable suspects, including the use of Appropriate Adults (AAs).

Finally, we will explore new street triage services; multiagency initiatives to respond to people with suspected mental health problems between police and health services.

MENTAL HEALTH AS AN INCREASINGLY CORE PART OF POLICE WORK

The police have long been involved with the mentally ill (Bittner, 1967). However, one of the many unforeseen consequences of the policy to close long-stay hospitals has been a shift in the role of key criminal justice agencies like the police, who have inevitably had to deal with increasing numbers of people experiencing mental health problems. Closure of the asylums required a growing number of people with mental disorder to live in the community, and this has potentially exacerbated the overlap between health and criminal justice services (Cummins, 2012). While some have previously argued that the available data are not sufficient enough to draw firm conclusions (Hiday, 1999), Cummins (2006:28) argues that one consequence of deinstitutionalisation is that the criminal justice system has become the de facto mental health care provider. Through a process of 'transinstitutionalisation', many people suffering mental ill-health have been moved to the penal estate with the police acting as gatekeepers to a variety of carceral institutions via legislation such as the MHA 1983 (as amended by the MHA 2007) (Prins, 2011) (see Chapter 3 for a discussion).

This situation has led some to argue that those with mental health problems risk being criminalised unfairly. Policing involves the exercise of significant discretion, particularly in the case of adults with mental health problems (Bittner, 1967) and this means that the police are key decision-makers in terms of what happens to people with mental health problems (see Hiday (1999) for a review). People with mental health problems are more likely to come into contact with the police and also more likely to be arrested (Teplin, 2000). This may be a consequence of those with severe mental health problems being easier to detect and therefore less likely to evade detection (Hiday, 1999). A recent study of mental health 'flagging', a process by which officers on the ground are alerted by the control room that an individual they are dealing with may have mental health problems, found that those who had been flagged were more likely to be charged with an offence, less likely to receive a caution and likely to spend longer in police custody, when compared to people suspected of similar offences (Kane et al., 2018). Following arrest, suspects with mental illness are less likely to understand their rights and more likely to make a false confession to the police (Redlich, 2004). Black people with mental health problems fare particularly badly with evidence of disproportionate use of police powers with this group (NACRO, 2007).

While it is important to interrogate the relationship between the police and those with mental health problems, Hiday (1999:515) also warns us that criticising the police for 'criminalising' those with mental health problems, 'connotes little appreciation for the role police play as "street-corner psychiatrists"'. This reminds us of the increasing role that police officers are having to take with those with mental health problems. Indeed, Menkes and Bendelow (2014:79) argue that as a result of the poor availability of mental health services, the 'police all too often take on the role of mental health carers, despite their lack of training and frequent competing demands for their time'. Faced with limited options or agencies to call for support, Markowitz (2011:41) asserts that the police may now 'have little choice but to use "mercy bookings" as a way to get persons into mental health treatment'. Moreover, some people experiencing a mental health crisis are positive about the care they receive from the police, with some even indicating that they regard it as superior to what they receive from specialist mental health services (Care Quality Commission (CQC), 2015).

It is estimated that between 15% and 25% of police incidents are related to mental health (Adebowale, 2013). These incidents include apprehending suspects with mental disorder, responding to individuals who are distressed and may be experiencing a mental health crisis, and dealing with those with mental health problems who have been victim or witness to a crime. Detainees in police custody have higher levels of physical and mental health problems than the general population (Rekrut-Lapa and Lapa, 2014) and approximately a third of those detained in police custody are thought to have mental health issues (Leese and Russell, 2017). Of those who die in police custody, more than half have mental health problems (Independent Office for Police Conduct (IOPC), 2018a).

This situation means that while police officers have always had a quasi-welfare role (Wolff, 2005), they are having to play an increasingly important role in responding to people who are experiencing difficulties with their mental health. As well as the prevention, detection and investigation of crime, policing now involves responding to a much broader set of social problems. However, questions have been raised about the extent to which police officers should be called upon as 'the service of first resort' (HMIC, 2017:8), with some police Chief Constables complaining that a high volume of mental health calls is restricting their ability to fulfil other policing functions including crime prevention and detection (BBC News, 2017).

DIVERSION AND POLICE POWERS UNDER THE MENTAL HEALTH ACT (MHA) 1983

Diverting offenders with mental health needs away from the criminal justice system into the care of health and social services has been a policy aim for some time (Department of Health and Home Office, 1992; Home Office, 1990, 1995b). More than 25 years ago, the Reed report recommended that there should be a nation-wide provision of properly resourced court assessment and diversion schemes to achieve this goal (Department of Health and Home Office, 1992). Following the Bradley report and his emphasis on the need for agencies to work together more effectively to meet the needs of vulnerable adults (Department of Health, 2009), there are now many liaison and diversion (L&D) schemes across England and Wales, many of which involve the police (see Chapter 3).

Diversion from criminal proceedings into the health care system can be achieved on an informal basis (via interdisciplinary agency protocols and local schemes) or formally under the MHA 1983 (as amended by the MHA 2007 and PCA 2017). Mentally disordered offenders may be diverted away from the criminal justice system by the police who, after dealing with an incident, may take no further action or may issue an informal caution. Alternatively, the MHA provides a range of diversionary powers, exercisable at various stages of the criminal justice process, and under this legislation, a police officer may remove a person who appears to be mentally disordered and is in need of immediate care and control to a 'place of safety'.

REMOVAL TO A PLACE OF SAFETY UNDER s135 AND s136 OF THE MHA 1983 (AS AMENDED)

Under s136 of the MHA 1983 (as amended) a person in a *public* place can be moved to a place of safety if they are suspected of having a mental health problem and are in need of immediate care or control. Under s135, a person in a *private* place can also be held in a place of safety if the same concerns are present. Once detained in a place of safety, an assessment should be undertaken by an Approved Clinician (AC) (a registered medical practitioner, ideally approved under s12 of the MHA 1983[2]) and an Approved Mental Health Professional (AMHP)[3] (a mental health professional, such as a social worker, nurse or social worker, who has been approved by their local social services authority to carry out certain duties under mental health law) to see whether the person requires admission to hospital for assessment or treatment (Sainsbury Centre for Mental Health, 2008).

Concerns about the use of police stations as a place of safety rather than a health-based place of safety (HBPOS)[4] such as a mental health unit, particularly for those under the age of 18, have long been raised by organisations including Mind, the Royal College of Psychiatrists and the Mental Health Alliance. Writing in 2008, the Sainsbury Centre for Mental Health estimated that around 11,000 people were detained in a police cell as a place of safety each year. The Royal College of Psychiatrists (1997:6) reported widespread feeling among police, social workers, service users and carers that police stations are inappropriate places for holding those with mental health problems. Highlighting some of the difficulties involved with trying to care for a mentally unwell person in the environment of a police custody suite, Cummins (2012:370) goes as far as to describe it as a 'nightmarish situation'. This reflects the view that a police cell is not a therapeutic environment for someone experiencing mental distress and has the potential to exacerbate mental health problems and delay access to effective treatment. In addition, others, including Bradley in his review of criminal justice and mental health diversion, identify that police custody 'has the effect of criminalising people for what is essentially a health need' and 'may exacerbate their mental state, and in the most tragic cases can lead to deaths in custody' (Department of Health, 2009:45). MS v UK (see Box 4.1) is sadly resonant of these concerns, and highlights that even when people are detained and suffering extreme mental distress, adequate crisis care may still not be available.

BOX 4.1 MS v UK 24527/08 [2012] ECHR 804

MS was taken to a police station under a section 136 as a result of suffering from a serious psychotic episode and having assaulted his aunt. While in police custody the Forensic Mental Examiner (FME) assessed him as unfit for interview and the local psychiatric intensive care unit (PICU) refused to admit him on the basis that he required a medium secure unit (MSU) but, for various reasons, there was a delay in transferring him there. This delay led to detention beyond the 72 hour limit of s136 (as was permitted prior to the PCA 2017). As his mental state worsened MS became more distressed. From his first day of detention, MS repeatedly banged his head against the wall and drank from his toilet, and by the end of the third day was smearing himself with his own excrement. MS took his case to the European Court of Human Rights (ECtHR), which found a breach of Article 3, the right against torture and inhuman or degrading treatment. The court found that his detention in a police cell under section 136, especially taking into account his acute vulnerability as a person suffering from mental illness, constituted 'an affront to human dignity'.

Following concerns about the use of s135 and s136 powers (see CQC, 2014; Department of Health and Home Office, 2014a, 2014b; HMIC, CQC, Her Majesty's Inspectorate of Prisons (HMIP) and Healthcare Inspectorate Wales (HIW), 2013 for a full review), significant changes have been brought about under the PCA 2017. In the discussion that follows, we outline the revised powers under s135 and s136 before considering some of the ongoing problems that the police face when exercising these powers.

Section 135(1) of the MHA 1983 gives magistrates the power to issue a warrant allowing a police officer to enter private premises to remove a mentally disordered person to a place of safety. Amendments made by the PCA 2017 now allow a mental health assessment to take place in private premises, including the person's home, under certain circumstances. Prior to this amendment there had been lack of clarity about whether or not, having gained entry with a warrant, it was legal to undertake the mental health assessment in the place where the warrant was executed rather than always having to remove the person of concern to a place of safety. Changes to the law under the PCA 2017 now make it clear that, with agreement of the person or householder, and if safe to do so, an assessment can take place in the home rather than removing the person to a HBPOS.

Section 136 of the MHA 1983 allows the police to remove an individual in a public space who appears to be having a mental health crisis and who are in need of immediate care or control to a place of safety. The exact wording of the legal aspects of section 136 is listed in Box 4.2. This wording reflects the amendments made by the PCA 2017, which removes the phrase 'place to which public has access' allowing s136 to be instigated anywhere other than a home (or any yard, garden or outhouse that is used in connection with the place where the person is living). The latter change allows for the police to exercise their powers under section 136 to protect people found in places such as railway lines, offices and rooftops which have previously not been considered as 'places to which the public have access'.

BOX 4.2 s136(1), MHA 1983: MENTALLY DISORDERED PERSONS FOUND IN PUBLIC PLACES

(1) If a person appears to a constable to be suffering from mental disorder and to be in immediate need of care or control, the constable may, if he thinks it necessary to do so in the interests of that person or for the protection of other persons –

(a) remove the person to a place of safety within the meaning of section 135 or

(b) if the person is already at a place of safety within the meaning of that section, keep the person at that place or remove the person to another place of safety.

(1A) The power of a constable under subsection (1) may be exercised where the mentally disordered person is at any place, other than–

(a) any house, flat or room where that person, or any other person, is living or

(b) any yard, garden, garage or outhouse that is used in connection with the house, flat or room, other than one that is also used in connection with one or more other houses, flats or rooms.

(1B) For the purpose of exercising the power under subsection (1), a constable may enter any place where the power may be exercised, if need be by force.

(1C) Before deciding to remove a person to, or to keep a person at, a place of safety under subsection (1), the constable must, if it is practicable to do so, consult –

(a) a registered medical practitioner,

(b) a registered nurse,

(c) an approved mental health professional, or

(d) a person of a description specified in regulations made by the Secretary of State.

[The full wording of section 136 can be found here: www.legislation.gov.uk/ukpga/1983/20/section/136]

POLICING AND CRIME ACT 2017: ARE THINGS ANY SAFER?

Sections 135 and s136 of the MHA 2007 are fundamental tools for police officers when managing situations involving persons with mental ill health (Turner, Ness and Imison, 1992). Moreover, for those with mental disorder, the police can sometimes represent an important link with mental health services. However, there is widespread regional variation in the use of these legislative powers (Department of Health and Home Office, 2014a). Social disadvantage, unemployment, lack of stable accommodation, belonging to a minority ethnic group, not being registered with a doctor, and psychiatric history have been identified as associated with increased detention under section 136 (Royal College of Psychiatrists, 2008). Of particular concern is the disproportionate use of s136 with black and minority ethnic groups (Department of Health and Home Office, 2014a), which has led to accusations of police racism (Browne, 2009; Rogers and Faulkner, 1987).

The main changes to s135 and s136 powers following the PCA 2017 are given in Box 4.3. The amendments now prevent those under the age of 18 from being taken to police stations as a place of safety in any circumstances, whereas adults should now only be taken to police stations as a place of safety in exceptional circumstances and in accordance with The Mental Health Act 1983 (Places of Safety) Regulations 2017. In addition, officers are required to consult, if practicable to do so, a registered medical practitioner, registered nurse or an AMHP before detaining a mentally disordered person. Amendments under the PCA 2017 have also reduced the period of detention under s136 from 72 to 24 hours (extended to 36 hours in only very specific situations).

BOX 4.3 MAIN CHANGES TO s135 AND s136 UNDER THE POLICING AND CRIME ACT 2017

- Section 136 powers may now be exercised anywhere other than in a private dwelling;
- it is now unlawful to use a police station as a place of safety for anyone under the age of 18 in any circumstances;
- a police station can now only be used as a place of safety for adults in specific circumstances, which are set out in regulations;
- the previous maximum detention period of up to 72 hours has been reduced to 24 hours (unless a doctor certifies that an extension of up to 12 hours is necessary);
- before exercising a section 136 power police officers must, where practicable, consult one of the health professionals listed in section 136(1C), or in regulations made under that provision;
- a person subject to section 135 or 136 can be kept at, as well as removed to, a place of safety. Therefore, where a section 135 warrant has been executed, a person may be kept at their home (if it is a place of safety) for the purposes of an assessment rather than being removed to another place of safety;
- a new search power allows police officers to search persons subject to section 135 or 136 powers for protective purposes.

Source: Department of Health and Home Office (2017:5)

These changes reflect a number of human rights concerns that have been raised about the use of sections 135 and 136. Concerns have included the use of police custody as an appropriate environment for people with mental disorder; the 72-hour period of detention; and the lack of any need to consult a person with medical training (Adebowale, 2013; Morgan and Paterson, 2017). The case law example in Box 4.1 illustrates well the problems associated with the way in which a section 136 has been traditionally used and the gap in mental health care provision for those experiencing crisis.

While amendments made by the PCA 2017 intend to alleviate some of these concerns, questions have been raised as to whether they go far enough. Some organisations, including the Police Federation, have called for a complete ban on the use of police custody as a place of safety (Liberty, 2016). While this has not materialised, the PCA 2017 does appear to have led to a reduction in the use of police stations as a place of safety. Prior to the legislative changes, the National Police Chiefs' Council (NPCC) (2016) reported that between 10% and 25% of s136 detentions involved the use of police custody. However, the latest figures for 2017–2018 report that only 2% of people detained under s136 were detained in a police station, with 85% taken to a HBPOS, and the remainder to Accident and Emergency (A&E) (Home Office, 2018). Of those taken to a police station, in 40% of cases this followed from there being no capacity in a HBPOS and in another 10% of cases because the HBPOS had refused admission (Home Office, 2018). In just over a quarter of cases, a police station had been used because of concerns about violence, and in a further 12% of cases because the person concerned had also been arrested for a substantive offence (Home Office, 2018).

While it is positive that there has been a reduction in the use of police custody as a place of safety for adults following the PCA 2017, it is important to also note that there has been a significant rise in the use of s136 over the last ten years (Loughran, 2018). Moreover, the use of s136 has continued to rise since the PCA 2017 with 29,662 uses of s136 recorded in 2017/18, representing a 5% increase on the year before (Home Office, 2018). Loughran (2018) suggests that a number of factors may be behind the rising use of s136, including changing police attitudes and as a result of limited resources among both police and mental health services. Of particular concern is that the strain currently being experienced by mental health services has 'resulted in a greater reliance on the police force as an access point to NHS care' (Loughran, 2018:268). Aside from raising concerns about the inappropriate use of s136, this also risks undermining the principle under the MHA 1983 of caring for people in the 'least restrictive' environment available (Loughran, 2018).

While making it illegal to remove a child, under the age of 18, to police custody as a place of safety is a welcomed amendment, this does have implications for place of safety provision. Clinical Commissioning Groups (CCGs) in England and Local Health Boards (LHBs) in Wales will need to consider their provision, ensuring that it equates with the standards set by the Royal College of Psychiatrists (2011). These standards, for example, indicate that place of safety provision should be able to manage situations where people may be exhibiting challenging behaviour.

The reduction to the period of detention under both s135 and s136 brings England and Wales in line with Scotland who capped place of safety detention at 24 hours under the Mental Health (Care and Treatment) (Scotland) Act 2003. However, it is this amendment that is likely to cause the most significant problems for mental health services who, despite the government's promises to improve services for people with mental health problems, are grossly under-funded and likely to remain so. Staffing problems or a lack of beds mean that people in need are either subject to long-waiting periods or even turned away from HBPOS (CQC, 2015; NPCC, 2017). While it has been exceptional for a s136 to last the maximum allowed time of 72 hours, it has been far from unknown for it to last more than 24 hours, especially if there has been a delay in assessment because the patient was unfit for interview or if a patient was detained outside of normal working hours. The CQC (2015) reports that the most common reason for delays follows from a lack of AMHP and specialist doctors. While there has been considerable criticism about the use of police custody as a place of safety, the police have often had no other choice because appropriate psychiatric facilities are simply unavailable (CQC, 2014). Without the proper resourcing of alternative places of safety, it is likely that this practice will continue.

SUPPORTING PEOPLE WITH MENTAL ILL HEALTH WHO COME INTO CONTACT WITH THE POLICE

HEALTH CARE PROFESSIONALS (HCPs)

While there are now restrictions on the use of police cells as places of safety under the PCA 2017, it is important to remember that the police must still process those who are arrested, rather than diverted from police custody. The detention of suspects is governed by PACE

1984, and in accordance with PACE Code C paragraph 9.5, the custody officer must ensure that appropriate medical attention is given as soon as practicable to any detainee who:

- Appears to be physically ill or injured
- Appears to be, they suspect, or have been told may be, experiencing mental ill health
- Appears to have a drug or alcohol dependence
- Appears to need medical attention
- Requests a medical examination.[5]

This means that if the custody sergeant suspects someone has a mental disorder s/he must seek services of a health care professional (HCP). HCPs in police custody include doctors (commonly referred to as Forensic Medical Examiners (FMEs)), nurses and paramedics. In recent years, Brooker et al. (2018) report that FMEs are increasingly being replaced by custody nurses within police custody. However, little is known about the HCP role in England and Wales, with considerable variation in the terminology used to describe HCPs who work in police custody (see Kennedy, Green and Payne-James (2017) for several examples). The role of a HCP is extensive and includes ascertaining if a detainee is fit to be detained and interviewed (Kennedy, Green and Payne-James, 2017). After examination, the HCP should record any initial finding relevant to their custodial care and directions in the custody record. Directions concerning the frequency of visits and any concerns must be made clear and precise. If the HCP considers admission to hospital may be appropriate, he or she may advise the custody sergeant to contact an AMHP to arrange an assessment under the MHA 1983 (as amended by the MHA 2007).

Despite these provisions, there are numerous problems with identifying, and then managing detainees with mental disorder in custody (Noga et al., 2015). While some HCPs have mental health training, there are no basic standards for HCPs, so others may have minimal forensic clinical experience (Payne-James, 2017). In addition, limited police training, along with high numbers of people in police custody under the influence of alcohol and drugs, makes the identification and response to mental health problems difficult (Cummins, 2016). The nature of the setting also means that the disclosure of serious mental health problems is unlikely (Public Health England, 2016). Indeed, people subject to police detention have indicated that they do not feel comfortable disclosing sensitive personal information about their physical or mental health at the custody desk (Revolving Doors Agency, 2013).

Once mental health problems are suspected, the police must work with a range of health practitioners to provide a high level of care. A mixture of private organisations, NHS services and police-led medical services are involved with the provision of care to detainees in police custody (Rekrut-Lapa and Lapa, 2014). However, the police and health services have sometimes been 'hesitant partners' (Heyman and McGeough, 2018:283) with the police frequently expressing concerns about the lack of support from partner agencies and difficulties involved with obtaining relevant information (Noga et al., 2015). Research also suggests there is wide variation in the provision of health care support to police custody as well as a lack of consistency in the recording and availability of information about these services (Payne-James et al., 2009:189). A recent review of deaths in police custody expressed concern about the poor quality of health care services within police custody (Angiolini, 2017).

As the first point of contact in the criminal justice system, police custody represents a good opportunity to screen detainees for mental health problems. Detention in police custody can also serve as a 'therapeutic opportunity' because detainees may be more receptive to medical assessment and intervention (Chariot and Heide, 2018). Police are 'crucial gatekeepers' to mental health services 'yet officers report they feel ill-equipped and under-resourced to judge when, and what interventions are appropriate' (Heyman and McGeough, 2018:283). Research also suggests that improvements in police custody health screening are needed (McKinnon and Grubin, 2012). Some argue that all suspects in police custody should be screened by L&D practitioners so that the identification of vulnerability and mental health needs is not left to police officers to identify (Justice, 2017).

Following the Bradley report, it was proposed that commissioning responsibility for health care services in custody be transferred from Police and Crime Commissioners (PCCs) to the NHS. However, this decision was halted in 2016, and as it stands, health services in custody are now the only part of the criminal justice pathway where services are not commissioned by the NHS. Unsurprisingly, several have expressed dissatisfaction at the decision not to proceed (Angiolini, 2017; Forrester, Valmaggia and Taylor, 2016; Kennedy, Green and Payne-James, 2017).

APPROPRIATE ADULT (AA) SCHEMES

In addition to consulting with an HCP, if the custody sergeant suspects someone has a mental disorder, s/he must also seek the services of an AA. The provision of AAs came about following concerns surrounding the treatment of juveniles in the Maxwell Confait case in 1972 (see Box 4.4) and the subsequent introduction of the PACE 1984 and its Codes of Practice. PACE 1984 is a key piece of legislation, that aims to reduce the potential for miscarriages of justice, by regulating how evidence should be gathered from suspects who are vulnerable and unwell.

BOX 4.4 1972 MAXWELL CONFAIT CASE

During the night of 21/22 April 1972, a fire took place at 27 Doggett Road, Catford in South East London. By the time the fire brigade had arrived the blaze had taken hold of both the basement and ground floor of the property. During an inspection of the property, the body of a man was found in one of the back bedrooms. As a result, the police were called and arrived a quarter of an hour later, followed shortly by the divisional police surgeon.

The police identified the body of a man called Maxwell Confait, a 26-year-old homosexual sex worker. In the circumstances, the police surgeon decided not to take a rectal temperature reading (as was the standard practice to determine the time of death) as this might compromise any activity relating to recent sexual activity. The pathologist also took the same decision when he arrived, although he did examine the body and noted that rigor mortis had already set in. The post mortem revealed that Confait had dies from asphyxia, having been strangled by a length of white electric flex found in his room.

Confait rented his bed-sit from a man called Winston Goode. Confait and Goode had become friends when they discovered that they both had an interest in wearing women's clothing. On the night in question, Goode claimed that he had been woken by the blaze and immediately raced to the railway station to raise the alarm. Goode was later interviewed by the police and he admitted that he knew Confait was planning to leave and set up home with another man. While he acknowledged he was jealous about this, he also denied any sexual relationship with Confait. Subsequently, Goode suffered a mental break down and was unable to remember any of the events of the weekend. He was then admitted to Bexley psychiatric hospital.

Soon after, the police apprehended three boys (Ronald Leighton, age 15, Colin Lattimore, age 18 and Ahmet Salih, age 14). All three boys were questioned (despite being underage) and readily admitted that they were responsible for the fire in question. Two of the boys (Leighton and Lattimore) confessed to the murder of Confait, whereas the third boy (Salih) admitted that he had been present when Confait was killed but that he was not involved. As a result of these confessions, Leighton and Lattimore were charged with murder and, together with Salih, were charged with setting fire to 27 Doggett Road. On 24th November 1972, Leighton was convicted of murder, Lattimore was convicted of manslaughter on the ground of diminished responsibility, and all three boys were convicted of arson.

Several years later, in the case of R v Lattimore and others, Lord Justice Scarman, Lord Justice Ormerod and Mr Justice Swanick concluded that all three convictions were 'unreliable in the light of expert evidence and so unsafe and unsatisfactory'. Their confessions had been false and were the combined result of their vulnerability and their treatment by police during detention and questioning.

The quashing of the convictions and the exoneration of the three boys led to a public debate about the 'judges rules'.* The case has been cited as one of the inspirations behind the PACE 1984 that eventually replaced the 'judges rules' with statutory provisions and made the tape recording of interviews compulsory.

---

* Judges' rules were developed in 1912 and governed the questioning of suspects.

Specifically, PACE Code C provided for the role of an AA to ensure that those who are identified as being particularly vulnerable – juveniles (aged 10–16), adults with mental health problems and adults with learning difficulties – are accompanied during a police interview (or other police procedures such as fingerprint identification and searching). This is in addition to the right to be represented by a solicitor. An AA can be: a relative, guardian or other person responsible for their care and custody; someone experienced with mentally disordered or mentally vulnerable people but who is not a police officer or employed by the police; or, failing these, some other responsible adult aged 18 or over who is not a police officer or employed by the police (PACE Code C, para. 1.7 (b)).

The PACE code refers to an AA being necessary for mentally vulnerable detainees who, because of mental state or capacity, may not understand the significance of what is said and of questions and their replies. The Home Office (2003) outlines the role of an AA as someone who: supports, advises and assists the detained person, particularly while they are being questioned; observes whether the police are acting properly, fairly and with respect for the rights of the detained person, and to tell them when they are not; assisting with communication between the detained person and the police; and ensuring that the detained person understands their rights.

There has been limited research concerning AAs and there are also considerable difficulties involved with obtaining clear figures about the use of AA schemes (Cummins, 2006; National Appropriate Adult Network (NAAN), 2010). However, evidence suggests that AAs are rarely used with adults despite the high levels of mental health problems among offenders (Cummins, 2011; NAAN, 2010). The NAAN (2015) reports that up to a quarter of a million adults with mental health issues are not being supported by an AA while in police custody and that there is huge variation across the country in the provision of this service. The NAAN (2015) estimates that 11% of adults detained by the police require an AA, but that an AA is only present in 1%–2% of police interviews. Additionally, they found that there was inadequate identification of suspects' vulnerabilities and their need for an AA, and in some areas no clear AA service in place (NAAN, 2015). This highlights that there are difficulties when it comes to identifying adults with mental health issues, especially by the police. The limited use of AA schemes raises concerns in regards to the rights of detainees being properly met and may also represent a missed opportunity to assess people's mental health and divert to appropriate services.

There have been calls to encourage more volunteers to attend as AAs (Audit Commission, 1996) in order to increase their availability (Home Office, 1995a). Research has indicated that the police sometimes have difficulty making contact with AAs and then ensuring they can attend the station for interview in a reasonable period of time (Littlechild, 1998). Research has also found that the police often become frustrated by the delays in obtaining an AA (Littlechild, 1995) and that opportunities to identify mental illness are potentially being missed in police custody (Department of Health, 2009). The police are more likely to identify vulnerability when they are aware of local AA schemes and therefore the decision to request an AA may be based on pragmatism and assumptions about availability (NAAN, 2014).

Identification of mental health problems is important because if they are not identified, no application for an AA will be made. Moreover, if the interviewing process is to be fair and just, it is essential that any mental health difficulties are identified (Gudjonsson, 2010).

While Young et al. (2013) found that custody risk assessment tools often identified that suspects had difficulties with reading and writing or their mental health, they also expressed concern that this information was not used effectively to allocate AAs. This is despite numerous initiatives and policies over the last 20 years to improve the safeguards for vulnerable people involved with the criminal justice system and a long-standing rhetoric of diversion.

Many have also highlighted the ambiguous role of the AA (Cummins, 2011; Pierpoint, 2008). Cummins (2011:308) suggests that the role can be contradictory and confusing on the basis that an AA is 'not quite an advocate, not quite a referee'. While Cummins (2011) generally advocates the protections that AAs afford to vulnerable detainees, he also reminds us that one potential counter argument and negative aspect of their role is that they may undermine the autonomy of the person they are trying to support. One way this can happen is if the AA insists on legal representation attending the station after the detainee has already waived their right to legal support.

To address some of the issues raised above, calls have been made for the role of AAs to be both extended and clarified (Pierpoint, 2011). To some extent, things are clearer with the provision of national standards from NAAN (2018). However, NAAN (2015) has long recommended that if we want to ensure the proper provision of AA services to those in need, statutory responsibility for AA services for vulnerable adults, must be placed on local authorities.[6]

STREET TRIAGE

Following the apparent success of two 'street triage' schemes in Leicestershire and Cleveland, the Department of Health invested £2 million into nine street triage pilots in 2013. Street triage refers to a range of initiatives that involves a joint policing and mental health services response to people who appear to require mental health support. In February 2014, a joint statement referred to as the Mental Health Crisis Care Concordat was agreed by health, social care, police, justice and local government (see Chapter 3). This statement set out how public services should work together to respond to people who are in crisis. The principle underlying the statement was that no one experiencing a mental health crisis should be turned away from services. Identified within this document were the street triage pilot schemes as examples of how the principles of the Crisis Care Concordat could be put into action.

Street triage models vary across the country. In some force areas, mental health nurses may be located with police officers in a patrol car where they can attend incidents together, while in others, nursing staff may based in a control centre in order to give telephone advice to police at the scene (House of Commons Home Affairs Committee, 2015). A recent review of the national provision of street triage by Kirubarajan et al. (2018) found that across the 41 street triage services they reviewed, 20% offered a telephone only service, 46% offered a mobile unit and 29% offered both.

While street triage models vary, they essentially aim to improve outcomes for people in a mental health crisis who come to the attention of the emergency services. While there may be some local variation in the terminology and the delivery of services, the typical objectives of street triage services are listed in Box 4.5. Street triage initiatives share similar aims in that they try to support improved access to mental health services and reduce the use of police cells as places of safety under s136 of the MHA 1983 (as amended). This is underpinned by real-time sharing of information, timely identification of appropriate care pathways and shared decision-making. The process also ensures that the police are supported in their decision-making with regards to vulnerable people.

BOX 4.5 STREET TRIAGE OBJECTIVES AS IDENTIFIED BY REVERUZZI AND PILLING (2016:14)

- Improved service user experience.
- Improved and prompt access to the crisis care pathway.
- Improved working relationships between health, police and other emergency services.
- Reductions in:

  o The use of police cells as places of safety for s136 detentions;
  o The numbers of individual service users being repeatedly detained under s136;
  o The use of health-based places of safety (HBPOS);
  o A&E attendance for those in crisis conveyed by the police or ambulance service; and,
  o The avoidable use of section 12 doctors, Approved Mental Health Professionals (AMHPs), police and other emergency services.

In an evaluation of the first street triage schemes in the UK, seven out of the nine areas implementing the pilot scheme observed a reduction in the use of s136 detentions when compared with an equivalent timeframe the previous year (Reveruzzi and Pilling, 2016). In addition, more people were placed in a HBPOS instead of police custody, while those placed in custody spent less time there than indicated in previous reports. Qualitative data have found that the police, mental health services and service users generally offer positive accounts of street triage schemes (Irvine, Allen and Webber, 2016; Oxford Health NHS Foundation Trust, 2015; Reveruzzi and Pilling, 2016), and perceive it to benefit individuals suffering with a mental health crisis in the community (Horspool, Drabble and O'Caithain, 2016). However, a number of challenges have also been identified, including perceived increases in demand on mental health services and the police, as well as difficulties in allocating staff for street triage duties, and the corresponding impact on the staffing and capacity of existing services (Horspool, Drabble and O'Caithain, 2016). These types of competing demands are, of course, compounded by the challenging financial situations confronted by both health and social care services and the police.

While street triage services are continuing to develop, they are now available in most areas across the country (Kirubarajan et al., 2018). However, there is still limited evidence about the impact of street triage schemes in England (Heyman and McGeogh, 2018) and considerable variation in their models, funding levels and provision of support (Kirubarajan et al., 2018). However, international research on Crisis Intervention Team (CIT) programmes in the US, where police officers receive specialist mental health training to respond to incidents (Oliva and Compton, 2008), illustrate that police officers have self-efficacy in their skills to handle mental health incidents, improved knowledge, better perceptions and a favourable attitude to mental health incidents (Ellis, 2014). There is also greater verbal engagement and lower levels of arrest (Compton et al., 2014), more referrals to mental health services (Watson et al., 2011) and officers may use less force in response to mental health scenarios (Compton et al., 2011).

THE VICTIMISATION OF THE MENTALLY DISORDERED

While the focus of this chapter has been on the experiences of people detained by the police we should not forget that despite common perceptions that those with mental disorder are dangerous, the evidence suggests that they are more likely to be a victim of crime than to harm others. A US study with community-based patients with schizophrenia by Brekke et al. (2001) found that they were 14 times more likely to be the victim of violent crime than to be arrested for a violent crime themselves. In a more recent study, and UK-based study, Khalifeh and colleagues (2015) found that crime was experienced by 40% of patients with mental illness in the last 12 months, compared to 14% in the control group. Patients with mental illness were three times more likely to be victim to non-violent crimes such as household acquisitive crime and criminal damage and five times more likely to become victims of assault (Khalifeh et al., 2015). Women fared particularly badly and were identified as being at particularly high risk of violence both within a domestic setting as well as the community (Khalifeh et al., 2015). Khalifeh et al.'s (2015) research also identifies that those with severe mental illness are more likely to report adverse psychological and social effects as a result of their victimisation. This suggests that people with mental health problems should be prioritised in public health policies on violence prevention.

Although police officers commonly interact with people who are mentally ill, the experiences of contact between those with mental health problems and the police is somewhat mixed. A recent study conducted in the UK suggested that while people's experiences with the police were both positive and negative, negative experiences were far more common (Koskela, Pettitt and Drennan, 2016). The deviant labelling and stigmatising attitudes of police officers have put forward as explaining factors for these negative experiences, particularly in terms of their propensity to dismiss, disbelieve or even blame a victim with mental health problems (Koskela, Pettitt and Drennan, 2016).

Sadly, there are occasions where negative police attitudes towards the mentally ill may contribute to a disproportionate use of force. One of the most high-profile cases, is that of Sean Rigg, a 40-year-old musician with a history of mental health problems, who suffered a fatal cardiac arrest in a holding area at Brixton police station in August 2008 before he was checked into custody. The inquest into his death found the police had used an 'unsuitable' level of force in their attempts to apprehend and detain him (Southwark Coroner's Court, 2012). While the Independent Police Complaints Commission (IPCC) originally concluded that the police were not guilty of any wrong doing, the Independent Office for Police Conduct (IOPC)[7] (2018b) later directed in 2018 that gross misconduct hearings should be held for five officers who were involved with the arrest and detention of Sean Rigg. A few years after Rigg's death in custody, in 2012, a similar tragedy occurred in Cornwall. Thomas Orchard, a 32-year-old church caretaker also died of a cardiac arrest following his arrest by police. Like Rigg, Orchard was known to suffer with mental health problems. Following concerns about his detention and restraint, six police officers are due to face misconduct hearings.

Despite a growing recognition that around half of those who die in police custody have some form of mental health problem (Docking, Grace and Bucke, 2008) and increasing scrutiny of the risks involved with detaining vulnerable people in police custody (Adebowale, 2013; Angiolini, 2017), in 2017–2018, deaths in police custody were at their highest for ten years (IOPC, 2018a). During this period, 23 people died while in police custody, up from 14 in 2016–2017, along with a further 57 apparent suicides following detention in police custody[8] (IOPC, 2018a). Of the 23 people who died in custody, more than half (12) had mental health problems, 18 had recently consumed alcohol or drugs at the time of their arrest, and four had been detained under s136 of the MHA 1983 (IOPC, 2018a).

POLICING IN TIMES OF AUSTERITY

In recent years, questions have been raised about the extent to which police officers should be called upon as 'the service of first resort' (HMIC, 2017:8). For example, the Office of the Police and Crime Commissioner for Staffordshire (2013) commissioned a review to identify the frontline impact of mental health issues and found that demand on the police to support people with mental health needs living independently was increasing. These findings are consistent with earlier comments made by Bean (1999:42) who has asked 'Would any other occupational group take on the task? The answer is surely no'. He further questions if any health profession would offer a 24-hour service to deal with the potential dangerousness of people with mental health problems in the community. This responsibility of the police to pick up people with mental disorder coupled with concerns about the 'policing of mental health' and the inability or lack of training among the police, reflects that the police are between a rock and a hard place when it comes to the mentally disordered.

Against this backdrop, there have been significant cuts to mental health provision and other services. In a recent report to the College of Policing, Weston and Cromar-Hayes (2017:4) found that many of the police officers interviewed expressed humanitarian concerns for the people who were requesting help and support and although resources were not always referred to, the narratives of officers moved to the inevitable conclusion that services were suffering from dire under-funding. This under-funding has resulted in the displacement of community mental health care to emergency services (Weston and Cromar-Hayes, 2017). HMIC (2016) reports that there are occasions when the police are having to act as first responders because of the lack of ambulances. Part of the problem is that the police are one of the few services that can respond to people in crisis around the clock. Very few A&E departments have around the clock support from a liaison mental health service, even though the peak hours for crisis are between 11pm and 7am, and this means that people continue to access mental health services and support via the police because there may be no other agency available at the time of crisis (Mental Health Taskforce, 2016). This has led HMIC (2017:24) to observe that 'the provision of mental health care has reached such a state of severity that police are often being used to fill the gaps that other agencies cannot'. Aside from diverting policing resources away from other priorities, this is also a 'profoundly improper way to treat vulnerable people' (HMIC, 2017:25).

TRAINING NEEDS OF POLICE OFFICERS

As we have learnt, police officers are increasingly expected to respond to rising demands caused by a shortage in mental health provision. The police officers interviewed in Weston and Cromar-Hayes' (2017:5) study reported how their role and responsibilities with regards to the management of situations involving people with mental ill health was much more than simply 'taking someone to the hospital'. Consistent with earlier research (Cummins, 2012), police officers expressed concerns about the increasing need to assess risk and make decisions based upon this assessment, despite not having the appropriate skills to make this type of judgement.

It has been suggested that if police officers were trained sufficiently enough to have the confidence and ability to de-escalate a situation, the need for specialist secondary care services, which are associated with higher costs, could be avoided. The need to prevent harm when confronted by situations involving persons with mental ill health is consistently expressed by police officers (Noga et al., 2015; Weston and Cromar-Hayes, 2017) yet mental health training for police staff is still lacking (Cummins, 2012). Moreover, in developing training packages, it is important to interrogate what type of training police officers want and need. Research suggests that police officers do not necessarily require more training regarding the different types of mental disorder but rather would like to know more about the type of local mental health services that are available (Bean,

1999). Given the renewed emphasis on diversion following the Bradley report (Department of Health, 2009) and the revisions made to s135 and s136 powers under the PCA 2017, a knowledge of local services is even more crucial.

There have been numerous attempts, both in the UK and elsewhere, to educate police officers about mental illness. Recent training guidance, developed by the College of Policing (2016) in England and Wales, has been designed to assist officers in identifying vulnerable victims and suspects so that they can get the right support. An important point to be made here is that the guidance has been developed as a form of 'assistance'. While dealing with mental health issues is an increasingly core part of policing, the College of Policing (2016) emphasises that the police are not mental health professionals and that health and welfare agencies should retain responsibility for those experiencing a mental health crisis.

DISCUSSION

Throughout this chapter we have focused on the role of the police in dealing with people with mental disorder. We have encouraged readers to consider the tools available to the police, such as the police powers under the MHA 1983 (as amended by the MHA 2007 and PCA 2017) and PACE 1984. However, as our discussions have revealed, many challenges remain when trying to exercise these powers.

The PCA 2017 set out to address some of the traditional challenges raised by the exercise of police powers under the MHA 1983 (as amended by the MHA 2007). The amendments made by the Act to prevent young people from being taken to police stations as a place of safety, and reductions to the period of detention under s135 and s136 down to 24 hours, are certainly to be welcomed. It is also positive that more people are now being held in HBPOS rather than police cells. When people are detained by the police as a result of a mental health crisis their experience can be a traumatic one and, therefore, an appropriate environment is essential for those in need of mental health care. However, it must also be recognised that, while controversial, s135 and s136 enable a key possibility for diversion from the criminal justice system and signposting of appropriate and beneficial medical care.

It seems, however, that the challenges overcome by the PCA 2017 have been replaced with others. The volume of calls received by the police has increased exponentially and, as we have shown, the police are often required to act as first responders to such situations. Inspector

Michael Brown, the mental health coordinator for the College of Policing has recently suggested that the inability of NHS services to cope with mental health problems has been 'a key factor in the rise of mental health calls to the police' and that

> most people in contact with the police about mental health issues don't need the police, they need a mental health professional … The inability to access a mental health professional is the problem, and that generates a lot of work for the police.
>
> (Quoted in Dodd, 2017)

While further police training, multiagency working and the interventions we have listed in this chapter can go some way to overcome some of these issues, the current situation nevertheless highlights the increasingly diverse nature of policing and the role of the police officer. Mental health has become a key aspect of police work. Alongside an increasing emphasis on dangerousness and risk, as identified in previous chapters, austerity measures have impacted exponentially on the role of those working with people experiencing a mental health crisis. As Morgan and Paterson (2017:9) suggest, there is an obligation on police officers, acting as street level experts, to 'engage appropriate statutory and community agencies to address complex social problems'. While the preoccupation with dangerousness and risk in the 1990s brought about the merging of aims and objectives of the police and probation services in particular – manifesting in the role of the 'polibation officer' (Nash, 1998) – the era of austerity combined with our continued preoccupation with dangerousness and risk may have resulted in what we might term the 'polipsy officer'. This type of officer not only has a role in protecting the public from the so-called 'dangerous' but also has a role in supporting the public where other relevant agencies may not have the capacity nor resources to do so.

FURTHER READING

Details about diversion are provided in Chapter 3 but for further reading see Home Office and Department of Health (1992) and Department of Health (2009). For a review about the problems surrounding s135 and s136 prior to the PCA 2017 see Department of Health and Home Office (2014a). For explanatory notes of the PCA 2017 see Home Office (2017). For a thorough reading of the evaluation of street triage see Reveruzzi and Pilling (2016).

REFERENCES

Adebowale, V. (2013) *Independent commission on mental health and policing report*, London: Independent Commission on Mental Health and Policing.

Angiolini, E. (2017) *Report of the independent review of deaths and serious incidents in police custody*, London: Home Office.

Audit Commission (1996) *Misspent youth: Young people and crime*, London: Audit Commission.

BBC News (2017) 'Mental health calls "stopping police preventing crime"', *BBC News*, 15 November 2017. Available from: www.bbc.co.uk/news/uk-wales-41998104 [Last accessed 22 April 2018].

Bean, P. (1999) 'The police and the mentally disordered in the community' in Webb, D. and Harris, R. (eds.) *Mentally disordered offenders: Managing people nobody owns*, London: Routledge.

Bittner, E. (1967) 'Police discretion in emergency apprehension of mentally ill persons', *Social Problems*, 14(3): 278–292.

Brekke, J.S., Prindle, C., Woo Bae, S. and Long, J.D. (2001) 'Risks for individuals with schizophrenia who are living in the community', *Psychiatric Services*, 52(10): 1358–1366.

Brooker, C., Tocque, K., Mitchell, D. and Pearce, M. (2018) 'Police custody in the north of England: Findings from a health needs assessment in Durham and Darlington', *Journal of Forensic and Legal Medicine*, 57: 91–95.

Browne, D. (2009) 'Black communities, mental health and the criminal justice system' in Reynolds, J., Muston, R., Heller, T., Leach, J., McCormick, M., Wallcraft, J. and Walsh, M. (eds.) *Mental health still matters*, Basingstoke: Palgrave Macmillan.

Care Quality Commission (CQC) (2014) *A safer place to be: Findings from our survey of health-based places of safety for people detained under section 136 of the Mental Health Act*, Newcastle-Upon-Tyne: CQC.

Care Quality Commission (CQC) (2015) *Right here, right now: People's experiences of help, care and support during a mental health crisis*, Newcastle-Upon-Tyne: CQC.

Chariot, P. and Heide, S. (2018) 'Custody medicine', *Journal of Forensic and Legal Medicine*, 57: 55–57.

College of Policing (2016) 'Public to gain from new police training and guidance in mental health', [Press release] 10 October 2016. Available from: www.college.police.uk/News/College-news/Pages/Mental-health-training-and-guidance.aspx [Last accessed 14 January 2018].

Compton, M., Broussard, B., Munetz, M., Oliva, J. and Watson, A. (2011) *The Crisis Intervention Team (CIT) model of collaboration between law enforcement and mental health*, New York: Nova Science Publishers.

Compton, M.T., Bakeman, R., Broussard, B., Hankerson-Dyson, D., Husbands, L., Krishan, S., Stewart-Hutto, T., D'Orio, B.M., Oliva, J.R., Thompson, N.J. and Watson, A.C. (2014) 'The police-based Crisis Intervention Team (CIT) model: II. Effects on level of force and resolution, referral and arrest', *Psychiatric Services*, 65(4): 523–529.

Cummins, I. (2006) 'A path not taken? Mentally disordered offenders and the criminal justice system', *Journal of Social Welfare and Family Law*, 28(3): 267–281.

Cummins, I. (2011) '"The other side of silence": The role of the Appropriate Adult post Bradley', *Journal of Ethics and Social Welfare*, 5(3): 306–312.

Cummins, I. (2012) 'Policing and mental illness in England and Wales post Bradley', *Policing*, 6(4): 365–376.

Cummins, I. (2016) *Mental health and the criminal justice system: A social work perspective*, Northwich: Critical Publishing Ltd.

Department of Health (2009) *The Bradley report. Lord Bradley's review of people with mental health problems or learning disabilities in the criminal justice system*, London: Department of Health.

Department of Health and Home Office (1992) *Review of health and social services for mentally disordered offenders and others requiring similar services – Final summary report*, London: Her Majesty's Stationery Office.

Department of Health and Home Office (2014a) *Review of the operation of sections 135 and 136 of the Mental Health Act 1983: A literature review*, London: Department of Health and Home Office.

Department of Health and Home Office (2014b) *Review of the operation of sections 135 and 136 of the Mental Health Act 1983: Review report and recommendations*, London: Department of Health and Home Office.

Department of Health and Home Office (2017) *Guidance for the implementation of changes to police powers and places of safety provisions in the Mental Health Act 1983*, London: Department of Health and Home Office.

Docking, M., Grace, K. and Bucke, T. (2008) *Police custody as a 'place of safety': Examining the use of section 136 of the Mental Health Act 1983*, London: Independent Police Complaints Commission.

Dodd, V. (2017) 'Police dealing with record level of phone calls on mental health', *The Guardian*, 28 August 2017. Available from: www.theguardian.com/society/2017/aug/28/police-phone-calls-mental-health-nhs [Last accessed 2 March 2018].

Ellis, H. (2014) 'Effects of a Crisis Intervention Team (CIT) training program upon police officers before and after Crisis Intervention Team training', *Archives of Psychiatric Nursing*, 28(1): 10–16.

Forrester, A., Valmaggia, L. and Taylor, P.J. (2016) 'Healthcare services in police custody in England and Wales', *British Medical Journal*, 353: i1994.

Gudjonsson, G.H. (2010) 'Psychological vulnerabilities during police interviews. Why are they important?', *Legal and Criminological Psychology*, 15(2): 161–175.

Her Majesty's Inspectorate of Constabulary (HMIC) (2017) *State of policing: The annual assessment of policing in England and Wales 2016*, London: HMIC.

Her Majesty's Inspectorate of Constabulary (HMIC), Care Quality Commission (CQC), Her Majesty's Inspectorate of Prisons (HMIP) and Healthcare Inspectorate Wales (HIW) (2013) *A criminal use of police cells? The use of police custody as a place of safety for people with mental health needs*, London: HMIC, CQC, HMIP and HIW.

Hiday, V. (1999) 'Mental illness and the criminal justice system' in Horwitz, A. and Scheid, T. (eds.) *The handbook of the sociology of mental health*, Cambridge: Cambridge University Press.

Heyman, I. and McGeough, E. (2018) 'Cross-disciplinary partnerships between police and health services for mental health care', *Journal of Psychiatric and Mental Health Nursing*, 25(5–6): 283–284.

Home Office (1990) *Home Office circular no. 66/90, Provision for mentally disordered offenders*, London: Home Office.

Home Office (1995a) *Appropriate adults: Report of review group*, London: Her Majesty's Stationery Office.

Home Office (1995b) *Home Office circular no. 12/95, Mentally disordered offenders: Inter-agency working*, London: Home Office.

Home Office (2003) *Guidance for appropriate adults*, London: Home Office.

Home Office (2017) *Explanatory notes: Policing and Crime Act 2017*, London: The Stationery Office.

Home Office (2018) *Police powers and procedures, England and Wales, year ending 31 March 2018*, London: Home Office.

Horspool, Drabble and O'Caithain (2016) 'Implementing street triage: A qualitative study of collaboration between police and mental health services', *BMC Psychiatry*, 16: 313.

House of Commons Home Affairs Committee (2015) *Policing and mental health. Eleventh Report of Session 2014–15*, London: The Stationery Office.

Independent Office for Police Conduct (IOPC) (2018a) *Deaths during or following police contact: Statistics for England and Wales 2017/18*, Sale: IOPC.

Independent Office for Police Conduct (IOPC) (2018b) 'Statement following judgment regarding suspension of Metropolitan Police officer', [Press release] 13 April 2018. Available from: www.policeconduct.gov.uk/news/statement-following-judgment-regarding-suspension-metropolitan-police-officer [Last accessed 01 September 2018].

Irvine, A., Allen, L. and Webber, M. (2016) *Evaluation of the Scarborough, Whitby and Ryedale street triage service*, York: University of York.

Justice (2017) *Mental health and fair trial: A report by Justice*, London: Justice.

Kane, E., Evans, E., Mitsch, J., Jilani, T., Quinlan, P., Cattell, J. and Khalifa, N. (2018) 'Police interactions and interventions with suspects flagged as experiencing mental health problems', *Criminal Behaviour and Mental Health*, 28(5): 424–432.

Kennedy, K.M., Green, P.G. and Payne-James, J.J. (2017) 'Complaints against health-care professionals providing police custodial and forensic medical/health-care services and sexual offence examiner services in England, Wales and Northern Ireland', *Medicine, Science and the Law*, 57(1): 12–32.

Khalifeh, M., Johnson, S., Howard, L.M., Borschmann, R., Osborn, D., Dean, K., Hart, C., Hogg, J. and Moran, P. (2015) 'Violent and non-violent crime against adults with severe mental illness', *British Journal of Psychiatry*, 206(4): 275–282.

Kirubarajan, A., Puntis, S., Perfect, D., Tarbit, M., Buckman, M. and Molodynski, A. (2018) 'Street triage services in England: Service models, national provision and the opinions of police', *BJPsych Bulletin*, published online 17 September 2018: 1–5. doi:10.1192/bjb.2018.62

Koskela, S.A., Pettitt, B. and Drennan, V.M. (2016) 'The experiences of people with mental health problems who are victims of crime with the police in England: A qualitative study', *British Journal of Criminology*, 56(5): 1014–1033.

Leese, M. and Russell, S. (2017) 'Mental health, vulnerability and risk in police custody', *The Journal of Adult Protection*, 9(5): 274–283.

Liberty (2016) *Liberty's briefing on the Policing and Crime Bill committee stage in the House of Lords – Part 4 Chapter 4, relating to sections 135 and 136 of the Mental Health Act 1983*, London: Liberty.

Littlechild, B. (1995) 'Reassessing the role of the appropriate adult', *Criminal Law Review*, July: 540–545.

Littlechild, B. (1998) 'An end to 'inappropriate adults'?', *Childright*, 144: 8–9.

Loughran, M. (2018) 'Detention under section 136: Why is it increasing?', *Medicine, Science and the Law*, 58(4): 268–274.

Markowitz, F.E. (2011) 'Mental illness, crime, and violence: Risk, context, and social control', *Aggression and Violent Behavior*, 16: 36–44.

McKinnon, I.G. and Grubin, D. (2012) 'Health screening of people in police custody – Evaluation of current police screening procedures in London, UK', *European Journal of Public Health*, 23(3): 399–405.

Menkes, D. and Bendelow, G. (2014) 'Diagnosing vulnerability and "dangerousness": Police use of section 136 in England and Wales', *Journal of Public Mental Health*, 13(2): 70–82.

Mental Health Taskforce (2016) *The five year forward view for mental health*, London: Mental Health Taskforce.

Morgan, M. and Paterson, C. (2017) '"It's mental health, not mental police": A human rights approach to mental health triage and section 136 of the Mental Health Act 1983', *Policing: A Journal of Policy and Practice*, pax047, doi: 10.1093/police/pax047

NACRO (2007) *Black communities, mental health and the criminal justice system*, London: NACRO.

Nash, M. (1998) 'Enter the polibation officer', *International Journal of Police Science and Management*, 1(4): 360–368.

National Appropriate Adult Network (NAAN) (2010) *Appropriate adult provision in England and Wales*, Ashford: NAAN.

National Appropriate Adult Network (NAAN) (2014) *NAAN briefing: Liaison and diversion and the provision of appropriate adults for mentally vulnerable adults*, Ashford: NAAN.

National Appropriate Adult Network (NAAN) (2015) *There to help: Ensuring provision of appropriate adults for mentally vulnerable adults detained or interviewed by the police*, Ashford: NAAN.

National Appropriate Adult Network (NAAN) (2018) *National standards for the development and provision of appropriate adult schemes in England and Wales*, Ashford: NAAN.

National Institute for Mental Health England (NIMHE) (2008) *Mental Health Act 2007: New roles. Guidance for approving authorities and employers on Approved Mental Health Professionals and Approved Clinicians*, London: NIMHE.

National Policing Improvement Agency (NPIA) (2008) *Review of literature on mentally disordered offenders*, London: NPIA.

National Police Chiefs' Council (NPCC) (2016) *Use of police cells for those in mental health crisis more than halves*, [Press release] 9 September 2016. Available from: https://news.npcc.police.uk/releases/use-of-police-cells-for-those-in-mental-health-crisis-more-than-halves [Last accessed 15 May 2018].

National Police Chiefs' Council (NPCC) (2017) *Thousands of people are suffering mental health issues may be unlawfully held by police due to delays accessing appropriate inpatient beds*, [Press release] 8 December 2017. Available from: https://news.npcc.police.uk/releases/thousands-of-people-suffering-mental-health-issues-may-be-unlawfully-held-by-police-due-to-lack-of-available-hospital-beds [Last accessed 28 June 2018].

Noga, H., Foreman, A., Walsh, E., Shaw, J. and Senior, J. (2015) 'Multi-agency action learning: Challenging institutional barriers in policing and mental health services', *Action Research*, 14(2): 132–150.

Office of the Police and Crime Commissioner for Staffordshire (2013) *Mental health review: Overview of statistical information and case scenario scoping*. Available from:https://staffordshire-pcc.gov.uk/wp-content/uploads/2013/07/Mental-Health-Report.pdf [Last accessed 30 January 2018].

Oliva, J. and Compton, M. (2008) 'A statewide Crisis Intervention Team (CIT) initiative: Evolution of the Georgia CIT program', *Journal of the American Academy of Psychiatry and the Law*, 36(1): 38–46.

Oxford Health NHS Foundation Trust (2015) *Oxfordshire mental health street triage pilot*, Oxford: Oxford Health NHS Foundation Trust.

Payne-James, J. (2017) 'Healthcare and forensic medical services in police custody – To degrade or to improve?', *Clinical Medicine*, 17(1): 6–7.

Payne-James, J.J., Anderson, W.R., Green, P.G. and Johnston, A. (2009) 'Provision of forensic medical services to police custody suites in England and Wales: Current practice', *Journal of Forensic and Legal Medicine*, 16(4): 189–195.

Pierpoint, H. (2008) 'Quickening the PACE? The use of volunteers as appropriate adults in England and Wales', *Policing and Society: An International Journal of Research and Policy*, 18(4): 397–410.

Pierpoint, H. (2011) 'Extending and professionalising the role of the appropriate adult', *Journal of Social Welfare and Family Law*, 33(2): 139–155.

Prins, S.J. (2011) 'Does transinstitutionalization explain the overrepresentation of people with serious mental illnesses in the criminal justice system?', *Community Mental Health Journal*, 47(6): 716–722.

Public Health England (PHE) (2016) *Rapid review of evidence of the impact on health outcomes of NHS commissioned health services for people in secure and detained settings to inform future health interventions and prioritisation in England*, London: PHE.

Redlich, A.D. (2004) 'Mental illness, police interrogations and the potential for false confession', *Psychiatric Services*, 55(1): 19–21.

Rekrut-Lapa, T. and Lapa, A. (2014) 'Health needs of detainees in police custody in England and Wales. Literature review', *Journal of Forensic and Legal Medicine*, 27: 69–75.

Reveruzzi, B. and Pilling, S. (2016) *Street triage. Report on the evaluation of nine pilot schemes in England, March 2016*, London: University College London.

Revolving Doors Agency (2013) *Healthcare in police custody: Users' views*, London: Revolving Doors Agency.

Rogers, A. and Faulkner, A. (1987) *A place of safety: MIND's research into police referrals to the psychiatric services*, London: MIND.

Royal College of Psychiatrists (1997) *Standards of places of safety under section 136 and the Mental Health Act 1983: Council Report CR61*, London: Royal College of Psychiatrists.

Royal College of Psychiatrists (2008) *Standards on the use of Section 136 of the Mental Health Act 1983*, London: Royal College of Psychiatrists.

Royal College of Psychiatrists (2011) *Guidance for commissioners: Service provision for section 136 of the Mental Health Act 1983*, London: Royal College of Psychiatrists.

Sainsbury Centre for Mental Health (2008) *Briefing 36: Policing and mental health*, London: Sainsbury Centre for Mental Health.

Southwark Coroner's Court (2012) *Inquisition at Southwark Coroner's Court, Jury's narrative verdict*, London: Southwark Coroner's Court. Available from: www.gardencourtchambers.co.uk/wp-content/uploads/old_site/File/Inquisition-for-Mr-Rigg.pdf [Last accessed 01 May 2017].

Teplin, L.A. (2000) 'Keeping the peace: Police discretion and mentally ill persons', *National Institute of Justice Journal*, 244: 8–15.

Turner, T., Ness, M.N. and Imison, C.T. (1992) 'Mentally disordered persons found in public places', *Psychological Medicine*, 22(3): 765–774.

Watson, A.C., Ottati, V.C., Draine, J.N. and Morabito, M. (2011) 'CIT in context: The Impact of mental health resource availability and district saturation on call outcomes', *International Journal of Law and Psychiatry*, 34(4): 287–294.

Wells, W. and Schafer, J.A. (2006) 'Officer perceptions of police responses to persons with a mental illness', *Policing: An International Journal of Police Strategies and Management*, 29(4): 578–601.

Weston, S. and Cromar-Hayes, M. (2017) *'This isn't just a case of taking someone to the hospital': Police approaches and management of situations involving persons with mental ill health*, Staffordshire: Keele University.

Wolff, N. (2005) 'Community reintegration of prisoners with mental illness: A social investment perspective', *International Journal of Law and Psychiatry*, 28(1): 43–58.

Young, S., Goodwin, E.J., Sedgwick, O. and Gudjonsson, G.H. (2013) 'The effectiveness of police custody assessments in identifying suspects with intellectual disabilities and attention deficit hyperactivity disorder', *BMC Medicine*, 11: 1–11.

NOTES

1   Now Her Majesty's Inspectorate of Constabulary and Fire & Rescue Services (HMICFRC).

2   For more information about s12(2) approvals see www.rcpsych.ac.uk/work inpsychiatry/divisions/london/resources/section12.aspx

3   AMHPs were introduced under the MHA 2007 and replaced Approved Social Workers (ASW). As the change in terminology suggests, a wider range

of professionals are now eligible to undertake this role. For more information about the role of AMHPs and ACs see National Institute for Mental Health England (2008).

4   For a map of current HBPOS across England, see www.cqc.org.uk/help-advice/mental-health-capacity/map-health-based-places-safety

5   For the latest revision of PACE 1984 Code C see https://assets.publishing.service.gov.uk/government/uploads/system/uploads/attachment_data/file/729842/pace-code-c-2018.pdf

6   Under s38 of the Crime and Disorder Act 1998, local authorities are legally required to ensure that an AA can be provided for all children via their Youth Offending Team (YOT) yet there is no such statutory duty on any agency to provide an AA for vulnerable adults with learning difficulties or mental health problems.

7   The IPCC was renamed as the IOPC in January 2018.

8   Apparent suicides following detention in police custody are recorded if they take place within two days.

CHAPTER 5

Mental health, offending and the courts

INTRODUCTION

The Mental Health Act (MHA) 1983 (as amended by the MHA 2007) provides a range of diversionary powers, exercisable at various stages of the criminal justice system. This chapter will systematically take the reader through the options available at court, where mental disorder raises a number of important questions for the judicial system. The chapter begins with some historical detail about culpability and our propensity to hold *only* those persons with sound mind responsible for their acts. This is followed by an outline of the various ways in which a defendant's mental disorder may impact on the decisions made at court, and their possible diversion from the criminal justice system. The first is the decision by the Crown Prosecution Service (CPS) about whether to prosecute or divert the suspect from court. A second set of decisions, assuming the individual has not been diverted, must assess the accused's fitness to plead (i.e. does the defendant have the capacity to understand what s/he is charged with and are they able to understand the consequences of submitting a guilty (or not guilty) plea) and if they are fit to stand trial. Assuming the case proceeds, the next issue to be decided by the court is whether the defendant is culpable and therefore responsible for the act they are accused of. Here, we will consider the defences that may be available during the trial including the insanity defence and diminished responsibility. The final area of court decision-making that is affected by mental disorder is sentencing and disposal and we therefore consider the range of disposals that are available to the court. The chapter ends by considering court liaison and diversion (L&D) schemes and the limited use of mental health courts in England and Wales.

PROSECUTING PEOPLE WITH MENTAL DISORDER AND DIVERSION FROM CRIMINAL PROCEDURES

HISTORY OF CULPABILITY

An act does not make a person legally guilty unless his or her mind is also legally blameworthy. A fundamental principle of criminal law is that a crime consists of both a mental and physical element. *Mens rea*, a person's awareness of the fact that his or her conduct is criminal, is the mental element, and *actus reus*, the act itself, is the physical element. In Anglo-Saxon jurisdictions, people are generally held responsible for their acts and adjudged capable of exercising control over them unless it is thought they did not have *mens rea*. This perception of culpability can be dated back as far as the Roman Empire who found that people *non-compos mentis* should not be held responsible for their crimes. Likewise, in thirteenth-century England, it seems to have been generally held that neither a child nor the 'insane' should be held liable for their crime. Like children, the insane were thought of as incapable of 'sinning' because they could not choose or distinguish the 'good from the evil'. Under this rule, the defendant would be found guilty if they knew the difference between good and evil at the time of the crime. This test was replaced in 1724 in the case of Rex v Arnold where the defendant had shot and attempted to kill a British lord. The trial judge instructed the jurors to acquit the defendant by reason of insanity if it was found that he was 'a man totally deprived of his understanding and memory, and doth not know what he was doing ... such a one is never the object of punishment'.

Further advancements to the insanity defence were made in 1800 in the case of R v Hadfield. On the 15th May 1800, Hadfield stood up in a theatre in London and fired a pistol at King George III missing his head by a foot. At the time, Hadfield was labouring under the illusion that God would destroy the world unless he sacrificed himself. Believing at that time that suicide was a sin, Hadfield decided to shoot at the king knowing that he would then be charged with treason and subsequently executed. He was put on trial only six weeks later where his lawyer, Erksine, produced evidence that while Hadfield knew he was breaking the law he was nevertheless insane because of a penetrating head wound that he had received while at war. Erskine's strategy in this case was to argue that madness could be partial. The jury was convinced by Erskine's arguments and Hadfield was acquitted. In deciding how Hadfield should be disposed of the judge gave the following statement:

> The prisoner for his own sake, and for the sake of society should not be discharged, for this is a case that concerns every man … from the King upon the throne to the beggar at the gate … therefore it is absolutely necessary that he should be properly disposed of.
>
> (Lord Kenyon, cited in Howell, 1800:1354)

The verdict caused political uproar and brought about an immediate change in the law through the Criminal Lunatics Act 1800, which allowed for Hadfield to be found 'not guilty by reason of insanity' and authorised the 'safe custody' of criminal lunatics 'at his majesty's pleasure'. Hadfield was, therefore, committed to Bethlam Hospital. In essence, the Criminal Lunatics Act ensured that someone found not guilty by reason of insanity was not set free but removed to a mental hospital.

While many of these laws have been replaced or amended, they nevertheless set out firm ideas about criminal responsibility. Before returning to how these laws have evolved, and the defences available to the mentally disordered offender, we will consider the various ways in which these individuals may be diverted before standing trial.

The Home Office and Department of Health and Social Security (1975:266) reported that

> where any apparent offender is clearly in need of psychiatric treatment and there is no risk to members of the public the question should always be asked whether any useful purpose would be served by prosecution … these remarks apply in cases of homicide or attempted homicide or grave bodily harm as in less serious cases.

In this regard, it is thought that, where possible, mentally disordered persons should receive care and treatment from health and social services. As we have already seen in Chapter 4, diversion from criminal proceedings into the health care system can be achieved on an informal basis or formally under the MHA 1983 (as amended by the MHA 2007). Having already dealt with the ways in which the police divert offenders from the criminal justice system, this chapter will outline the ways in which diversion may happen after an individual has been charged with an offence. First, the CPS may decide not to prosecute. Second, the court might decide to remand the individual to a suitable hospital for assessment and care. Third, the court may decide that the individual is unfit to plead or stand trial. In the event that a trial proceeds, a number of defences may be available to the individual concerned and, subsequently, a number of disposals are available to the court to impose.

THE CROWN PROSECUTION SERVICE (CPS) AND THE DECISION TO PROSECUTE

The Code for Crown Prosecutors notes that

> prosecutors should also have regard to whether the suspect is, or was at the time of the offence, affected by any significant mental or physical ill health or disability, as in some circumstances this may mean that it is less likely that a prosecution is required.
>
> (CPS, 2018)

In accordance with the Code for Crown Prosecutors, the CPS requires any evidence of an accused's mental health problems at the earliest opportunity in order to review the case. To inform their decision, they will use information from the police who have a number of key responsibilities as set out in the Home Office circular 12/95 (see Box 5.1).

BOX 5.1 HOME OFFICE CIRCULAR 12/95: RESPONSIBILITIES OF THE POLICE

- Where the police have been advised of the defendant's condition and prognosis by the Social Services, Probation Service, psychiatrists or other professionals, who may advocate a particular approach or disposal, the advising agency should be encouraged to set out their views in writing. Where this is not possible, the police should summarise any views expressed to them orally;
- The police should include on the file a brief summary of their reasons for starting proceedings or their views as to whether the suspect should be prosecuted;

- The CPS should be informed if the defendant has been seen by a psychiatrist or arrangements have been made to have him or her assessed;
- If the police want to release the defendant on unconditional bail on the understanding that he or she will accept certain conditions (such as treatment or residence) they should be advised to keep the period of bail to a minimum. Preferably, the defendant should be bailed to the next available court for bail arrangements to be reviewed as soon as possible. Any informal conditions should be clearly stated on the CPS file;
- If there is a bail information scheme operating, advice from outside agencies regarding factors in favour of bail or available placements should be passed to the CPS via the Bail Information Officer. Where such procedures are not operating, such information should be given in writing by the authorised person via the police. It is important that any such information or advice from outside agencies is reliable, accurate and authoritative. You should avoid being lobbied in court with sensitive and important information given orally.

Source: Crown Prosecution Service (2017).

Irrespective of whether a suspect may have mental disorder or not, a prosecution should only start if the CPS is satisfied that both stages of the Full Code Test have been passed. The first stage of the Full Code Test, the evidential stage, requires prosecutors to assess if there is sufficient evidence on which to proceed. Once prosecutors have considered the evidence, they must then consider the second stage – the public interest stage – and if it is in the public interest to proceed with a prosecution. When considering the public interest stage, the CPS (2018) advises prosecutors that 'the greater the suspect's level of culpability the more likely it is that a prosecution is required'. However, when considering the public interest stage with a suspect with possible mental disorder, prosecutors must also 'consider how serious the offence was, whether the suspect is likely to reoffend and the need to safeguard the public or those providing care to such persons' (CPS, 2018). In cases where the offence committed by the suspect with mental disorder is minor, prosecutors may decide that it is not in the public interest to proceed. However, where the offence is serious or there are concerns about public safety, a prosecution will almost certainly proceed.

PRE-TRIAL REMAND TO HOSPITAL

Section 35 of the MHA 1983 may be used for defendants pending trial before the Crown Court or having been convicted before the magistrates' court. Specifically, the provision allows a remand to hospital so that a report may be written on the defendant's mental health. Section 36 may be used by the Crown Court to remand a person to hospital for treatment pending their appearance for trial. This section is available for all offences punishable by imprisonment, except for murder proceedings. The provisions of sections 35 and 36 of the MHA 1983 are not used extensively, mainly because of the preferred policy of diversion from the criminal justice system at the earliest opportunity (Hotopf et al., 2000).

FITNESS TO PLEAD AND STAND TRIAL

If a defendant's mental disorder is so severe that they cannot understand the proceedings, have not got the ability to instruct counsel, or cannot exercise their right to challenge a juror, they may be able to put forward a defence of being under disability in relation to trial. Fitness to plead is concerned with the question of an accused's mental state at the time of his or her trial and not at the time of the offence. The criteria regarding fitness to plead were laid out in the 1836 Pritchard case and recently updated following the R v M (John) [2003] EWCA Crim 3452 case (see de Lacy (2016) for an extended discussion). The defendant in the Pritchard case was deaf, could not speak, and was standing trial for what was then the capital offence of bestiality. In directing the jury, the judge highlighted

> there are three points to be enquired into; firstly whether the defendant is mute of malice or not, secondly whether he can plead to the indictment or not, and thirdly whether he is of sufficient intellect to comprehend the course of proceedings on the trial so as to make a proper defence to know that he might challenge any of you to whom he might object and to comprehend the details of the evidence.
>
> (R v Pritchard (1836) 7 C&P 303)

Expert witnesses who assess whether the accused is unfit to plead must give evidence on the extent to which the accused is able to meet these criteria. An inability to meet any one of the criteria is sufficient to render an accused person unfit to plead. The accused not being capable of making decisions which are in his or her best interests will not be enough to conclude that he or she is unfit to plead.

Although MacKay, Mitchell and Howe (2007) show that the number of findings of unfitness to plead is rising, Rogers et al. (2009:817) observe that 'formal findings of unfitness under the test ... are extremely rare' meaning that 'significant numbers of the mentally ill continue to undergo trial and may be doing so unfairly'. The fitness to plead test has been criticised on many grounds (Law Commission, 2010). First, there have been suggestions that it only deals with extreme cases of a particular type – usually relating to cognitive deficiency – and sets too high a threshold for finding an accused unfit to plead. Second, it fails to cover all aspects of the trial process (e.g. the ability to give evidence) and therefore has the practical effect of limiting the number of people who are found to be unfit to plead.

In recent years, there has been an attempt to update the criteria to make them more consistent with the modern trial process. In R v M (John) [2003] EWCA Crim 3452, the appellant had been convicted of rape, indecent assault on a female, indecency with a child and taking indecent photographs of a child. At trial, the defence contended that the defendant suffered from a serious impairment to his short-term memory, known as anterograde amnesia, which rendered him incapable of following the proceedings and giving evidence in his own defence. It was argued therefore that he was unfit to plead, and the issue was contested before the jury. Two of the psychiatrists giving evidence concluded that the defendant was unfit to plead while the third was of the view that he was fit, although this psychiatrist had previously noted that special steps would be required to deal with his memory problems. The trial judge directed the jury, suggesting that it was sufficient for the defence to persuade them on the balance of probabilities that any one of the following things was beyond the defendant's capability: (1) understanding the charges, (2) deciding whether to plead guilty or not, (3) exercising his right to challenge jurors, (4) instructing solicitors and counsel, (5) following the course of proceedings and (6) giving evidence in his own defence.

The jury found that the defendant was fit to plead and therefore to stand trial. He was convicted and appealed. The first ground of appeal was that the judge had misdirected the jury by setting the test for fitness to plead too low with the result that it was too easily met. In addition, it was argued that the first two of the six items (understanding the charges and deciding whether or not to plead guilty) should not have been included. The appeal was dismissed. The Court of Appeal approved the trial judge's direction that the jury could find unfitness to plead if the defence could establish on a balance of probabilities any one of six things that was beyond the appellant's capabilities.

If a defendant is found to be unfit to plead, the court will proceed to a trial of the facts in order to ascertain if the defendant did the act or made the omission constituting the *actus reus* of the offence charged against him. This is decided by a jury under section 4A of the Criminal Procedures (Insanity) Act (CPIA) 1964.

If it is decided that the defendant did the act, as it is not a criminal trial, a criminal disposal cannot be given. Instead, the sentencing options available to the court are as follows: (1) a hospital order under s37 of the MHA 1983 (with or without a restriction under s41) (to be discussed in further detail below under the section 'Disposals at court'), (2) a supervision order or (3) an order for an absolute discharge. If a supervision order is made under Schedule 1a of the CPIA 1964, the defendant will be required to be under the supervision of a social worker or probation officer for a period not exceeding two years as specified in the order and may include a requirement that the offender submits to treatment with a view to improvement of the medical condition and a residence requirement.

The law is silent on whether there is an issue to resume the prosecution of an offender who becomes fit to plead following one of these disposals. Section 4A(2) of the CPIA 1964 provides that a finding of unfitness will have the effect that the trial 'shall not proceed or proceed further'. Although the fitness to plead procedure can result in an acquittal, a finding that the offender did the act will not amount to a conviction and will not result in a criminal charge.

In R v Birch [1989] 11 Cr App R (S) 202, the Court of Appeal held that

> once the offender is admitted to hospital pursuant to a hospital order without restriction on discharge, his position is almost exactly the same as if he were a civil patient. In effect, he passes out of the penal system and into the hospital regime. Neither the court nor the Secretary of State has any say in his disposal.

However, these comments were made when a hospital order was the only order available following a finding of unfitness. Amendments made to the CPIA 1964 by the Criminal Procedure (Insanity and Unfitness to Plead) Act (CPIA) 1991 and Domestic Violence, Crime and Victims Act (DVCVA) 2004 made available the supervision order and absolute discharge. These statutes neither restrict nor allow the court to postpone the trial of an offender who becomes fit to plead after an order is made. Moreover, there is no duty on the Responsible

Clinician (RC)[1] or supervising officer to advise the CPS if an offender subject to a hospital order (without a restriction order) or supervision order becomes fit to plead. In practice this means that it is unlikely that the CPS will be made aware of such circumstances. However, such a situation may come to light if a person is subsequently charged with a further offence and their previous unfitness to plead becomes known. In such cases, prosecutors may consider whether the public interest requires a prosecution for the original offence, although the original decision that a restriction order was not necessary may indicate that the offence was not so serious as to now require prosecution, and that the public interest has been satisfied by treatment rather than punishment.

The law relating to fitness to plead has recently been reviewed. A report published by the Law Commission (2016) sets out new tests that would establish a defendant's ability to enter a plea and whether they are able to participate effectively in their trial. These changes would represent a shift in focus from the existing criteria, which prioritises intellectual ability. At the time of writing, the Law Commission is still awaiting a final response from government to their proposals, but for a comprehensive analysis of the proposed reforms to this complex and poorly understood area of law, readers are encouraged to consult Loughnan (2016).

ASSESSING A DEFENDANT'S CULPABILITY AND RESPONSIBILITY AT COURT

THE INSANITY DEFENCE

The insanity defence was developed as a consequence of the 1843 case of Daniel McNaughten, a Scottish woodturner, who fatally wounded Edward Drummond, the private secretary of the Prime Minister Robert Peel. Believing that he was being persecuted by the Conservative government, McNaughten bought a pair of pistols and on the 20th January 1843, mistaking Drummond for Peele, followed him up Whitehall to his bank and shot him in the back. Drummond died five days later. McNaughten was arrested, taken to the police station and gave the following statement to the police:

> The Tories in my native city have compelled me to do this, they follow and persecute me where ever I go and have entirely destroyed my peace of mind, they've followed me to France and to Scotland, all over England. In fact, they follow me wherever I go. They've

accused me of crimes of which I am not guilty. In fact, they wish to murder me, it can be proved by evidence, that is all I have to say.

(McNaughten, 1843, cited in West and Walk, 1977)

On the 3rd March 1843, McNaughten went on trial where questions were raised about whether his mental disorder was so severe that he did not know what he was doing at the time he committed the offence. The judge directed the jury that they should find McNaughten guilty if they believed he could distinguish right from wrong. The jury returned a not guilty verdict by reason of insanity. Amidst public outcry, the House of Lords were tasked with questioning the judiciary whose responses were shaped into the McNaughten rules. They followed that, if a defence is to be upheld, the court must be satisfied that at the time of the alleged offence, the defendant did not know what s/he was doing, or that what s/he was doing was wrong due to a 'defect of reason' arising from a 'disease of mind' (Moran, 1985). The rules state that

[e]very man is presumed to be sane and to possess a sufficient degree of reason to be responsible for his crime until the contrary is proved to their satisfaction; and that to establish a defence of insanity, it must be clearly proved that, at the time of committing the act, the party accused was labouring under such a defect of reason from disease of mind, as not to know the nature and quality of his act he was doing; or if he did know it, that he did not know what he was doing wrong.

(Lord Chief Justice Tindal, 1843, cited in Holmes, 1895:6)

While there is a perception that many defendants seek the insanity defence out to avoid taking responsibility for their actions (Perlin, 2016), there is evidence that many defendants may wish to distance themselves from such a classification (Peay, 2017). Indeed, defendants often seek to avoid a finding of insanity and may even change a plea to guilty in order to avoid a finding of insanity (Perlin, 2016). In the US it has been found that defendants who have asserted the insanity defence at trial, and who were ultimately found guilty of their charges, served significantly longer than defendants tried on similar charges who did not assert the insanity defence (Perlin and Cucolo, 2016). Similarly, research in Ireland has found that those detained under mental health legislation spent longer in detention when compared to those given a prison sentence (Davoren et al., 2015).

The defence of insanity is a general defence which is available to all crimes. It is unique in that it may be raised by the prosecution and judge in addition to the defence. In England and Wales, the defence has declined in importance since the abolition of the death penalty and the introduction of the diminished responsibility defence for murder.

DIMINISHED RESPONSIBILITY

Diminished responsibility was not available as a defence in the UK until the introduction of the Homicide Act 1957. It came into being because it was thought that the McNaughten rules were too rigid. The defence allows a charge of murder to be reduced to manslaughter if the accused person can show that they are suffering from an abnormality of the mind that has substantially impaired their responsibility, as judged by individual medical experts a jury. Section 2 of the Act states:

> [w]here a person kills or is party to the killing of another, he shall not be convicted of murder if he was suffering from such abnormality of mind (whether arising from a condition of arrested or retarded development of mind or any inherent causes or induced by disease or injury) as substantially impaired his mental responsibility for his acts or commissions in doing or being party to the killing.

However, diminished responsibility is not always easy to establish without further testing whether such impairments affect a given individual, and if so, whether they interfere with that individual's local, particular and context-specific decisions in a 'substantial' way. It is these types of questions that invoke great difficulties for the law on the one hand and psychiatry on the other, particularly where experts are called upon to give evidence about an individual's mental state, as can be seen in the case of David Copeland. Copeland, also known as the London nail bomber, killed three people and injured 139 by using homemade nail bombs in a series of attacks in 1999. He pleaded not guilty to murder but guilty to manslaughter on the grounds of diminished responsibility. At Copeland's trial, one of the psychiatric experts called upon, John Gunn, argued that there was no doubt that Copeland had severe schizophrenia (a diagnosis also confirmed by the team at the hospital where Copeland had previously received treatment). This assessment was supported by five other psychiatrists all arguing that Copeland was suffering from paranoid schizophrenia at the time of the bombing and so acted 'like a robot' who was incapable of taking full responsibility for his actions (Hopkins, 2000:1). However, the prosecution expert said that Copeland 'had overwhelming anxiety over his sexual orientation and intense rage and hatred of others that led to extreme views and a desire to destroy' (Hopkins, 2000:1), and argued that Copeland was not suffering from schizophrenia but had a personality disorder. The jury favoured this minority view and Copeland was convicted for murder and sentenced to life imprisonment.

Gunn (2002) argues that the decision made in Copeland's case was reminiscent of that made in the case of Peter Sutcliffe. Sutcliffe was charged in January 1981 with the murder of 13 women and attempted murder of seven more. After his arrest he was found to have been experiencing lucid hallucinations which instructed him to kill the women and was considered to have a diagnosis of schizophrenia. His delusional system embraced the idea that God had given him a mission to rid the world of prostitutes. So clear-cut was the evidence that the prosecution was prepared to accept the plea of diminished responsibility on all 13 counts of murder. However, the judge was not prepared for this outcome and ordered that the argument for diminished responsibility be put to a jury. The prosecution called one of the psychiatrists who had previously assessed Sutcliffe again, who then argued that 'in the light of the present knowledge of schizophrenia we believe that he [Sutcliffe] should be kept in custody for the rest of his natural life'. While the jury concurred that Sutcliffe was suffering from schizophrenia, they decided that the case had not been made for abnormality of mind under Section 2 of the Homicide Act. A majority verdict of 10:2 resulted in a mandatory sentence of 20 concurrent terms of life imprisonment. While in prison it became immediately apparent that all of the psychiatrists who had assessed him had been right, and that Sutcliffe needed to be detained in hospital so his schizophrenia could be treated. Two years after his trial Sutcliffe was transferred to Broadmoor hospital.

What these cases illustrate is that the concept of mental disorder in the legal arena belongs to the legal profession, not necessarily the medical profession. Gunn (2002:62) asserts:

[o]n many occasions, due deference is given by lawyers and jury-men to medical opinion, thus conferring apparent power to psychiatrists. This is an illusion because the power is on loan and can be withdrawn when the politics of a case, usually a high-profile case, demand it. The mental-abnormality excuse used to mitigate many crimes of homicide is not available for cases deemed inexcusable by the newspapers, politicians and public opinion. If by some skilful advocacy by the newspapers, politicians and public opinion. If by some skilful advocacy an 'inexcusable' crime is excused, then a public outcry occurs after the trial. In the case of Daniel

McNaughton the whole legal profession was put under pressure to change the rules and duly did so ... More recently both Peter Sutcliffe and David Copeland terrorised whole communities and were the target of intense feelings of public vengeance; any excusing of their crimes on medical grounds would have led to a public outcry which the courts and their jurymen circumvented.

There is a tension in the reaction of the public to murderers such as Copeland and Sutcliffe. On the one hand, there is often a tendency to think that the killer 'must be mad' to commit such heinous crimes. On the other hand, there is an overwhelming desire for retribution. The killer 'must be punished' in the appropriate way, with psychiatric treatment not perceived as a sufficient response to severe crimes. Retributivist intuitions and the desire to punish are strong and extremely resistant to change. In cases of emotionally shocking crimes, these types of motivations easily over-ride the intuitions that (a) horrendous crimes must be the consequence of some sort of mental malfunctioning and that (b) people with mental illness may not be morally responsible for the crimes they commit. Commenting on the Anders Breivik case in Norway, Wessely (2012:1563) exposes two common misconceptions about psychiatry: the first is that 'outrageous crimes must mean mental illness', and the second is that 'the purpose of psychiatry is to get people off'. As Wessely (2012) suggests, these positions are badly supported by evidence, blind us to the important details of individual cases, and lead to excessively polarised debates on mental health and moral and legal responsibility.

DISPOSALS AT COURT

Guidance on remand and the sentencing options available to the court is set out by the Ministry of Justice (2008).[2] Under s157 of the Criminal Justice Act (CJA) 2003, a medical report should be obtained by the court before passing sentence on a defendant who is suspected of having a mental disorder. In order to make its decision the court can also request information about available hospital treatment facilities in the defendant's local area from the relevant Clinical Commissioning Group (CCG) (or Local Health Board (LHB) in Wales).

Several sentencing options are set out under the MHA 1983 (as amended by the MHA 2007) and CPIA 1964 although notable changes have also been generated by the Crime (Sentences) Act (C(S)A) 1997, the CJA 2003 and the DVCVA 2004. In this next section, we set out the main options available to the courts, including an interim hospital order under s38 of the MHA 1983, a hospital order under s37 of the MHA 1983 (with or without restrictions under s41); a hospital and limitation direction (HLD) under s45A of the MHA 1983 (as inserted by the C(S)A 1997 and amended by the MHA 2007); and a community order under the CJA 2003, which may include a 'mental health treatment requirement' (MHTR).

According to the latest available statistics about detention under the MHA 1983 (as amended by the MHA 2007), overall detentions under Part III of the Act (i.e. as a result of criminal proceedings) have been in decline since 2011–2012 from 2,130 to 1,696 in the year 2015–2016 (NHS Digital, 2016) (see Table 5.1). In 2015, Birmingham, Awonogun and Ryland (2017:379) report that of the 1,238,917 sentences passed by the courts, only '12,992 were dealt with by way of restriction orders, hospital orders, guardianship orders[3] and related disposals'. This amounts to little over 1% of all court disposals in 2015, and therefore lends little support to the public perception that those with mental health problems are disproportionately responsible for serious crime as well as commonly diverted (or 'let off') from punishment.

INTERIM HOSPITAL ORDER UNDER s38 MENTAL HEALTH ACT 1983

If a defendant has been found guilty of an offence, the first option available to the court is an interim hospital order under s38 of the MHA 1983. The interim order can be imposed by the courts initially for a period of 12 weeks and it may be then renewed for a period of between 28 days and 12 months. If, while a patient is detained under a s38, the court is provided with information that leads it to conclude that a full hospital order under s37 (see below) is required they can make it a substantive order without bringing the patient back before the court.

HOSPITAL ORDER UNDER s37 MENTAL HEALTH ACT 1983

Those who have been convicted of an offence punishable by imprisonment, but are thought to be mentally disordered and in need of hospital treatment at the time of sentencing, can be made the subject of a hospital order under section 37 of the MHA 1983. The order lasts for six months, can be renewed for a further six months and can then be renewed annually. Both the magistrates' and Crown courts have the power to make the order, but they must have medical evidence from two doctors that the convicted person is mentally disordered and requires treatment in hospital. Such an order is made on the basis of how the person is at the time of sentencing. Therefore, it is possible that a person may have been unwell at the time the offence was committed but by the time of sentencing has recovered sufficiently to make a hospital order inappropriate. Once the court has made a hospital order an appropriate bed must be found for the patient within 28 days.

If an offender is given a hospital order by the court its duration is not specified (as it would be with a prison sentence). This means that there is 'no correlation between seriousness of offence and duration of hospital stay' and in contrast to other countries, no difference between the forensic and civil mental health system (Schneider, 2010:204). The Ministry of Justice (2008) makes clear that this is because a hospital order is not for the purpose of punishment. This means that neither the court nor the Secretary of State have any further say in the patient's disposal (unless they are also subject to a s41, described in the next section) on the basis that

> once the offender is admitted to hospital pursuant to a hospital order without restriction on discharge, his [sic] position is almost exactly the same as if he were a civil patient. In effect he [sic] passes out of the penal system and into the hospital regime.
>
> (R v Birch [1989] 11 Cr App R (S) 202)

The use of hospital orders (including those restricted under s41) has been in decline, falling from 981 in 2011–2012 to 638 in 2015–2016 (NHS Digital, 2016) (see Table 5.1). Bickle (2009) attributes this decline to the expansion of indeterminate sentences and argues that

Table 5.1 Detentions under s37 and s37/41 of the MHA 1983 between 2011/12 and 2015/16

	2011– 2012	2012– 2013	2013– 2014	2014– 2015	2015– 2016
Detentions under Part III of the Mental Health Act	2,130	1,788	1,847	1,930	1,696
37 (without s41 restrictions)	459	326	315	307	223
37 (with s41 restrictions)	522	435	448	486	415
47 (without s49 restrictions)	41	41	43	60	32
47 (with s49 restrictions)	427	404	414	429	385
48 (with s49 restrictions)	398	371	394	440	465

Source: NHS Digital (2016).

it has led to a corresponding increase in the numbers of prisoners with mental disorder. Others have observed, that even when a hospital order may be the preferred option of the court, circumstances such as a lack of hospital beds, may force judges to send an offender to prison even though a therapeutic disposal would have been desirable (Easton and Piper, 2016; Harrison, 2011).

RESTRICTION ORDER UNDER s41 MENTAL HEALTH ACT 1983

If the defendant eligible for a hospital order at the time of sentencing is thought to pose a risk of serious harm to others, the Crown Court may impose a restriction order under section 41 of the MHA 1983. Only the Crown Court is able to impose a restriction order. However, if the magistrates' court decides that a patient's risk is sufficiently serious, the case may be sent to the Crown Court for consideration. To make a restriction order, a Crown Court must hear oral evidence from a doctor in addition to the two written medical recommendations required for a section 37 hospital order. A restriction order is made on the grounds of public protection and imposes obligations both on the patient and on their RC. The patient can only be discharged on the order of the Ministry of Justice or a mental health tribunal.[4] Thus, a patient subject to a section 37 hospital order without restriction may be discharged by their RC, but the RC of a patient detained under a hospital order with restrictions can only make a recommendation for discharge (to either the Ministry of Justice or a Tribunal).

HOSPITAL AND LIMITATION DIRECTION (HLD) UNDER s45A MENTAL HEALTH ACT 1983

Where there is a conviction by the Crown Court of an offence, the sentence for which is not fixed by law, the defendant may be given a HLD under section 45A of the MHA 1983 (inserted under the C(S) A 1997). The disposal allows the judge to direct someone's removal to hospital after conviction for the offence as long as two clinicians are satisfied that: s/he is suffering from mental disorder, that the mental disorder from which the offender is suffering is of a nature or degree which makes it appropriate for him to be detained in a hospital for medical treatment, and that appropriate medical treatment is available. Once the treatment is no longer necessary, a HLD allows the Secretary of State for Justice to direct a person's removal to prison to serve any remaining part of their sentence if their RC indicates that continued treatment in hospital is no longer necessary. Any subsequent decisions about release will then be made by the Parole Board (PB), rather than a Tribunal. This is in contrast to a hospital order, which would allow the patient to be released once the RC is satisfied the individual no longer requires hospital treatment (or for those also restricted under s41, following discharge by a Tribunal).

When the HLD was first inserted by the C(S)A 1997 it only applied to defendants who were thought to suffer from 'psychopathic disorder'. Following the amendments brought about by the MHA 2007 (and specifically, the removal of the separate legal category of psychopathic disorder), the provision is now available to all defendants thought to suffer from mental disorder. Section 45A orders cannot apply to anyone found unfit to plead or stand trial, those found not guilty by reason of insanity, or people convicted of murder (for which the sentence is fixed by law as a mandatory life sentence). However, it may still apply to people who are convicted of manslaughter on the grounds of diminished responsibility.

Unsurprisingly, use of the so-called 'hybrid order' has increased since its remit was expanded by the MHA 2007 (Delmage, Exworthy and Blackwood, 2015). Following the Vowles judgment (see R(Vowles) v SSJ [2015] EWCA Crim 45), many interpreted this case law as suggesting that a s45A should be given precedence over a s37 hospital order (with or without s41 restrictions) (see Peay (2016) for a discussion).[5] However, a more recent judgement by the Court of Appeal in R v Edwards [2018] EWCA Crim 595 has clarified that '[s]ection 45A and the judgment in Vowles do not provide a "default" setting of imprisonment'. Instead, a sentencing judge who is considering the use of a hospital order must, before making such an order, consider all the powers at its disposal, including a s45A HLD. Should the judge consider a hospital order to be most appropriate, s/he must then provide 'sound reasons' for not imposing a sentence with a penal element, as would be the usual course.

The HLD has been subject to considerable criticism. Eastman and Peay (1998) suggest that the 'hybrid order' was created by the government, not on the basis of empirical research evidence, but as a reaction to a small number of high-profile cases where patients released from hospital went on to reoffend. In a review, the Sainsbury Centre for Mental Health (2010) identifies a range of financial, clinical and ethical problems with the legal provision. The first issue they raise is the blurring of blame and responsibility that the 'hybrid order' generates. When the order was first introduced, they note that judges were concerned about how 'partial' responsibility and tariffs may be worked out. The Sainsbury Centre for Mental Health (2010:40) also argues that the HLD is 'fundamentally anti-therapeutic'. On this point, they cite Eastman (1996) who observes 'it may be that giving such a "double message" (of treatment and punishment) is correct in logic but it may be psychologically confusing or unhelpful to a patient' (cited in Sainsbury Centre for Mental Health, 2010:40). The HLD blurs the boundary between patient and prisoner and has the potential to mean that psychiatrists are serving as jailers (Sainsbury Centre for Mental Health, 2010). Drawing on the work of Eastman, the Sainsbury Centre for Mental Health (2010) also expresses concern that the widening use of the HLD may create an 'avalanche effect' with implications for mental health and prison services, as well as the staff cultures within them (see Eastman (1996) for a full discussion).

Before the MHA 2007 amendments, the disposal was rarely used, presumably because it put psychiatrists in an invidious position in court whereby he or she had to make decisions that would inform decisions made by the court about whether the punishment was warranted or not. Concerns about the 'treatability' of those with personality disorder also meant that 'many clinicians and psychiatric services were unwilling or unable to provide treatment' (Sainsbury Centre for Mental Health, 2010:32). With the removal of the 'treatability test' and the expansion to cover all disorders rather than only psychopathic disorder (see Chapter 3 for a discussion), psychiatrists have been unable to avoid answering questions about culpability and punishment.

COMMUNITY ORDER UNDER THE CRIMINAL JUSTICE ACT 2003

In an attempt to provide the courts with greater flexibility, a single community order to simplify and replace earlier community sentence options was introduced under the CJA 2003. Magistrates and judges now have a range of different 'requirements' that can be added to a community order. One is the MHTR,[6] although an order may consist of a range of requirements including unpaid work, curfews and probation supervision. The MHTR is one of several treatment options available to the court, along with the drug rehabilitation requirement (DRR), alcohol treatment requirement (ATR) and a rehabilitation activity requirement (RAR).

A MHTR requires an offender to receive treatment for up to 36 months from a registered medical practitioner. In order for a MHTR to be added to a community order, the court must be satisfied that the offender has a mental disorder, that suitable treatment is available and that the offender will consent to this treatment. The court must also be satisfied that the offender does not require admission to hospital and that the treatment can be completed in the community.

Despite the high levels of mental health problems among people who offend, and evidence that MHTRs are effective at reducing the reoffending of those with mental health problems (Hillier and Mews, 2018), use of the MHTR has been very limited. In 2012–2013, less than 1% of community orders had an attached MHTR (National Offender Management Service (NOMS), 2014). While some optimism surrounded the introduction of the Legal Aid, Sentencing and Punishment of Offenders Act (LASPO) 2012, which broadened the range of professionals who can assess mental health for a MHTR and removed the prerequisite of having a psychiatric report before a MHTR can be issued, use still appears to be very limited.

There are many reasons for the limited uptake of the MHTR. Scott and Moffatt (2012) highlight that there has been a lack of clarity about who should receive a MHTR as well as uncertainty about how breaches of community orders should be managed. A recent review by Public Health England (2016:36) reports that MHTRs are difficult to implement because of 'the inability to enforce compliance with treatment, the lack of trained/willing health professionals to administer this and access to appropriate services'. Research has also identified divergent professional views about the MHTR and some considerable regional differences in its use (Pakes and Winstone, 2012). Some psychiatrists in Durcan's (2016) research expressed concerns about the implications of MHTRs for their workload. A lack of confidence among the courts and probation may also explain the limited uptake (Canton, 2008 cited in Harrison, 2011) as well as a populist preference for imprisonment over alternatives in the community (Harrison, 2011). There is also evidence of confusion among commissioners and providers between the MHTR of a 'community order' and 'community treatment orders' under the MHA 2007 (NOMS, 2014; see also Chapter 7). However, a recent review of mental health and criminal justice concludes that the biggest barrier to increasing the use of MHTRs is the lack of mainstream community mental health care services available at the point of sentencing (Durcan, 2016; see also Scott and Moffatt, 2012).

Following the Offender Rehabilitation Act (ORA) 2014, a court may now also include a RAR when making a community order. A RAR is a requirement that makes the defendant participate in activity to reduce the possibility of reoffending. The precise activity to be engaged in is only decided once a more in-depth assessment has been made. There is evidence that RARs have been popular with the courts with Her Majesty's Inspectorate of Probation (2017:7) noting they have become the 'vehicle for most rehabilitative activity'. However, this popularity may serve to continue the limited use of more specific and appropriate interventions, such as those that could be undertaken as part of a MHTR. Given the high levels of mental health problems among those under probation supervision in the community (see Chapter 7 for a discussion), the limited use of the MHTR is of concern. However, as we discuss later in the chapter, the new community treatment requirement protocol being piloted in some areas of England may change this.

COURT LIAISON AND DIVERSION (L&D) SCHEMES

To reiterate previous discussions, policies to divert people with mental health problems from the criminal justice system have been around for some time. The Home Office (1990, 1995) circulars 66/90 and 12/95 encouraged and reinforced the need for cooperation between the criminal justice, health and social services to ensure that those suffering from a mental disorder received appropriate care and treatment, whether or not proceedings were brought. Similarly, the Reed Report (Department of Health and Home Office, 1992) suggested that high-quality care should be provided by health and social services (not in the criminal justice system) according to individual need, close to the patient's home or family, and in conditions of no greater security than is justified. The central implications being for patients that they should not be disadvantaged by their status as offenders, and that

> [t]here should be nationwide provision of properly resourced court assessment and diversion schemes and the further development of bail information schemes ... The longer-term future of many schemes is not yet assured but experience increasingly suggests that, where diversion schemes became established, these come to provide a broader multi-agency focus which, of itself, can make effective disposals easier.
>
> (Department of Health and Home Office, 1992: para 5.3.6)

Yet many years post Reed, reviews of the diversion initiatives put in place suggested that the national picture was far from ideal (Department of Health, 2009; NACRO, 2005). In 2009 Lord Bradley reported that while policy developments across both the health and criminal justice sectors had created a much more receptive background for diversion, the implementation of these initiatives had been inconsistent (Department of Health, 2009).

While there were many examples of good practice in the 'first wave' of diversion schemes that followed the Bradley report, the provision of mental health specialists in key locations, including courts, was still only patchy (Pakes and Winstone, 2010). Across the country there was significant variability in the composition and scope of services and that this led to significant variation in the reach and associated outcomes of L&D services (Dyer, 2013). The failure to successfully, and consistently, implement diversion schemes has been attributed to poor strategic and operational support, funding and provision of staffing that can support multiagency working (de Lacy, 2016). L&D schemes have often also failed because of competition within and between services for resources and disagreements about the best philosophical approach (Dyer, 2013). Another common criticism of L&D schemes is that the 'liaison' rather than 'diversion' aspect is generally more developed, with far more needing to be done in terms of actual diversion to health services (Public Health England, 2016).

These concerns aside, improvements do appear to have been made in the last five years. Between 2011 and 2013 the Department of Health developed a national L&D model (see NHS England (2014) for further details about this national model and its core aims) and in April 2014 ten pilot L&D schemes were launched across the country. Responsibility for the L&D programme also moved to NHS England in the same month. An evaluation of the implementation of this national model across ten pilot areas was generally positive, noting several significant changes (Disley et al., 2016). In terms of their impact on the courts, they found that judges and magistrates reported that the volume and quality of information provided to the court had improved, and that this information was making its way to the court in a more timely manner (Disley et al., 2016). The clearer provision of information gave some magistrates greater confidence in the decisions they were making, while the quicker availability of information helped to speed up court processes and may have contributed to less adjournments (Disley et al., 2016).

Following positive findings about these L&D services, extra injections of funding and further L&D initiatives have been implemented across the country (see Chapter 3). At the time of writing, it is estimated that there is approximately 75% of the country has access to L&D services, with the aim of achieving full coverage by 2020 (NHS England, 2016). L&D services take many forms, but common activities include: identification, screening, assessment and referral (see Box 5.2).

BOX 5.2 MAIN ACTIVITIES OF LIAISON AND DIVERSION (L&D) SERVICES

Identification: Criminal justice agencies working at the Police and Courts stages of the pathway are trained to recognise possible signs of vulnerability in people when they first meet them. They then alert their local L&D service about the person.

Screening: Once someone is identified as having a potential vulnerability, the L&D practitioner can go through screening questions to identify the need, level of risk and urgency presented. It also helps determine whether further assessment is required.

Assessment: Using approved screening and assessment tools, an L&D practitioner will undertake a more detailed assessment of the person's vulnerability. This provides more information on a person's needs and also whether they should be referred on for treatment or further support.

Referral: The L&D practitioner may refer someone to appropriate mainstream health and social care services or other relevant interventions and support services that can help. A person is also supported to attend their first appointment with any new services and the outcomes of referrals are recorded. L&D services will also provide a route to treatment for people whose offending behaviour is linked to their illness or vulnerability.

Source: www.england.nhs.uk/commissioning/
health-just/liaison-and-diversion/about/

MENTAL HEALTH COURTS

In more recent years, the traditional revolving door of adversarial criminal courts is gradually giving way to 'solution focused' courts that recognise psychosocial challenges, such as addiction and mental illness, along with problems with accommodation and unemployment, all contribute towards offending behaviour. New principles of 'therapeutic jurisprudence' utilise legal systems to incentivise offenders to actively engage with social agencies as a means of addressing the causes of their offending (McKenna, Skipworth and Pillai, 2017).

Mental health courts follow the 'therapeutic court' model of drug courts. Based upon ideas of therapeutic jurisprudence, they use various creative methods to enforce compliance with treatment in the community such as 'pre-adjudication suspension of prosecution of charges; post-plea strategies that suspend sentencing; and probation' (Griffin, Steadman and Petrila, 2002:1285). Mental health courts are dedicated to the processing of people with mental illness. The court has a 'mental health judge' with a particular interest in the area and cases are referred across from other courts if there is 'voluntary' agreement of the accused to participate. The court will liaise with mental health agencies and mandate participation in treatment programmes, mainly in the community. The court retains control and monitors the progress of the case. If the person fails to comply, the court can apply sanctions, either by continuing with the prosecution in cases where the process has been suspended at the pre-adjudication stage or by adopting another form of sentence in post-plea cases, including custodial sentences.

Mental health courts initially gained popularity in the US, growing from only 4 in 1997 to over 300 in 2017. This growth was due to the suggestion that many people with mental illnesses are 'overlooked, turned away or intimidated by the mental health system' and as a result 'landing in the criminal justice system at an alarming rate' (Council of State and Local Governments, 2002:xiii). While mental health courts have been popular, questions have been raised in the US about whether a court-based diversion programme that requires a person to be arrested to participate – and that might even send them to prison for non-compliance – fairly addresses the over-representation of people with serious mental illnesses in the criminal justice system (Seltzer, 2005).

While there are many methodological challenges involved with assessing the impact of mental health courts (Honegger, 2015), international evidence suggests that mental health courts can contribute to a reduction in reoffending (Centre for Justice Innovation, 2015). However, the UK has not experienced the same growth in mental health courts as the US. In 2009, in response to Lord Bradley's review of people with mental health problems or learning disabilities in the criminal justice system, pilot schemes were introduced in Brighton and Stratford. These schemes adopted a problem-solving approach to offenders with mental disorders while operating in the regular magistrates' court. In Stratford, a dedicated mental health court operated one day a week while in Brighton cases were heard among normal court lists (Winstone and Pakes, 2010:2).

The stated aims of the mental health court pilot projects were to develop a model for identifying offenders with mental disorders to help ensure that they receive appropriate treatment and to determine the potential costs of operating such a court (Winstone and Pakes,

2010). The pilot courts also sought to reduce recidivism among the mentally ill, to halt the revolving-door syndrome which persists and to improve access to treatment for offenders (Winstone and Pakes, 2010:1). All defendants are screened at the charge stage, resulting in a combined 4000 screenings during 2009–2010, with 547 deemed to require further assessment (Winstone and Pakes, 2010:10). Referrals were most often made by the police but could also be made by defence solicitors, the court, probation officers and custody officers. Self-referrals and referrals by friends and family were also permitted (Winstone and Pakes, 2010:15).

The initial findings from these pilots were promising and identified the core requirements for a nation-wide mental health court scheme (Winstone and Pakes, 2010:31). Of the 55 offenders given a MHTR as part of their community order, only nine were found to have breached (Winstone and Pakes, 2010). However, since the pilot, funding for the expansion of the project has not been forthcoming with James (2010:246) suggesting that the mental health court model is unlikely to find a place in England, since other diversion mechanisms, along with the law, enable more directly interventionist solutions to be adopted. Similarly, the Sainsbury Centre for Mental Health (2010) argues, in line with Bradley (Department of Health, 2009), that if L&D services are rolled out nationally (as is currently underway) there would be little need for dedicated mental health courts.

COMMUNITY TREATMENT REQUIREMENT PROTOCOL

While dedicated mental health courts have not materialised in England, other schemes to divert offenders away from custody do appear to be emerging. In August 2018, the Justice Secretary, David Gauke, announced plans to address the underlying cause of offending for those with mental health, alcohol and substance misuse (Ministry of Justice, 2018). Across five pilot areas, criminal justice and health services have signed up to a new protocol that will help to divert relevant offenders away from the frequently ineffective short-term custodial offences and towards treatment. The first of these pilot schemes began in Milton Keynes in October 2017. The other four sites are based in Birmingham, Plymouth, Sefton and Northampton.

The pilot sites aim to improve training and multiagency collaboration at the court stage to give sentencers greater confidence to make use of the treatment requirements that can be used as part of a community order (Ministry of Justice, 2018). The scheme allows psychologists to be present in court to assess offenders whose crime makes them eligible for a community order. Each pilot site is also supported a multidisciplinary group of staff from the National Probation Service (NPS), Community Rehabilitation Companies (CRCs), along with local third sector, L&D services and substance misuse providers (Ministry of Justice and Department of Health and Social Care, 2018).

Together, the government reports that the partnerships between these key agencies are helping to enable 'strong community and communication links along with the provision of services required to provide appropriate clinical interventions and support to this vulnerable group' (Ministry of Justice and Department of Health and Social Care, 2018:2). While it would be premature to try and evaluate the success of the five pilots, reports indicate that fewer short-term sentences, which are known to be ineffective at reducing recidivism, have been issued since the scheme was implemented.

DISCUSSION

While only a very small proportion of defendants receive a mental health disposal at court (Birmingham, Awonogun and Ryland, 2017), this chapter has highlighted a number of complex questions and processes that surround the prosecution, diversion and sentencing of defendants with mental disorder. The presumption of innocence, a defendant's right to a fair trial and the adversarial system are all well-established principles in the English legal system. However, the presence of mental disorder before and during trial, raises many very difficult challenges for the court. One of the key challenges is well captured by Peay (2016:1) who notes that

> for the courts the quandaries seem to revolve primarily around management of the perceived future risk posed by mentally disordered offenders. For the psychiatrists, they concern primarily the ethically problematic issue of contributing to decisions about punishment.

Another fundamental challenge is that while the court is required to make a series of binary decisions (e.g. fit/not fit to plead; guilty/not guilty; prison/hospital), medical practitioners (such as psychiatrists and psychologists) giving evidence and advice to the court tend to understand issues surrounding mental disorder and offending in terms of 'degrees'. It is thought to be rare for mental illness to completely deprive sufferers of rationality or control (Hudson, 1993) and as a result judges must juggle 'a series of imponderable dilemmas' that are raised by partial culpability and risk prediction (Peay, 2015:1).

The task is inherently problematic, especially the diversity of opinion among practitioners in the context of an adversarial legal process. As Harris (1999:12–13) observes, 'the idea that fine distinctions can be reliably drawn between the rational and the irrational, with precise degrees of responsibility ascribed to some configuration of person, incident, time and place, appears a little optimistic'. Similarly, Appelbaum (2008:197) warns against 'treading on morally perilous terrain' by attempting to offer evidence in court on the so-called 'ultimate issue', namely, criminal responsibility. The information provided by a medical professional at court may lead to a defendant receiving a longer than usual sentence because of heightened concerns about risk following a psychiatry or psychology report (McMurran, Khalifa and Gibbon, 2009). Psychiatry's role in sentencing may serve, not to divert offenders to the treatment they need, but may aggravate the punitiveness of sentencing (Peay, 2000:72). This situation inevitably makes it harder for psychiatrists to practice according to the ethical principle of acting in the best interests of the patient, weakening the doctor-patient relationship – an important point that we shall return to in Chapter 8.

FURTHER READING

For an accessible guide to mental health law in England and Wales see Barber, Brown and Martin (2017). For the Crown Prosecution Service guidance about the proper procedure when dealing with mentally disordered offenders see www.cps.gov.uk/legal/l_to_o/mentally_disordered_offenders/. For more information about the sentencing options available to the courts see Ministry of Justice (2008). For an interesting discussion of the tensions between the law and psychiatry see Wessely (2012). We have not included the latest (2016–2017 and 2017–2018) figures for the number of detentions made under Part III of the MHA 1983 (as amended by the MHA 2007) as these are incomplete, but for information about these see NHS Digital (2018).

REFERENCES

Appelbaum, P. (2008) 'Ethics and forensic psychiatry: Translating principles into practice', *Journal of the American Academy of Psychiatry and the Law*, 36(2): 195–200.

Barber, P., Brown, R. and Martin, D. (2017) *Mental health law in England and Wales: A guide for mental health professionals (Third edition)*, London: Sage.

Bickle, A. (2009) 'The interface between dangerous offender sentencing and psychiatry', *Mental Health Review Journal*, 14(1): 20–23.

Birmingham, L., Awonogun, O. and Ryland, H. (2017) 'Diversion from custody: An update', *BJPsych Advance*, 23(6): 375–384.

Centre for Justice Innovation (2015) *Problem-solving courts: An evidence review*, London: Centre for Justice Innovation.

Council of State and Local Governments (2002) *Criminal justice / mental health consensus project*, Kentucky: Council of State and Local Governments.

Crown Prosecution Service (CPS) (2017) *Mentally disordered offenders: Legal guidance*, London: CPS.

Crown Prosecution Service (CPS) (2018) *The code for Crown Prosecutors*, London: CPS.

Davoren, M., Byrne, O., O'Connell, O., O'Neill, H., O'Reilly, K. and Kennedy, H.G. (2015) 'Factors affecting length of stay in forensic hospital setting: Need for therapeutic security and course of admission', *BMC Psychiatry*, 15: 301.

de Lacy, C. (2016) 'The role of the mental health clinical nurse specialist in the Crown Court setting: Towards a best practice model' in Winstone, J. (ed.) *Mental health, crime and criminal justice*, Basingstoke: Palgrave Macmillan.

Delmage, E., Exworthy, T. and Blackwood, N. (2015) 'The "hybrid order": Origins and usage', *Journal of Forensic Psychiatry and Psychology*, 26(3): 325–336.

Department of Health (2009) *The Bradley Report. Lord Bradley's review of people with mental health problems or learning disabilities in the criminal justice system*, London: Department of Health.

Department of Health and Home Office (1992) *Review of health and social services for mentally disordered offenders and others requiring similar services – Final summary report*, London: Her Majesty's Stationery Office.

Disley, E., Taylor, C., Kruithof, K., Winpenny, E., Liddle, M., Sutherland, A., Lilford, R., Wright, S., McAteer, L. and Francis, V. (2016) *Evaluation of the offender liaison and diversion trial schemes*, Cambridge: RAND Corporation.

Durcan, G. (2016) *Mental health and criminal justice: Views from consultations across England and Wales*, London: Centre for Mental Health.

Dyer, W. (2013) 'Criminal justice diversion and liaison services: A path to success?' *Social Policy and Society*, 12(1): 31–45.

Eastman, N. (1996) 'Hybrid orders: An analysis of their likely effects on sentencing practice and on forensic psychiatric practice and services', *Journal of Forensic Psychiatry*, 7(3): 481–494.

Eastman, N. and Peay, J. (1998) 'Sentencing psychopaths: Is the 'Hospital and Limitation Direction' an ill-considered hybrid?', *Criminal Law Review*, February: 93–108.

Easton, S. and Piper, C. (2016) *Sentencing and punishment (Fourth edition)*, Oxford: Oxford University Press.

Fennell, P. and Yeates, V. (2002) '"To serve which master?" – Criminal justice policy, community care and the mentally disordered offender' in Buchanan, A. (ed.) *Care of the mentally disordered offender in the community*, Oxford: Oxford University Press.

Griffin, P., Steadman, H. and Petrila, J. (2002) 'The use of criminal charges and sanctions in mental health courts', *Psychiatric Services*, 53: 1285–1289.

Gunn, J. (2002) 'No excuses', *Journal of the Royal Society of Medicine*, 95(2): 61–63.

Harris, R. (1999) 'Mental disorder and social order: Underlying themes in crime management' in Webb, D. and Harris, R. (eds.) *Mentally disordered offenders: Managing people nobody owns*, London: Routledge.

Harrison, K. (2011) *Dangerousness, risk and the governance of serious sexual and violent offenders*, Abingdon: Routledge.

Her Majesty's (HM) Inspectorate of Probation (2017) *The implementation and delivery of Rehabilitation Activity Requirements*, Manchester: HM Inspectorate of Probation.

Hillier, J. and Mews, A. (2018) *Do offender characteristics affect the impact of short custodial sentences and court orders on reoffending*, London: Ministry of Justice.

Holmes, R. (1895) 'Insanity as a defence in criminal law', *Historical Theses and Dissertations Collection*, Paper 68.

Home Office (1990) *Home Office circular no. 66/90, Provision for mentally disordered offenders*, London: Home Office.

Home Office (1995) *Home Office circular no. 12/95, Mentally disordered offenders: Inter-agency working*, London: Home Office.

Home Office and Department of Health and Social Security (1975) *Committee on mentally abnormal offenders*, London: Her Majesty's Stationery Office.

Honegger, L.N. (2015) 'Does the evidence support the case for mental health courts? A review of the literature', *Law and Human Behaviour*, 39(5): 478–488.

Hopkins, N. (2000) 'Bomber gets six life terms', *The Guardian*, 1 July 2000. Available from: www.theguardian.com/uk/2000/jul/01/uksecurity.nickhopkins [Last accessed 1 December 2017].

Hotopf, M., Wall, S., Buchanan, A., Wessely, S. and Churchill, R. (2000) 'Changing patterns in the use of the Mental Health Act 1983 in England, 1984–1996', *British Journal of Psychiatry*, 176: 479–484.

Howell, T. (1800) 'Trial of James Hadfield for high treason' in *27 Howell's State Trials 1281*, London: T.C. Hansard.

Hudson, B.A. (1993) *Understanding justice: An introduction to ideas, perspectives and controversies in modern penal theory*, Buckingham: Open University Press.

James, D. (2010) 'Diversion of mentally disordered people from the criminal justice system in England and Wales: An overview', *International Journal of Law and Psychiatry*, 33(4): 241–248.

Law Commission (2010) *Unfitness to plead. The Law Commission consultation paper no. 197*, London: Law Commission.

Law Commission (2016) *Unfitness to plead, Volume 1: Report*, London: Law Commission.

Loughnan, A. (2016) 'Between fairness and "dangerousness": Reforming the law on unfitness to plead', *Criminal Law Review*, 7: 451–466.

MacKay, R. Mitchell, B. and Howe, L. (2007) 'A continued upturn in unfitness to plead – More disability in relation to trial under the 1991 Act', *Criminal Law Review*, July: 530–545.

McKenna, B., Skipworth, J. and Pillai, K. (2017) 'Mental health care and treatment in prisons: A new paradigm to support best practice', *World Psychiatry*, 16(1): 3–4.

McMurran, M., Khalifa, N. and Gibbon, S. (2009) *Forensic mental health*, Cullompton: Willan Publishing.

Ministry of Justice (2008) *Mental Health Act 2007: Guidance for the courts on remand and sentencing powers for mentally disordered offenders*, London: Ministry of Justice.

Ministry of Justice (2018) 'Vulnerable offenders steered towards treatment' [Press release], 10 August 2018. Available from: www.gov.uk/government/news/vulnerable-offenders-steered-towards-treatment [Last accessed 19 October 2018].

Ministry of Justice and Department of Health and Social Care (2018) *Community sentence treatment requirement protocol*, London: Ministry of Justice and Department of Health and Social Care.

Moran, R. (1985) 'The modern foundation for the insanity defence: The cases of James Hadfield (1800) and Daniel McNaughten (1843)', *Annals of the American Academy of Political and Social Science*, 477(1): 31–42.

NACRO (2005) *Findings of the 2004 survey of court diversion / criminal justice liaison schemes for mentally disordered offenders in England and Wales*, London: NACRO.

National Health Service (NHS) Digital (2016) *Inpatients formally detained in hospital under the Mental Health Act 1983, and patients subject to supervised community treatment. Uses of the Mental Health Act: Annual statistics 2015/16*, London: NHS Digital.

National Health Service (NHS) Digital (2018) *Mental Health Act statistics, Annual figures 2017/18*, London: NHS Digital.

National Health Service (NHS) England (2016) *Implementing the five year forward view for mental health*, London: NHS England.

National Offender Management Service (NOMS) (2014) *Supporting Community Order treatment requirements*, London: NOMS.

Pakes, F. and Winstone, J. (2012) 'The mental health treatment requirement: The promise and the practice' in Pycroft, A. and Clift, S. (eds.) *Risk and rehabilitation: Management and treatment of substance misuse and mental health problems in the criminal justice system*, Bristol: Polity Press.

Peay, J. (2000) 'Surviving psychiatry in an era of 'popular punitiveness', *Acta Psychiatrica Scandinavica*, 101: 72–76.

Peay, J. (2015) 'Sentencing mentally disordered offenders: Conflicting objectives, perilous decisions and cognitive insights', *LSE Law, Society and Economy Working Papers*, 1/2015.

Peay, J. (2016) 'Responsibility, culpability and the sentencing of mentally disordered offenders: Objectives in conflict', *Criminal Law Review*, 3: 152–164.

Peay, J. (2017) 'Mental health, mental disabilities and crime' in Liebling, A., Maruna, S. and McAra, L. (eds.) *The Oxford handbook of criminology (Sixth edition)*, Oxford: Oxford University Press.

Perlin, M. (2016) 'The insanity defense: Nine myths that will not go away' in White, M.D. (ed.) *The insanity defense: Multidisciplinary views on its history, trends, and controversies*, Santa Barbara, CA: Praeger.

Perlin, M. and Cucolo, H. (2016) *Mental disability law: Civil and criminal*, Newark, New Jersey: Lexis Law Publishing.

Public Health England (2016) *Rapid review of evidence of the impact on health outcomes of NHS commissioned health services for people in secure and detained settings to inform future health interventions and prioritisation in England*, London: Public Health England.

Rogers, T., Blackwood, N., Farnham, F., Pickup, G. and Watts, M. (2009) 'Reformulating fitness to plead: A qualitative study', *Journal of Forensic Psychiatry and Psychology*, 20(6): 815–816.

Sainsbury Centre for Mental Health (2010) *Blurring the boundaries: The convergence of mental health and criminal justice policy, legislation, systems and practice*, London: Sainsbury Centre for Mental Health.

Schneider, B. (2010) *Hearing (our) voices: Participatory research in mental health*, Toronto: University of Toronto Press.

Scott, G. and Moffatt, S. (2012) *The Mental Health Treatment Requirement: Realising a better future*, London: Centre for Mental Health.

Seltzer, T. (2005) 'Mental health courts: A misguided attempt to address the criminal justice system's unfair treatment of people with mental illnesses'. *Psychology, Public Policy, and Law*, 11(4): 570–586.

Wessely, S. (2012) 'Anders Breivik, the public and psychiatry', *The Lancet*, 379(9826): 1563–1564.

West, D. and Walk, A. (1977) *Daniel McNaughton: His trial and the aftermath*, Kent: Gaskell Books.

Winstone, J. and Pakes, F. (2010) *Process evaluation of the Mental Health Court pilot*, London: Ministry of Justice.

NOTES

1   A Responsible Clinician (RC) has overall responsibility for a patient's case under the MHA 1983 (as amended by the MHA 2007). These responsibilities include making decisions about treatment, assessing if the criteria for detention are met, granting leaves of absence and authorizing discharge from detention (providing the patient is not restricted). Following changes under the MHA 2007 (which replaced the Responsible Medical Officer (RMO) with the RC), a range of staff other than doctors can now undertake this role, including psychologists, nurses, social workers and occupational therapists.

2   This guidance is available at www.gov.uk/government/publications/remand-and-sentencing-powers-for-mentally-disordered-offenders

3   Guardianship orders are where a guardian is appointed to help support someone with a mental disorder to live in the community, as an alternative to sectioning them and detaining them in hospital.

4   Patients in England will have their case heard by the First-tier Tribunal (Mental Health) in England. Patients in Wales will have their case heard by the Mental Health Review Tribunal for Wales.

5   The judgment states:

> in cases where medical evidence suggests mental disorder, the offending is party or wholly attributable to that disorder, treatment is available and a hospital order may be appropriate, the court should consider (and, if appropriate make) a s45A order before considering making a hospital order.

6   The option of requiring an offender to undertake mental health treatment has been around since the Criminal Justice Act 1948. Prior to the MHTR, the courts could make a Probation Order with a requirement for psychiatric treatment (see Fennell and Yeates (2002) for a brief review).

CHAPTER 6

Mental health, offending and secure detention

INTRODUCTION

Many people in prison have mental health problems and imprisonment is often thought to contribute to poor mental health. While the Mental Health Act (MHA) 1983 (as amended by the MHA 2007) allows for prisoners to be transferred to the mental health system for care, in practice, very few people will be transferred to hospital, and therefore the majority of prisoners with mental health problems will remain in prison. This chapter begins by examining the rates of mental disorder, self-harm and suicide in prisons before considering the key challenges involved with caring for those with mental disorder in a prison environment. The chapter outlines how people can be transferred from prison to secure mental health services in England and Wales, and then explores the challenges involved with detaining and treating offenders in these health settings. Throughout the chapter we explore the many conflicts that arise across these secure settings, as practitioners try to achieve a difficult balance between care and control.

RATES OF MENTAL DISORDER, SELF-HARM AND SUICIDE AMONG PRISONERS

On the 9th November 2018, 83,190 men and women were detained in prison in England and Wales. Ninety-five per cent of this figure was made up of men (79,361) and just under 5% (3,829) women (Ministry of Justice, 2018a). While prisoners are thought to have considerably higher rates of mental illness than the general population (Bebbington et al., 2017; Fazel and Seewald, 2012; Singleton et al., 1998), there are limited data about the *actual* level of mental health need among prisoners (National Audit Office, 2017). Many still rely on data published by the Office for National Statistics (ONS) in 1998 (Singleton et al., 1998); which aside from being more than 20 years old, has been criticised for using a very broad definition of mental disorder (National Audit Office, 2017).

Whatever the true picture, there is little dispute that prisoners have high levels of mental health problems. A recent study assessed 80% of women and 70% of male prisoners to have at least one mental health treatment need (Jakobowitz et al., 2017). Despite known challenges with access to and provision of mental health services in the community, a quarter of people in prison have used mental health services in the 12 months prior to their imprisonment (Bebbington et al., 2017). Using data from two London prisons, Bebbington et al. (2017) found that 12% of prisoners met the criteria for psychosis, 34.2% personality disorder, 53.8% for a depressive disorder and 26.8% an anxiety disorder. Nearly 70% of prisoners met the criteria for two or more disorders (Bebbington et al., 2017). In addition to having a higher prevalence of mental health problems, people in prison also experience mental health problems of a much higher severity, when compared to those in the general population (Bebbington et al., 2017).

Suicidal ideation and attempts have been linked to previous or current mental illness (Singleton et al., 1998). Therefore, the high levels of mental health problems in prison are thought to impact on the high levels of self-harm and suicide (Fazel et al., 2016). Self-harm and suicide in prison have increased significantly in the last few years, with a record high of over 40,000 self-harm incidents recorded across the prison estate in 2016 (Ministry of Justice, 2017b). These figures reflect a 73% increase of self-harm incidents in prisons between 2012 and 2016 (National Audit Office, 2017). Self-inflicted deaths have also more than doubled since 2013 with 113 self-inflicted deaths recorded between March 2016 and March 2017 (Ministry of Justice, 2017b).

Prisoners also have high levels of comorbidity (Brooker, Sirdifield and Gojkovic, 2007; Singleton et al., 1998) with around a third of prisoners dependent on alcohol and nearly 60% on illegal drugs (Bebbington et al., 2017). In addition, prisoners have a shorter life expectancy than the general population, reflecting more problems with their physical health (Zlodre and Fazel, 2012). Seven per cent of the prison population have a marked disability, 25% a borderline disability (Talbot, 2008) and nearly 50% a history of brain injury (Pitman, Haddlesy and Fortescue, 2013). Many health problems go undetected or untreated because offenders in prison often have poor access to (or poor engagement with) health services in the community. This is reflected by the fact that only about half of all prisoners are registered with a GP prior to their imprisonment (Social Exclusion Unit, 2002).[1]

PRISONS AND MENTAL HEALTH POLICY

Many changes have been made to prison mental health policy in the last 20 years. During the 1990s there were increasing calls to move the responsibility for prison health care from the Home Office to the National Health Service (NHS) (Department of Health and Home Office, 1992; Her Majesty's (HM) Inspectorate of Prisons, 1996; HM Prison Service and NHS Executive Working Group, 1999). In 1999 a formal partnership between HM Prison Service and the NHS was established along with the National Service Framework (NSF) for Mental Health (Department of Health 1999). Full responsibility for prison health care was eventually transferred from the prison service to NHS Primary Care Trusts (PCTs) in April 2006.[2] Responsibility for prison health care now rests with NHS England, who took over responsibility for the commissioning of health care services for prisoners (including drug and alcohol services but not emergency and/or out of hours services) from PCTs in April 2013. A National Partnership Agreement (NPA) to improve mental health care in prisons has been made between NHS England, Her Majesty's Prison and Probation Service (HMPPS) and Public Health England (who are responsible for advising HMPPS and NHS England) (HM Government and NHS England, 2018), and it is believed that this has improved the engagement of each of these agencies (Public Health England, 2016).

While the transfer of responsibility for health care commissioning to the NHS is generally thought to be positive and as having contributed to significant improvements in health outcomes (Hayton and Boyington, 2006; Public Health England, 2016), Hales et al. (2016) assert that these developments reflect an increasing acceptance that many offenders with mental health problems can remain in prison for treatment. This is evidenced by the proliferation of guidelines to support prison mental health care, including the Department of Health and National Institute for Mental Health in England's (NIMHE) (2015) *Offender Mental Health Care Pathway*, Royal College of Psychiatrists (2015) quality standards for prison mental health care and National

Institute for Health and Care Excellence (NICE) (2017) guidelines concerning the mental health of adults in contact with the criminal justice system. Importantly, government policy has long been that the health care provided in prisons should be of an 'equivalent' standard to that provided in the community (HM Government and Department of Health, 2011; HM Prison Service and NHS Executive Working Group, 1999; World Health Organization, 2013) and that 'prisoners should have access to the same range and quality of services appropriate to their needs as are available to the general population' (Department of Health and HM Prison Service, 2001:5).

While improvements in provision can be observed since the NHS took over responsibility for prison mental health, in-reach services continue to fall short of community equivalence (Patel, Harvey and Forrester, 2018). One of the key challenges with achieving 'equivalence' is that it is 'not clear what an "equivalent service" means in practice or how this could be measured' (National Audit Office, 2017:7). One of the reasons for this is that the original NSF in 1999 did not indicate how the standards should be applied within a prison setting and, in fact, made no reference to prisons (Prisons and Probation Ombudsman, 2016). An additional challenge is identified by Senior, Appleby and Shaw (2014:58) who argue that 'equivalence cannot simply be taken to mean the same' because prisons need to be more adaptive to the different levels and types of mental disorder and suicide risk found in prisons. Prisoners experience considerable social inequality in their wider social environments and this structural determinate has an important impact on the quality of care they receive in prison (de Viggiani, 2007). The higher levels of need in prisons and the lack of corresponding funding led the majority of staff in Caulfield and Twort's (2012:11) research to express doubts that equivalence could be achieved. Prisons are 'likely to be burdened with more frequent consultation for less important medical conditions than in an equivalent community setting', in part, because prisoners have less opportunities for self or informal care (Marshall, Simpson and Stevens, 2007:855). While prisoners are often not registered with a GP in the community (Social Exclusion Unit, 2002), in prison, they are five times more likely than persons of the same age to consult a doctor (Marshall, Simpson and Stevens, 2007).

In addition to some of these practical challenges, it is important to be mindful that the system of imprisonment in England and Wales has historically been structured around the principle of 'less eligibility' and the notion that those incarcerated in prison should not have a better standard of living than those who do not offend in the community. Pycroft and Green (2016:151) argue that the 'principle of less eligibility is a powerful socio-political and ideological process that discriminates most profoundly against already vulnerable people'. It is difficult to imagine how a system historically structured on a principle of less eligibility, and one that is subject to regular public and political scrutiny in terms of its cost, can deliver a system truly based on equivalence.

IDENTIFICATION AND ASSESSMENT OF MENTAL HEALTH PROBLEMS IN PRISON

When a prisoner is received into custody, an assessment of their health care needs should be undertaken within 24 hours by an appropriately trained member of health care staff. Efforts should be made to gather relevant information from previous health care services including the prisoner's GP. If the prisoner is suspected of having mental health difficulties, appropriate referrals should be made and if a prisoner is particularly unwell, consideration should be given to a hospital transfer under the MHA 1983 (as amended by the MHA 2007).

Some improvements in prison health care and the identification of mental health problems have been made since the Bradley report (Public Health England, 2016). For example, Brown et al. (2015) found that relatively inexpensive local provisions, such as the use of Community Psychiatric Nurses (CPNs) in prison receptions, had served to improve prison mental health pathways. Similarly, mechanisms to support the early detection of mental health problems among a sample of young people in prison has been reported by Evans et al. (2017) to have had a positive impact on mental health outcomes and a reduction in returns to prison.

Unfortunately, and despite improved screening procedures on arrival to prison, many challenges with identifying mental health needs in prisons remain (Prisons and Probation Ombudsman, 2016). While prisoners are screened by prison and health care staff when they arrive in prison, this screening does not always identify mental health problems (National Audit Office, 2017). One of the reasons for this may follow from the fact that screening may be undertaken by staff without a primary mental health expertise and/or those without specific training, such as Registered General Nurses (RGNs) (Wright, Jordan and Kane, 2014). If mental health problems are not picked up when prisoners arrive in prison they should be identified during a prisoner's sentence. However, health care staff in Wright, Jordan and Kane's (2014:183) research expressed concerns that prison health care is 'mainly reactive in nature and lacking a preventative care pathway'. As a result, there is an over-reliance on screening for mental disorder at reception and insufficient opportunities at other points of a prisoner's sentence to identify mental health needs (Wright, Jordan and Kane, 2014).

Of course, one of the problems is that a prisoner's mental health will vary over time (Haney, 2017) and while changes in mental health may sometimes be recognised by prison staff, staffing and resource challenges make this more difficult and less likely (National Audit Office, 2017). In addition, there is evidence that mental health knowledge among prison staff may be inadequate (Wright, Jordan and Kane, 2014) and that more needs to be done to support early intervention services (Public Health England, 2016).

Another challenge for the identification of mental health problems in prisons follows from the challenges involved with information sharing. Samele et al. (2017) report that once people arrive in prison, any prior information about their mental health may not necessarily be passed from the police or the court to the prison. While the sharing of health information between different prisons is reported to have improved following the introduction of SystmOne (a clinical IT system that is used in prisons) (Durcan, 2016), Slade et al. (2016) report that mental health information is not always recorded on this system. As a result of concerns about the reliability of computer systems and anxieties about the confidentiality of prisoners, Wright, Jordan and Kane (2014:183) found evidence of 'a hierarchal inter- and intra-professional desire to not share data and retain ownership of it'. This means that only minimal information about prisoners with mental health problems is recorded on electronic systems (Wright, Jordan and Kane, 2014). While informal communication can often work well it can also lead to a lack of structured and formally recorded documentation (Wright, Jordan and Kane, 2014). Moreover, 'amicable joint-working in these settings is not standard practice but is instead both personnel and personality dependent' (Wright, Jordan and Kane, 2014:184). This raises important implications in terms of equity and equivalence of provision as well as for the continuity of care for those with mental health problems detained in prison.

PROVISION OF MENTAL HEALTH TREATMENT IN PRISONS

Prisons usually have two levels of health care services: primary and secondary. Primary health care services in prison are made up of the same elements as found in the community and usually consist of GPs, dentists and nursing staff, whereas secondary mental health care in prisons is mainly comprised of mental health in-reach teams (MHITs) (sometimes referred to as Secondary Mental Health Teams) (Durcan, 2016). MHITs in prisons were introduced in 2004 to try and improve mental health provision for those detained in prison (Sharpe et al., 2016; Steel et al., 2007). All prisons should have MHITs as part of the *Offender Mental Health Care Pathway* (Department of Health and NIMHE, 2005).

Following assessment, prisoners may be offered medication for their mental health problems. In addition to, or as an alternative to medication, prisoners may also be offered psychological therapies for their mental health problems. Those with particularly severe mental health problems, including those awaiting transfer to the mental health system, may be detained in an inpatient health care facility within the prison. It is important to remember, however, that these prison-based facilities are not regarded as hospitals under the MHA 1983 (as amended by the MHA 2007) and therefore compulsory treatment cannot be given.

OTHER TREATMENT SERVICES AVAILABLE IN PRISON

Offenders with mental health problems may also access a number of other treatment services in prison. These include drug and alcohol treatment services which are commonly provided by the Counselling, Assessment, Referral, Advice and Throughcare (CARAT) team. Another service, the Integrated Drug Treatment System (IDTS), aims to ensure that drug users in prison can access the same treatment as in the community.

To address their offending behaviour, prisoners with mental health problems may be offered accredited Offending Behaviour Programmes (OBPs). However, there are concerns that these programmes may be less effective because their focus is often quite general and they often have not been adapted for use with people with mental health problems (Harrison, 2011) (see Chapter 1 for a discussion). In any case, prisoners with mental health problems may also find themselves excluded from such interventions on the basis of having been diagnosed with a mental health problem.

In addition to the provision of accredited OBPs, there are a limited number of therapeutic communities (TC) within the prison estate. Places are usually reserved for offenders with complex offending and/ or mental health problems who are willing to engage with treatment. The most famous is Grendon Underwood which opened in 1962.[3]

Often described as a 'psychiatric prison', 'every aspect of prison life is an important component' under the TC model and offender treatment does not happen in isolation from the wider regime (Brookes, 2010:103). While limited research has been undertaken with TCs and mentally disordered offenders, the results have been promising (Knabb, Welsh and Graham-Howard, 2011). TCs have been celebrated for their lower rates of problematic institutional behaviour, self-harm and reconviction rates in comparison to similar security prisons and for their embodiment of welfarist values that seek to minimise harm and offer opportunities for offenders to change as part of a 'wider system of inclusive social justice' (Bennett and Shuker, 2017:23). However, most TCs have been developed in the psychiatric system, and despite some rejuvenation of their promise with personality disorder, they remain marginal in the penal system (McBride, 2017).

The Offender Personality Disorder (OPD) pathway emerged in 2011 and followed from the dismantling of the controversial DSPD Programme (see Chapter 3). Part of this initiative has involved an increasing focus on 'psychologically informed' and 'enabling environments'. Enabling environments are not specific to prisons or the OPD pathway but are settings that follow standards set out by the Royal College of Psychiatrists (2013). Bennett and Shuker (2017:23) argue that these standards represent 'an attempt to formalise, disseminate and promote elements of TCs that can influence wider institutional practices'. Examples of these new environments include new 'Psychologically Informed Planned Environments' (PIPEs) which have been set up across the male and female prison estate and in a small number of approved premises (APs) in the community. PIPEs aim to provide a supportive environment for prisoners with possible personality disorder to 'prepare' for treatment or 'consolidate' what they have learnt following treatment. A national evaluation of their effectiveness is currently underway, but early qualitative findings about their value can be found in Turley, Payne and Webster (2013).

CHALLENGES INVOLVED WITH MENTAL HEALTH IN PRISONS

OVER-RELIANCE ON MEDICATION

Historically, interventions in prison have been criticised for being structured by security and control rather than treatment and rehabilitation (Sim, 1990). One method of controlling prisoners has been the use of medication (Sim, 1990) and prior to the introduction of MHITs the 'main psychiatric interventions came from the medication cabinets of prison healthcare wings' (Noyce, 2012:58). This reflects how the prison service has often placed a greater priority on treating offenders with medication rather than therapeutic alternatives (Harrison, 2011). While the growth of psychological therapies in prisons may lead some to argue this has changed, research undertaken by the Howard League for Penal Reform and Centre for Mental Health (2016) found that prisoners regarded mental health services in prison to still mainly revolve around the provision of medication. While most people in prison report having a free choice as to whether to take their medication, some may nevertheless feel coerced into taking medication in order to avoid the threat of sanctions and to ensure they are regarded positively by the Parole Board (Mills et al., 2011). Indeed, research suggests that some prisoners are mistrusting of the use of medication and regard it as a mechanism of control rather than support (Howard League for Penal Reform and Centre for Mental Health, 2016).

POOR TREATMENT AVAILABILITY

Even when mental health problems are identified, access to appropriate support and services may still be difficult. Unmet needs are high in prison, with a recent study finding that 32% of prisoners have unmet medication needs, and 51% unmet needs for psychological treatment (Jakobowitz et al., 2017). Part of the problem is that early identification alone is unlikely to improve access to treatment (Caulfield and Twort, 2012). While many prison staff are sufficiently trained to provide good healthcare the barriers to them succeeding are often structural and related to the establishment (Jordan, 2017). Prisons represent an 'unpredictable working environment' with a high turnover of clients who may be eligible for health care (Jordan, 2017). Moreover, access problems follow from the limited resources available and because the demand for mental health support is far higher than these resources permit (Durcan, 2016). Durcan (2016) argues that primary mental health care in prisons is currently the weakest element of mental health support because they have limited provision to address a skewed population with very high level of needs. Consequently, the quality of primary health care can be affected by the size of the prison and the specific characteristics of the prisoners, as well as by organisational issues including the commitment to health care among senior management (Fraser, 2014). Wright, Jordan and Kane (2014:182) also remind us that 'mental illness does not confine itself to office hours' and this can create problems in prisons when specialist mental health provision usually only operates between 9 and 5 pm during the working week. Prisoners experiencing out-of-hours crises may be particularly disadvantaged (Wright, Jordan and Kane, 2014).

MHITs have been criticised for being under resourced, weighed down with referrals and for offering only a limited range of treatment interventions (Sainsbury Centre for Mental Health, 2006). In practice, only a small number of prisoners with serious mental illness are reviewed by the MHIT (Senior et al., 2013). MHITs are supposed to operate as a secondary specialist provision; however, some have merged with primary health care services which has led to mission 'creep' or 'stretch' (Durcan, 2016:23). In addition, psychological interventions for prisoners with mental health problems appear to be a 'relatively rare commodity' (Durcan, 2016:21; see also Brooker and Gojkovic, 2009). As a result of many prisoners not meeting the threshold for a referral to mental health services, many people who still have a high level of need, receive little support during their imprisonment (Howard League for Penal Reform and Centre for Mental Health, 2016). This is important because unmet needs have implications for the welfare of the individual prisoner and the functioning of the criminal justice system (Jakobowitz et al., 2017; Public Health England, 2016).

STAFFING AND RESOURCES IN PRISONS

In a review of prison mental health services, Brooker and Webster (2017:48) note that resources have grown significantly and 'have never been better'. While prison mental health work can be challenging for staff (Smith, 2010) enjoyment, feelings of safety and job satisfaction are also reported by prison staff (Jordan, 2017). However, between 2010 and 2016, the National Offender Management Service (NOMS) (now HMPPS) budget was reduced by nearly a quarter (NOMS, 2016a) and the number of operational frontline staff in prisons reduced by 26% (Ministry of Justice, 2017a). In the same period, the number of inexperienced frontline prison staff is reported to have risen (Prison Reform Trust, 2017). These staffing challenges have had a negative impact on safety (Howard League for Penal Reform and Centre for Mental Health, 2016) and affect not only the order of a prison but also its legitimacy (Crewe, Liebling and Hulley, 2014).

To add to some of the staffing challenges surrounding frontline custodial staff, there are also problems with the numbers and quality of health care staff. Forrester et al. (2013) report that there is approximately one nurse for every 500 prisoners and one doctor for more than 3,700. This reflects that resources continue to be a key challenge, and that the lack of adequate funding and staff has made it difficult to properly implement adequate prison mental health care (Caulfield and Twort, 2012). Public Health England (2016:41) reports that prisons are highly dependent on agency staff and that this represents poor value for money in terms of cost as well as the 'continuity of care/ working knowledge of local systems'. In addition, changes in the prison estate have sometimes not been communicated well enough to NHS England and this has led to problems with provision (National Audit Office, 2017).

In addition to the challenges surrounding the levels and experience of frontline staff, concerns have also been expressed about their lack of training, supervision and support. The National Audit Office (2017) reports that prison officers do not undertake regular mental health training while prison staff in Durcan's (2008) research indicate that even when mental health awareness courses are offered, they are poorly attended. To address concerns around the inadequacy of staff training, the Justice Secretary announced in March 2018 that the government was investing in mental health awareness training for prison staff (Ministry of Justice, 2018b) with all new prison officers to be given improved suicide and self-harm prevention training (HMPPS, 2018).

A HEALTHY ENVIRONMENT TO DELIVER TREATMENT?

By offering prisoners an opportunity for respite from their often chaotic and unpredictable lives in the community, prison can act as a 'stabiliser' (Durcan, 2008:31). Some offenders report that imprisonment can be positive in that it also affords them clearer opportunities for treatment and support (Douglas et al., 2009; Harner and Riley, 2012; Trebilcock, 2011). Prison may enable people to access mental health care (Jordan, 2017), while the structure afforded by the prison routine may increase compliance with medication (Mills et al., 2011). Accessing health care in the prison environment may also be easier than in the community and prisoners may find it preferable to spend time in a waiting room than in their cell (Marshall, Simpson and Stevens, 2007:853). While the prison environment, culture and regime may serve as a barrier to good health, prisons may also offer an opportunity for 'effective and sustained contact' with health care (Public Health England, 2016:30). Moreover, the prison environment may be positive for its ability to set boundaries and encourage offenders to 'confront the unacceptability of their offending and to take responsibility for their actions' (Department of Health, 2009:15).

However, concerns remain about the significant challenges involved with looking after mentally disordered offenders in prison. Anxieties about the impact of imprisonment on an individual's well-being and mental health can be traced back to the emergence of the prison system (Johnston, 2016:30–31). The two systems of mental health and imprisonment are 'inextricably intertwined' and it would be both impossible and irresponsible to try and study the nature of prison life without acknowledging the large amounts of mental illness that are involved (Haney, 2017:312). Despite recognition of this point, and a considerable growth in the literature about imprisonment and mental health, the challenges of providing mental health care in the prison environment have often received 'no more than a tokenistic mention' (Mills and Kendall, 2016:187). However, there is generally a consensus in the literature that the prison environment is unlikely to be conducive to, or support, good mental health (Goomany and Dickinson, 2015). The characteristics of the prison environment have been shown to influence suicide (van Ginneken et al., 2017) and 'in comparison with other penalties, imprisonment is associated with the highest levels of reoffending and the deterioration of inmates' mental health and social exclusion' (Player, 2017:2). Indeed, 'prisons epitomise the antithesis of a healthy setting' (de Viggiani, 2007:115).

The prison environment itself can undermine efforts to address mental health problems because many of the facilities are old (having been built a long time ago and without modern health care in mind) (National Audit Office, 2017). The environment is also under considerable pressure as cuts to public service have taken hold (Durcan, 2016). Lower staffing levels can impact on operational issues such as the amount of time prisoners spend out of their cells, and this can limit prisoner access to health care (Public Health England, 2016). The inflexibility of prison routines can create difficulties for treatment adherence (Mills et al., 2011) while moves around the prison estate can undermine treatment efforts (National Audit Office, 2017). Staff interviewed as part of a Public Health England (2016:42) rapid review of evidence felt that health care services in prisons were '"clock/regime centred" rather than "person centred"'. The size of the prison population, population turnover and the prison's level of security have all been found to impact on the rates of suicide at individual establishments (van Ginneken et al., 2017).

The prison system has been consistently overcrowded every year since 1994 (Prison Reform Trust, 2017), and this adds to the challenge of trying to support prisoners with mental health problems. It can limit the availability of key resources, including those that may help with rehabilitation and reducing reoffending. Moreover, staff shortages (Howard League for Penal Reform and Centre for Mental

Health, 2016), too much time in cell and a lack of purposeful activity (Harris, 2015), are thought to contribute to the rates of suicide in prison. Conviction and imprisonment may precipitate feelings of hopelessness and depression as prisoners process their deprivation of liberty (Marshall, Simpson and Stevens, 2007:836).

Other features of the environment are of note. The rise of 'legal highs', in particular synthetic cannabis is creating numerous problems for prisons (Durcan, 2016). The use of these new psychoactive substances has contributed to increasing violence (Shafi et al., 2017). Assaults have also reached a record high with 26,022 incidents recorded in the 12 months to December 2016 and the number of serious assaults on staff and prisoners having trebled since 2012 (Ministry of Justice, 2017b). This data suggests that victimisation, including bullying, is a largely 'taken for granted' aspect of imprisonment and something that is widespread (Gooch and Treadwell, 2015).

There are also considerable challenges involved with providing mental health treatment in a prison setting (Jordan, 2011). Smedley (2010) identifies many of these including practical issues that follow from the prison routine or as a result of prisoner movement between different establishments, demand outstripping supply, information sharing and issues surrounding confidentiality. It is also important to remember that a high number of prisoners have suffered from past trauma (Krammer et al., 2017) and 'typically have extensive trauma histories that include chronic poverty and deprivation, severe forms of emotional, physical and sexual abuse, and abject neglect' (Haney, 2017:312). Given that imprisonment itself can re-invoke past trauma (Short and Barber 2004) the challenges involved with promoting good mental health in prison are clear.

While the provision of specialist units appear to provide promising treatment possibilities, the relationship between specialist units and their host institutions can sometimes be a source of tension within the prison system (Cooke, Stephenson and Rose, 2017; Trebilcock and Weaver, 2010). Tensions also sometimes arise between different staff groupings. In a qualitative study of a specialist personality disorder treatment unit, Cooke, Stephenson and Rose (2017) identify a number of tensions that can arise between disciplinary and clinical staff. Disciplinary staff identified that they sometimes felt clinical staff could be condescending as well as naïve to security issues while clinical staff indicated that disciplinary staff could undermine therapeutic efforts. In other research, Wright, Jordan and Kane (2014) found that difficult working relationships exist throughout the prison with some mental health staff characterising other prison staff as unrealistic about what mental health services could be provided.

Despite the challenges with providing treatment, many prisons have become default placements for the mentally ill in the absence of more appropriate and humane settings to treat them (Haney, 2017). In the US, Markowitz (2011:38) argues that prisons have become 'dysfunctional alternatives to psychiatric hospitals'. This is especially the case for prisoners held in solitary confinement in the US where prisons have become *de facto* mental health facilities to cope with the level of unmet mental health needs (Jeffreys, 2016; see also Haney, 2017:321). Suicide attempts and self-harm can in themselves be treated as disciplinary infractions and prisoners may find themselves in segregation as a result (Haney, 2017). Isolation in prison causes additional mental pain and suffering (Haney, 2017) and 'many of the direct negative psychological effects of isolation mimic or parallel specific symptoms of mental illness' thereby exacerbating a prisoner's mental illness (Haney, 2017:322) (see also Shalev, 2008).

It is for many of the reasons above that imprisonment is thought to exacerbate mental health problems. Many health problems arise as a direct consequence of the conditions of imprisonment (de Viggiani, 2007), with the nature of imprisonment likely to cause distress and worsen the mental state of those detained (Marshall, Simpson and Stevens, 2007). While this review may lead some to advocate that more treatment in the secure mental health system should be offered to offenders who need it, there are considerable challenges with accessing this scarce resource. Moreover, this parallel system of secure care has its own set of challenges, as we explore in the sections that now follow.

DETENTION OF OFFENDERS IN SECURE MENTAL HEALTH SERVICES

Those with particularly acute mental health needs may be transferred from prison to the secure mental health system for assessment or specialist care. However, this is only one route into secure mental health services and people who have offended may also arrive from court or the community. Most patients in secure mental health services are detained under the MHA 1983 (as amended by the MHA 2007), but some may be admitted informally, and not under mental health legislation.

On the 31st March 2016 NHS Digital (2016) reports that 20,151 were detained in hospital under the MHA 2007, the highest number since NHS Digital began collecting publishing statistics in 2005–2006. Seventy per cent (n=14,197) were detained in NHS facilities and the remaining 30% (n=5,954) were detained in privately run facilities, reflecting a continuing increase in the number of patients detained in independently run secure mental health services (NHS Digital, 2016).

Those who are formally detained can be admitted to hospital under a range of different powers under the MHA 1983 (as amended by the MHA 2007). Part II of the MHA 1983 sets out the main provisions for compulsory admission to hospital under the Act for 'civil' patients, that is, people not involved with criminal proceedings. The main provisions allow for individuals to be admitted for 28 days for assessment under section 2 of the Act, initially for six months for treatment under section 3 or for up to 72 hours in an emergency under section 4. Those involved with criminal proceedings are usually detained under Part III of the MHA 1983. The main provisions in Part III of the MHA 2007 include the following: s35/s36 remand to hospital for assessment/treatment, s37 hospital order, s45A hospital and limitations direction, and s47/s48 transfers from prison. Further information about s35-s45A has already been given in Chapter 5, so we limit our discussion here to s47/48.

Section 47 of the MHA 1983 allows a sentenced prisoner to be transferred to hospital for assessment and treatment, whereas s48 enables the transfer to hospital of a prisoner on remand. In 2016–2017, 1,081 people with mental illness were transferred to a secure hospital from prison (National Audit Office, 2017). The most common diagnosis among those transferred to hospital under s47 or s48 is schizophrenia, followed by a depressive disorder (Marshall, Simpson and Stevens, 2007). Guidance stipulates that prisoners eligible to be admitted to a secure hospital should be transferred within 14 days (Department of Health, 2011). Transfers are approved by the Mental Health Casework Section in HMPPS. However, delays in transferring prisoners to hospital are common, and often far exceed the 14-day target (Bartlett et al., 2012; Sharpe et al., 2017) with only 34% of cases transferred in this time during 2016–2017 (National Audit Office, 2017). Numerous reasons for delays can be identified including problems with transport, communication, the transfer of patient records and challenges with identifying a suitable bed (Forrester et al., 2009, 2010). The process of transferring prisoners to hospital is complex and the relevant government departments (HMPPS/NHS England) are unable to report how many prisoners are currently waiting transfer (National Audit Office, 2017). Prior to transfer under s47, these offender-patients often have high levels of behavioural problems, adjudications and self-harm (Shaw et al., 2008) so long delays may negatively impact on a person's mental health and increase the likelihood of them being held in an unsuitable prison location, such as a segregation unit, while they wait for a bed to be found.

Jewesbury and McCulloch (2002:53) report that there was a measurable and large increase in the number of prisoners transferred to the mental health system in the early 1990s, after which it remained fairly stable at around 750 per year until the time of their analysis. From 2003, Birmingham, Awonogun and Ryland (2017) report that transfers to hospital under s47/48 began to rise steadily again. Recent statistics about detention under the MHA published by NHS Digital (2016) reports that detentions under Part III have declined since 2011–2012 from 2,130 to 1,696 in 2015–2016. However, this decline is mainly explained by the courts using less s37 hospital orders. Indeed, a recent analysis of the rates of detention under the MHA 1983 (as amended by the MHA 2007) by Keown et al. (2018) reports that between 1984–1985 and 2015–2016 the use of court orders fell by 37% while transfers from prison increased by 717%.

Section 37 hospital orders and s47 transfers from prison may also be restricted under s41 or s49 of the MHA 1983. A restriction order means that a patient cannot be given a leave of absence, transferred or discharged by the Responsible Clinician (RC) (the practitioner with overall responsibility for the care and treatment of someone detained under the MHA) without the permission of the Secretary of State. Beswick and Gunn (2017:68) highlight that its duration is indefinite and that it is 'the closest mental health equivalent to a life sentence'. A s49 means that it is possible to return to the patient to prison if they get better and that they will not be released by the hospital to the community unless their prison sentence has expired. At the end of October 2016, there were 7,171 restricted patients in the system; 4,690 were detained in hospital, and 2,481 were in the community following a conditional discharge (NOMS, 2016b). For more information about restricted patients in England and Wales see Ministry of Justice and HMPPS (2017).

Each year approximately 7,700 secure beds in the mental health system are commissioned by NHS England. Secure mental health beds are provided in three different levels of security: high, medium and low with each providing 'a range of physical, procedural and relational security measures to ensure effective treatment and care whilst providing for the safety of the individual and others including other patients, staff and the general public' (NHS England, 2016:5). There are also a range of other inpatient-based services which are less secure, including acute and long-stay wards for adults, as well as specialised wards for women, children and adolescents, older people, and those with a learning disability (Care Quality Commission

(CQC), 2017). While the number of NHS-funded mental health beds has fallen substantially in the last 30 years from nearly 70,000 in 1987 to only 18,700 in March 2017 (Kentish, 2017; see also Galappathie, Khan and Hussain, 2017), the number of secure mental health beds has been increasing (Centre for Mental Health, 2011:23). It is of note that much of this growth has been in medium security services (Abbott et al., 2005) which may explain the limited investment in lower security and community services (Centre for Mental Health, 2011).

HIGH SECURITY HOSPITALS

Despite their long history, high security hospitals remain largely misunderstood (Gatawa, 2016). There are currently three high security hospitals in England and Wales: Broadmoor, Ashworth and Rampton. The population of the high security hospital estate declined during the 1990s and 2000s, leaving approximately 800 beds across the three hospitals in 2007 (Rutherford and Duggan, 2007). Since this time the number of high secure beds has stayed consistent with approximately 800 commissioned each year by NHS England (2017). High secure beds are an expensive resource, especially when compared to prison beds, with the average annual cost per high security bed in 2013 estimated to range from £251,000 per year at Rampton to £325,000 per year at Broadmoor (House of Commons debate, 25 April 2013, c1106W).

The criteria for admission to high security mental health services is set out in the National Health Service Act 2006 which states that those admitted to a high security hospital should 'require treatment under conditions of high security on account of their dangerous, violent or criminal propensities'.[4] Patients in the high security hospital estate are usually detained under Part III of the MHA 1983 (as amended by the MHA 2007) and will often be subject to a restriction order. Following the Tilt et al. (2000) report, the three high security hospitals are required to be as secure as a Category B prison, reflecting that secure mental health services tend to be more restrictive in England compared to other European countries (Salize and Dressing, 2007). While specialist services for personality disorder, women and learning disabilities are available within the high security estate (McMurran, Khalifa and Gibbon, 2009), most patients have a diagnosis of schizophrenia (Darjee, Øfstegaard and Thomson, 2017). The average length of stay in a high security hospital is approximately eight years (Völlm et al., 2017).

MEDIUM AND LOW SECURITY MENTAL HEALTH SERVICES

Medium and lower security provision is harder to describe, in part because of its location across a wide range of providers in the public and private sectors. However, approximately 3,200 medium security and 3,700 low security beds are commissioned each year (NHS England, 2017) with an approximate cost of £1.1 billion per annum (NHS England, 2016).[5] Patients in medium secure services will usually have been transferred from the courts, high security services or prison, although some patients may also have been transferred from less secure settings (or even community services) following concerns about their mental health and/or the safety of others. More than two thirds of patients in medium secure services are detained under Part III of the MHA 1983 (as amended by the MHA 2007) (Coid et al., 2001). Schizophrenia is the most common diagnosis among medium security hospital patients (Coid et al., 2001).

The development of medium secure services since they were first proposed in the 1970s has been difficult and they have struggled to meet the demands placed on them leading to blockages with patient pathways and unmet needs (Cree and Hodgins, 2007). The model of medium secure units (MSU) in England has been criticised by Wilson, James and Forrester (2011:9786) who argue that their inflexibility and inability to keep up with the pace of change has led them to 'resemble the Special Hospitals ... [they were] ... designed to replace'.

There is a lack of clarity about what constitutes low security services, but they are generally comprised of low secure units and Psychiatric Intensive Care Units (PICU) (Pereira, Dawson and Sarsam, 2006). There are a number of pathways into low secure mental health services including admission from the courts or prison, stepping down from more secure mental health services or from adult inpatient or community services (NHS England, 2017). There are approximately 150 low secure units in England (Joint Commissioning Panel for Mental Health, 2013) and 170 PICU (Chaudhry and Pereira, 2009). Low security units are usually managed by Community Mental Health Teams (CMHTs) (McMurran, Khalifa and Gibbon, 2009), while PICU are specialist mental health wards, run by general adult mental health services with the aim of managing patients that are difficult to manage on ordinary, open wards. They usually have higher staffing levels and a number of security features (such as locked doors and restricted access to facilities like the kitchen). They are often highly specialised and designed to treat patients who cannot be managed on other wards because of their violent behaviour (Bowers et al., 2008).

T̶R̶E̶A̶T̶M̶E̶N̶T̶ IN THE SECURE MENTAL HEALTH SYSTEM

Multidisciplinary working should underpin the service a patient receives in the mental health system and once in hospital, patients can expect to be looked after a range of staff including psychiatrists, psychologists, nurses, social workers and occupational therapists. Any treatment in hospital must comply with Part 4 of the MHA 1983 (as amended by the MHA 2007) and the Mental Capacity Act (MCA) 2005. Consent to treatment under the mental health legislation is complex (McMurran, Khalifa and Gibbon, 2009) and beyond the scope of this text. However, while the MCA 2005 states no one should be assumed to lack capacity to make treatment decisions, this right is waived once a patient is detained under the MHA 1983 (as amended by the MHA 2007) (Spandler and Calton, 2009). For more information see Beswick and Gunn (2017).

Treatment in secure mental health settings may take several forms including medication, psychological therapy and occupational therapy. Medication may include anti–depressants, anti–psychotics and/or anti–libidinal medication. Psychological therapies may focus on mental health awareness, emotional regulation, hearing voices groups, and relapse prevention. In forensic services, psychological therapies also usually seek to understand the patient's index offence and address issues surrounding risk (Glorney et al., 2010). Patients in secure services may also undertake specific offence related interventions. These may be undertaken on a 1:1 basis or in groups and may address a range of areas including: anger management, violence, sex offending and/or substance misuse. Interventions are structured by a range of psychological approaches including cognitive behavioural therapy (CBT), dialectical behaviour therapy (DBT), schema therapy and mentalisation based therapies. Patients in secure mental health services may also be offered a range of occupational therapies to support their treatment.

CARE PROGRAMME APPROACH (CPA)

Patients can expect regular reviews of their case under the Care Programme Approach (CPA). This should be used to make an assessment of a patient's need and to help plan, coordinate and review their care (Sizmur and McCulloch, 2016). The CPA should also provide a framework 'that facilitates an assessment and treatment approach that combines an understanding of both a patient's mental health and their potential risks' (Gournay et al., 2008:531). The weight of expectation on the planning and coordination of care is heavier than ever

(Coffey, Hannigan and Simpson, 2017). However, a recent review by the CQC (2018) found that in nearly a third of cases there was no evidence of patients having been involved in their care planning. Similarly, Simpson et al. (2016) found that patients were not adequately involved with their care planning, with care plans rarely consulted and considered to be a burden in terms of administration. Problems with poor clinical information systems (CQC, 2017) and inconsistent use of the CPA across different health settings (Sizmur and McCulloch, 2016) have also been reported.

CHALLENGES WITH SECURE MENTAL HEALTH PATHWAYS AND PROGRESSION

In contrast to the prison service, Gournay et al. (2008:530) observe that it 'would be a mistake to assume that patients in England seamlessly travel down levels of security until final discharge to community care'. Many patients in the mental health system have difficulty accessing the services they need in a timely manner (CQC, 2017). While the Department of Health (1999) *NHS Framework for Mental Health* advises a patient should be held in a level of security that is as least restrictive as possible, in practice this is not consistently adhered to (Markham, 2018). A recent study by Völlm et al. (2017:v) found that long-stay patients had particularly complex treatment pathways with many 'moving "around" between settings rather than moving forward'. It can be difficult for patients to get a transfer to less restrictive settings and as a result the length of stay for forensic patients can be very long (Sharma et al., 2015). Moreover, transfer from high to medium security services in the mental health system is a critical transition point and patients who are not ready, risk being returned to high security after an unsuccessful move to medium security services (Tetley et al., 2011). Low security beds are often not available when needed and this adds to the difficulties of enabling a patient to progress through the different levels of security (McMurran, Khalifa and Gibbon, 2009).

The Centre for Mental Health (2011) discusses a number of challenges that make the pathways through secure care more difficult for patients in the mental health system. These challenges include: assessment procedures, that can be lengthy, unnecessarily duplicated and sometimes undertaken out of area; limited funding for services, high MSU occupancy and limited bed capacity; risk aversion and debates over the appropriate level of security; lack of step-down facilities in secure and community settings; unwillingness of general services to take forensic patients; and anxiety on the part of the patient. The Centre for Mental Health (2011:13–14) also highlights the lack of clear entry criteria for secure care, concluding that 'as "low secure" is poorly defined, it is difficult to establish what it consists of and how many patients it supports'. This creates problems in offender pathways because there is a lack of clarity about how low security services should be used. In addition, a lack of clear criteria means that admission decisions can be arbitrary. This is because they are affected by discretionary professional judgements made by clinicians who have a range of values, experiences and contextual pressures (Grounds et al., 2004).

The progression of patients through secure mental health services is also affected by a range of staffing challenges. For example, a recent CQC (2017) report has highlighted that many mental health services are suffering from a lack of qualified mental health nurses. This can lead to restricted access to therapies and day time activities for the patients. A lack of nursing staff also leads to a reliance on agency staff and this means patient movements are restricted and staff are unable to take breaks because of the limited provision of staff (CQC, 2017).

DISCUSSION

Working with mentally disordered offenders in secure settings is without doubt challenging. A key challenge follows from the fact that prisons are primarily set up to provide punishment and serve as a deterrent; quite different aims to those involved with psychiatric care (Howells, Day and Thomas-Peter, 2004). While prisons are required to deliver health care services that are 'equivalent' to those provided in the community, ultimately, 'security and custodial issues hold precedence over health care' (Sainsbury Centre for Mental Health, 2006:21; see also Sim, 1990). This highlights that the restrictive nature of the prison environment can impact on therapeutic efforts by the staff (Cooke, Stephenson and Rose, 2017). While health care staff are primarily concerned with providing care for prisoners (Jordan, 2017) 'even well-trained and dedicated mental health staff must work in and against punitive prison norms, counter-therapeutically structured environments, and long-standing correctional practices that undermine their ability to provide caring and effective treatment' (Haney, 2017:313).

These challenges reflect how the relationship between prisons and the NHS represents somewhat of 'an "arranged marriage" of two very different ideologies: with the prison service being based on security and deprivation of liberty, and the NHS being based on healing and promoting wellbeing' (Sainsbury Centre for Mental Health, 2006:12). Such a marriage is also unequal, since the over-riding dominance of security concerns serves to disrupt patient care and place mental health at the 'bottom of the pile' of priorities (Caulfield and Twort, 2012:12–13). It is within this context that many different staff with different professional backgrounds, training, principles, expertise, priorities and ultimately responsibilities, must come together. Limited funding and resources serve to make things harder for these staff who are often trying to achieve multiple aims without the colleagues, training and resources to support them.

To add to this, prison staff are commonly exposed to distressing and traumatic events (Howard League for Penal Reform and Centre for Mental Health, 2016). The impact of self-harm, violence and offender mental health on staff is likely to be significant, especially given recent, and substantial, increases across the prison estate. Violence is also common in mental health services (Duxbury et al., 2008) with health care staff far more likely than most occupational groups to experience workplace violence (Bowers et al., 2011). Frontline staff such as prison officers and nurses are at particular risk and may feel the 'draining effects' of working with offenders more intensely as a result of their increased contact time (Cooke, Stephenson and Rose, 2017). However, staff in secure services may feel obliged to present themselves as unaffected by traumatic incidents, and therefore may also feel unable to access support (Walker et al., 2017). In addition to the detrimental impact that violence can have on workforce morale, Howells, Daffern and Day (2008) remind us that it can lead to a poor therapeutic climate, which, in turn, will limit the reductions in risk that detained patients and prisoners are able to make. This reminds us that while achieving a balance between security and therapy can be difficult, they are also dependent on one another, and without a secure and safe environment, providing effective treatment is unlikely to occur.

FURTHER READING

See Seddon (2007) for an excellent and detailed overview of the imprisonment of people with mental health problems. See also Senior and Shaw (2008) for a historical overview of prison mental health care. For a review of mental health issues in prisons see National Audit Office (2017). For more information about the restricted patient system see Ministry of Justice and HMPPS (2017). For an interesting insight into one of the high security hospitals (Ashworth) see Pilgrim (2007).

REFERENCES

Abbott, P., Davenport, S., Davies, S., Nimmagadda, S.R., O'Halloran, A. and Tattan, T. (2005) 'Potential effects of retraction of the high secure hospitals', *The Psychiatrist*, 29(11): 402–406.

Bartlett, A., Somers, N., Reeves, C. and White, S. (2012) 'Women prisoners: An analysis of the process of hospital transfers', *Journal of Forensic Psychiatry and Psychology*, 23(4): 538–553.

Bebbington, P., Jakobowitz, S., McKensie, N., Killaspy, H., Iveson, R., Duffield, G. and Kerr, M. (2017) 'Assessing needs for psychiatric treatment in prisoners: 1. Prevalence of disorder', *Social Psychiatry and Psychiatric Epidemiology*, 52(2): 221–229.

Bennett, J. and Shuker, R. (2017) 'The potential of prison-based democratic therapeutic communities', *International Journal of Prison Health*, 13(1): 19–24.

Beswick, J. and Gunn, M. (2017) 'The law in England and Wales on mental health treatment in the community' in Buchanan, A. and Wootton, L. (eds.) *Care of the mentally disordered offender in the community (Second edition)*, Oxford: Oxford University Press.

Birmingham, L., Awonogun, O. and Ryland, H. (2017) 'Diversion from custody: An update', *BJPsych Advance*, 23: 375–384.

Bowers, L., Jeffrey, D., Bilgin, H., Jarrett, M., Simpson, A. and Jones, J. (2008) 'Psychiatric intensive care units: A literature review', *International Journal of Social Psychiatry*, 54(1): 56–68.

Bowers, L., Stewart, D., Papadopoulos, C., Dack, C., Ross, J., Khanom, H. and Jeffrey, D. (2011) *Inpatient violence and aggression: A literature review*, London: Kings College.

Brooker, C. and Gojkovic, D. (2009) 'The second national survey of mental health in-reach services in prisons', *Journal of Forensic Psychiatry and Psychology*, 20(1): S11–S28.

Brooker, C., Sirdifield, C. and Gojkovic, D. (2007) *Mental health services and prisoners: An updated review*, Lincoln: Centre for Clinical and Academic Workforce Innovation.

Brooker, C. and Webster, R. (2017) 'Prison mental health in-reach teams, serious mental illness and the Care Programme Approach in England, *Journal of Forensic and Legal Medicine*, 50: 44–48.

Brookes, M. (2010) 'Putting principles into practice: The therapeutic regime at HMP Grendon and its relationship with the "good lives" model' in Shuker, R. and Sullivan, E. (eds.) *Grendon and the emergence of forensic Therapeutic Communities: Developments in research and practice*, Chichester: Wiley-Blackwell.

Brown, K., Cullen, A., Kooyman, I. and Forrester, A. (2015) 'Mental health expertise at prison reception', *Journal of Forensic Psychiatry and Psychology*, 26(1): 107–115.

Care Quality Commission (CQC) (2017) *The state of care in mental health services 2014 to 2017 Findings from CQC's programme of comprehensive inspections of specialist mental health services*, Newcastle-Upon-Tyne: CQC.

Care Quality Commission (CQC) (2018) *Monitoring the Mental Health Act in 2016/17*, Newcastle-Upon-Tyne: CQC.

Caulfield, L.S. and Twort, H. (2012) 'Implementing change: Staff experiences of changes to prison mental healthcare in England and Wales', *International Journal of Prisoner Health*, 8(1): 7–15.

Centre for Mental Health (2011) *Pathways to unlocking secure mental health care*, London: Centre for Mental Health.

Chaudhry, K. and Pereira, S. (2009) 'A comparison of NHS and private psychiatric intensive care units: Unit and patient characteristics', *Journal of Psychiatric Intensive Care*, 5(1): 5–13.

Coffey, M., Hannigan, B. and Simpson, A. (2017) 'Care planning and coordination: Imperfect solutions in a complex world', *Journal of Psychiatric Mental Health Nursing*, 24(6): 333–334.

Coid, J., Kahtan, N., Gault, S., Cook, A. and Jarman, B. (2001) 'Medium secure forensic psychiatry services: Comparison of seven English health regions', *British Journal of Psychiatry*, 178(1): 55–61.

Cooke, E., Stephenson, Z. and Rose, J. (2017) 'How do professionals experience working with offenders diagnosed with personality disorder within a prison environment?', *Journal of Forensic Psychiatry and Psychology*, 28(6): 841–862.

Cree, A. and Hodgins, S. (2007) 'Services for the treatment of mentally disordered offenders – From reaction to pro-action', *The Mental Health Review*, 12(1): 7–15.

Crewe, B., Liebling, A. and Hulley, S. (2014) 'Heavy-light, absent-present: Rethinking the 'weight' of imprisonment', *British Journal of Sociology*, 65(3): 387–410.

Darjee, R., Øfstegaard, M. and Thomson, L. (2017) 'Schizophrenia in a high security hospital: Long-term forensic, clinical, administrative and social outcomes', *Journal of Forensic Psychiatry and Psychology*, 28(4): 525–547.

de Viggiani, N. (2007) 'Unhealthy prisons: Exploring structural determinants of prison health', *Sociology of Health and Illness*, 29(1): 115–135.

Department of Health (1999) *National Service Framework for mental health*, London: Department of Health.

Department of Health (2009) *The Bradley report. Lord Bradley's review of people with mental health problems or learning disabilities in the criminal justice system*, London: Department of Health.

Department of Health (2011) *Good practice procedure guide: The transfer and remission of adult prisoners under s47 and s48 of the Mental Health Act*, London: Department of Health.

Department of Health and Her Majesty's (HM) Prison Service (2001) *Changing the outlook – A strategy for developing and modernising mental health services in prisons*, London: Department of Health and HM Prison Service.

Department of Health and Home Office (1992) *Review of health and social services for mentally disordered offenders and others requiring similar services*, London: Department of Health and Home Office.

Department of Health and National Institute for Mental Health in England (NIMHE) (2005) *Offender mental health care pathway*, London: Department of Health and NIMHE.

Douglas, N., Plugge, E. and Fitzpatrick, R. (2009) 'The impact of imprisonment on health: What do women prisoners say?' *Journal of Epidemiology and Community Health*, 63(9): 749–754.

Durcan, G. (2008) *From the inside: Experiences of prison mental health care*, London: Centre for Mental Health.

Durcan, G. (2016) *Mental health and criminal justice: Views from consultations across England and Wales*, London: Centre for Mental Health.

Duxbury, J., Hahn, S., Needham, I., and Pulsford, D. (2008) 'The Management of Aggression and Violence Attitude Scale (MAVAS): A cross-national comparative study', *Journal of Advanced Nursing*, 62(5): 596–606.

Evans, C., Forrester, A., Jarrett, M., Huddy, V., Campbell, C.A., Byrne, M., Craig, T. and Valmaggia, L. (2017) 'Early detection and early intervention in prison: Improving outcomes and reducing prison returns', *Journal of Forensic Psychiatry and Psychology*, 28(1): 91–107.

Fazel, S., Hayes, A.J., Bartellas, K., Clerici, M. and Trestman, R. (2016) 'Mental health of prisoners: Prevalence, adverse outcomes, and interventions', *Lancet Psychiatry*, 3(9): 871–881.

Fazel, S. and Seewald, K. (2012) 'Severe mental illness in 33,588 prisoners worldwide: Systematic review and meta-regression analysis', *British Journal of Psychiatry*, 200(5): 364–373.

Forrester, A., Chiu, K., Dove, S. and Parrott, J. (2010) 'Prison health-care wings: Psychiatry's forgotten frontier', *Criminal Behaviour and Mental Health*, 20(1): 51–61.

Forrester, A., Exworthy, T., Olumoroti, O., Sessay, M., Parrott, J., Spencer, S. and Whyte, S. (2013) 'Variations in prison mental health services in England and Wales', *International Journal of Law and Psychiatry*, 36(3–4): 326–332.

Forrester, A., Henderson, C., Wilson, S., Cumming, C., Spyrou, M. and Parrott, J. (2009) 'A suitable waiting room? Hospital transfer outcomes and delays from two London prisons', *Psychiatric Bulletin*, 33(11): 409–412.

Fraser, A. (2014) 'Primary health care in prisons' in Møller, L., Stöver, H., Jürgens, R., Gatherer, A. and Nikogosian, H. (eds.) *Health in prisons: A WHO guide to the essentials in prison health*, Copenhagen, Denmark: World Health Organization Regional Office for Europe.

Galappathie, N., Khan, S.T. and Hussain, A. (2017) 'Civil and forensic patients in secure psychiatric settings: A comparison', *BJPsych Bulletin*, 41(3): 156–159.

Gatawa, T. (2016) 'Prosecuting the persecuted: Forgive them, they know not what they do' in Winstone, J. (ed.) *Mental health, crime and criminal justice*, Basingstoke: Palgrave Macmillan.

Glorney, E., Perkins, D., Adshead, G., McGauley, G., Murray, K., Noak, J. and Sichau, G. (2010) 'Domains of need in a high secure hospital setting: A model for streamlining care and reducing length of stay', *International Journal of Forensic Mental Health*, 9(2): 138–148.

Gooch, K. and Treadwell, J. (2015) *Prison bullying and victimisation*, Birmingham: Birmingham Law School.

Goomany, A. and Dickinson, T. (2015) 'The influence of prison climate on the mental health of adult prisoners: A literature review', *Journal of Psychiatric and Mental Health Nursing*, 22(6): 413–422.

Gournay, K., Benson, R. and Rogers, P. (2008) 'Inpatient care and management' in Soothill, K., Rogers, P. and Dolan, M. (eds.) *Handbook of forensic mental health*, Cullompton: Willan Publishing.

Grounds, A., Gelsthorpe, L., Howes, M., Melzer, D., Tom, B.D.M., Brugha, T., Fryers, T., Gatward, R. and Meltzer, H. (2004) 'Access to medium secure psychiatric care in England and Wales. 2: A qualitative study of admission decision-making', *Journal of Forensic Psychiatry and Psychology*, 15(1): 32–49.

Hales, H., Dixon, A., Newton, Z. and Bartlett, A. (2016) 'Assaults by mentally disordered offenders in prison: Equity and equivalence', *Bioethical inquiry*, 13(2): 317–326.

Haney, C. (2017) '"Madness" and penal confinement: Some observations on mental illness and prison pain', *Punishment and Society*, 19(3): 310–326.

Harner, H.M. and Riley, S. (2012) 'The impact of incarceration on women's mental health: Responses from women in a maximum-security prison', *Qualitative Health Research*, 23(1): 26–42.

Harris, T. (2015) *Changing prisons, saving lives: Report of the independent review into self inflicted deaths in custody of 18–24 year olds*, London: Her Majesty's Stationery Office.

Harrison, K. (2011) *Dangerousness, risk and the governance of serious sexual and violent offenders*, Abingdon: Routledge.

Hayton, P. and Boyington, J. (2006) 'Prisons and health reforms in England and Wales', *American Journal of Public Health*, 96(10): 1730–1733.

Her Majesty's (HM) Government and Department of Health (2011) *No health without mental health: A cross-government mental health outcomes strategy for people of all ages*, London: HM Government and Department of Health.

Her Majesty's (HM) Government and National Health Service (NHS) England (2018) *National Partnership Agreement for prison healthcare in England 2018–2021*, London: HM Government and NHS England.

Her Majesty's (HM) Inspectorate of Prisons (1996) *Patient or prisoner?*, London: HM Inspectorate of Prisons.

Her Majesty's Prison and Probation Service (HMPPS) (2018) *Her Majesty's Prison and Probation Service annual report and accounts 2017–18*, London: HMPPS.

Her Majesty's (HM) Prison Service and NHS Executive Working Group (1999) *The future organisation of prison healthcare*, London: Department of Health.

House of Commons debate, 25 April 2013, c110gW. Available from: https://publications.parliament.uk/pa/cm201213/cmhansrd/cm130425/text/130425w0003.htm#130425w0003.htm_spnew46 [Last accessed 04 January 2018].

Howard League for Penal Reform and Centre for Mental Health (2016) *Preventing prison suicide: Perspectives from the inside*, London: Howard League for Penal Reform and Centre for Mental Health.

Howells, K., Daffern, M. and Day, A. (2008) 'Aggression and violence' in Soothill, K., Rogers, P. and Dolan, M. (eds.) *Handbook of forensic mental health*, Cullompton: Willan Publishing.

Howells, K., Day, A. and Thomas-Peter, B. (2004) 'Changing violent behaviour: Forensic mental health and criminological models compared', *Journal of Forensic Psychiatry and Psychology*, 15(3): 391–406.

Jakobowitz, S., Bebbington, P., McKenzie, N., Iveson, R., Duffield, G., Kerr, M. and Killaspy, H. (2017) 'Assessing needs for psychiatric treatment in prisoners: 2. Met and unmet need', *Social Psychiatry and Psychiatric Epidemiology*, 52(2): 231–240.

Jeffreys, D.S. (2016) 'Segregation and supermax confinement: An ethical evaluation' in Jewkes, Y., Crewe, B. and Bennett, J. (eds.) *Handbook on prisons (Second edition)*, London: Routledge.

Jewesbury, I. and McCulloch, A. (2002) 'Public policy and mentally disordered offenders in the UK' in Buchanan, A. (ed.) *Care of the mentally disordered offender in the community*, Oxford: Oxford University Press.

Johnston, H. (2016) 'Prison histories, 1770–1950s. Continuities and contradictions' in Jewkes, Y., Crewe, B. and Bennett, J. (eds.) *Handbook on prisons (Second edition)*, London: Routledge.

Joint Commissioning Panel for Mental Health (2013) *Guidance for commissioners of forensic mental health services*, London: Joint Commissioning Panel for Mental Health.

Jordan, M. (2011) 'The prison setting as a place of enforced residence, its mental health effects, and the mental healthcare implications', *Health and Place*, 17(5): 1061–1066.

Jordan, M. (2017) '"The will's there and the skill's there": Prison mental health care' in Hughes, M. and Jordan, M. (eds.) *Mental health uncertainty and inevitability: Rejuvenating the relationship between social science and psychiatry*, Basingstoke: Palgrave Macmillan.

Kentish, B. (2017) 'Number of mental health patients treated hundreds of miles from home hits new high', *The Independent*, 5 March 2017. Available from: www.independent.co.uk/news/mental-health-patients-out-of-area-placements-theresa-may-psychosis-anorexia-schizophrenia-a7611571.html [Last accessed 14 July 2017].

Keown, P., Murphy, H., McKenna, D. and McKinnon, I. (2018) 'Changes in the use of the Mental Health Act 1983 in England 1984/85 to 2015/16', *British Journal of Psychiatry*, 213(4): 295–299.

Knabb, J.J., Welsh, R.K. and Graham-Howard, M.L. (2011) 'Treatment alternatives for mentally disordered offenders: A literature review', *Psychology*, 2(2): 122–131.

Krammer, S., Eisenbarth, H., Hügli, D., Liebrenz, M. and Kuwert, P. (2017) 'The relationship between childhood traumatic events, social support, and mental health problems in prisoners', *Journal of Forensic Psychiatry and Psychology*, 29(1): 72–85.

Markham, S. (2018) 'Red-teaming the panopticon (mobilising adaptive change in secure and forensic settings)', *Journal of Forensic Psychiatry and Psychology*, 29(1): 16–36.

Markowitz, F.E. (2011) 'Mental illness, crime, and violence: Risk, context, and social control', *Aggression and Violent Behavior*, 16(1): 36–44.

Marshall, T. Simpson, S. and Stevens, A. (2007) 'Chapter 11: Health care in prisons' updated version of a chapter in The Health Care Needs Assessment series, funded by the Department of Health/National Institute for Health and Clinical Excellence (NICE), Birmingham: University of Birmingham.

McBride, R. (2017) 'On the advancement of therapeutic penality: Therapeutic authority, personality science and the therapeutic community', *Sociology of Health and Illness*, 39(7): 1258–1272.

McMurran, M., Khalifa, N. and Gibbon, S. (2009) *Forensic mental health*, Cullompton: Willan Publishing.

Mills, A., Lathlean, K., Bressington, D., Forrester, A., Van Veenhuyzen, W. and Gray, R. (2011) 'Prisoners' experiences of antipsychotic medication: Influences on adherence', *Journal of Forensic Psychiatry and Psychology*, 22(1): 110–125.

Mills, H. and Kendall, K. (2016) 'Mental health in prisons' in Jewkes, Y., Crewe, B. and Bennett, J. (eds.) *Handbook on prisons (Second edition)*, London: Routledge.

Ministry of Justice (2017a) *National Offender Management Service workforce statistics: March 2017*, London: Ministry of Justice.

Ministry of Justice (2017b) *Safety in custody statistics bulletin, England and Wales. Deaths in prison custody to March 2017, assaults and self-harm to December 2016*, London: Ministry of Justice.

Ministry of Justice (2018a) *Population and capacity briefing for Friday 9th November 2018*, London: Ministry of Justice.

Ministry of Justice (2018b) Prisons reform speech [Press statement] 6 March 2018 Available from: www.gov.uk/government/speeches/prisons-reform-speech [Last accessed 25 June 2018].

Ministry of Justice and Her Majesty's Prison and Probation Service (HMPPS) (2017) *Mentally disordered offenders – The restricted patient system. Background briefing*, London: Ministry of Justice and HMPPS.

National Audit Office (2017) *Mental health in prisons*, London: National Audit Office.

National Health Service (NHS) Digital (2016) *Inpatients formally detained in hospital under the Mental Health Act 1983, and patients subject to supervised community treatment. Uses of the Mental Health Act: Annual statistics 2015/16*, London: NHS Digital.

National Health Service (NHS) England (2016) *Consultation guide: New service specifications for adult secure low and medium mental health services*, London: NHS England.

National Health Service (NHS) England (2017) *Draft adult medium secure service specification*, London: NHS England.

National Institute for Health and Care Excellence (NICE) (2017) *Mental health of adults in contact with the criminal justice system*, London: NICE.

National Offender Management Service (NOMS) (2016a) *Annual report and accounts 2015/16*, London: The Stationery Office.

National Offender Management Service (NOMS) (2016b) *Mental Health Casework Section stakeholder engagement framework*, London: NOMS.

Noyce, G. (2012) 'The Mental Health Act: Dual diagnosis, public protection and legal dilemmas in practice' in Pycroft, A. and Clift, S. (eds.) *Risk and rehabilitation: Management and treatment of substance misuse and mental health problems in the criminal justice system*, Bristol: The Policy Press.

Patel, R., Harvey, J. and Forrester, A. (2018) 'Systemic limitations in the delivery of mental health care in prisons in England', *International Journal of Law and Psychiatry*, 60: 17–25.

Pereira, S., Dawson, P. and Sarsam, M. (2006) 'The national survey of PICU and low secure services: 2. Unit characteristics', *Journal of Psychiatric Intensive Care*, 2(1): 13–19.

Pilgrim, D. (2007) (ed.) *Inside Ashworth: Personal accounts of institutional life*, London: Radcliffe Medical Press.

Pitman, I., Haddlesy, C. and Fortescue, D. (2013) *Briefing: The prevalence of traumatic brain injury among adult male offenders in the UK*, Wakefield: The Disabilities Trust Foundation.

Player, E. (2017) 'The offender personality disorder pathway and its implications for women prisoners in England and Wales', *Punishment and Society*, 19(5): 1–22.

Prison Reform Trust (2017) *Bromley briefings prison factfile autumn 2017*, London: Prison Reform Trust.

Prisons and Probation Ombudsman (PPO) (2016) *Learning from PPO investigations: Prisoner mental health*, London: PPO.

Public Health England (PHE) (2016) *Rapid review of evidence of the impact on health outcomes of NHS commissioned health services for people in secure and detained settings to inform future health interventions and prioritisation in England*, London: PHE.

Pycroft, A. and Green, A. (2016) 'Challenging the cultural determinants of dual diagnosis in the criminal justice system' in Winstone, J. (ed.) *Mental health, crime and criminal justice*, Basingstoke: Palgrave Macmillan.

Royal College of Psychiatrists (2013) *Enabling environments standards*, London: Royal College of Psychiatrists.

Royal College of Psychiatrists (2015) *Standards for prison mental health services*, London: Royal College of Psychiatrists.

Rutherford, M. and Duggan, S. (2007) *Forensic mental health services: Facts and figures on current provision*, London: Sainsbury Centre for Mental Health.

Sainsbury Centre for Mental Health (2006) *London's prison mental health services: A review*, London: Sainsbury Centre for Mental Health.

Salize, H.J. and Dressing, H. (2007) 'Placement and treatment of mentally-ill offenders – Legislation and practice in member states', *Psychiatrische Praxis*, 34(8): 388–394.

Samele, C., Urquia, N., Slade, K. and Forrester, A. (2017) 'Information pathways into prison mental health care', *Journal of Forensic Psychiatry and Psychology*, 28(4): 548–561.

Seddon, T. (2007) *Punishment and madness: Governing prisoners with mental health problems*, Abingdon: Routledge-Cavendish.

Senior, J., Appleby, L. and Shaw, J. (2014) 'The management of mental health problems among prisoners in England and Wales', *International Psychiatry*, 11(3): 56–58.

Senior, J., Birmingham, L., Harty, M.A., Hassan, L., Hayes, A.J., Kendall, K., King, C., Lathlean, J., Lowthian, C., Mills, A., Webb, R., Thornicroft, G. and Shaw, J. (2013) 'Identification and management of prisoners with severe psychiatric illness by specialist mental health services', *Psychological Medicine*, 43(7): 1511–1520.

Senior, J. and Shaw, J. (2008) 'Mental healthcare in prisons' in Soothill, K., Rogers, P. and Dolan, M. (eds.) *Handbook of forensic mental health*, Cullompton: Willan Publishing.

Shafi, A., Gallagher, P., Stewart, N., Martinotti, G. and Corazza, O. (2017) 'The risk of violence associated with novel psychoactive substance misuse in patients presenting to acute mental health services', *Human Psychopharmacology: Clinical and Experimental*, 32(3): e2606.

Shalev, S. (2008) *A sourcebook on solitary confinement*, London: Mannheim Centre for Criminology, London School of Economics.

Sharma, A., Dunn, W., O'Toole, C. and Kennedy, H.G. (2015) 'The virtual institution: Crosssectional length of stay in general adult and forensic psychiatry beds', *International Journal of Mental Health Systems*, 9: 25.

Sharpe, R., Völlm, B., Akhtar, A., Puri, R. and Bickle, A. (2016) 'Transfers from prison to hospital under sections 47 and 48 of the Mental Health Act between 2011 and 2014', *Journal of Forensic Psychiatry and Psychology*, 27(4): 459–475.

Shaw, J., Senior, J., Hayes, A., Roberts, A., Evans, G., Rennie, C., James, C., Mnyamana, M., Senti, J., Trwoga, S., Whittaker, I., Taylor, P., Maslin, L., de Viggiani, N. and Jones, G. (2008) *An evaluation of the Department of Health's 'Procedure for the transfer of prisoners to and from hospital under sections 47 and 48 of the Mental Health Act 1983' initiative: Project report*, Manchester: Offender Health Research Network.

Short, J. and Barber, M. (2004) 'Troubled inside: Vulnerability in prison' in Jeffcote, N. and Watson, T. (eds.) *Working therapeutically with women in secure mental health settings*, London: Jessica Kingsley Publishers.

Sim, J. (1990) *Medical power in prisons: The prison medical service in England 1774–1989*, Buckingham: Open University Press.

Simpson, A., Hannigan, B., Coffey, M., Barlow, S., Cohen, R., Jones, A., Všetečková, J., Faulkner, A., Thornton, A. and Cartwright, M. (2016) 'Recovery-focused care planning and coordination in England and Wales: A cross-national mixed methods comparative case study', *BMC Psychiatry*, 16(1): 1–18.

Singleton, N., Meltzer, H., Gatward, R., Coid, J., Deasy, D. (1998) *Psychiatric morbidity among prisoners in England and Wales*, London: Office for National Statistics.

Sizmur, S. and McCulloch, A. (2016) 'Differences in treatment approach between ethnic groups', *The Mental Health Review*, 21(2): 73–84.

Slade, K., Samele, C., Valmaggia, L. and Forrester, A. (2016) 'Pathways through the criminal justice system for prisoners with acute and serious mental illness', *Journal of Forensic and Legal Medicine*, 44: 162–168.

Smedley, K. (2010) 'Cognitive behaviour therapy with adolescents in secure settings' in Harvey, J. and Smedley, K. (eds.) *Psychological therapy in prisons and other settings*, Abingdon: Willan Publishing.

Smith, E. (2010) 'Care versus custody: Nursing in the prison service', *Practice Nurse*, 40, 33–35.

Social Exclusion Unit (2002) *Reducing re-offending by ex-prisoners*, London: Social Exclusion Unit.

Spandler, H. and Calton, T. (2009) 'Psychosis and human rights: Conflicts in mental health policy and practice', *Social Policy and Society*, 8(2): 245–256.

Steel, J., Thornicroft, G., Birmingham, L., Brooker, C., Mills, A., Harty, M. and Shaw, J. (2007) 'Prison mental health in reach services', *British Journal of Psychiatry*, 190(5): 373–374.

Talbot, J. (2008) *No one knows: Report and final recommendations – Experiences of the criminal justice system by prisoners with learning disabilities and difficulties*, London: Prison Reform Trust.

Tetley, E., Evershed, S. and Krishnan, G. (2011) 'The transition from high secure to medium secure services for people with personality disorder: Patients and clinicians experiences', *Journal of Forensic Psychiatry and Psychology*, 22(3): 321–339.

Tilt, R., Perry, B., Martin, C., Maguire, N. and Preston, M. (2000) *Report of the review of security at the high security hospitals*, London: Department of Health.

Trebilcock, J. (2011) *No winners: The reality of short term prison sentences*, London: Howard League for Penal Reform.

Trebilcock, J. and Weaver, T. (2010) *Multi-method Evaluation of the Management, Organisation and Staffing (MEMOS) in high security treatment services for people with Dangerous and Severe Personality Disorder (DSPD)*, London: Ministry of Justice.

Turley, C. Payne, C. and Webster, S. (2013) *Enabling features of Psychologically Informed Planned Environments*, London: Ministry of Justice.

van Ginneken, Esther F J C, Sutherland, A. and Molleman, T. (2017) 'An ecological analysis of prison overcrowding and suicide rates in England and Wales, 2000–2014', *International Journal of Law and Psychiatry*, 50: 76–82.

Völlm, B., Edworthy, R., Holley, J., Talbot, E., Majid, S., Duggan, C., Weaver, T. and McDonald, R. (2017) 'A mixed-methods study exploring the characteristics and needs of long-stay patients in high and medium secure settings in England: Implications for service organisation', *Health Services and Delivery Research*, 5(11): 1–233.

Walker, T., Shaw, J., Hamilton, L., Turpin, C., Reid, C. and Abel, K. (2017) '"Coping with the job": Prison staff responding to self-harm in three English female prisons: A qualitative study', *Journal of Forensic Psychiatry and Psychology*, 28(6): 811–824.

Wilson, S., James, D. and Forrester, A. (2011) 'The medium-secure project and criminal justice mental health', *The Lancet*, 378(9786): 110–111.

World Health Organization (WHO) (2013) *Good governance for prison health in the 21st century: A policy brief on the organization of prison health*, Geneva, Switzerland: WHO.

Wright, N., Jordan, M. and Kane, E. (2014) 'Mental health/illness and prisons as place: Frontline clinicians' perspectives of mental health work in a penal setting', *Health and Place*, 29: 179–185.

Zlodre, J. and Fazel, S. (2012) 'All cause and external mortality in released prisoners: Systematic review and meta-analysis', *American Journal of Public Health*, 102(12): 67–75.

NOTES

1   For a thorough review of the health care needs of those in prison see Marshall, Simpson and Stevens (2007).

2   England has the longest history of health commissioning in Western Europe and is often cited as a model of good practice. Most Western European countries continue to commission prison health care via their justice ministries, although notable exceptions now include France, Italy,

Norway, Sweden and Finland. Full responsibility for prison health care in England transferred to the NHS in April 2006, and this was followed in Scotland from November 2011 and Northern Ireland from April 2012 (Public Health England, 2016).

3   See Bennett and Shuker (2017) for a recent overview of the work of HMP Grendon.

4   For more information about the high-security mental health services see the most recent services specifications published by NHS England www.england.nhs.uk/wp-content/uploads/2013/06/c02-high-sec-mh.pdf

5   For more information about the medium and low security mental health services see the most recent services specifications published by NHS England www.england.nhs.uk/publication/service-specification-medium-secure-mental-health-services-adult/ www.england.nhs.uk/publication/service-specification-low-secure-mental-health-services-adult/

CHAPTER 7

Mental health, offending and the community

INTRODUCTION

Care in the community has a relatively short, but difficult history in England and Wales. This chapter explores how offenders with mental health problems are supervised, punished and cared for in the community. The chapter begins with a brief overview of the history of mental health care in the community before turning to outline the key services available to, and responsible for, those who offend, have mental disorder and reside in the community. Specific issues surrounding punishment, treatment and supervision will be explored through closer examination of community mental health teams (CMHTs), community treatment orders (CTOs) and Multi-Agency Public Protection Arrangements (MAPPA). Decisions about discharge and release from secure settings along with the related challenges involved with providing safe aftercare and supervision in the community, will also be considered. Here, we highlight the importance of continuity of care, inter-agency communication and the proper provision of services. While criticisms have often been made about the inadequacy of community care for those with mental disorder, it is important to remember that the community can offer important opportunities for both preventive and rehabilitative work if it is properly resourced.

THE EMERGENCE OF COMMUNITY HEALTH CARE

After the asylum system began to break down, community became a key term in national policy, offering a way for psychiatry to not only 'modernise itself' but also divest itself from the carceral features of the asylum and 'their custodial and controlling role' (Rose, 2002:15). Until the 1980s mental health care in the community was a localised affair, experimental and driven by psychiatrists; it did not follow any structured models of practice, and there was little scientific evaluation of these localised practices (Burns, 2014). Instead, 'clinicians, predominantly psychiatrists, tried things out and drew conclusions on what seemed to work' (Burns, 2014:337). Although usually led by clinicians (in part to meet the legal status afforded to Responsible Medical Officers (RMOs)[1] under mental health legislation at the time) most community outreach work was undertaken by social workers and nurses. From the 1980s diagnosis and treatment became increasingly scientific and community care more evidence based as new service alternatives such as CMHTs and the effectiveness of psychosocial interventions with community mental health patients began to emerge (Burns, 2014).

In the 1990s a legislative framework for care in the community also developed. This began, significantly, with the National Health Service and Community Care Act 1990 and the introduction of the Care Programme Approach (CPA) a year later. While the development of community services was encouraged by other policy at the time, such as the Reed Report (Department of Health and Home Office, 1992), the development of alternative community provision following asylum closures was often slow, and not reflective of a proper reallocation of resources (see Chapter 3 for a discussion). Initially, CMHTs were based on a sectorised model of services in clearly defined catchment areas, but this changed following the millennium as a functional model of community care with a plethora of teams with specialised remits (such as assertive outreach and early intervention teams) began to emerge (Holloway and Davies, 2017).

MENTAL HEALTH SERVICES IN THE COMMUNITY

The provision of mental health services in the community is complex, and while it is difficult to provide a simple description or map, Crisp, Smith and Nicholson (2016:37)[2] suggest that services can be usually be categorised under the following five groups:

1. Primary care services provided by GPs to help support people live at home or in other residential care.
2. Community services to help with day-to-day living such as CMHTs, Assertive Outreach Teams (AOTs), drugs and alcohol teams, housing services and the Improving Access to Psychological Therapies (IAPT) programme.
3. Crisis care to respond to urgent needs such as Crisis Resolution and Home Treatment (CRHT) teams (or Crisis Resolution Teams CRT) and other programmes such as street triage.
4. Acute inpatient services
5. Specialist inpatient services including forensic services (such as those described in the last chapter) and services for children, eating disorders and mother and baby facilities.

The majority of offenders receiving care for their mental disorder in the community are managed by generic services but, when resources permit, some CMHTs are differentiated into teams with different functions. In practice, Holloway and Davies (2017:318) suggest that four distinct but overlapping models are in operation. The first is a generic CMHT model where the offender is managed by non-specialist services. The second involves a consultation/liaison model where specialist practitioners offer support to the CMHT. The third model is a specialist team with a forensic focus, and the fourth is where a forensic psychiatrist works independently from an institutional base with ad hoc support from other community and criminal justice practitioners (Holloway and Davies, 2017:318). These different models reflect that forensic community mental health services have developed in an ad hoc manner, with different service structures and referral criteria, influenced by local clinical and commissioning decisions (Royal College of Psychiatrists, 2013).

CMHTs are usually staffed by clinical staff such as psychologists or psychiatrists, social workers and community psychiatric nurses (CPNs).[3] The extent to which CMHTs have contact with specialist forensic staff depends on local policies and resources (Holloway, 2002; Thornicroft and Tansella, 2004). Some areas also have dedicated forensic CMHTs[4] and while debates about the value of specialised versus generic community mental health services are ongoing, specialist community services appear to be growing (Royal College of Psychiatrists, 2013). Changes in commissioning arrangements under the Health and Social Care Act 2012 have contributed to the different ways in which local forensic community mental health services have developed (Royal College of Psychiatrists, 2013). Mental health services in the community are now usually commissioned by Clinical

Commissioning Groups (CCGs)[5] (or Local Health Boards (LHB) in Wales) unless they are highly specialised or secure, when they are commissioned by National Health Service (NHS) England (Wright, 2017).

While the configuration of multidisciplinary mental health teams may differ across different settings, they are often remarkably similar (Burns, 2006). While there are different models of community-based forensic mental health care (i.e. parallel, integrated and hybrid), and greater understanding about the structure, scope and role of forensic community mental health services is still needed, the core functions of forensic community mental health services are usually:

1. 'Consultation and liaison with local mental health teams and other agencies to provide specialist advice
2. Management of a defined caseload of high-risk individuals in the community and patients on restriction orders with complex needs
3. Providing a resource to multiagency public protection arrangements (MAPPA) in the area.
4. Education and training to other services
5. Some court liaison and diversion arrangements
6. Oversight of patients in secure hospitals'

(Royal College of Psychiatrists, 2013:16)

Referrals to CMHTs may come from a range of services including those in primary care, other secondary mental health services, secure mental health facilities and the criminal justice system (Royal College of Psychiatrists, 2013). Referrals to community mental health services may be made for mental health assessments, in an attempt to develop better understandings of the risk posed by service users, and to explore if service users can access appropriate treatment interventions. Forensic service users will usually be those who have been discharged from a secure mental health facility, patients under a CTO (discussed below), or those who cannot be managed in other community mental health services because of their level of risk (Royal College of Psychiatrists, 2013).

When under the care of community mental health services, patients should be managed under the CPA, which should be supported by structured risk assessment tools such as the HCR-20 (Royal College of Psychiatrists, 2013) (see Chapter 1 for more details about risk assessment tools). While the CPA is criticised by Cummins (2016:39) for being unduly focused on bureaucracy and audit, Burns (2006:191) argues that 'whatever the criticisms of some of the clumsy terminology and bureaucracy of the CPA, it has sharpened up CMHT practice and introduced reflective thought into who should, and should not, be maintained on caseloads'.

As part of their case management, service users may be offered a range of assessments or structured interventions (including cognitive and dialectical therapies) (Royal College of Psychiatrists, 2013). These are usually provided on an out-patient basis, but for those with acute needs, four types of inpatient service in the community also exist: high dependency inpatient rehabilitation, community rehabilitation units, long-term high dependency units and long-term complex care units (Wright, 2017). These sit alongside the three tiers of secure mental health services (high, medium and low) that were outlined in Chapter 6.

CHILD AND ADOLESCENT MENTAL HEALTH SERVICES (CAMHS)

Child and Adolescent Mental Health Services (CAMHS) are spread across secure and community settings. Forensic CAMHS in England are provided within a range of medium and low secure services (including psychiatric intensive care) and are commissioned nationally (Peto et al., 2015). However, there is patchy geographical provision of forensic mental health services for young people across England and Wales (Peto et al., 2015) and long waiting times (Public Health England, 2016). Some young offenders involved with CAMHS have also expressed particularly negative views about the care they receive, with complaints that some workers do not take enough time to get to know them (Heath and Priest, 2016). While inpatient facilities for young people have significantly improved in the last ten years, community-based services have 'lagged behind' (Peto et al., 2015:284). Given the substantial reduction of young people in prison custody in the same period, this lack of provision is concerning (Peto et al., 2015). For more information about current policies and reforms relating to young people and mental health see Parkin, Long and Bate (2018).

UNANTICIPATED CONSEQUENCES OF THE SHIFT TO COMMUNITY CARE

Two unexpected developments occurred as community mental health care developed (Burns, 2014). The first has been the growing special-ism of mental health services in the community to address the different stages of a person's mental illness (e.g. early intervention and crisis services). This development has contributed to a long-standing debate about the relationship between forensic and general mental health ser-vice and the extent to which they should be integrated or run parallel to one another (Jewesbury and McCulloch, 2002; Tighe, Henderson and Thornicroft, 2002; Turner and Salter, 2008).[6] One of the problems with this debate is that there is a lack of agreement among staff about what terms like integrated and parallel mean in practice (Royal College of Psychiatrists, 2013). There is also a lack of consensus about whether generic or specialised services are most appropriate to deal with forensic (and non-forensic) community mental health patients (Wootton et al., 2017). In practice, many community mental health services combine features of both and operate on a continuum or in a 'hybrid' model (Royal College of Psychiatrists, 2013). However, this can be problematic since there is 'a lack of permeability between generic and forensic services' with the boundaries between them 'fraught with conceptual complexity' (Holloway and Davies, 2017:305–306).

Buchanan (2002) reminds us that specialised services can be desirable for their ability to provide expertise, specialised skills, recognition of clinical need that may be overlooked elsewhere as well as specialised treatment. Many of the challenges posed by mentally disordered offenders cannot be adequately addressed by generic CMHTs (Holloway, 2002). In addition, Ministry of Justice case workers (who have responsibility for the discharge of restricted patients) indicate that specialist forensic mental health services in the community are preferable over generic or integrated service models because community staff have a better understanding of the provision of secure care and how to access it, they report changes in behaviour to Ministry of Justice case workers in a more timely manner, and they have a greater understanding of the restricted patients system (Royal College of Psychiatrists, 2013). The Royal College of Psychiatrists (2013) also reports that the introduction of dedicated forensic CMHTs in two areas of London led to a reduction in the length of stay in secure beds. General mental health services may struggle to have the same understanding of service users with complex forensic backgrounds and needs, and this lack of experience and understanding may lead to blockages, miscommunication, failed discharges and delays (Royal College of Psychiatrists, 2013:19). Integrated services can also result in higher CMHT workloads and a corresponding decline in staff morale (Simpson et al., 2016).

However, parallel models are thought to cost more (Centre for Mental Health, 2011) and Turner and Salter (2008) argue that general and forensic psychiatric services in the community should be reintegrated, with the money allocated to specialist services, redistributed to CMHTs. There is a risk that specialised mental health services for those who offend lead people to become more marginalised from mainstream services, and this can negatively impact on service users as well as staff recruitment and morale (Wotton et al., 2017). One consequence of an increasing focus on functionalised and specialist teams is 'a disintegration of services' from the perspective of the service user (England and Lester, 2005) and 'increasing fragmentation of care and erosion of continuity as more and more specialized teams have been established' (Burns, 2014:340; see also Gilburt, 2015). This means that patients have been increasingly likely to fall between the referral criteria of different services (Wootton et al., 2017). Specialised services also risk leading the patient, particularly if the services are designed to deal with high risk, to experience considerable stigma and this can impact on their future care pathways (Trebilcock, 2009).

The second unanticipated development has been an increase in coercion and compulsion in the delivery of community care (Burns, 2014). As we have already seen in Chapter 3, several high-profile crimes involving mental health patients in the community in the late 1980s and early 1990s led to the introduction of compulsory homicide inquiries and greater supervision powers (Department of Health, 1994, 1996). These policy developments reflect that as the asylums closed and demands on CMHTs increased, there was a corresponding increase in 'popular and political expectations' that the risk posed by patients with mental health problems should be adequately managed in the community (Holloway, 2002:225). These expectations have led to a number of coercive measures in the community including compulsory supervision and treatment, as well as an increase in the use of compulsory inpatient treatment (Burns, 2014). Mental health practitioners and services are now commonly criticised for their *lack* of control, rather than their over-use of control and there is growing recognition that coercion is a key feature of community mental health care (Rugkåsa, Molodynski and Burns, 2016).

PROBATION SERVICES IN THE COMMUNITY

In addition to forensic community mental health staff such as psychiatrists, psychologists, social workers and nurses, offenders with mental health problems in the community will inevitably encounter probation staff. Probation staff work in a range of secure and community settings with offenders who have mental health problems. Probation staff may be involved with the supervision (and punishment) of offenders with mental health problems at all stages of the criminal justice system and must therefore work with other health and social care agencies to identify mental health needs, support access to services and to inform health care commissioning (Sirdifield and Owen, 2016). At court, probation staff may be required to provide information that is used to inform decisions about diversion from prosecution, bail and sentencing (Sirdifield and Owen, 2016). After court, probation staff occupy a number of other spaces including prisons, approved premises (APs) and the community. In the community, contact with probation staff usually takes the form of routine appointments, although probation staff will sometimes also be involved with group work and one-to-one interventions (Bridges and Torchia, 2014). In practice, a large proportion of probation staff time is spent ensuring that clients are being compliant with their sentence or license requirements, with accredited programmes and group work only occupying a 'finite period' of an offender's community order or supervision (Bridges and Torchia, 2014:11). While their use has been limited, probation staff may nevertheless work closely with forensic clinicians, when supervising an offender with a mental health treatment requirement (MHTR) or where engagement with mental health treatment is part of an offender's license condition on release from a prison sentence (Royal College of Psychiatrists, 2013).

Offenders involved with probation services in the community may either be serving a community 'punishment' such as a community order (see Chapter 5) or subject to probation 'supervision' in the community following their release from prison. However, there is limited knowledge about the extent of mental health problems among those on probation (Brooker and Ramsbotham, 2014) and limited research about the probation supervision of offenders with mental disorder (Brooker, Denney and Sirdifield, 2014). While limited research and a range of methodological problems make prevalence difficult to establish (Brooker et al., 2012), offenders under probation supervision are thought to have high levels of mental illness and comorbidity (Sirdifield, 2012). Research in a single probation trust found 39% of those under probation supervision to have a current mental health problem (Brooker et al., 2012). In the same sample, nearly 50% were found to have a past or lifetime disorder, with the most prevalent mental disorder identified as 'likely' personality disorder in 47% of cases (Brooker et al., 2012). Offenders under the supervision of probation services also have high levels of comorbidity with 72.3% of those screening positive for a mental illness also thought to have a substance misuse problem (Brooker et al., 2012). Those under probation supervision also have higher levels of physical and general health issues (Plugge et al., 2014), a higher risk of suicide (Ministry of Justice, 2017) and a higher mortality rate (Howard League for Penal Reform, 2012) when compared to the general population. Mental health problems are thought to be particularly acute for women serving community sentences since they often have higher levels of mental health problems than men serving similar sentences (Palmer, Jinks and Hatcher, 2010; Sirdifield, 2012).

While the prevalence of mental health problems among those subject to probation supervision is thought to be high, the provision of mental health training and support to probation staff is often reported to be low. There are also concerns that probation services in urban areas such as London are struggling to adequately support the mental health needs of those they supervise (London Assembly Health Committee, 2017). Changes brought about by the introduction of Community Rehabilitation Companies (CRCs) are also likely to have had a significant impact on the ways in which offenders with mental health problems experience probation supervision (Sirdifield and Owen, 2016). The Bradley report identified that many probation staff were unsure how they should manage offenders with mental health problems, with some unclear about the types of local services that they could refer offenders on their caseload to (Department of Health, 2009). Information sharing between probation and other agencies can be difficult and this means that staff do not always have the information they need (Department of Health, 2009:148). As a result of the historically limited provision of liaison and diversion (L&D) services, it falls to untrained probation staff to identify signs of mental health and learning disability in offenders. In a review of one probation trust Sirdifield and Owen (2016) found that probation staff received very little formal mental health training, relying instead on other sources of understanding including personal experience and things they had learnt 'on the job'. In practice, this meant that staff went about identifying mental health problems and then referring to services in different ways, meaning staff were reliant on 'individualised referral networks and processes' (Sirdifield and Owen, 2016:192). The lack of appropriate provision in the community means that probation staff are often left to manage offenders who may be residing in APs, and this 'places an unnecessary strain on probation officers, who may be untrained in mental health awareness' (Department of Health, 2009:67).

Plugge et al. (2014) remind us that being under probation supervision in the community can be a stressful experience. Some offenders report that serving a prison sentence can be 'easier' because of the security of provision (e.g. shelter and food) and the certainty of the experience (e.g. standardised induction processes and for those serving short sentences, a clear timetable in terms of detention) (Plugge et al., 2014; see also Trebilcock, 2011). Others remind us that while punishment in the community may 'create the illusion of liberty', in practice, anxieties about being breached for non-compliance and the possibility of being sent to prison hang over offenders (van Ginneken and Hayes, 2017:70). This reveals that there are a number of 'pains' involved with being under probation supervision and that supervision requirements can generate significant obstacles for reintegration (Durnescu, 2011). These 'pains' may be particularly acute for those with a mental health problem.

Given these observations, the relationship between probation staff and offenders is therefore very important. Research suggests that high-quality relationships between an offender manager and offender are predictive of compliance with probation supervision (Kennealy et al., 2012). Offenders are often 'hypersensitive to perceived injustice and are unusually astute in recognising when stringent risk management has lost its focus' (Craissati, 2007:227). Higher quality relationships between staff and offender increase the likelihood of an offender being open and honest and the chances of probation staff identifying when someone is in need of support (Sirdifield and Owen, 2016). Moreover, offenders who are kept well informed by their offender managers, are more likely to comply with supervision requirements (Kemshall and Wood, 2007).

LEAVING SECURE DETENTION FOR THE COMMUNITY

The majority of patients under the care of forensic community mental health services are likely to have spent time in a secure setting. Given this, the chapter now briefly considers the mechanisms of release from prison and discharge from secure mental health facilities. After outlining the ways by which prisoners may leave prison and patients may leave secure mental health services, the chapter explores the importance of aftercare and resettlement along with the provision of supervision and risk management in the community.

RELEASE FROM PRISON TO THE COMMUNITY

The date of a prisoner's release from custody will depend on the type of sentence they are serving. The majority of people in prison are serving short prison sentences (of 12 months and under) and will be automatically released once they have served half of their sentence in custody. Those serving longer determinate sentences of up to four years may also be released at the half way point. Some offenders serving sentences of less than four years may be eligible for 'early' release under the Home Detention Curfew (HDC) scheme, where they will be subject to an electronic 'tag' in the community. If the offender does not comply with the set curfew they can be recalled to prison. Following the Offender Rehabilitation Act (ORA) 2014 all adults released from prison following a sentence of more than one day are now subject to statutory supervision in the community. This is made up of a license period and post-sentence supervision.

All prisoners serving a 'life' or 'indeterminate' sentences, along with those serving determinate (4+ years) or 'extended' sentences will have their release reviewed by the Parole Board (PB). Under the CJA 1991 and the C(S)A 1997 the PB are responsible for carrying out risk assessments of prisoners in England and Wales and making decisions about their release. Eligibility for parole is a complex area and dependent on the sentence handed down by the court (i.e. determinate or indeterminate), the date of that sentence (under what CJA the sentence was passed) and the length of sentence (as specified by the courts and/or Home Secretary). For further information about PB law and practice see Arnott and Creighton (2013); Her Majesty's (HM) Prison Service (2012, 2017). See also the Parole Board Rules 2016 (as amended by Parole Board (Amendment) Rules 2018).

Following the Supreme Court's judgement in the case of R(Osborn) v Parole Board [2013] UKSC 61, the system of parole has become fairer and prisoners have enjoyed greater rights. However, while the rights of prisoners may have improved, the PB has become increasingly sensitive to risk, especially following a number of high-profile inquiries into their decision-making. Following two high-profile reviews into offences that were committed by two men who had been released by the PB (HM Inspectorate of Probation, 2006a, 2006b), Shute (2007:22) argues that the PB has moved away from: 'considerations of rehabilitation balanced against risk ... [to] an approach that is plainly in tune with the public protection agenda'. The recent high-profile review of the PBs decision to release John Worboys (now known as John Radford), a taxi driver convicted of 19 serious sexual offences, by the High Court and decision to quash the release decision, may also increase the caution with which the PB reviews offenders.

Harrison (2011:194) argues that mentally disordered offenders in the prison service have an 'even steeper mountain to climb' when it comes to satisfying the PB because they are less likely than other prisoners to have had access to, or been able to, successfully complete offending behaviour programmes. Research also suggests that they are more likely to be assessed in a negative manner than other prisoners applying for parole (Fitzgibbon, 2009; Trebilcock and Weaver, 2012). And if they are released on parole, mentally disordered offenders may find themselves subject to overly restrictive community conditions that do not adequately support their treatment and rehabilitation (Fitzgibbon, 2009). This, in turn, may increase their likelihood of recall to prison.

DISCHARGE FROM SECURE MENTAL HEALTH CARE TO THE COMMUNITY

For the majority of patients, discharge from hospital is a process rather than a single event, and for patients held in high or medium secure mental health facilities, there is usually an expectation that they will travel through the different levels of security before being considered for discharge to the community. In order to assess how well patients may cope in the community, many are given a leave of absence under s17 of the MHA 1983 (as amended by the MHA 2007) before being discharged (Bartlett and Sandland, 2014). Under s17 the Responsible Clinician (RC) (the practitioner with overall responsibility for the care and treatment of someone detained under the MHA) can grant leave to unrestricted patients. With Ministry of Justice agreement, restricted patients can also be granted leave.[7] Section 17 leave may be granted for a number of reasons including trial periods or treatment at another hospital; on compassionate grounds such as funeral attendance; and, for short periods in the community in order to assess the patient's ability to cope and to enhance their prospects of rehabilitation (McMurran, Khalifa and Gibbon, 2009:19). Conditions for the leave of absence can be set by the RC if they are deemed necessary for the safety of the patient or others and a patient can be recalled to hospital under s17(4).

Patients may also leave hospital following review by a mental health tribunal. The First-tier Tribunal (Mental Health) is responsible for reviewing the detention of those detained under the MHA 1983 in England.[8] In many respects, the tribunal performs a similar role to the PB in their role of deciding when it is safe for a patient to be released (Harrison, 2011). However, their remit is different and under s73 of the MHA 2007 the tribunal is generally required to discharge the patient from hospital unless they are satisfied that

- the patient is suffering from a mental disorder of a nature or degree that makes it appropriate for the patient to be liable to be detained in hospital for medical treatment; or
- the medical treatment is necessary for the patient's health and safety or for the protection of other persons, or
- appropriate medical treatment is available for the patient.

The tribunal also has a wider range of powers and options available to them than the PB. In addition to recommending that a patient is discharged from hospital, they can also recommend that a patient be given a leave of absence, supervised community treatment and transferred to another (lower security) hospital. If a tribunal discharges a patient who is still under sentence they will be returned to prison where their release will be decided in the usual way (which may include review by the PB).

In 2015–2016 there were a total of 29,808 applications to the First-tier Tribunal (Mental Health) (Care Quality Commission (CQC), 2016). Of these applications, 3,417 were from restricted patients and, of these, 669 restricted patients were recommended for a discharge (most often conditional or deferred conditional) by the tribunal (CQC, 2016). A recent review of tribunal decision-making, reports that patients who have undertaken unescorted community leave, have a RC recommendation for discharge and are under a restricted MHA section were more likely to be recommended for discharge by the tribunal (Jewell et al., 2017). Patients with higher HCR-20 scores, recent episodes of acute illness and reports of agitated behaviour or inpatient violence were least likely to be recommended for discharge (Jewell et al., 2017). Tribunals also hear applications against CTOs (discussed in the next section), although patients seeking a discharge from a CTO may be disappointed since these are rarely granted by a tribunal (CQC, 2016). While 4,317 applications against a CTO were made to the tribunal in 2015–2016, only 132 patients were discharged (CQC, 2016). These figures suggest that tribunals prefer to recommend transfer rather than discharge (Holloway and Grounds, 2003; Peay, 1989) and that through the process and performance of a tribunal 'a clear expectation is signalled to both patients and workers that continued and ongoing aftercare monitoring is necessary' (Coffey, 2011:751).

Approximately 1,500 conditionally discharged patients are under supervision in the community (Cummins, 2016:70). Under s41(3) of the MHA 1983 specific conditions can be added to the conditional discharge of a restricted patient. These may include a requirement to engage with treatment and to reside in a particular location (Beswick and Gunn, 2017). If a conditionally discharged patient does not engage with treatment, they remain liable to recall to hospital where treatment can be enforced. Patients may also be subject to a range of supervision requirements including attendance at treatment or other daytime activities, restrictions on travel and/or restrictions on contacting key individuals (Coffey, 2012). The supervision of those released from the forensic mental health system is undertaken by the 'social supervisor', commonly a social worker or probation officer (Prins, 2016). Service users will also find themselves under the care of a named clinical practitioner, their RC, commonly a psychiatrist or psychologist, although they may also have contact with other staff involved with the provision of community mental health care, such as community mental health nurses (Prins, 2016). Together, the social supervisor and the RC have a statutory duty to manage restricted patients who have been discharged to the community (Royal College of Psychiatrists, 2013).[9] Within 28 days of discharge the social supervisor must prepare a report about how the service user is doing in the community, addressing key issues surrounding rehabilitation and risk and submit this report to the Ministry of Justice and the RC.

MENTAL HEALTH 'TREATMENT' IN THE COMMUNITY

CTOs were introduced in November 2008 following the insertion of s17A–17HG into the MHA 1983 by the MHA 2007.[10] A CTO allows an unrestricted patient (i.e. s3, s37 and s47) to be discharged from hospital to the community, where they will be subject to supervised treatment. However, the patient can be recalled to hospital at any time if there are concerns about risk to the patient, others or if the patient is found to have breached any of the conditions attached to the CTO. Harrison (2011:203) observes that CTOs are designed for mentally disordered offenders 'who have a history of non-compliance, relapse and re-admission, and is an attempt to break the "revolving door" of detention' (see also Bartlett and Sandland, 2014). Under s17A(5) of the MHA 2007 five criteria must be satisfied for a CTO to be made:

a. the patient is suffering from mental disorder of a nature or degree which makes it appropriate for him to receive medical treatment;
b. it is necessary for his health or safety or for the protection of other persons that he should receive such treatment;
c. subject to his being liable to be recalled as mentioned in paragraph (d) below, such treatment can be provided without his continuing to be detained in a hospital;
d. it is necessary that the RC should be able to exercise the power under section 17E(1) below to recall the patient to hospital; and
e. appropriate medical treatment is available for him.

Several discretionary conditions can be added to a CTO which commonly include agreeing to take medication and/or engaging with services in the community (e.g. attending assessments or treatment sessions). It is important to highlight that CTOs do not permit forcible treatment in the community. However, those who fail to engage with community based treatment are likely to be recalled to hospital if their mental health is felt to be at risk of deterioration or if there are concerns about the safety of others (Weich et al., 2018).

As we described in Chapter 3, the introduction of CTOs under the MHA 2007 was met with considerable resistance. Unfortunately, the government 'grossly underestimated the clinical and risk management appeal of CTOs' (Rawala and Gupta, 2014:15; see also Mental Health Alliance, 2010) and despite limited evidence of their effectiveness and their impact on patient autonomy, CTOs have been extensively used (Beswick and Gunn, 2017). Following their introduction in 2008 when the MHA 2007 came into force, the number of people subject to a CTO has steadily increased. On 31st March 2016, 5,426 people were subject to a CTO in the community (NHS Digital, 2016). Nearly twice as many men as women are subject to a CTO (NHS Digital, 2017) and when using broad ethnic groups, those categorised as 'black', are nearly nine times more likely to receive a CTO than those who are 'white' (NHS Digital, 2017).

Although many point to the challenges that CTOs pose for civil liberties, some highlight that their introduction was motivated by a desire to reduce the number of 'revolving door' patients and to facilitate treatment in the 'least restrictive' setting (Churchill et al., 2007). While CTOs were partly designed to try and reduce the problem of revolving door patients (Bartlett and Sandland, 2014), research in England and Wales has concluded that CTOs do not reduce readmission to hospital (Burns et al., 2016; Maughan et al., 2014) and therefore do not 'justify the significant curtailment of patients' personal liberty' (Burns et al., 2013:1627). Concerns have also been expressed that they may lead to people being discharged from hospital too early in order to free up beds (Mental Health Alliance, 2010). The recent independent review of the MHA 1983 has recommended that a number of reforms are made to CTOs in order to reduce their use and to give greater protection to those who are subject to them (Department of Health and Social Care, 2018b).

MULTI-AGENCY PUBLIC PROTECTION ARRANGEMENTS AND OFFENDERS WITH MENTAL DISORDER

MAPPA place a statutory duty on the police, probation and prison services (the 'Responsible Authority'), to establish procedures to identify and reduce the risk posed by violent and sexual offenders. Other agencies, including health and local authority social services, also have a statutory duty to cooperate with the Responsible Authority. Together, these agencies are responsible for the following functions: identification of MAPPA offenders; assessment of their risk; management of the risks they pose; and effective information sharing between relevant agencies. MAPPA eligible offenders (defined by s327 Criminal Justice Act (CJA) 2003) include those sentenced to 12 months or more in prison following conviction for a specified sexual or violent offence (under Schedule 15 of the CJA 2003) and registered sex offenders (under the Sexual Offences Act (SOA) 2003). MAPPA may also apply to some offenders who are subject to provisions of the MHA 2007. This means that clinical staff working in mental health services will often be required to provide expertise to, and work in collaboration with MAPPA. Indeed, it is not uncommon for community forensic mental health teams to be recorded as the Single Point of Contact (SPOC) for MAPPA (Royal College of Psychiatrists, 2013).

While agency cooperation has long been a feature of criminal justice policy (Clift, 2012), much debate has surrounded the question of what a duty to cooperate should actually entail (Snowden and Ashim, 2008). Mental health professionals have expressed particular concerns about information sharing, with some arguing that the duty to cooperate 'threatens historical understandings of patient confidentiality' (Hales et al., 2016:319). This has led to some resistance among mental health staff on the basis that MAPPA are primarily focused on risk and public protection rather than care, and may consequently have a negative impact on the quality of therapeutic relationships (Yakeley and Taylor, 2011).

A number of practical challenges have also been identified. Despite having a duty to cooperate, health services are not provided with additional funding to help implement MAPPA (Snowden and Ashim, 2008). Harrison (2011:194) questions if those responsible for supervising offenders under MAPPA are sufficiently trained to comment on an offender's mental health while Yakeley and Taylor (2011) report that there have been difficulties with trying to combine different agency-based assessments of risk.

While MAPPA will have certainly helped to manage the risk posed by some offenders with mental disorder, the arrangements also work to further blur the boundaries between criminal justice and mental health care. This has sometimes meant that mental practitioners have found themselves in the difficult position of having to prioritise risk over the needs and rights of their patients. It is for this reason that

Yakeley, Taylor and Cameron (2012) have called for clear guidelines to help address the challenges surrounding their use with offenders with mental health problems.

AFTERCARE AND MENTAL HEALTH

As we have learnt in the last few sections, managing the risk that people may pose following their release from prison or discharge from secure mental health care is a key priority. Ensuring that patients adhere to their treatment plan and take their medication in the community has also been an increasing feature of mental health 'aftercare' in England. However, it is important to ensure that offenders are involved in their own commitment to change (Shuker and Bates, 2015; Weaver, 2014). Moreover, the successful reintegration of offenders is dependent not just on managing risk but also by giving sufficient attention to throughcare and resettlement (Trebilcock and Worrall, 2018). In the next section we consider some of the policies in place to support aftercare as well as the challenges surrounding them.

AFTERCARE FOR PEOPLE RELEASED FROM PRISON

Chapter 6 highlighted the very high prevalence of mental disorder among people in prison. If we are to address this we need to think beyond the prison, and remember that the mental health needs of prisoners will 'always remain greater than the capacity, unless mental health and community services outside prison are improved' (HM Inspectorate of Prisons, 2007:5). It is also important to be mindful that 'leaving prison can be as traumatic as entering' (London Assembly Health Committee, 2017:1). Recognising that the principles of the offender mental health care pathway (see Department of Health and National Institute for Mental Health England, 2005) cannot be achieved without adequate mental health services in the community, the Bradley review called for improvements in community mental health services to be made (Department of Health, 2009). But, while there has been increasing investment in L&D services, there are still many problems with the aftercare that prisoners may receive following their release.

As part of the *Transforming Rehabilitation* (TR) reforms Through the Gate (TTG) resettlement services were introduced in 2015 to ensure that offenders are supported in their transition from prison to the community (Ministry of Justice, 2013). Despite the focus on resettlement, the National Audit Office (2017:9) reports that 'prisoners do not routinely receive continuity of care on release' while the HM Inspectorate of Probation (2017:57) has described TTG resettlement planning as 'woefully inadequate'. Far from helping prisoners to reintegrate back into the community, a recent case study of one resettlement prison warns that the current operation risks enhancing resentment and 'deepening the sense of a penal crisis' (Taylor et al., 2017:116). Problematically, neither the National Offender Management Service (NOMS) (which was replaced by Her Majesty's Prison and Probation Service (HMPPS) in April 2017) nor NHS England monitors whether this care is provided (National Audit Office, 2017), and this adds to the challenges of ensuring TTG services are funded and in place. In addition, health information is not routinely shared with CRCs and this causes inevitable difficulties when trying to plan a prisoner's release from prison (National Audit Office, 2017). It is clear that further improvements to the relationship between prison regimes and health care as well as with the wider community are needed (Public Health England, 2016).

AFTERCARE ARRANGEMENTS FOR PATIENTS LEAVING HOSPITAL

Under s117 of the MHA 1983, local authorities have a statutory duty to provide aftercare for patients discharged from sections 3 (civil admission), 37 (hospital order), 45A (hospital and limitations direction), 47 and 48 (transfers to hospital from prison) of the Act. The CPA must be followed and aftercare will continue until those involved with the care jointly agree that the individual no longer needs it. However, a recent review by CQC (2018) found that 24% of care plans had no evidence of discharge planning. In addition, they found there had been no patient involvement in 32% of care plans (CQC, 2018). Given that being discharged from hospital can lead to increased anxiety for mental health patients (Coffey, 2012), this is particularly concerning. Limited funding and availability of community-based step-down services have also led to delays for patients waiting for transfer to the community (Royal College of Psychiatrists, 2013). Once discharged, patients in the community have expressed dissatisfaction with issues such as housing and the lack of 'back up services', including daytime activities and sheltered work (Royal College of Psychiatrists, 2013:15). Some also considered weekly appointments to be intrusive rather than supportive (Royal College of Psychiatrists, 2013:15) suggesting that there may sometimes be too much of a focus on managing risk rather than providing care and support. Taken together, these findings suggest that more needs to be done to recognise the different needs that patients leaving secure care have, and to target discharge planning accordingly (Conlin and Braham, 2018; Nolan, Bradley and Brimblecombe, 2011).

MENTAL HEALTH AFTERCARE AS CHALLENGING FOR SERVICE USERS

Aftercare arrangements need to address the many causes of reoffending (Appleby, Roscoe and Shaw, 2015) and are essential for mentally disordered offenders. Aside from the fact that prisoners have an increased mortality rate after release from prison (Zlodre and Fazel, 2012), offenders with mental illness have multiple needs (Anderson, 2011) and are more likely to have problems with housing (Boardman, 2016) and employment (Burns, 2014). Less than a third of prisoners, for example, have a job (or alternative place in education or training) following their release from prison (Samele, Keil and Thomas, 2009). Release from prison is a critical point when offenders with mental health problems need a range of support (Durcan, 2016) yet, bare essentials like housing, work, health and good relationships are areas that are often not met with offenders with mental health problems (Göbbels, Thaker and Ward, 2016). Resettlement efforts can also be undermined when prisoners are released a long way from home (perhaps because of victim and/or resource issues) and/or when they are released very quickly and without adequate support mechanisms in place.

We should also remember how vulnerable people with mental health problems in the community can be. One unforeseen consequence of aftercare arrangements is that they draw attention to people with mental health problems in the community (Coffey, 2012). Aftercare and monitoring of patients after discharge is often dominated by concerns about risk and that this can generate iatrogenic risks for its ability to undermine the service user's efforts to start a new life in the community as a result of them being 'unmasked' to the community and characterised as someone who must be supervised (Coffey, 2012; see also Holloway and Davies, 2017). Some service users find aftercare arrangements more intrusive and restrictive than their detention in hospital (Coffey, 2012). This leads Coffey (2012:465) to warn that 'intensive aftercare handled without regard for its wider visibility may work to jeopardise these attempts'. Association with mental health services, made visible through home visits and monitoring by statutory services, can increase the stigma and anxiety experienced by service users in the community (Coffey, 2012). Efforts to reintegrate into the community are made more difficult as a result of the social isolation experienced by this group and the length of time that many mentally disordered offenders will have spent in secure institutions, often far away home (Coffey, 2012). The prioritisation of public protection over social support and help with reintegration may lead service users to disengage from services, and in addition, by focusing on the possible risk of the discharged patient, the risks the patient is exposed to can be overlooked (Coffey, 2012). As we learnt in Chapter 4, the victimisation of those with mental health problems is disproportionately high. Aside from adverse psychological and social effects that may follow from such victimisation (Khalifeh et al., 2015), victimisation can increase the likelihood of a mentally disordered offender committing further offences (Sadeh, Binder and McNiel, 2014).

OTHER KEY CHALLENGES INVOVLED WITH MANAGING OFFENDERS WITH MENTAL HEALTH PROBLEMS IN THE COMMUNITY

The Royal College of Psychiatrists (2013) highlights a number of key challenges involved with the provision of care in the community to forensic services users, including: a limited evidence base regarding clinical and cost-effectiveness, geographical variability of service models and structure, disagreement about the definition of community forensic services, and debate about who services should be for, and for how long. In addition, it is known that mental health practitioners in the community experience high levels of stress (Carson and Fagin, 1996; Johnson et al., 2012). Community mental health staff often work under extreme time pressures and are likely to have higher caseloads than those in secure services (Holloway and Davies, 2017). Such workload pressures, along with a lack of resources, are frequently cited by staff as key sources of stress (Onyett, 2011).

CONTINUITY OF CARE

Our previous discussion about the importance of aftercare reminds us of the importance of 'continuity of care' for mentally disordered offenders. Indeed, continuity of care has been recognised as essential by both criminal justice and health policies (Department of Health,

2005, 2009; HM Prison Service, 2006; Ministry of Justice, 2013). In a review, Weaver, Coffey and Hewitt (2017) highlight how 'continuity' can take many different forms including: how effective coordination is between different services (cross-boundary continuity), the extent to which it is delivered by as few professionals as possible with minimal gaps (longitudinal continuity), the quality of the therapeutic relationship (relational continuity), communication of information between services (informational continuity), the context in which care is delivered in the community and supported by things like day centres and housing (contextual continuity) and the flexibility of care (flexible/responsive continuity). As we have seen throughout this chapter, mentally disordered offenders are at risk of experiencing multiple problems across these different forms of continuity.

INTER-AGENCY COMMUNICATION

If community mental health services are to work well it is essential that CMHTs have good links with other services including general community mental health services and secure forensic mental health services (Royal College of Psychiatrists, 2013). However, the engagement of general adult mental health services with mentally disordered offenders is reported to be problematic, with many not wanting involvement with forensic service users because of the core issues of 'stigma, fear, different approach and emphasis around risk' (Royal College of Psychiatrists, 2013:13). In addition, good links must be established between health services and criminal justice agencies such as prisons and probation. However, communication between prison in reach teams and community mental health services is reported to be problematic (Caulfield and Twort, 2012) while challenges with inter-agency communication between probation and health and social services can serve as a barrier to facilitating effective offender engagement with services (Sirdifield and Owen, 2016).

GAPS IN SERVICE PROVISION

Despite increasing recognition that the prevalence of mental health problems among offenders on probation, Brooker and Ramsbotham (2014) remind us that the availability of services is problematic. One reason for this is that commissioning is difficult, in part because of the challenges involved with establishing prevalence (Plugge et al., 2014).

Essentially the size and the scale of the problem is not fully understood or known. However, there is agreement, that there are many gaps in provision for offenders with mental disorder. This is particularly true for those with comorbidity and substance misuse issues. This is because local substance misuse services are unlikely to be closely integrated with adult mental health services. Weston (2017) found a lack of knowledge about local mental health services among drug treatment practitioners with staff also complaining that CMHT referral processes were unclear and that their clients with comorbid mental health issues were often not getting the help they needed. Moreover, support for those with mental health and alcohol problems is particularly poor (Institute of Alcohol Studies and Centre for Mental Health, 2018). Given the high prevalence of drug and alcohol issues among those under probation supervision in the community, this represents a significant problem.

For those in need of crisis intervention or inpatient care, access to services from the community is also reported to be problematic. Crisp, Smith and Nicholson (2016:11) report that 'access to acute care for severely ill adult mental health patients in England is inadequate and, in some cases, potentially dangerous'. Between 1998 and 2012 the number of adult inpatient psychiatric beds fell by 39% (Mental Health Taskforce, 2016). Limited early intervention and crisis care have led to patients being transferred long distances in order to access beds (Mental Health Taskforce, 2016:9). This highlights two interconnected problems of gaining access to psychiatric wards as well as problems surrounding the adequate provision of alternative care in the community (Crisp, Smith and Nicholson, 2016). These points reflect that local rehabilitation and inpatient mental health services have been depleted (Centre for Mental Health, 2017).

As a result of some these gaps, and the low availability of services, people in the community may often find that they are turned away from services. One way this is achieved is with strict eligibility criteria, which represent a significant barrier for those with complex needs (Public Health England, 2016). Drawing on the work of New (1996), Holloway and Davies (2017:316) set out five possible ways that health services may respond when faced with high demand and limited resources:

> These include *deterrence* (characterised by service charges, gatekeeping by primary care, unfriendly staff, inconvenient appointment times, poor quality care environments and prolonged duration between appointments); *deflection* (passing referrals to other agencies, shifting between 'health' and 'social' care or between generic,

forensic and learning disability mental health services); *dilution* (thinly spreading serving provision, adopting minimal standards of care, reducing skill–mix in a nursing team); *delay* (waiting lists, which for psychological treatments can become infinitely long); and *denial* (which involves not providing a treatment at all for more or less justifiable reasons).

Holloway and Davies (2017) assert that most mental health professionals working in the community will recognise these strategies and that mentally disordered offenders are most likely to experience deterrence, deflection and denial when referred to generic mental health services. With limited resources, CMHTs may be reluctant to accept referrals of patients with a 'forensic' label (Holloway and Davies, 2017) reflecting a culture among mental health professionals that is 'prone to de-legitimising the mentally abnormal offender by labelling them offender not patient' which often leads to people being rejected from services (Mullen, 2002:xvi).

DISCUSSION

While mental health services in the community may be criticised for failing to control patients under their care; surveillance and crime control should not be the primary concern of these services (Buchanan, 2002). However, mental health service users are increasingly defined in terms of their potential risk factors 'rather than in terms of their needs and rights' (Langan and Lindow, 2004:2) and in practice, the conditional discharge of patients from forensic services to the community only offers limited freedom to service users (Coffey, 2012). While the use of compulsory powers may increase service user compliance with medication and treatment in the community, such measures also risk undermining the therapeutic alliance (Coffey and Jenkins, 2002) and fracturing the relationships between practitioners and service users (Hannigan and Coffey, 2011).

Establishing a good relationship between the mentally disordered offender and those involved with their community management and care is essential. While considerable resources continue to be attached to the most secure services in the country, if these services are not supported by adequate services in the community, attempts at rehabilitation and recovery in the community are highly likely to fail. This reminds us of the importance of continuity of care, and that practitioners in the community need to focus on aftercare and support as well as issues of risk.

Along with being a key site for rehabilitation, the community also represents a key site for diversion and for keeping people out of secure services in the first place. However, more needs to be done in terms of prevention (Public Health England, 2016). Too often mental health services are reactionary rather than proactive in tackling people's poor mental health. This often follows from limited resources but has significant consequences since people often do not receive care until they have become very unwell (and in some cases, only following their contact with the criminal justice system).

Only about half of CMHTs are reported to offer a 24/7 crisis service and only a small number of A&E departments have 24/7 liaison with mental health services and this means that too many in people in crisis are having to be picked up by the police (Mental Health Taskforce, 2016). Aside from questions about whether this is a good use of police time (especially in the context of their own resource constraints), increased police involvement with vulnerable people experiencing a mental health crisis, may serve to criminalise them or add to the stigma and discrimination that they face.

Given this, it is positive to note that in 2018 the government announced that £15 million would be used to help fund the *Beyond Places of Safety* scheme, which involves the provision of crisis cafés, clinics and other community services with the aim of helping prevent people with mental health problems reaching crisis point (Department of Health and Social Care, 2018a).[11] Along with these 'safe havens' in the community, it is promised that funding will support a new mental health crisis service that will provide a 24-hour hotline, comprehensive support in all A&E departments, a national crisis teams for young people, and more mental health ambulances (HM Treasury, 2018). Such schemes may have an important role to play in preventing people's mental health problems from escalating to a point where they come to the attention of criminal justice services, improve the outcomes of those in crisis, and help reduce the demands made on emergency services including the police.

FURTHER READING

For further information about the emergence of community mental health care see Burns (2014). For a comprehensive overview of the care of mentally disordered offenders in the community see the edited collections by Buchanan and Wooton (2017), Molodynski et al. (2016) and Ashmore and Shuker (2014). Readers interested in the community management of mental health patients outside the UK should consult Molodynski et al. (2016).

REFERENCES

Anderson, S. (2011) *Complex responses: Understanding poor frontline responses to adults with multiple needs: A review of the literature and analysis of contributing factors*, London: Revolving Doors Agency.

Appleby, L., Roscoe, A. and Shaw, J. (2015) 'Services for released prisoners should address the many causes of reoffending', *Lancet Psychiatry*, 2: 853–854.

Arnott, H. and Creighton, S. (2013) *Parole Board hearings (Third edition)*, London: Legal Action Group.

Ashmore, Z. and Shuker, R. (2014) (eds.) *Forensic practice in the community*, Abingdon: Routledge.

Bartlett, P. and Sandland, R. (2014) *Mental health law: Policy and practice (Fourth edition)*, Oxford: Oxford University Press.

Beswick, J. and Gunn, M. (2017) 'The law in England and Wales on mental health treatment in the community' in Buchanan, A. and Wootton, L. (eds.) *Care of the mentally disordered offender in the community (Second edition)*, Oxford: Oxford University Press.

Boardman, J. (2016) *More than shelter. Supported accommodation and mental health*, London: Centre for Mental Health.

Bridges, A. and Torchia, K. (2014) 'Overview of forensic services in the community' in Ashmore, Z. and Shuker, R. (eds.) *Forensic practice in the community*, Abingdon: Routledge.

Brooker, C., Denney, D. and Sirdifield, C. (2014) 'Mental disorder and probation policy and practice: A view from the UK', *International Journal of Law and Psychiatry*, 37(5): 484–489.

Brooker, C. and Ramsbotham, D. (2014) 'Probation and mental health: Who cares?' *British Journal of General Practice*, 64(621): 170–171.

Brooker, C., Sirdifield, C., Blizard, R., Denney, D. and Pluck, G. (2012) 'Probation and mental illness', *Journal of Forensic Psychiatry and Psychology*, 23(4): 522–537.

Buchanan, A. (2002) 'Who does what? The relationship between generic and forensic psychiatric service' in Buchanan, A. (ed.) *Care of the mentally disordered offender in the community*, Oxford: Oxford University Press.

Buchanan, A. and Wootton, L. (2017) (eds.) *Care of the mentally disordered offender in the community*, Oxford: Oxford University Press.

Burns, T. (2006) 'An introduction to Community Mental Health Teams (CMHTs): How do they relate to patients with personality disorders?' in Sampson, M., McCubbin, R. and Tyrer, P. (eds.) *Personality disorder and Community Mental Health Teams: A practitioner's guide*, Chichester: John Wiley and Sons Ltd.

Burns, T. (2014) 'Community psychiatry's achievements', *Epidemiology and Psychiatric Sciences*, 23(4): 337–344.

Burns, T., Rugkåsa, J., Molodynski, A., Dawson, J., Yeeles, K., Vazquez-Montes, M., Voysey, M., Sinclair, J. and Priebe, S. (2013) 'Community treatment orders for patients with psychosis (OCTET): A randomised controlled trial', *The Lancet*, 381(9878):1627–1633.

Burns, T., Rugkåsa, J., Yeeles, K. and Catty, J. (2016) 'Coercion in mental health: A trial of the effectiveness of community treatment orders and an investigation of informal coercion in community mental health care', *Programme Grants for Applied Research*, 4(21): 1–353. www.ncbi.nlm.nih.gov/books/NBK401969/pdf/Bookshelf_NBK401969.pdf

Care Quality Commission (CQC) (2016) *Monitoring the Mental Health Act in 2015/16*, Newcastle-Upon-Tyne: CQC.

Care Quality Commission (CQC) (2018) *Monitoring the Mental Health Act 2016/17*, Newcastle Upon Tyne: CQC.

Carson, J. and Fagin, L. (1996) 'Stress in mental health professionals: A cause for concern or an inevitable part of the job?', *International Journal of Social Psychiatry*, 42(2): 79–81.

Caulfield, L.S. and Twort, H. (2012) 'Implementing change: Staff experiences of changes to prison mental healthcare in England and Wales', *International Journal of Prisoner Health*, 8(1): 7–15.

Centre for Mental Health (2011) *Pathways to unlocking secure mental health care*, London: Centre for Mental Health.

Centre for Mental Health (2017) *Briefing 51: Long-stay rehabilitation services*, London: Centre for Mental Health.

Churchill, R., Owen, G., Singh, S. and Hotopf, M. (2007) *International experiences of using community treatment orders*, London: Department of Health.

Clift, S. (2012) 'Risk, assessment and the practice of actuarial criminal justice' in Pycroft, A. and Clift, S. (eds.) *Risk and rehabilitation: Management and treatment of substance misuse and mental health problems in the criminal justice system*, Bristol: The Policy Press.

Coffey, M. (2011) 'Resistance and challenge: Competing accounts in aftercare monitoring', *Sociology of Health and Illness*, 33(5): 748–760.

Coffey, M. (2012) 'A risk worth taking? Value differences and alternative risk constructions in accounts given by patients and their community workers following conditional discharge from forensic mental health services', *Health, Risk and Society*, 14(5): 465–482.

Coffey, M. and Jenkins, E. (2002) 'Power and control: Forensic community mental health nurses perceptions of team-working, legal sanction and compliance', *Journal of Psychiatric and Mental Health Nursing*, 9(5): 521–529.

Conlin, A. and Braham, L. (2018) 'Comparison of outcomes of patients with personality disorder to patients with mental illness, following discharge from medium secure hospital: Systematic review', *Journal of Forensic Psychiatry and Psychology*, 29(1): 124–145.

Craissati, J. (2007) 'The paradoxical effects of stringent risk management' in Padfield, N. (ed.) *Who to release? Parole, fairness and criminal justice*, Cullompton: Willan Publishing.

Crisp, N., Smith, G. and Nicholson, K. (2016) *Old problems, new solutions – Improving acute psychiatric care for adults in England (The Commission on Acute Adult Psychiatric Care, 2016)*, London: Royal College of Psychiatrists.

Cummins, I. (2016) *Mental health and the criminal justice system: A social work perspective*, Northwich: Critical Publishing Ltd.

Department of Health (1994) *Introduction of supervision registers for mentally ill people from 1 April 1994, HSG (94)*, London: Department of Health

Department of Health (1996) *Guidance on supervised discharge (Aftercare under supervision and related provisions)*, London: Department of Health.

Department of Health (2005) *Offender mental healthcare pathway*, London: Department of Health.

Department of Health (2009) *The Bradley Report. Lord Bradley's review of people with mental health problems or learning disabilities in the criminal justice system*, London: Department of Health.

Department of Health and Home Office (1992) *Review of health and social services for mentally disordered offenders and others requiring similar services*, London: Her Majesty's Stationery Office.

Department of Health and National Institute for Mental Health England (NIMHE) (2005) *Offender mental health care pathway*, London: Department of Health and NIMHE.

Department of Health and Social Care (2018a) '£15 million boost for local mental health crisis services', [Press Release] 25 May 2018, London: Department of Health and Social Care.

Department of Health and Social Care (2018b) *Modernising the Mental Health Act: Increasing choice, reducing compulsion. Final report of the independent review of the Mental Health Act 1983*, London: Department of Health and Social Care.

Durcan, G. (2016) *Mental health and criminal justice: Views from consultations across England and Wales*, London: Centre for Mental Health.

Durnescu, I. (2011) 'Pains of probation: Effective practice and human rights', *International Journal of Offender Therapy and Comparative Criminology*, 55(4): 530–545.

England, E. and Lester, H. (2005) 'Integrated mental health services in England: A policy paradox?', *International Journal of Integrated Care*, 5(3): 1–8.

Fitzgibbon, W. (2009) 'Mentally disordered offenders and the parole process', *Eris Web Journal*, Available at: http://periodika.osu.cz/eris/dok/2010-01/mentally_disordered_offenders.pdf [Last accessed 03.01.2017].

Gilburt, H. (2015) *Mental health under pressure*, London: The King's Fund.

Göbbels, S., Thakker, J. and Ward, T. (2016) 'Desistance in offenders with mental illness' in Winstone, J. (ed.) *Mental health, crime and criminal justice*, Basingstoke: Palgrave Macmillan.

Gunn, J. (1977) 'Management of the mentally abnormal offender: Integrated or parallel?', *Proceedings of the Royal Society of Medicine*, 70: 877–880.

Hales, H., Dixon, A., Newton, Z. and Bartlett, A. (2016) 'Assaults by mentally disordered offenders in prison: Equity and equivalence', *Bioethical inquiry*, 13: 317–326.

Hannigan, B. and Coffey, M. (2011) 'Where the wicked problems are: The case of mental health', *Health Policy*, 101(3): 220–227.

Harrison, K. (2011) *Dangerousness, risk and the governance of serious sexual and violent offenders*, Abingdon: Routledge.

Heath, R.A. and Priest, H.M. (2016) 'Examining experiences of transition, instability and coping for young offenders in the community: A qualitative analysis', *Clinical Child Psychology and Psychiatry*, 21(2): 224–239.

Her Majesty's (HM) Inspectorate of Prisons (2007) *The mental health needs of prisoners: A thematic review of the care and support of prisoners with mental health problems*, London: HM Inspectorate of Prisons.

Her Majesty's (HM) Inspectorate of Probation (2006a) *An independent review of a serious further offence case: Damien Hanson and Elliott White*, London: HM Inspectorate of Probation.

Her Majesty's (HM) Inspectorate of Probation (2006b) *An independent review of a serious further offence case: Anthony Rice*, London: HM Inspectorate of Probation.

Her Majesty's (HM) Inspectorate of Probation (2017) *2017 Annual report*, Manchester: HM Inspectorate of Probation.

Her Majesty's (HM) Prison Service (2006) *Prison Service Order (PSO) 3050: Continuity of healthcare for prisoners*, London: HM Prison Service.

Her Majesty's (HM) Prison Service (2012) *Prison Service Order (PSO) 6000: Parole, release and recall*, London: HM Prison Service.

Her Majesty's (HM) Prison Service (2017) *Prison Service Order (PSO) 4700: Indeterminate sentences manual*, London: HM Prison Service.

Her Majesty's Treasury (2018) *Budget 2018: Philip Hammond's speech*. Available from: www.gov.uk/government/speeches/budget-2018-philip-hammonds-speech [Last accessed 01 November 2018].

Holloway, F. (2002) 'Mentally disordered offenders and the community mental health team' in Buchanan, A. (ed.) *Care of mentally disordered offenders in the community*, Oxford: Oxford University Press.

Holloway, F. and Davies, T. (2017) 'The Community Mental Health Team and the mentally disordered offender' in Buchanan, A. and Wootton, L. (eds.) *Care of the mentally disordered offender in the community (Second edition)*, Oxford: Oxford University Press.

Holloway, K. and Grounds, A. (2003) 'Discretion and the release of mentally disordered offenders' in Gelsthorpe, L. and Padfield, N. (eds.) *Exercising discretion: Decision-making in the criminal justice system and beyond*, Cullompton: Willan Publishing.

Howard League for Penal Reform (2012) *Deaths on probation: An analysis of data regarding people dying under probation supervision*, London: The Howard League for Penal Reform.

Institute of Alcohol Studies and Centre for Mental Health (2018) *Alcohol and mental health: Policy and practice in England*, London: Institute of Alcohol Studies and Centre for Mental Health.

Jewell, A., Dean, K., Fahy, T. and Cullen, A.E. (2017) 'Predictors of Mental Health Review Tribunal (MHRT) outcome in a forensic inpatient population: A prospective cohort study', *BMC Psychiatry*, 17: 25.

Jewesbury, I. and McCulloch, A. (2002) 'Public policy and mentally disordered offenders in the UK' in Buchanan, A. (ed.) *Care of mentally disordered offenders in the community*, Oxford: Oxford University Press.

Johnson, S., Osborn, D.P., Araya, R., Wearn, E., Paul, M., Stafford, M., Wellman, N., Nolan, F., Killaspy, H., Lloyd-Evans, B., Anderson, E. and Wood, S.J. (2012) 'Morale in the English mental health workforce: Questionnaire survey', *British Journal of Psychiatry*, 201(3): 239–246.

Kemshall, H. and Wood, J. (2007) 'Beyond public protection: An examination of community protection and public health approaches to high-risk offenders', *Criminology and Criminal Justice*, 7(3): 203–222.

Kennealy, P.J., Skeem, J.L., Manchak, S.M. and Eno Louden, J. (2012) 'Firm, fair and caring officer-offender relationships protect against supervision failure', *Law and Human Behavior*, 36(6): 496–505.

Khalifeh, M., Johnson, S., Howard, L.M., Borschmann, R., Osborn, D., Dean, K., Hart, C., Hogg, J. and Moran, P. (2015) 'Violent and non-violent crime against adults with severe mental illness', *British Journal of Psychiatry*, 206(4): 275–282.

Langan, J. and Lindow, V. (2004) *Living with risk: Mental health service user involvement in risk assessment and management*, Bristol: The Policy Press.

London Assembly Health Committee (2017) *Offender mental health*, London: London Assembly Health Committee.

Maughan, D., Molodynski, A., Rugkåsa, J. and Burns, T. (2014) 'A systematic review of the effect of community treatment orders on service use', *Social Psychiatry and Psychiatric Epidemiology*, 49(4): 651–63.

McMurran, M., Khalifa, N. and Gibbon, S. (2009) *Forensic mental health*, Cullompton: Willan Publishing.

Mental Health Alliance (2010) *Briefing paper 2: Supervised community treatment*, London: Mental Health Alliance.

Mental Health Taskforce (2016) *The five year forward view for mental health*, London: Mental Health Taskforce.

Ministry of Justice (2009a) *Guidance for clinical supervisors*, London: Ministry of Justice.

Ministry of Justice (2009b) *Guidance for social supervisors*, London: Ministry of Justice.

Ministry of Justice (2013) *Transforming rehabilitation: A strategy for reform*, London: Ministry of Justice.

Ministry of Justice (2017) *Deaths of offenders in the community 2016/17. Annual statistics bulletin England and Wales*, London: Ministry of Justice.

Molodynski, A., Rugkåsa, J. and Burns, T. (2016) (eds.) *Coercion in community mental health care*, Oxford: Oxford University Press.

Mullen, P. (2002) 'Introduction' in Buchanan, A. (ed.) *Care of the mentally disordered offender in the community*, Oxford: Oxford University Press.

National Audit Office (2017) *Mental health in prisons*, London: National Audit Office.

National Health Service (NHS) Digital (2016) *Inpatients formally detained in hospital under the Mental Health Act 1983, and patients subject to supervised community treatment. Uses of the Mental Health Act: Annual statistics 2015/16*, London: NHS Digital.

National Health Service (NHS) Digital (2017) *Mental Health Act statistics. Annual figures 2016/17*, London: NHS Digital.

Nolan, P., Bradley, E. and Brimblecombe, N. (2011) 'Disengaging from acute inpatient psychiatric care: A description of service users' experiences and views', *Journal of Psychiatric and Mental Health Nursing*, 37(2): 271–288.

Onyett, S. (2011) 'Revisiting job satisfaction and burnout in community mental health teams', *Journal of Mental Health*, 20(2): 198–209.

Ozdural, S. (2006) 'The role of a community forensic mental health team', *Psychiatric Bulletin*, 30(1): 36.

Palmer, E.J., Jinks, M. and Hatcher, R.M. (2010) 'Substance use, mental health, and relationships: A comparison of male and female offenders serving community sentences', *International Journal of Law and Psychiatry*, 33(2): 89–93.

Parkin, E., Long, R. and Bate, A. (2018) *Children and young people's mental health – Policy, services, funding and education, Briefing paper number 07196, 1 August 2018*, London: House of Commons Library.

Peay, J. (1989) *Tribunals on trial: A study of decision-making under the Mental Health Act 1983*, Oxford: Oxford University Press.

Peto, L.M., Dent, M., Griffin, M. and Hindley, N. (2015) 'Community-based forensic child and adolescent services in England, Scotland and Wales: A national mapping exercise', *Journal of Forensic Psychiatry and Psychology*, 26(3): 283–296.

Plugge, E., Annes Ahmed, A.P., Maxwell, J. and Holland, S. (2014) 'When prison is "easier": Probationers' perceptions of health and wellbeing', *International Journal of Prisoner Health*, 10(1): 38–46.

Prins, H. (2016) *Offenders, deviants and patients: An introduction to clinical criminology (Fifth edition)*, Hove: Routledge.

Public Health England (PHE) (2016) *Rapid review of evidence of the impact on health outcomes of NHS commissioned health services for people in secure and detained settings to inform future health interventions and prioritisation in England*, London: PHE.

Rawala, M. and Gupta, S. (2014) 'Use of community treatment orders in an inner-London assertive outreach service', *Psychiatric Bulletin*, 38(1): 13–18.

Rose, N. (2002) 'Society, madness and control' in Buchanan, A. (ed.) *Care of mentally disordered offenders in the community*, Oxford: Oxford University Press.

Royal College of Psychiatrists (2013) *Standards for community forensic mental health services*, London: Royal College of Psychiatrists.

Rugkåsa, J., Molodynski, A. and Burns, T. (2016) 'Introduction' in Molodynski, A., Rugkåsa, J. and Burns, T. (eds.) *Coercion in community mental health care*, Oxford: Oxford University Press.

Sadeh, N., Binder, R.L. and McNiel, D.E. (2014) 'Recent victimization increases risk for violence in justice-involved persons with mental illness', *Law and Human Behavior*, 38(2): 119–125.

Samele, C., Keil, J. and Thomas, S. (2009) *Securing employment for offenders with mental health problems. Towards a better way*, London: Sainsbury Centre for Mental Health.

Shuker, R. and Bates, A. (2014) 'Offender behaviour programmes: Managing the transition from prison into the community' in Ashmore, Z. and Shuker, R. (eds.) *Forensic practice in the community*, Abingdon: Routledge.

Shute, S. (2007) 'Parole and risk assessment' in Padfield, N. (ed.) *Who to release? Parole, fairness and criminal justice*, Cullompton: Willan Publishing.

Simpson, A., Hannigan, B., Coffey, M., Barlow, S., Cohen, R., Jones, A., Všetečková, J., Faulkner, A., Thornton, A. and Cartwright, M. (2016) 'Recovery-focused care planning and coordination in England and Wales: A cross-national mixed methods comparative case study', *BMC Psychiatry*, 16(1): 1–18.

Sirdifield, C. (2012) 'The prevalence of mental health disorders amongst offenders on probation: A literature review', *Journal of Mental Health*, 21(5): 485–498.

Sirdifield, C. and Owen, S. (2016) 'Probation's role in offender mental health', *International Journal of Prisoner Health*, 12(3): 185–199.

Snowden, P. and Ashim, B. (2008) 'Release procedures and forensic mental health' in Soothill, K., Rogers, P. and Dolan, M. (eds.) *Handbook of forensic mental health*, Cullompton: Willan Publishing.

Taylor, S., Burke, L., Millings, M. and Ragonese, E. (2017) '*Transforming Rehabilitation* during a penal crisis: A case study of *Through the Gate* services in a resettlement prison in England and Wales', *European Journal of Probation*, 9(2): 115–131.

Thornicroft, G. and Tansella, M. (2004) 'Components of a modern mental health service: A pragmatic balance of community and hospital care', *British Journal of Psychiatry*, 185(4): 283–290.

Tighe, J., Henderson, C. and Thornicroft, G. (2002) 'Mentally disordered offenders and models of community care provision' in Buchanan, A. (ed.) *Care of the mentally disordered offender in the community*, Oxford: Oxford University Press.

Trebilcock, J. (2009) *Journeys through managing the unknowable: Making decisions about dangerous patients and prisoners with severe personality disorder*, PhD thesis, Keele: Keele University.

Trebilcock, J. (2011) *No winners: The reality of short term prison sentences*, London: Howard League for Penal Reform.

Trebilcock, J. and Weaver, T. (2012) '"Everybody knows that the prisoner is going nowhere"': Parole Board (PB) members views about the conduct and outcome of PB reviews with Dangerous and Severe Personality Disorder (DSPD) prisoners', *International Journal of Criminology and Sociology*, 1:141–150.

Trebilcock, J. and Worrall, A. (2018) 'The importance of throughcare and resettlement for working with violent and sexual offenders' in Ireland, J.L., Ireland, C.A. and Birch, P. (eds.) *Violent and sexual offenders: Assessment, treatment and management*, London: Routledge.

Turner, T. and Salter, M. (2008) 'Forensic psychiatry and general psychiatry: Re-examining the relationship', *Psychiatric Bulletin*, 32: 2–6.

van Ginneken, E.F.J.C. and Hayes, D. (2017) '"Just" punishment? Offenders' views on the meaning and severity of punishment', *Theoretical Criminology*, 17(1): 62–78.

Weaver, B. (2014) 'Control or change? Developing dialogues between desistance research and public protection practices', *Probation Journal*, 61(1): 8–26.

Weaver, N., Coffey, M. and Hewitt, J. (2017) 'Concepts, models and measurement of continuity of care in mental health services: A systematic appraisal of the literature', *Journal of Psychiatric and Mental Health Nursing*, 24(6): 431–450.

Weich, S., Duncan, C., Bhui, K., Canaway, A., Crepaz-Keay, D., Keown, P., Madan, J., McBride, O., Moon, G., Parsons, H., Singh, S. and Twigg, L. (2018) 'Evaluating the effects of community treatment orders (CTOs) in England using the Mental Health Services Dataset (MHSDS): Protocol for a national, population based study', *BMJ Open*, 8: e024193.

Weston, S. (2016) 'The everyday work of the drug treatment practitioner: The influence and constraints of a risk-based agenda', *Critical Social Policy*, 36(4): 511–530.

Wootton, L., Fahy, T., Wilson, S. and Buchanan, A. (2017) 'The interface of general psychiatric and forensic psychiatric services' in Buchanan, A. and Wootton, L. (2017) (eds.) *Care of the mentally disordered offender in the community*, Oxford: Oxford University Press.

Wright, E. (2017) *Briefing 51: Long-stay rehabilitation services*, London: Centre for Mental Health.

Yakeley, J. and Taylor, R. (2011) 'Multi-Agency Public Protection Arrangements (MAPPA): Can we work with them?' in Rubitel, A. and Reiss, A. (eds.) *Containment in the community: Supportive frameworks for thinking about antisocial behaviour and mental health*, London: Karnac Books Ltd.

Yakeley, J., Taylor, R. and Cameron, A. (2012) 'MAPPA and mental health – 10 years of controversy', *The Psychiatrist*, 36(6): 201–204.

Zlodre, J. and Fazel, S. (2012) 'All cause and external mortality in released prisoners: Systematic review and meta-analysis', *American Journal of Public Health*, 102(12): 67–75.

NOTES

1   Mental health legislation now refers to Responsible Clinicians (RCs) rather than RMOs.

2   See Buchanan (2002) for a discussion of earlier service models.

3   For more information about the role of different CMHT staff see www.rcpsych.ac.uk/healthinformation/treatmentsandwellbeing/mentalhealth-inthecommunity.aspx

4   See Ozdural (2006) for a discussion about the role of CFMHTs.

5   In April 2013 CCGs took over responsibility for the majority of offender healthcare commissioning in the community from Primary Care Trusts (PCTs).

6   The distinction between integrated and parallel mental health services was first made by John Gunn (1977) and became a central issue in 1980s and 1990s models of community care (Jewesbury and McCulloch, 2002).

7   For more information about s17 for restricted patients see https://assets.publishing.service.gov.uk/government/uploads/system/uploads/attachment_data/file/595085/mhcs-guidance-s17-leave_.pdf

8   The First-tier Tribunal (Mental Health) was introduced under the Tribunals, Courts and Enforcement Act 2007 and replaced the Mental Health Review Tribunal. Patients in Wales will have their case heard by the Mental Health Review Tribunal for Wales.

9   Social and clinical supervisors have strict reporting requirements as set out by the Ministry of Justice (2009a, 2009b).

10   CTOs replaced the supervised discharge of patients under s25A. s25A followed an amendment to the MHA 1983 by the Mental Health (Patients

in the Community) Act 1995 which introduced the supervision of non-restricted patients following their discharge from hospital. See www.mentalhealthlaw.co.uk/Supervised_Community_Treatment_replaces_Supervised_Discharge for more information. For more information about CTOs see the MHA 2007 Code of Practice and Beswick and Gunn (2017).

11 A list of schemes that have been awarded provisional grants is available here: https://s16878.pcdn.co/wp-content/uploads/2018/06/BPOS-Awards-Table.pdf

Care, coercion and control: Exploring the key themes raised by mental health and offending

INTRODUCTION

Despite a long history of curiosity and concern about people with mental disorder, their needs have commonly been neglected in policy, treatment and research. While high-profile cases in the 1990s (such as the Christopher Clunis and Michael Stone cases) repositioned the priority given to the mentally disordered offender (see Chapter 3), the policies and measures that have followed, have often prioritised security and risk rather than patient autonomy and care. While renewed attempts to divert mentally disordered offenders away from the criminal justice system and to achieve a parity of esteem with physical health services are to be welcomed, austerity measures in England and Wales have led to significantly reduced funding within mental health and criminal justice services, thereby potentially undermining these aims.

Against this backdrop, there has been an increasing convergence of mental health and criminal justice legislation and policy. The need for mental health and criminal justice systems to work together for the care, support, rehabilitation and punishment of people with mental health problems who have, or are suspected of having, offended is now embedded in a range of policy initiatives and interventions. Good examples of this convergence include: criminal justice liaison and diversion (L&D), the mental health treatment requirement (MHTR), the hospital and limitation direction (HLD) and the Dangerous and Severe Personality Disorder (DSPD) programme (Sainsbury Centre for Mental Health, 2010). Under these developments, it is no surprise that the roles of mental health professionals have become increasingly blurred (Hannigan and Allen, 2010).

Drawing many earlier discussions in the book together, this final chapter highlights some of the key themes that are raised by mental health and offending. Beginning with the ethical issues raised by working at the intersection of health and criminal justice, we revisit the core challenge of trying to balance public protection with the rights of the individual offender with mental disorder, along with related challenges surrounding the 'care', 'control' and 'coercion' of offenders with mental health problems. Here, we learn that care, control and coercion are inevitable features of the ways in which this heterogeneous population is governed, and that just as there are 'bad' forms of care, there may be 'good' forms of control. The chapter then considers some of the key staffing and organisational challenges presented by working with mentally disordered offenders, identifying a number of iatrogenic effects of working at the intersection of health and criminal justice. The chapter ends by considering several subgroups of mentally disordered offenders, who are often subject to disproportionate criminal justice and mental health attention while sometimes also being excluded or overlooked by these same agencies.

BALANCING THE RIGHTS OF THE PATIENT WITH DEMANDS FOR PUBLIC PROTECTION

There are multiple ethical challenges for practitioners involved with mental health clients (Szmulker, 2009). Having to deal with mentally disordered offenders 'places practitioners at the meeting point of two quite different paradigms of thinking: respectively those of healthcare and criminal justice' (McGuire, 2016:49) and, in practice, health care practitioners must straddle both systems (Ward, 2013). Medical ethics are structured by the principles of beneficence (doing good), non–maleficence (avoiding harm), autonomy and justice (see Beauchamp and Childress, 1999 for a discussion). Clinicians must also work under professional guidance from the General Medical Council (GMC) (2013), and this means they are expected to ensure that the care of their patient is their primary concern. As a consequence, pressures to prioritise public safety over the welfare of an offender raise a number of conflicts for mental health practitioners because their work is guided by a concern for offender beneficence and autonomy (Ward, 2013).

In practice, many staff working with mentally disordered offenders must serve 'two masters' (Robertson and Walter, 2008) and operate as 'double agents' to ensure the safety of their clients and the public (Blackburn, 2004). This 'dual relationship problem' can occur at many stages of the criminal justice system, including expert testimony of experts in court about a defendant's mental health, and with the preparation of therapeutic reports for the Parole Board (PB) (Ward, 2013). Such activities raise questions about the balance that should be given to public protection, individual autonomy and welfare, and can generate considerable challenges in terms of confidentiality and therapeutic trust.

While many accept that clinical staff working with the mentally disordered have a dual role of protecting the service user's rights and need for treatment on the one hand, and concerns for the safety of the wider community on the other, there is often disagreement about the emphasis that should be placed on either (Robertson, Barnao and Ward, 2011). In addition to the conflict between the rights of the public to protection and the rights of the service user, the practitioner may experience internal value conflicts between personal, professional and universal norms (Ward, 2013). A fundamental challenge for those who work with offenders with mental health problems is that while professional standards and ethical codes of practice may help '*describe* or *label* the problem, arguably they do not provide ways of navigating past the obstacles' (Ward, 2013:94, emphasis in original).

Conflict between different values can make it harder for professionals to decide on, and justify, particular courses of action (Ward, 2013) which, in turn, has important implications for the legitimacy and safety of interventions. This situation was observed in the independent inquiry into the temporary discharge and absconsion of John Barrett, a man with a history of violence and schizophrenia, who stabbed Dennis Finnegan to death in Richmond park in 2004. The inquiry report concluded that the 'interventions did not give sufficient weight to the risk John Barrett could pose to the public' and 'there was a tendency to emphasise unduly the desirability of engaging John Barrett rather than intervening against his wishes to reduce risk' (National Health Service (NHS) London, 2006:9). This case highlights how an overemphasis on patient rights can lead to risks being inadequately managed (Kemshall, 2008:18).

This example also reminds us that risk prevention can represent a 'legitimate activity' when it constitutes part of a mentally disordered offender's treatment (Mullen, 2000). While risk assessment may restrict a patient's freedom, it may also have clear benefits for the patient including closer supervision and the use of proactive interventions (Duggan, 2008). In any case, Douglas et al. (2017:135) argue that 'the view that medical professionals ought never to act against a patient's best interests can be contested' since there may be circumstances when it is just and appropriate for a clinician to act in a way that protects others. Even when a risk assessment leads to an offender being detained in secure services for longer, this may still be seen in the 'best interests' of this person, since detention may prevent a relapse of their symptoms, reoffending and future periods of hospitalisation (Douglas et al., 2017).

While public protection may be a legitimate aim, some still express concern that mental health policies are dominated by concerns about risk, rather than humanitarian concerns for the welfare of those with mental illness (Peay, 2011). Problematically, Hudson (2003) reminds us that when a focus on risk comes to structure criminal justice, offender rights and core principles such as proportionality can be sidestepped. This may reflect that 'despite well-meaning attempts at humane interpretations, once the issue of potential dangerousness to the public is raised, then liberal intentions are shelved' (Duggan, 2008:519). In practice, and as evidenced by many of the high-profile inquiries involving mental health patients since the move from asylum to community care, 'the prevailing criticism of psychiatry in our age is not its excess of social control, but its failures of social control and public protection' (Grounds, 1997:135).

Paradoxically, a preoccupation with public protection can not only increase public anxiety but also direct resources at the wrong targets, thereby making the public less safe (Kitzinger, 2004). Moreover, overly restrictive measures may reduce offender compliance. As Craissati (2007:227) acknowledges, there is a 'fine line between control and persecution' and the social exclusion that follows from risk management may trigger greater levels of offending. Heightened attention to risk may also incapacitate key decision-makers in the criminal justice system (Trebilcock and Weaver, 2012). Moreover, a preoccupation with risk can lead to a situation where key aspects of recovery, such as self-management and responsibility, are overlooked and therefore not supported (Coffey et al., 2016; see also Trebilcock and Worrall, 2018).

This discussion highlights both the ethical dilemmas faced by mental health practitioners as well as the significant ideological and cultural differences between health and criminal justice. Consequently,

> the question that emerges when medicine takes over traditionally legal domains or vice versa is how the resulting social control arrangements satisfy both the inhabitants of the borderland and those at the different centres of expertise.
>
> (Timmermans and Gabe, 2003:7)

The solutions that emerge can be particularly precarious since the social control measures that may be used may contain elements from both health and criminal justice but cannot be reduced (and therefore traced/justified) to either one (Timmermans and Gabe, 2003). However, we are reminded by Kemshall (2008:113) that key stakeholders in the criminal justice system, including members of the judiciary and practitioners, are able to 'exercise resistance' to the overwhelming demands of public protection by bringing 'their own values and ideologies to bear on policy interpretation and delivery'.

CHALLENGES INVOLVED WITH DETERMINING THE RESPONSIBILITY OF MENTALLY DISORDERED OFFENDERS

As noted in Chapter 5, determining responsibility has a long history, and is an issue that raises complex questions for both lawyers and clinicians. While the increasing involvement of psychiatric and psychological expertise in the judicial system has been 'applauded as a desirable humanization of legal processes', it is also feared for its 'infringement on legal standards of culpability' and for its ability to violate principles of proportionality (Oosterhuis and Longnan, 2014:3). Traditionally, if an offender is found not guilty of an act for reason of insanity, it is not considered appropriate under the law to punish them. However, as we have seen with the likes of Peter Sutcliffe, it is difficult to debate the normality of individual offenders when they behave in particularly dangerous ways (Hollin, 1989, cited in Harris, 1999). Moreover,

> if virtually any crime committed by the mentally disordered involved exoneration through insanity or alleviation of guilt through diminished

responsibility, the socio-political choice would be between giving the offender a blank cheque to offend and making a response geared not to the traditional purposes of justice or punishment (which can scarcely be appropriate if volition is denied) but to public protection, with a consequential elevation of security over rights.

(Harris, 1999:12)

When we try to consider the responsibility of people with different mental disorders, these uncertainties become even more pronounced. For example, Hare (1998:205) highlights that in most jurisdictions, psychopathy is considered as an aggravating rather than mitigating factor when determining criminal responsibility. This has resulted in harsher judicial sentencing (Zinger and Forth, 1998) and, in some locations, has been used to justify the death penalty rather than life imprisonment (Edens, Petrilla and Buffington-Vollum, 2001). Similarly, the diagnosis of post-traumatic stress disorder (PTSD), has been used as a mitigating factor in sentencing (Friel, White and Hull, 2008). These outcomes are particularly concerning given the inaccuracies associated with predicting future violence for these populations (Sparr and Atkinson, 1986). Despite the 'implicit logic of every system of law: that the reach of the law extends only to creatures able to comprehend its terms and abide by prescriptions' (Robinson, 1996:233), it is discomforting to observe that in modern times, society seems to be significantly less tolerant towards those with mental illness who are not considered to be fully responsible for their actions (Stuckenberg, 2016).

CARE: CHALLENGES SURROUNDING TREATMENT AND REHABILITATION

Interventions with mentally disordered offenders have a 'chequered history' as a result of the experimental nature by which the different 'psy' (psychiatry, psychology, psychoanalysis) professions have developed (Knight and Stephens, 2009, cited in Harrison, 2011). As we have highlighted in several chapters across the book, there are concerns about the over-reliance of treating mental health problems with medication, alongside limited evidence of the effectiveness of psychological treatments.

The reliance on medicating psychiatric problems, especially schizophrenia, is argued to follow not only from a 'dominant psychiatric epistemology' but also the policies and guidelines that surround the management of schizophrenia, including those produced by the National Institute for Health and Care Excellence (NICE) (Spandler and Calton, 2009). Psychiatric medication, compared to hospitalisation, has also been popular because it represents an 'effective, inexpensive and less invasive way' to care for people with mental health problems in the community (Klassen, 2017:362). However, the dominance of psychiatric medication may lead to an overwhelming focus on treatment compliance and mandatory medication at the expense of other treatment options (Spandler and Calton, 2009).

While psychological treatments have potential, their success with mentally disordered offenders is dependent on many factors. Vossler et al. (2017:16–21) remind us that therapeutic endeavours can be affected by institutional security concerns, offender engagement with therapy, the extent to which offenders are prepared to disclose information, and the imbalance of power between an offender and those charged with providing treatment. There is also a risk that psychological therapies may re-traumatise service users as they re-experience previous traumas, and this can make establishing effective therapeutic relationships difficult (Mueser et al., 2002). This reminds us that the quality of therapeutic relationships is key to improving outcomes (Hewitt and Coffey, 2005). However, many factors can impact on the therapeutic relationship including: offender perceptions of staff availability and accessibility (MacInnes et al., 2014), trust (Yamashita, Forchuk and Mound, 2014) and offender involvement in their treatment (Johnstone and Dallos, 2014).

In any case, Player (2017:17) warns against automatically viewing the provision of treatment as an 'unmitigated good'. This is an important warning, and according to Player (2017), a neglected perspective given research has found that treatment can sometimes make things worse. For example, Rice, Harris and Cornier (1992) found that treatment increased the antisocial and criminal behaviour of patients with personality disorder after their release. Others have also found that starting treatment too early (and then subsequently dropping out) can elevate the risk that people pose (McMurran and Theodosi, 2007). Individuals 'might be harmed more by being offered services than being denied them' because of the further stigmatisation and damage to their self-esteem that might follow from treatment 'failure' (Duggan, 2008:5133). Failure to complete treatment may, in turn, lead to subsequent exclusion from other services (Duggan, 2008).

A recent review by Völlm et al. (2018) reports that while the evidence base is weak, there is some evidence that better outcomes are achieved by psychiatric care when compared to criminal justice detention alone. This may reflect some of the challenges involved with offering effective interventions in prison. Traditionally, mental health care in prisons has tended to be structured around security and control rather than treatment and rehabilitation (Sim, 1990). In addition, many features of imprisonment serve to worsen mental health, leading Ben-Moshe (2017:282) to argue that treatment in such a setting is an oxymoron. The structure of secure services for mentally disordered offenders can generate iatrogenic damage as patients try to fight against the system and find themselves in a spiral of 'service user rebellion provoking a more controlling institutional response, which stimulates further rebellion' (Davies et al., 2006:1104).

CONTROL AND THE MISUSE OF POWER: THE POLITICS OF MENTAL HEALTH AND DETENTION

Much of the discussion so far has focused on the compromises that have been made by mental health practitioners. However, there are a number of ways in which the powers of psychiatry can be easily misused (Gunn, 2006). During the first half of the twentieth century, chemical constraint with the use of sedatives and hazardous untested treatments, such as electroconvulsive therapy (ECT) and brain surgery, challenge the idea that psychiatrists always protect a patient's 'best interests' (Carpenter, 2009:218). Along with some questionable treatments, Parker (1985:15) highlights that in the 600 years or so that we have been detaining those with mental health problems,

> the forms of security employed have changed little over the period; perimeter security, internal locks and bars and individual restraint by both physical and chemical means have been in continuous use to a greater or lesser degree in various guises up the present day.

Historically, Soviet Russia gained a reputation for many political abuses of psychiatry with political dissidents often locked up in mental health facilities without any medical diagnosis, intervention or legal framework to challenge. In a recent paper, van Voren (2014) argues that the number of cases where psychiatry has been used in a political manner in Russia is on the rise again. This reminds us that we should not assume that historical cruelties and abuses of power are consigned to the past; instead, history should demonstrate the importance of keeping sight of the ethical issues surrounding the care and control of the mentally disordered (Canton, 2016). Indeed, a leading community psychiatrist in the UK, observes that

> sadly psychiatry continues to provide good reasons for mistrust although the specific practices that attract opprobrium (restraints, caged beds, seclusion and forced medication) vary markedly from country to country, as does the strength of the opposition.
>
> (Burns, 2014:341)

In one secure hospital (Ashworth), Adshead (2009:306) illustrates some of the difficulties mental health staff experience when attempting to balance care, on the one hand, and control, on the other. In the early 1990s, Blom-Cooper et al. (1992) found that staff had been physically abusive to patients in the name of 'control' but by the end of the decade, another inquiry in the hospital by Fallon et al. (1999) found that control had been lost 'in the name of "care"', with patients on one ward found to have been involved with running businesses and the grooming of a young child (Adshead, 2009:306). Examples like these lead Adshead (2009) to argue that mental health practitioners require enhanced clinical competencies if they are to safely manage the boundaries between their roles as a 'carer' and a 'controller'. But achieving this balance has proven stubborn. In a recent Care Quality Commission (CQC) (2017) review of core mental health services, 36% of NHS and 34% of independent services were categorised as needing to improve safety. Conversely, the report also expressed concern about examples of 'outdated and sometimes institutionalised care' in the form of locked rehabilitation wards, an over-reliance on seclusion and restraint, and that some services were staffed by people without the skills to support proper recovery (CQC, 2017:5). Concerns about the use of force in mental health services have also come to the fore in recent years and at the time of writing a Private Members' Bill – the Mental Health Units (Use of Force) Bill – is currently being reviewed by the House of Lords (Bate, Parkin and Strickland, 2018).

Before we move on, it is important to observe there are 'good' and 'bad' forms of power, and that when used for the right reasons, power can lead to positive outcomes (Crewe, Liebling and Hulley, 2014:393). In the context of prisons, prisoners do not necessarily prefer prisons where power can be characterised as 'light', can recognise the negative effects of a light-approach and accept that power is 'often necessary, desirable and legitimate' (Crewe, Liebling and Hulley, 2014:401). Prisoners in 'light-absent' prisons may struggle with a lack of clarity and consistency from staff, increased opportunities for violence, greater struggles with regulating their own behaviour and complain that less staff interference can be accompanied by less support from staff too (Crewe, Liebling and Hulley, 2014:399–401).

Similar themes can be drawn from the supervision and compulsory treatment of patients in the community (Dixon, 2015; Molodynski, Rugkåsa and Burns, 2010). Indeed, problems can follow from under- and over- supervision of mental health patients (Molodynski, Rugkåsa and Burns, 2010). In a similar way that prisoners in Crewe, Liebling and Hulley's (2014) research valued disciplinary measures, patients in the community, especially those with previous alcohol or drug problems, may value the threat of recall to hospital as a useful deterrent (Dixon, 2015). Moreover, some patients in Dixon's (2015) research viewed a s41 restriction order positively because they regarded it as a mechanism for receiving treatment and support from staff. This was because the legal framework was 'seen to obligate mental health professionals to provide treatments as well as placing obligations on service users to access that treatment' (Dixon, 2015:1309). Some patients valued a legal restriction order for its ability to 'limit staff autonomy' and its ability to enable patients to 'exercise a degree of control over staff' (Dixon, 2015:1308).

COERCION: AN ESSENTIAL MECHANISM OF CARE AND CONTROL

The conventional wisdom is that coercion should be avoided and patients should volunteer for treatment if it is to be effective (Duggan, 2008). However, coercion in mental health services is endemic (Duggan, 2008) and service users commonly report that they experience mental health services as coercive (Newton-Howes, 2010; Pescosolido, Gardner and Lubell, 1998). While the coercion of mental health patients is most commonly associated with the secure mental health system, there is growing recognition that coercion is a key feature of *community* mental health care (Rugkåsa, Molodynski and Burns, 2016). This reflects that coercion can be experienced in many ways and is not simply associated with compulsory admission for treatment (Holloway, 2002). Indeed, the majority of people with mental health problems are now looked after in the community and therefore most coercive practices occur in this location (Rugkåsa, Molodynski and Burns, 2016). Much of this coercion operates informally and outside of legal processes (Rugkåsa, Molodynski and Burns, 2016) and in order to encourage psychiatric patients to comply with their treatment plan, a number of 'leverages' may be used by staff (Monahan et al., 2005).

This reminds us of the need to distinguish between formal (i.e. admission under the MHA) and informal (the use of 'leverages' to encourage treatment adherence) uses of coercion (Burns et al., 2016). While formal detentions under the MHA 1983 (as amended by the MHA 2007) have risen significantly and are now more than three times higher than they were in the early 1980s (Keown et al., 2018), increases in the use of informal coercion can also be observed. For example, there have been growing concerns about the rise of 'de facto detention' where patients are 'deprived of liberty without legal authority' (CQC, 2016:59). This situation can arise when informal patients are held on locked wards and are not fully aware of their rights to leave (CQC, 2016). In the community there have been many efforts to encourage treatment compliance, most recently evidenced by the introduction of CTOs under the MHA 2007. Policies such as these reflect that care in the community has been 'predicated not only on the efficacy of medication, but also the ability of psychiatric services to use compulsion, and in particular, to enforce medication compliance' (Spandler and Calton, 2009:248).

Ultimately, coercion is an essential part of the care and control of mentally disordered offenders. However, feelings of coercion may lead to more negative treatment outcomes as treatment adherence and high-quality therapeutic relationships become more problematic (Kaltiala-Heino, Laippala and Salokangas, 1997). We are reminded by Lidz et al. (1995) that a patient is less likely to feel coerced if they have been 'respectfully included in a fair decision-making process, allowed a 'voice' in the process and has been treated with respect, concern and good faith (in a manner which has been termed "procedural justice"' (cited by Holloway and Davies, 2017:311). Coffey and Jenkins (2002:527) argue that 'if compulsion is used it must be on the basis of reciprocity or else compulsion assumes its own inherent utility, devoid of any therapeutic content or process'. Duggan (2008) also argues that the principle of reciprocity may mitigate against some of the challenges surrounding coercion. This means that if treatment is effective and properly resourced, being coerced into engaging with it or being preventatively detained to receive it, may be regarded as more legitimate (Duggan, 2008). However, the problem is that treatment is not always effective and resources are not always available (Duggan, 2008).

STAFFING AND ORGANISATIONAL CHALLENGES

Reflecting the increasing convergence between the mental health and criminal justice systems, a considerable number of agencies now come

BOX 8.1 KEY PARTNERSHIPS INVOLVED IN THE PROVISION OF CARE TO OFFENDERS WITH MENTAL DISORDER

- NHS England
- High secure and low secure services
- NHS / independent / third sector providers
- Local mental health services (including PICUs and community mental health services)
- Advocacy services
- Carer support services
- Department of Health (DoH)
- Ministry of Justice (MoJ)
- Courts
- Police
- Her Majesty's Prison and Probation Service (HMPPS)
- Multi Agency Public Protection Arrangements (MAPPA)
- Health and Justice commissioned offender health services
- Offender Personality Disorder (OPD) services
- Social Care Agencies
- Care Quality Commission (CQC)
- Appropriate Regulators
- Housing associations and other providers of accommodation

Source: NHS England (2018)

together in the provision of forensic mental health care, as demonstrated in Box 8.1. Mental health services in both secure settings and the community draw on a range of disciplines and specialities including psychiatry, psychology, nursing, social work and occupational therapy (McMurran, Khalifa and Gibbon, 2009). However, mental health work takes place within a 'seismic zone' where multiple agencies with different aims intersect, in a sometimes conflicting and unstable manner (McGuire, 2002). Research with mental health staff confirms the challenges already discussed about achieving a balance between therapeutic aims and the management of risk (Roberts, 1994). In addition, different training and organisational aspects of service provision affect multiagency working (McGuire, 2002). The contrasting theoretical and empirical bases of the different disciplines involved and the ways in which these different models are applied in a legal context also add to the difficulties of multiagency working (McGuire, 2002). Importantly, intradisciplinary differences of opinion may also exist

(Davies et al., 2006). It is within this context that we now explore several iatrogenic effects that are generated by the need to work at the intersection of health and criminal justice.

THE IATROGENIC EFFECTS OF WORKING AT THE INTERSECTION OF HEALTH AND CRIMINAL JUSTICE I.: CONFLICT AND POWER AMONG MULTIDISCIPLINARY STAFF

Experiences of power can exist between staff and patients but also between different groups of staff (Coffey and Jenkins, 2002). The interdependency of, and competition for, power, status and resources, means that the relationships between different professional groups can be in a state of 'constant flux' (Davies et al., 2006). The different status of staff groups can also mean that some practitioners are overlooked. Key actors, such as forensic psychiatrists, have more status and cultural capital than other staff as a result of their access to higher levels of training, education and expertise (McDonald, Furtado and Völlm, 2016) and this can lead to the dominance of the medical model (Davies et al., 2006; see also Coffey and Jenkins, 2002). Many different and distinct disciplines and professional groupings can come under the 'psy' umbrella, including psychiatry, psychology and psychoanalysis, but traditionally, psychiatry has held more prestige than these other 'psy' disciplines, despite the considerable (and growing) contribution made by psychology (Pickersgill, 2012). This highlights that the relationship between them is complex, with 'these traditions being at once competitors and collaborators' (Pickersgill, 2012:556).

Elsewhere in forensic mental health settings, nursing staff, despite their often heavy involvement with the supervision of offender-patients, report that their opinions are not always sought by other members of the multidisciplinary team (Coffey and Jenkins, 2002). Some also feel that their input is not recognised and that they are devalued (Coffey and Jenkins, 2002). However, Prins (2016) remarks that there has been a shift in thinking and practice in the management of the mentally disordered following the introduction of Approved Mental Health Practitioners (AMHP) under the MHA 2007. Prins (2016:106) emphasises the wide range of professionals that are permitted to act in this role, including nurses, occupational therapists (OTs), and chartered psychologists, and argues that this reflects an 'acknowledgement of the importance of a team approach' to the management of mentally disordered offenders. However, he also reminds us that this inclusion of a wider range of staff makes many of the boundary disputes and ethical challenges described in this chapter, more likely to occur.

THE IATROGENIC EFFECTS OF WORKING AT THE INTERSECTION OF HEALTH AND CRIMINAL JUSTICE II.: DIVERGENCE OF PERSPECTIVES ABOUT THE PRIMARY TASK

There is wide variation in the nature of multidisciplinary team working (West et al., 2012). While different disciplines can make a valuable contribution to the care and treatment of mentally disordered offenders, the divergence of perspectives and 'absence of an overarching framework for integrating the different disciplinary perspectives and knowledge' can be problematic (Robertson, Barnao and Ward, 2011:482). Different disciplines can bring unique perspectives to the table but, as Robertson, Barnao and Ward (2011:482) note, the 'diversity of perspectives offered by multidisciplinary teams often falls short of providing a cohesive understanding of an individual and his or her rehabilitation needs, and, at worst, results in tensions and conflicts among different perspectives'. Research suggests that effective multidisciplinary working can be hindered by a lack of clarity about the roles of different staff and the purpose of multidisciplinary activities (Nic et al., 2016). One of the many challenges that follows from the blurred boundaries between health and criminal justice is the lack of consensus regarding key definitional issues, responsibility of different practitioners and agencies, and what is thought to be an appropriate disposal for the mentally disordered offender. Moreover, different practitioners will not only perceive risk in different ways but will also wish to act and manage it differently (Kemshall et al., 2005).

Due to this variation, it is of no surprise that staff working within mental health settings have reported difficulties in identifying the primary task and desired outcomes (Roberts, 1994). Kurtz and Jeffcote (2011:251) identify many difficulties in identifying a primary task in forensic mental health services, where a complex clinical task is set against the background of inherent tension between therapeutic activity and the management of risk. Davies et al. (2006) observe that nursing staff in forensic mental health services are most likely to adopt a criminogenic perspective and focus on the safety and security of the ward. Nurses in one medium secure unit were characterised by one staff participant as either 'hawks' or 'doves' with the former behaving in ways most often characterised as being like a prison officer and the latter 'so loose and liberal that they've lost the plot' (nurse manager quoted in Davies et al., 2006:1102). Other practitioners in Davies et al.'s (2006) research, such as OTs, often emphasised the iatrogenic consequences of nursing staff being too strict, but conversely OTs were commonly seen by nursing staff as blind to security issues.

As we saw in Chapter 6, similar themes have been found in the prison officer literature, further highlighting the intradisciplinary nature of forensic mental health services. Smith (2010:35) observes that working as a nurse for a health organisation within a different organisation such as a prison can be difficult, especially when it comes to resources. Other prison staff, such as custodial officers, especially those involved with therapeutic efforts in prisons such as Psychologically Informed Planned Environments (PIPES), are increasingly required to attend to offender needs, and expected to be 'more tolerant, empathetic and "psychologically aware"' (McBride, 2017:1268). Other criminal justice practitioners are also facing changing demands. For example, the role of probation staff has changed under the OPD pathway, as they are increasingly required to take a prominent role in the development of case formulations of their clients (Shaw, Higgins and Quarty, 2017); a task historically undertaken by qualified psychologists.

THE IATROGENIC EFFECTS OF WORKING AT THE INTERSECTION OF HEALTH AND CRIMINAL JUSTICE III.: ACCOUNTABILITY AND BLAME

Douglas (1992:16) argued some time ago that there now exists a system that 'is almost ready to treat every death as chargeable to someone's account, every accident as caused by someone's criminal negligence, every sickness a threatened prosecution. Whose fault? Is the first question?' This situation has inevitably had an impact on the day-to-day work of the practitioners responsible for managing mentally disordered offenders. The more risk avoidant and litigious society has become, the greater the expectations on mental health practitioners to minimise risk and public outcry (Holloway and Davies, 2017). In trying to meet these expectations, practitioners responsible for offenders with mental disorder are forced to work within a blame-prone culture where assumptions are often made about the care individuals have received. For example, Holloway and Davies (2017) argue that the inquiries that are undertaken when a patient with a history of contact with mental health services commits a homicide, are predicated on the belief that there must have been shortcomings in the patient's clinical care. These inquires, along with professional standards, serve not only to regulate the professional conduct of mental health staff but also hold them responsible when things go wrong (Rose, 1996). As a result, concerns about the potential harm that a patient may do to themselves or others 'preoccupies and potentially distorts the work of mental health professionals' (Holloway and Davies, 2017:303) (see Chapter 3 for further discussion).

Mullen (2002:xiv) suggests that the shift towards a risk management approach should enable practitioners to improve the patient's situation, but instead is usually driven by a desire to reduce the liability of the organisation and the professionals involved. This situation arises because when things go wrong, blame is commonly shifted from 'politicians and administrators, responsible for poorly financed and inadequately managed services, to individual clinicians, who are judged to have failed to follow procedures' (Mullen, 2002:xiv). The anxieties that follow from practitioners being held accountable for the risks their patients may pose is problematic because it 'excludes a broader consideration of risks *to* risky individuals' and commonly positions those with mental health problems as 'solely risk makers' rather than a group that can also be 'at risk' (Coffey, 2012:467). Given the disproportionate levels of victimisation experienced by those with mental health problems (see Chapter 4), the preoccupation with accountability and blame may have a number of iatrogenic effects for service users.

THE IATROGENIC EFFECTS OF WORKING AT THE INTERSECTION OF HEALTH AND CRIMINAL JUSTICE IV.: FAILURES IN COMMUNICATION AND INFORMATION SHARING

Poor communication and information sharing between different agencies is commonly identified as a key failure in mental health work (see e.g. Prisons and Probation Ombudsman, 2016). For example, the inquiry into the murder of Naomi Bryant in 2005 following the release of Anthony Rice, a man with personality disorder, from prison 'found a number of deficiencies, in the form of mistakes, misjudgements and miscommunications at various stages throughout the whole process of this case that amount to … a cumulative failure' (Her Majesty's (HM) Inspectorate of Probation, 2006:2).

Given the meeting of and attempt to 'conjoin two very different structures' of criminal justice and health, Duggan (2009:xi) argues that the poor communication between different agencies involved with mentally disordered offenders 'ought not to surprise us'. These different agencies have very different histories, differing objectives and different protocols when it comes to confidentiality and information sharing (McMurran, Khalifa and Gibbon, 2009).

Disclosure of information between agencies is now enshrined in UK legislation (Kemshall, 2008) and the 'the closer working relationship between health and criminal justice agencies may enhance safety, but it challenges established clinical roles' (Hales et al., 2016:319). The right to privacy under Article 8 of the European Court of Human

Rights is frequently sidestepped on paternalistic grounds when it comes to the care of the mentally disordered offender because sensitive information may be shared without their consent (Holloway and Davies, 2017:312). As a result, professionals may struggle to promote patient autonomy in the face of the 'therapeutic gaze of the state' (Holloway and Davies, 2017:313).

For example, the 'role' of health care provider becomes contested when 'health' information is then extracted and used against defendants in a court of law (Timmermans and Gabe, 2003). Following a psychiatry or psychology report, a defendant may receive a longer than usual sentence because of heightened concerns about risk and this raises ethical dilemmas for the professionals involved (McMurran, Khalifa and Gibbon, 2009). Information sharing, especially when no consent has been sought, also risks undermining key therapeutic relationships. Similarly, mandatory reporting requirements as part of the community supervision of offenders with mental health problems can raise clear challenges for health and criminal justice staff (Timmermans and Gabe, 2003:9). These challenges lead Holloway and Davies (2017:312) to observe that once someone is classified as a mentally disordered offender, 'it would seem that ... traditional rights to confidentiality should be waived – a potentially disturbing and destructive development'.

THE IATROGENIC EFFECTS OF WORKING AT THE INTERSECTION OF HEALTH AND CRIMINAL JUSTICE IV.: FUNDING, PRIVATISATION AND CHALLENGES SURROUNDING SERVICE COMMISSIONING

Mental health services have long suffered from chronic underfunding (Mental Health Taskforce, 2016) and this adds to the challenges of working at the intersection of health and criminal justice. To add to these challenges, commissioning arrangements in England and Wales have undergone considerable change and reform in recent years and are now particularly complex. Research has found that 'fragmentation in commissioning and provision can lead to a lack of clarity and/or competition regarding the roles and responsibilities for staff' (Wright, Jordan and Kane, 2014:181). Others report that some tendering and procurement exercises have been 'incredibly disruptive' and this has generated much confusion about who is responsible for what (Durcan, 2016). Another key problem with commissioning follows from 'the discrepancy between a cost-saving for one organisation and the spend of another' (Public Health England, 2016:41). In practice, this means that an NHS funded intervention may help to reduce reoffending but such benefits may be seen in the criminal justice system rather than health services. In any case, Durcan (2016) reports that few clinical commissioning groups

(CCGs) are prepared to prioritise health care provision for people in contact with criminal justice services. Worse still, there is evidence that some CCGs are unaware of their commissioning responsibilities towards people involved with the criminal justice system, such as those under probation supervision in the community (Brooker et al., 2017).

CHALLENGES OF INCLUSION, EXCLUSION AND OVERLOOKING

The historical and contemporary treatment of the mentally disordered offender no doubt illustrates their position as 'outliers' (Harris, 1999), 'unwanted packages' in a game of 'pass the parcel' (George, 1998) and as a group that 'nobody owns' (Webb and Harris, 1999). As Trebilcock (2009:40) reminds us,

> years of debate have failed to clarify who these people are, who should take responsibility for their care and management, whether they should be punished or treated, and perhaps most problematically, if they can be treated at all.

While the distinction between punishment and treatment is presented as straightforward, 'in reality it is not clear that there is such clear water between the two' (Bartlett and Sandland, 2014:278). In any case, mentally disordered offenders are a heterogeneous and complex population, and people with different characteristics require different health care solutions rather than a one size fits all approach (Public Health England, 2016). Their diverse and wide-ranging characteristics have important implications for the provision of care and the need to manage potential risk to the public. However, mentally disordered offenders occupy a highly liminal position since they are still positioned as outsiders but also expected to reintegrate into and recover within the communities in which they reside (Warner and Gabe, 2004). In addition, there are many subgroups of mentally disordered offenders that are either disproportionately involved with mental health and criminal justice services, or excluded and overlooked by these same services, as a result of their diagnosis or socio-demographic status.

EXCLUSION RELATED TO DIAGNOSIS, NEEDS OR OFFENDING BEHAVIOUR

Some mentally disordered offenders, especially those with personality disorder, comorbid drug and alcohol problems, those who have committed sexual offences, and/or those with learning disabilities, have been denied treatment and passed between a number of services. This situation may reflect how 'there is, and always has been, a tendency in psychiatry to divide patients into those we want to treat and those we do not' (Bennett, 1973:61). Staff in forensic mental health services may make judgements about what constitutes 'genuine' mental illnesses (Davies et al., 2006), may be pessimistic about the potential outcomes of working with such individuals (Harris, 1999), and may even actively dislike the particular individuals concerned (Lewis and Appleby, 1988). Hence, the rejection of patients from services can be related to struggles between different practitioners who may 'attempt to draw the boundaries of patient eligibility in ways that suit their interests' (Griffiths, 2001:679).

Traditionally, there have been many concerns that patients with personality disorder may be excluded from mental health services on the basis of 'untreatability' and from prison treatment programmes on the basis that treatment may serve to increase their risk. It is important to remember that patients with personality disorder and patients with mental illness who are detained in the mental health system are likely to have very different care pathways (Centre for Mental Health, 2011). Where offending behaviour programmes have been evaluated and/or modified for use with offenders with mental illness, they have tended to cater for those with schizophrenia, with limited attention directed towards comorbidity or offenders with personality disorder (Barnao and Ward, 2015). Given the high numbers of offenders with personality disorder and substance misuse problems and the general consensus that both of these characteristics are significant risk factors for reoffending, this has important implications for offenders in terms of equity and equality, as well as for assessments of risk made by the PB.

Although Lewis and Appleby (1988) famously wrote a paper entitled 'Personality disorder: the patients psychiatrists dislike', Maier (1990:776) argues that clinicians have been slow to recognise and address their potential biases. Indeed,

> psychiatrists have denied the hatred they feel for psychopaths and criminals, and thus have been unable to treat psychopaths adequately because their conceptual bases for treatment have been distorted by unconscious, denied feelings from the start.
>
> (Maier, 1990:776)

To counter this rejection, we have learnt in previous discussions (see especially Chapter 3) that an unprecedented amount of funding has been channelled into personality disorder services. While the majority of developments are now occurring in the criminal justice system, mental health services have also been encouraged not to exclude patients with personality disorder from services (National Institute for Mental Health England (NIMHE), 2003b). Despite this, Coid et al. (2015:73) suspect that patients with personality disorder continue to be rejected from medium secure services in England because their characteristics are viewed as unattractive by clinicians.

Those with dual diagnosis of drug and alcohol problems and mental health difficulties are also liable to fall through the net of care (Department of Health, 2009; Pycroft and Green, 2016). People with dual diagnosis are often regarded as challenging to work with (Pycroft and Green, 2016) and have been routinely excluded from services as a result (Social Exclusion Unit, 2002). Pycroft and Green (2016) argue that dual diagnosis has become a 'term of convenience' that masks the considerable heterogeneity of people who have substance misuse issues and mental health problems. Traditionally, mental health and drug policies have often not been linked because services and the legislation that supports them have been developed separately (Pycroft and Green, 2016). However, since the early 2000s, the Department of Health has developed several dual diagnosis policy guidelines (Department of Health, 2002, 2006). Yet, as Pycroft and Green (2016:150) acknowledge, 'clinical guidelines are only as good as the people implementing them' and lack the 'strength and the ability to influence commissioners and mental health and substance misuse services at a local level'.

It is well known that those with learning disabilities are more likely to develop a mental disorder than those without (McMurran, Khalifa and Gibbon, 2009). They are also more likely to come to the attention of the criminal justice system because those without learning disabilities may be more likely to avoid detection (McMurran, Khalifa and Gibbon, 2009). However, the provision of services for patients with mental disorder and learning disabilities remains very patchy (Holloway and Davies, 2017). It also appears that offenders with intellectual disabilities may have more negative care pathways. Indeed, Butwell et al. (2000) report that these patients often have longer lengths of stay and experience more problems with progression as a result of it being more difficult to transfer them to conditions of lower security.

EXCLUSION RELATED TO BLACK, ASIAN AND MINORITY ETHNIC (BAME) STATUS

Men and women from BAME groups are over-represented in the prison population (Ministry of Justice, 2016). However, the learning difficulties and mental health problems of BAME individuals are less likely to be identified on reception at prison (Lammy, 2017) and people from BAME groups are far less likely to access mental health services in prison (Prins et al., 2012). Black people are also over-represented in secure mental health services (de Taranto et al., 1998; Gajwani et al., 2016) with recent statistics indicating that those with black ethnicity are ten times more likely than those with a White British ethnicity to be detained under mental health legislation (NHS Digital, 2018).

While there is some evidence of increased prevalence of mental disorders among some BAME communities, evidence also exists to suggest that discrimination, poverty and social exclusion contribute to the higher detention rates of some ethnic minority groups (Department of Health and Social Care, 2018). Sizmur and McCulloch (2016) remind us that those from ethnic minority groups experience greater than average social deprivation and, in addition to contributing to poor mental health, such factors will also affect treatment outcomes. Despite the apparent commitment to equal services for equal need, inequitable access, along with poor experiences and outcomes, have been documented for many BAME groups across NHS mental health care (NIMHE, 2003a).

Once in the system, those from ethnic minority backgrounds are more likely to have negative care pathways (Morgan et al., 2005), poorer mental health provision and insufficient access to psychological treatments (Rabiee and Smith, 2014). A recent report by the Prison Reform Trust (2017) explicitly considers women from ethnic minority backgrounds in the criminal justice system and identifies that in addition to the disproportionate use of custody with this group, they are also more likely to feel unsafe in prison and have less access to mental health support. The tragic case of Sarah Reed, who died at Holloway prison in 2016, reflects some of these concerns, and demonstrates how the convergence of race, gender and mental health can generate to a 'a vortex of race discrimination and institutional indifference' (Jasper, 2017).

There is also evidence that once in secure care, those from BAME communities may feel that their care is not culturally sensitive and that many staff lack appropriate cultural awareness (Department of Health and Social Care, 2018). Worse still, the Department of Health (2003) has previously acknowledged that there is an undue emphasis on coercive models of treatment with BAME patients. Young black men are disproportionately affected and more likely to be found in the most coercive and specialised mental health services (Sizmur and McCulloch, 2016). Black men who experience a breakdown are also more likely to be segregated in prison (Ben-Moshe, 2017). The disproportionate detention of BAME people indicates 'a systemic failure to provide effective crisis care for these groups' (Mental Health Task-force, 2016:9) and their treatment once detained, reveals a 'racial and gender bias in the interpretation and diagnosis of mental health differences' (Ben-Moshe, 2017:281). Together, psychiatry and criminal justice services have 'played a key role in creating the racist stereotype of the psychically aggressive violent black male' (Cummins, 2015:168). Sadly, such stereotypes may contribute to the misuse of force with those with mental health problems, as seen in a number of cases over the last 25 years including the deaths of Orville Blackwood (Prins et al., 1993), David 'Rocky' Bennett (Norfolk, Suffolk and Cambridgeshire Strategic Health Authority, 2003) and Sean Rigg (Southwark Coroner's Court, 2012).

In recent years, concerns have emerged about the prevalence of mental health problems among foreign national prisoners (Borrill and Taylor, 2009; Bosworth, 2016; Sen, Exworthy and Forrester, 2014; Shaw, 2016). Foreign national offenders, held in HM Prison Service and Her Majesty's Prison and Probation Service (HMPPS) operated immigration removal centres (IRCs) now represent 11% of the total prison population (Ministry of Justice, 2017). Many of these will have been detained because of trying to enter the UK without adequate documentation (an offence under the Asylum and Immigration Act 2004) and may therefore be suffering from trauma brought on by their asylum experience (Baluchi, 1999 cited in Browne, 2009). Such trauma is likely to be exacerbated by detention in an IRC (Durcan, Stubbs and Boardman, 2017). Moreover, immigration detention has been associated with high levels of mental health problems as well as poor level of provision (Bosworth, 2016; Durcan, Stubbs and Boardman, 2017).

There has been a long-standing and serious failure by mental health services and other statutory agencies to effectively deal with 'racial inequalities'. Despite the disproportionate use of secure detention for some BAME people, as well as calls for separate provision (Bhui and Sashidharan, 2003 cited in McMurran, Khalifa and Gibbon, 2009), there are currently no separate or specialised forensic mental health services for BAME patients. While the Department of Health's *Delivering Race Equality in Mental Health* (Department of Health, 2005) action plan, that was published following the death of David 'Rocky' Bennett, sought to address inequalities in mental health provision to those from ethnic minority groups, the strategy was not sufficiently resourced or sustained by the government and other agencies (RAWorg, 2010). Sewell and Waterhouse (2012) argue that a tight financial climate, in combination with significant changes in the health and social care system, has negatively impacted on the attention paid to race inequality.

EXCLUSION RELATED TO GENDER

Although there are far more men in prison and secure mental health services compared to women, more than 50% of women in prison receive medication for mental health issues (Harrison, 2011). This reflects that women in prison have higher levels of mental health problems (Home Office, 2007; Light, Grant and Hopkins, 2013) and higher rates of suicide and self-harm, when compared to men (World Health Organization, 2009). While women only make up around 5% of the prison population, they represent between 20% and 25% of the secure mental health population (Logan and Taylor, 2017), where three-quarters of them have a history of self-harm (National Confidential Inquiry into Suicide and Safety in Mental Health (NCISH), 2018).

Concerns about the criminal justice response to women are long standing (Carlen, 2002; Dominelli, 1984; Gelsthorpe and Sharpe, 2015; Hedderman and Gelsthorpe, 1997; Smart, 1976; Zedner, 1991). Yet, despite these concerns, criminal justice provision has often failed to be gender-responsive and take into account the trauma that has frequently played a part in women's offending and substance use (Petrillo, 2016). Women often have histories of extensive abuse (MacDonald, 2013) and this inevitably impacts on their well-being, as well as their experiences of imprisonment. Crewe, Hulley and Wright (2017), in their work with women serving long sentences, highlight how the prison experience itself, can reproduce some of the dynamics of abuse so often already experienced by these women. For example, women can be re-traumatised by intrusive prison practices such as internal body searches (Ben-Moshe, 2017). Other aspects of imprisonment may be more negatively experienced by women. For example, two-thirds of women in prison have children under the age of 18 (Epstein, 2014) and may lose custody of them, as well as their homes, as a result of their imprisonment (NACRO, 2009). Women are more likely than men to be detained further away from their home areas as well as on release (HM Inspectorate of Probation, 2017).

To address these issues, Bloom and Covington (2008) call for a gender-responsive approach that should take the content and context of women's lives into account. Women, they suggest, should not be treated in isolation from their social support networks and a continuity of care model should include links to substance abuse, trauma and mental health. Calls have also been made for the development of more gender specific services in secure mental health services (Long, Fulton and Hollin, 2008). While the imprisonment of women has received increasing academic attention, Bartlett and Hollins (2018) criticise recent NICE guidelines (2017) regarding people with mental health problems in contact with the criminal justice system, along with the Royal College of Psychiatrist's (2015) prison quality standards, for making minimal reference to gender specific needs. At the time of writing, gender-specific standards for women in prison have been published by Public Health England (2018) along with a new female offender strategy (Ministry of Justice, 2018), but it remains to be seen how these will lead to changes in practice.

One attempt to provide gender-responsive and therapeutic pathways for women is the OPD pathway (Petrillo, 2016). It is targeted at women who have committed a violent or sexual offence and are assessed as high risk of committing another serious offence. Logan and Taylor (2017) argue that there are a number of features that distinguish it from the male pathway. However, Player (2017:584) is less persuaded, concluding that it has 'followed the well-worn tradition' of adapting policies designed for men. While Player (2017:573) accepts that the OPD Pathway has attempted to be 'gender responsive' she rightly criticises the initiative for its 'significant lack of attention to the intersection of gender with race and ethnicity, as well as other sources of oppression and inequality'. Player (2017:583) is also concerned that the OPD Pathway may lead to women's risk of harm being up-tariffed.

EXCLUSION RELATED TO SEXUALITY

There is growing evidence that those from lesbian, gay, bisexual and trans (LGBT) communities may also experience mental health inequalities (Hickson et al., 2017) and that there may be a higher prevalence of mental health problems among those who do not identify as heterosexual (Chakraborty et al., 2011; Semlyen et al., 2016). There is limited research in this area, but one reason LGBT communities may be more susceptible to mental health problems is because of the discrimination that they experience (Chakraborty et al., 2011). Little is also known about the experience LGBT communities may have with mental health services. However, a recent study in Ireland with LGBT service users found that two-thirds considered mental health services to be unable to respond to their mental health needs (McCann and Sharek, 2014).

EXCLUSION RELATED TO YOUNG AGE

Young people, including those who offend, often 'experience multiple risk factors for poor mental health, exacerbated by services that are experienced as "hard to-reach", leading to wide health inequalities'

(Durcan, Zlotowitz and Stubbs, 2017:1). Children brought up in families with low incomes are three times more likely to develop a mental health problem (Mental Health Taskforce, 2016) and often have a range of challenges in their lives regarding living arrangements, relationships (particularly with family and support services) as well as clear histories of violence and conflict (Heath and Priest, 2016). Yet, they are less likely than adults to recognise that they have a mental health problem and may need support (Centre for Mental Health, 2016). Consequently, most children and young people receive no support for their mental health problems (Mental Health Taskforce, 2016).

In recent years, the number of young people in custody has undergone significant decline, with 861 young people under the age of 18 held in custody in September 2018 (HMPPS, 2018). Young offenders are thought to have particularly poor mental health with one study reporting that 95% of young people in custody have at least one mental health problem (Lader, Singleton and Meltzer, 2000). Despite this high prevalence, young people in custody do not appear to get access to the support and treatment that they need (Harris, 2015). The mental health needs of young people involved with the youth justice system are often unmet because of challenges with identification and continuity of care (Harrington and Bailey, 2005). This reflects the lack of services for young people with mental health problems generally, and for those involved with the criminal justice system (Office of the Children's Commissioner for England, 2011). Young BAME offenders (who are over-represented) may have greater challenges with accessing appropriate services (NACRO, 2001).

Youth justice liaison diversion (YJLD) schemes, to enhance health provision for young people with mental health and developmental problems, have had some success (Haines et al., 2014). Following contact with YJLD schemes, Haines et al. (2014) observed reductions in overall needs, levels of depression and levels of self-harm. However, levels of reoffending remained the same. To prevent future offending among young people with mental health and developmental problems, Chitsabedan and Hughes (2016) suggest the need for early identification and responsive interventions based on an increased awareness among a range of professionals and services regarding how behaviour might be influenced or explained by mental health conditions, particularly regarding neurodevelopmental impairment.

In October 2016, 400 young people (under the age of 18) were detained under the MHA in hospital, although only a very small number (10) of these patients were detained under a forensic section under Part III of the Act (CQC, 2016:29). For those who are very unwell, one key problem is the limited availability of inpatient beds, and this may mean that young people are either detained a long way from home or temporarily within adult wards (CQC, 2018); neither a satisfactory response to a young person who is so unwell. This reflects that the provision of forensic mental health services for young people across the UK is patchy (Peto et al., 2015) and that young people who require inpatient care may be detained anywhere in the country (Mental Health Taskforce, 2016). A full review of the challenges involved with detaining young people with mental health problems is beyond the scope of this chapter, but for a recent review about the mental health of young people in custody and their transfer to the mental health system see Hill, Mitchell and Leipold (2017) and for a review of mental health services (inpatient and community) see CQC (2018).

EXCLUSION RELATED TO OLDER AGE

While the number of young people in custody has been falling, the rate of older prisoners has been significantly rising. The prevalence of mental health problems among older people involved with the criminal justice system is significantly higher than the general population (Fazel et al., 2001) with those aged over 60 representing the fastest growing group in prison (Cornish et al., 2016). Rates of detention under mental health legislation also rise once people reach age 65 (NHS Digital, 2018).

Despite a high prevalence of mental health problems, very few studies have focused on the mental health needs of older adults in the criminal justice system (Maschi, Suftin and O'Connell, 2012). Older prisoners are a marginalised group within prisons (Crawley, 2005) and have high levels of unmet needs because of both under-diagnosis and under-treatment (Fazel et al., 2004). Mental health problems include dementia, which is a growing and 'hidden problem' in prisons, with legal and social systems unprepared to handle it (Cipriani et al., 2017). Older prisoners also have higher levels of physical health problems than younger prisoners (Fazel et al., 2004) but imprisonment makes it difficult to address the medical and palliative care required by older prisoners (Marti, Hostettler and Richter, 2017; Turner, Payne and Barbarachild, 2011). These points reflect that the prison estate is not set up to properly address the needs of older prisoners, leading Cornish et al. (2016:21) to argue that a national strategy for older prisoners needs to be devised to try and 'offset the risk of unjust disparities'.

DISCUSSION

Managing the mentally disordered offender inevitably requires mental health practitioners to adopt a philosophy of care that is at significant odds with the traditional focus of the health care professional. Ward (2013:94) advises that it might be useful to think of the dual relationship problem as a problem that follows from 'value pluralism'. This is helpful for reminding us that it is far more complex than simply having to navigate between two schools of thought. In the field of forensic mental health, where there are many uncertainties, there are many disagreements and different values that guide people's work, and these may conflict within and between professional groups of staff. In seeking to resolve these challenges, Appelbaum (1997) argues that forensic psychiatry should follow the principles of 'truth telling' and 'respect for persons' rather than the traditional medical ethical principles of beneficence (doing good), non-maleficence (avoiding harm), autonomy and justice. However, Ward (2013) argues that his proposals side step the dual relationship problem and instead advocates that a 'hybrid ethical code' is developed that acknowledges the dual relationship faced by many forensic practitioners.

Whatever the solution, this chapter has revealed a number of overlapping and complex ethical challenges that are faced by a range of practitioners involved with the care and control of offenders with mental health problems. We have seen that care, control and coercion are inevitable features of the ways in which this heterogeneous population is governed. We have also learnt that just as too much of a focus of public protection, risk and control can be undesirable, neglecting these issues can have very serious consequences. The chapter has similarly highlighted that treatment (and care) may not always represent unmitigated goods, and that there are occasions where people with mental health problems may value the restrictions placed on their behaviour, for their ability to help support recovery as well as regulate the behaviour of staff. This reveals the very intractable and complex nature of striking the right balance with people with mental health problems who also offend. Furthermore, it reminds us that just as there are 'bad' forms of care, there may be 'good' forms of control.

FURTHER READING

For an overview of the key themes raised by 'mentally disordered offenders' see Harris (1999). For a comprehensive overview of the challenges raised by 'mentally disordered offenders' see Peay (2017).

For an excellent case study example of the conflicting discourses of psychiatry and the law see Greig (2002) and her book about the Garry David case in Australia.

REFERENCES

Adshead, G. (2009) 'Ethical issues in secure care' in Bartlett, A. and McGauley, G. (eds.) *Forensic mental health: Concepts, systems and practice*, Oxford: Oxford University Press.

Appelbaum, P.S. (1997) 'A theory of ethics for forensic psychiatry', *Journal of the American Academy of Psychiatry and the Law*, 25: 233–247.

Barnao, M. and Ward, T. (2015) 'Sailing unchartered seas without a compass: A review of interventions in forensic mental health', *Aggression and Violent Behavior*, 22: 77–86.

Bartlett, A. and Hollins, S. (2018) 'Challenges and mental health needs of women in prison', *British Journal of Psychiatry*, 212: 134–136.

Bartlett, P. and Sandland, R. (2014) *Mental health law: Policy and practice (Fourth edition)*, Oxford: Oxford University Press.

Bate, A., Parkin, E. and Strickland, P. (2018) *Mental Health Units (Use of Force) Bill 2017–19: Committee stage report, Briefing paper number 08088*, London: House of Commons Library.

Beauchamp, T.L. and Childress, J.F. (2009) *Principles of biomedical ethics (Sixth edition)*, Oxford: Oxford University Press.

Ben-Moshe, L. (2017) 'Why prisons are not "the new asylums"', *Punishment and Society*, 19(3): 272–289.

Bennett, D. (1973) 'Community psychiatry', *Community Health*, 5: 58–64.

Blackburn, R. (2004) '"What works" with mentally disordered offenders', *Psychology, Crime and Law*, 10(3): 297–308.

Blom-Cooper, L., Brown, M., Dolan, R. and Murphy, E. (1992) *Report of the committee of inquiry into the personality disorder unit, Ashworth Special Hospital*, London: Stationery Office.

Bloom, B. and Covington, S. (2008) 'Addressing the mental health needs of female offenders' in Gido, R. and Dalley, L. (eds.) *Women's mental health issues across the criminal justice system*, Columbus, Ohio: Prentice Hall.

Borrill, J. and Taylor, D.A. (2009) 'Suicides by foreign national prisoners in England and Wales 2007: Mental health and cultural issues', *Journal of Forensic Psychiatry and Psychology*, 20(6): 886–905.

Bosworth, M. (2016) *Mental health in immigration detention: A literature review. Review into the welfare in detention of vulnerable persons, Cm 9186*, London: Her Majesty's Stationery Office.

Brooker, C., Sirdifield, C., Ramsbotham, L.D. and Denney, D. (2017) 'NHS commissioning in probation in England – On a wing and a prayer', *Health and Social Care in the Community*, 25(1): 137–144.

Browne, D. (2009) 'Black communities, mental health and the criminal justice system' in Reynolds, J., Muston, R. and Heller, T. (eds.) *Mental health still matters*, Basingstoke: Palgrave MacMillan.

Burns, T. (2014) 'Community psychiatry's achievements', *Epidemiology and Psychiatric Sciences*, 23(4): 337–344.

Burns, T., Rugkåsa, J., Yeeles, K. and Catty, J. (2016) 'Coercion in mental health: A trial of the effectiveness of community treatment orders and an investigation of informal coercion in community mental health care', *Programme Grants for Applied Research*, 4(21): 1–353. www.ncbi.nlm.nih.gov/books/NBK401969/pdf/Bookshelf_NBK401969.pdf

Butwell, M., Jamieson, E., Leese, M. and Taylor, P. (2000) 'Trends in special (high security) hospitals: 2: Residency and discharge episodes, 1986–1995', *British Journal of Psychiatry*, 176(3): 260–265.

Canton, R. (2016) 'Troublesome offenders, undeserving patients? The precarious rights of mentally disordered offenders' in Winstone, J. (ed.) *Mental health, crime and criminal justice*, Basingstoke: Palgrave Macmillan.

Carlen, P. (2002) *Women and imprisonment: The struggle for justice*, Cullompton: Willan.

Care Quality Commission (CQC) (2016) *Monitoring the Mental Health Act in 2015/16*, Newcastle-Upon-Tyne: CQC.

Care Quality Commission (CQC) (2017) *The state of care in mental health services 2014 to 2017 Findings from CQC's programme of comprehensive inspections of specialist mental health services*, Newcastle-Upon-Tyne: CQC.

Care Quality Commission (CQC) (2018) *Review of children and young people's mental health services. Phase one report*, Newcastle-Upon-Tyne: CQC.

Carpenter, M. (2009) 'A third wave, not a third way? New Labour, human rights and mental health in historical context', *Social Policy and Society*, 8(2): 215–230.

Centre for Mental Health (2011) *Pathways to unlocking secure mental health care*, London: Centre for Mental Health.

Centre for Mental Health (2016) *Missed opportunities. A review of recent evidence into children and young people's mental health*, London: Centre for Mental Health.

Chakraborty, A., McManus, S., Brugha, T., Bebbington, P. and King, M. (2011) 'Mental health of the non-heterosexual population of England', *British Journal of Psychiatry*, 198(2): 143–148.

Chitsabesan, P. and Hughes, N. (2016) 'Mental health needs and neurodevelopmental disorders amongst young offenders: Implications for policy and practice' in Winstone, J. (ed.) *Mental health, crime and criminal justice*, Basingstoke: Palgrave Macmillan.

Cipriani, G., Carlesi, C., Danti, S. and Di Fiorino, M. (2017) 'Old and dangerous: Prison and dementia', *Journal of Forensic and Legal Medicine*, 51: 40–44.

Coffey, M. (2012) 'A risk worth taking? Value differences and alternative risk constructions in accounts given by patients and their community workers following conditional discharge from forensic mental health services', *Health, Risk and Society*, 14(5): 465–482.

Coffey, M., Cohen, R., Faulkner, A., Hannigan, B., Simpson, A. and Barlow, S. (2016) 'Ordinary risks and accepted fictions: How contrasting and competing priorities work in risk assessment and mental health care planning', *Health Expectations: An International Journal of Public Participation in Health Care and Health Policy*, 20(3), 471–483.

Coffey, M. and Jenkins, E. (2002) 'Power and control: Forensic community mental health nurses perceptions of team-working, legal sanction and compliance', *Journal of Psychiatric and Mental Health Nursing*, 9(5): 521–529.

Coid, J.W., Yang, M., Ullrich, S., Hickey, N., Kahtan, N. and Freestone, M. (2015) 'Psychiatric diagnosis and differential risks of offending following discharge', *International Journal of Law and Psychiatry*, 38: 68–74.

Cornish, N., Edgar, K., Hewson, A. and Ware, S. (2016) *Social care or systematic neglect? Older people on release from prison*, London: Prison Reform Trust and Restore Support Network.

Craissati, J. (2007) 'The paradoxical effects of stringent risk management' in Padfield, N. (ed.) *Who to release? Parole, fairness and criminal justice*, Cullompton: Willan Publishing.

Crawley, E. (2005) 'Institutional thoughtlessness in prisons and its impacts on the day-to-day prison lives of elderly men', *Journal of Contemporary Criminal Justice*, 21(4): 350–363.

Crewe, B., Hulley, S. and Wright, S. (2017) 'The gendered pains of life imprisonment', *British Journal of Criminology*, 6(1): 1359–1378.

Crewe, B., Liebling, A. and Hulley, S. (2014) 'Heavy-light, absent-present: Rethinking the 'weight' of imprisonment', *British Journal of Sociology*, 65(3): 387–410.

Cummins, I. (2015) 'Discussing race, racism and mental health: Two mental health inquiries reconsidered', *International Journal of Human Rights in Healthcare*, 8(3): 160–172.

Davies, J.P., Heyman, B., Godin, P.M., Shaw, M.P. and Reynolds, L. (2006) 'The problems of offenders with mental disorders: A plurality of perspectives within a single mental health care organization', *Social Science and Medicine*, 63(4): 1097–1108.

de Taranto, N., Bester, P., Czhniak, P.P., McCallum, A. and Kennedy, H. (1998) 'Medium secure provision in NHS and private units', *Journal of Forensic Psychiatry*, 9(2): 369–378.

Department of Health (2002) *Dual diagnosis good practice policy*, London: Department of Health.

Department of Health (2003) *Inside out: Improving mental health services for black and minority ethnic communities in England*, Leeds: Department of Health.

Department of Health (2005) *Delivering race equality in mental health care: An action plan for reform inside and outside services and the government's response to the independent inquiry into the death of David Bennett*, London: Department of Health.

Department of Health (2006) *Closing the gap: A capability framework for dual diagnosis*, London: Department of Health.

Department of Health (2009) *The Bradley report. Lord Bradley's review of people with mental health problems or learning disabilities in the criminal justice system*, London: Department of Health.

Department of Health and Social Care (2018) *The independent review of the Mental Health Act. Interim report*, London: Department of Health and Social Care.

Dixon, J. (2015) 'Treatment, deterrence or labelling: Mentally disordered offenders' perspectives on social control', *Sociology of Health and Illness*, 37(8), 1299–1313.

Dominelli, I. (1984) 'Differential justice: Domestic labour, community service and female offenders', *Probation Journal*, 31(3): 100–103.

Douglas, M. (1992) *Risk and blame: Essays in cultural theory*, London: Routledge.

Douglas, T., Pugh, J., Singh, I., Savulescu, J. and Fazel, S. (2017) 'Risk assessment tools in criminal justice and forensic psychiatry: The need for better data', *European Psychiatry*, 42: 134–137.

Duggan, C. (2008) 'Focusing on treatment: The main interventions and their implications' in Soothill, K., Rogers, P. and Dolan, M. (eds.) *Handbook of forensic mental health*, Cullompton: Willan Publishing.

Duggan, C. (2009) 'Foreword' in McMurran, M., Khalifa, N. and Gibbon, S. (2009) *Forensic mental health*, Cullompton: Willan Publishing.

Durcan, G. (2016) *Mental health and criminal justice: Views from consultations across England and Wales*, London: Centre for Mental Health.

Durcan, G., Stubbs, J. and Boardman, J. (2017) *Immigration removal centres in England: A mental health needs analysis*, London: Centre for Mental Health.

Durcan, G., Zlotowitz, S. and Stubbs, J. (2017) *Meeting us where we're at: Learning from INTEGRATE's work with excluded young people*, London: Centre for Mental Health.

Edens, J., Petrilla, J. and Buffington-Vollum, J. (2001) 'Psychopathy and the death penalty: Can the Psychopathy Checklist-Revised identity offenders who represent "a continuing threat to society"?', *Journal of Psychiatry and Law*, 29(4): 433–481.

Epstein, R. (2014) *Mothers in prison: The sentencing of mothers and the rights of the child*, London: Howard League.

Fallon, P., Bluglass, R., Edwards, B. and Daniels, G. (1999) *Report of the committee of inquiry into the personality disorder unit, Ashworth Special Hospital*, London: The Stationery Office.

Fazel, S., Hope, T., O'Donnell, I. and Jacoby, R. (2001) 'Hidden psychiatric morbidity in elderly prisoners', *British Journal of Psychiatry*, 179(6): 535–539.

Fazel, S., Hope, T., O'Donnell, I. and Jacoby, R. (2004) 'Unmet treatment needs of older prisoners: A primary care survey', *Age Ageing*, 33(4): 396–398.

Friel, A., White, T. and Hull, A. (2008) 'Posttraumatic stress disorder and criminal responsibility', *Journal of Forensic Psychiatry and Psychology*, 19(1): 64–85.

Gajwani, R., Parsons, H., Birchwood, M. and Singh, S.P. (2016) 'Ethnicity and detention: Are Black and minority ethnic (BME) groups disproportionately detained under the Mental Health Act 2007?', *Social Psychiatry and Psychiatric Epidemiology*, 51(5): 703–711.

Gelsthorpe, L. and Sharpe, G. (2015) 'Women and sentencing: Challenges and choices' in Roberts, J. (ed.) *Exploring sentencing practice in England and Wales*, Basingstoke: Palgrave Macmillan.

General Medical Council (GMC) (2013) *Good medical practice: Guidance for doctors – The duties of a doctor*, London: General Medical Council.

George, S. (1998) 'More than a pound of flesh: A patient's perspective' in Mason, T. and Mercer, D. (eds.) *Critical perspectives in forensic care*, Basingstoke: Macmillan Press Ltd.

Greig, D. (2002) *Neither bad nor mad: The competing discourses of psychiatry, law and politics*, London: Jessica Kingsley Publishers.

Griffiths, L. (2001) 'Categorising to exclude: The discursive construction of cases in community mental health teams', *Sociology of Health and Illness*, 23(5): 678–700.

Gunn, J. (2006) 'Abuse of psychiatry', *Criminal Behaviour and Mental Health*, 16: 77–86.

Haines, A., Lane, S., McGuire, G. Perkins, E. and Whittington, T. (2014) 'Offending outcomes of mental health youth diversion pilot scheme in England', *Criminal Behaviour and Mental Health*, 25(1): 126–140.

Hales, H., Dixon, A., Newton, Z. and Bartlett, A. (2016) 'Assaults by mentally disordered offenders in prison: Equity and equivalence', *Bioethical Inquiry*, 13: 317–326.

Hannigan, B. and Allen, D. (2010) 'Giving a fig about roles: Policy, context and work in community mental health care', *Journal of Psychiatric and Mental Health Nursing*, 18(1): 1–8.

Hare, R. (1998) 'Psychopaths and their nature', in Millon, T., Simonsen, E., Birkett-Smith, M. and Davis, R. (eds.) *Psychopathy: Anti-social, criminal and violent behaviour*, New York: The Guildford Press.

Harrington, R. and Bailey, S. (2005) *Mental health needs and effectiveness of provision for young people in the youth justice system*, London: Youth Justice Board.

Harris, R. (1999) 'Mental disorder and social order: Underlying themes in crime management' in Webb, D. and Harris, R. (eds.) *Mentally disordered offenders: Managing people nobody owns*, London: Routledge.

Harris, T. (2015) *The Harris review: Changing prisons, saving lives. Report of the independent review into self inflicted deaths in custody of 18–24 year olds*, London: Her Majesty's Stationery Office.

Harrison, K. (2011) *Dangerousness, risk and the governance of serious sexual and violent offenders*, Abingdon: Routledge.

Heath, R.A. and Priest, H.M. (2016) 'Examining experiences of transition, instability and coping for young offenders in the community: A qualitative analysis', *Clinical Child Psychology and Psychiatry*, 21(2): 224–239.

Hedderman, C. and Gelsthorpe, L. (1997) *Understanding the sentencing of women. Home Office Research Study 170*, London: Home Office.

Her Majesty's (HM) Inspectorate of Probation (2006) *An independent review of a Serious Further Offence case: Anthony Rice*, London: HM Inspectorate of Probation.

Her Majesty's (HM) Inspectorate of Probation (2017) *Probation hostels' (Approved Premises) contribution to public protection, rehabilitation and resettlement*, London: HM Inspectorate of Probation.

Her Majesty's Prison and Probation Service (HMPPS) (2018) *Youth custody data, September 2018*, London: HMPPS.

Hewitt, J. and Coffey, M. (2005) 'Therapeutic working relationships with people with schizophrenia: Literature review', *Journal of Advanced Nursing*, 52(5): 561–570.

Hickson, F., Davey, C., Reid, D., Weatherburn, P. and Bourne, A. (2017) 'Mental health inequalities among gay and bisexual men in England, Scotland and Wales: A large community-based cross-sectional survey', *Journal of Public Health*, 39(2): 266–273.

Hill, S.A., Mitchell, P. and Leipold, A. (2017) 'Transfers of mentally disordered adolescents from custodial settings to psychiatric hospital in England and Wales 2004–2014', *Journal of Forensic Psychiatry and Psychology*, 28(1): 1–9.

Holloway, F. (2002) 'Mentally disordered offenders and the community mental health team' in Buchanan, A. (ed.) *Care of the mentally disordered offender in the community*, Oxford: Oxford University Press.

Holloway, F. and Davies, T. (2017) 'The Community Mental Health Team and the mentally disordered offender' in Buchanan, A. and Wootton, L. (eds.) *Care of the mentally disordered offender in the community (Second edition)*, Oxford: Oxford University Press.

Home Office (2007) *The Corston report: A report by Baroness Jean Corston of a review of women with particular vulnerabilities in the criminal justice system*, London: Home Office.

Hudson, B. (2003) *Justice in the risk society*, London: Sage.

Jasper, L. (2017) 'Those who failed Sarah Reed must be held to account', *The Guardian*, 24 July 2017. Available from: www.theguardian.com/commentis-free/2017/jul/24/sarah-reed-death-avoidable-mental-illness-holloway-prison [Last accessed 12 August 2018].

Johnstone, L. and Dallos, R. (2014) *Formulation in psychology and psychotherapy: Making sense of people's problems*, London: Routledge.

Kaltiala-Heino, R., Laippala, P. and Salokangas, R.K. (1997) 'Impact of coercion on treatment outcome', *International Journal of Law and Psychiatry*, 20(3): 311–322.

Kemshall, H. (2008) *Understanding the community management of high-risk offenders*, Maidenhead: Open University Press.

Kemshall, H., Wood, J., Mackenzie, G., Bailey, R. and Yates, J. (2005) *Strengthening multi-agency public protection arrangements (MAPPA)*, London: Home Office.

Keown, P., Murphy, H., McKenna, D. and McKinnon, I. (2018) 'Changes in the use of the Mental Health Act 1983 in England 1984/85 to 2015/16', *British Journal of Psychiatry*, 213(4): 295–299.

Kitzinger, J. (2004) *Framing abuse: Media influence and public understanding of sexual violence against children*, London: Pluto Press.

Klassen, A.L. (2017) 'Spinning the revolving door: The governance of non-compliant psychiatric subjects on community treatment orders', *Theoretical Criminology*, 21(3): 361–379.

Kurtz, A. and Jeffcote, N. (2011) '"Everything contradicts in your mind": A qualitative study of forensic mental health staff in two contrasting services', *Criminal Behaviour and Mental Health*, 21(4): 245–258.

Lader, D., Singleton, N. and Meltzer, H. (2000) *Psychiatric morbidity among young offenders in England and Wales*, London: Office for National Statistics.

Lammy, D. (2017) *The Lammy review: An independent review into the treatment of, and outcomes for, Black, Asian and Minority Ethnic individuals in the criminal justice system*, London: Ministry of Justice.

Lewis, G. and Appleby, L. (1988) 'Personality disorder: The patients psychiatrists dislike', *British Journal of Psychiatry*, 153(1): 44–49.

Light, M., Grant, E. and Hopkins, K. (2013) *Gender differences in the substance misuse and mental health amongst prisoners: Results from the Surveying Prisoner Crime Reduction (SPCR) longitudinal cohort study of prisoners*, London: Ministry of Justice.

Logan, C. and Taylor, J.L. (2017) 'Working with personality disordered women in secure care: The challenge of gender-based service delivery', *Journal of Forensic Psychiatry and Psychology*, 28(2): 242–256.

Long, C.G., Fulton, B. and Hollin, C.R. (2008) 'The development of a 'best practice' service for women in a medium-secure psychiatric setting: Treatment components and evaluation', *Clinical Psychology and Psychotherapy*, 15(5): 304–319.

MacDonald, M. (2013) 'Women prisoners, mental health, violence and abuse', *International Journal of Law and Psychiatry*, 36: 293–303.

MacInnes, D., Courtney, H., Flanagan, T., Bressington, D. and Beer, D. (2014) 'A cross sectional survey examining the association between therapeutic relationships and service user satisfaction in forensic mental health setting', *BMC Research Notes*, 7: 657.

McBride, R. (2017) 'On the advancement of therapeutic penality: Therapeutic authority, personality science and the therapeutic community', *Sociology of Health and Illness*, 39(7): 1258–1272.

McCann, E. and Sharek, D. (2014) 'Survey of lesbian, gay, bisexual, and transgender people's experiences of mental health services in Ireland', *International Journal of Mental Health Nursing*, 23(2): 118–127.

McDonald, R., Furtado, V. and Völlm, B. (2016) 'Managing madness, murderers and paedophiles: Understanding change in the field of English forensic psychiatry', *Social Science and Medicine*, 164: 12–18.

McGuire, J. (2002) 'Multiple agencies with diverse goals' in Buchanan, A. (ed.) *Care of the mentally disordered offender in the community*, Oxford: Oxford University Press.

McGuire, J. (2016) 'Interventions and outcomes: Accumulating evidence' in Winstone, J. (ed.) *Mental health, crime and criminal justice*, Basingstoke: Palgrave Macmillan.

McMurran, M., Khalifa, N. and Gibbon, S. (2009) *Forensic mental health*, Cullompton: Willan Publishing.

McMurran, M. and Theodosi, E. (2007) 'Is treatment non-completion associated with increased reconviction over no treatment', *Psychology, Crime and Law*, 13(4): 333–343.

Maier, G. (1990) 'Psychopathic disorders: Beyond counter-transference', *Current Opinion in Psychiatry*, 3(6): 766–769.

Marti, I., Hostettler, U. and Richter, M. (2017) 'End of life in high-security prisons in Switzerland: Overlapping and blurring of "care" and "custody" as institutional logics', *Journal of Correctional Health Care*, 23(1): 32–42.

Maschi, T. Suftin, S. and O' Connell, B. (2012) 'Aging, mental health, and the criminal justice system: A content analysis of the literature', *Journal of Forensic Social Work*, 2(2–3): 162–185.

Mental Health Taskforce (2016) *The five year forward view for mental health*, London: Mental Health Taskforce.

Ministry of Justice (2016) *Black, Asian and Minority Ethnic disproportionality in the criminal justice system in England and Wales*, London: Ministry of Justice.

Ministry of Justice (2017) *Offender management statistics quarterly: January to March 2017*, London: Ministry of Justice.

Ministry of Justice (2018) *Female offender strategy*, London: Ministry of Justice.

Molodynski, A., Rugkasa, J. and Burns, T. (2010) 'Coercion and compulsion into community mental health care', *British Medical Bulletin*, 95(1): 105–119.

Monahan, J., Redlich, A.D., Swanson, J., Robbins, P.C., Appelbaum, P.S., Petrila, J., Steadman, H.J., Swartz, M., Angell, B. and McNiel, D.E. (2005) 'Use of leverage to improve adherence to psychiatric treatment in the community', *Psychiatric Services*, 56(1): 37–44.

Morgan, C., Mallett, R., Hutchinson, G., Bagalkote, H., Morgan, K., Fearon, P., Dazzan, P., Boydell, J., Mckenzie, K., Harrison, G., Murray, R., Jones, P., Craig, T. and Leff, J. (2005) 'Pathways to care and ethnicity. 2: Source of referral and help-seeking: Report from the AeSOP study', *British Journal of Psychiatry*, 186(4): 290–296.

Mueser, K.T., Rosenberg, S.D., Goodman, L.A. and Trumbetta, S.L. (2002) 'Trauma, PTSD, and the course of severe mental illness: An interactive model', *Schizophrenia Research*, 53(1–2): 123–143.

Mullen, P. (2000) 'Forensic mental health', *British Journal of Psychiatry*, 176: 307–311.

Mullen, P. (2002) 'Introduction' in Buchanan, A. (ed.) *Care of the mentally disordered offender in the community*, Oxford: Oxford University Press.

NACRO (2001) *Youth offending teams, race and justice: After the watershed (Part one)*, London: NACRO.

NACRO (2009) *Information needs of women in prison with mental health issues*, London: NACRO.

National Confidential Inquiry into Suicide and Safety in Mental Health (NCISH) (2018) *National confidential inquiry into suicide and safety in mental health annual report 2018*, Manchester: NCISH.

National Health Service (NHS) Digital (2018) *Mental Health Act statistics, Annual figures England, 2017–18*, London: NHS Digital.

National Health Service (NHS) England (2018) *Service specification: Medium secure mental health services*, London: NHS England.

National Health Service (NHS) London (2006) *Report of the independent inquiry into the care and treatment of John Barrett*, London: NHS London.

National Institute for Mental Health England (NIMHE) (2003a) *Inside outside: Improving mental health services for black and minority ethnic communities in England*, London: NIMHE.

National Institute for Mental Health in England (NIMHE) (2003b) *Personality disorder – No longer a diagnosis of exclusion. Policy implementation guidance for development of services for people with personality disorder*, London: NIMHE.

Newton-Howes, G. (2010) 'Coercion in psychiatric care: Where are we now, what do we know, where do we go?', *The Psychiatrist*, 34(6): 217–220.

Nic, A.B., Xanthopoulou, P., Black, G., Michie, S., Pashayan, N. and Raine, R. (2016) 'Multidisciplinary team meetings in community mental health: A systematic review of their functions', *Mental Health Review Journal*, 21(2): 119–140.

Norfolk, Suffolk and Cambridgeshire Strategic Health Authority (2003) *Independent Inquiry into the death of David Bennett*. Available from: http://image. guardian.co.uk/sys-files/Society/documents/2004/02/12/Bennett.pdf [Last accessed 21 April 2017].

Office of the Children's Commissioner for England (2011) *I think I must have been born bad: Emotional well-being and mental health of children and young people in the youth justice system*, London: Office of the Children's Commissioner for England.

Oosterhuis, H. and Loughnan, A. (2014) 'Madness and crime: Historical perspectives on forensic psychiatry', *International Journal of Law and Psychiatry*, 37: 1–16.

Parker, E. (1985) 'The development of secure provision' in Gostin, L. (ed.) *A review of special services for the mentally ill and mentally handicapped in England and Wales*, London: Tavistock.

Peay, J. (2011) *Mental health and crime*, Abingdon: Routledge.

Peay, J. (2017) 'Mental health, mental disabilities and crime' in Liebling, A., Maruna, S. and McAra, L. (eds.) *The Oxford handbook of criminology (Sixth edition)*, Oxford: Oxford University Press.

Pescosolido, B.A., Gardner, C.B. and Lubell, K.M. (1998) 'How people get into mental health services: Stories of choice, coercion and "muddling through" from "first-timers"', *Social Science and Medicine*, 46(2): 275–286.

Peto, L.M., Dent, M., Griffin, M. and Hindley, N. (2015) 'Community-based forensic child and adolescent services in England, Scotland and Wales: A national mapping exercise', *Journal of Forensic Psychiatry and Psychology*, 26(3): 283–296.

Petrillo, M. (2016) '"It made my mind unwell": Trauma-informed approaches to the mental health needs of women in the criminal justice system' in Winstone, J. (ed.) *Mental health, crime and criminal justice*, Basingstoke: Palgrave Macmillan.

Pickersgill, M. (2012) 'Standardising antisocial personality disorder: The social shaping of a psychiatric terminology', *Sociology of Health and Illness*, 34(4): 544–559.

Player, E. (2017) 'The offender personality disorder pathway and its implications for women prisoners in England and Wales', *Punishment and Society*, 19(5): 1–22.

Prins, H. (2016) *Offenders, deviants or patients? An introduction to clinical criminology*, London: Routledge.

Prins, H., Blacker-Holst, T., Francis, E. and Keitch, I. (1993) *Report of the committee of inquiry into the death in Broadmoor hospital of Orville Blackwood and a review of the deaths of two other Afro Caribbean patients. Big, black and dangerous*, London: Special Hospitals Service Authority.

Prins, S.J., Osher, F.C., Steadman, H.J., Clark Robbins, P. and Case, B. (2012) 'Exploring racial disparities in the brief jail mental health screen', *Criminal Justice and Behavior*, 39: 635–645.

Prisons and Probation Ombudsman (PPO) (2016) *Learning from PPO investigations: Prisoner mental health*, London: PPO.

Prison Reform Trust (2017) *Counted out: Black, Asian and minority ethnic women in the criminal justice system*, London: Prison Reform Trust.

Public Health England (PHE) (2016) *Rapid review of evidence of the impact on health outcomes of NHS commissioned health services for people in secure and detained settings to inform future health interventions and prioritisation in England*, London: PHE.

Public Health England (PHE) (2018) *Gender specific standards to improve health and wellbeing for women in prison in England*, London: PHE.

Pycroft, A. and Green, A. (2016) 'Challenging the cultural determinants of dual diagnosis in the criminal justice system' in Winstone, J. (ed.) *Mental health, crime and criminal justice*, Basingstoke: Palgrave Macmillan.

Rabiee, F. and Smith, P. (2014) 'Understanding mental health and experience of accessing services in African and African Caribbean users and carers in Birmingham, UK', *Journal of Diversity and Ethnicity in Health and Care*, 11: 125–134.

RAWorg (2010) *The end of delivering race equality? Perspectives of frontline workers and service-users from racialised groups*, London: Mind.

Rice, M.E., Harris, G.T. and Cornier, C.A. (1992) 'An evaluation of a maximum security therapeutic community for psychopaths and other mentally disordered offenders', *Law and Human Behaviour*, 16(4): 399–412.

Roberts, Z. (1994) 'The organisation of work: Contributions from open systems theory' in Obholzer, A. and Roberts, V. (eds.) *The unconscious at work*, London: Routledge.

Robertson, M. and Walter, G. (2008) 'Many faces of the dual-role dilemma in psychiatric ethics', *Australian and New Zealand Journal of Psychiatry*, 42(3): 228–235.

Robertson, P., Barnao, M. and Ward, T. (2011) 'Rehabilitation frameworks in forensic mental health', *Aggression and Violent Behaviour*, 16(6): 472–484.

Robinson, D.N. (1996) *Wild beasts and idle humours: The insanity defense from antiquity to the present*, Harvard: Harvard University Press.

Rose, N. (1996) 'Psychiatry as a political science: Advanced liberalism and the administration of risk', *History of the Human Sciences*, 9(2): 1–23.

Royal College of Psychiatrists (2015) *Standards for prison mental health services*, London: Royal College of Psychiatrists.

Rugkåsa, J., Molodynski, A. and Burns, T. (2016) 'Introduction' in Molodynski, A., Rugkåsa, J. and Burns, T. (eds.) *Coercion in community mental health care*, Oxford: Oxford University Press.

Sainsbury Centre for Mental Health (2010) *Blurring the boundaries: The convergence of mental health policy, legislation, systems and practice*, London: Sainsbury Centre for Mental Health.

Semlyen, J., King, M., Varney, J. and Hagger-Johnson, G. (2016) 'Sexual orientation and symptoms of common mental disorder or low wellbeing: Combined meta-analysis of 12 UK population health surveys', *BMC Psychiatry*, 16: 67.

Sen, P., Exworthy, T. and Forrester, A. (2014) 'Mental health care for foreign national prisoners in England and Wales', *Journal of Mental Health*, 23(6): 333–339.

Sewell, H. and Waterhouse, S. (2012) *Making progress on race equality in mental health*, London: Mental Health Network NHS Confederation.

Shaw, J., Higgins, C. and Quartey, C. (2017) 'The impact of collaborative case formulation with high risk offenders with personality disorder', *Journal of Forensic Psychiatry and Psychology*, 28(6): 777–789.

Shaw, S. (2016) *Review into the welfare in detention of vulnerable persons*, London: Her Majesty's Stationery Office.

Sim, J. (1990) *Medical power in prisons: The prison medical service in England 1774–1989*, Buckingham: Open University Press.

Sizmur, S. and McCulloch, A. (2016) 'Differences in treatment approach between ethnic groups', *The Mental Health Review*, 21(2): 73–84.

Smart, C. (1976) *Women, crime and criminology*, London: Routledge.

Smith, E. (2010) 'Care versus custody: Nursing in the prison service', *Practice Nurse*, 40, 33–35.

Social Exclusion Unit (2002) *Reducing re-offending by ex-prisoners*, London: Social Exclusion Unit.

Southwark Coroner's Court (2012) *Inquisition at Southwark Coroner's Court, Jury's narrative verdict*, London: Southwark Coroner's Court. www.gardencourtchambers. co.uk/wp-content/uploads/old_site/File/Inquisition-for-Mr-Rigg.pdf

Spandler, H. and Calton, T. (2009) 'Psychosis and human rights: Conflicts in mental health policy and practice', *Social Policy and Society*, 8(2): 245–256.

Sparr, L.F. and Atkinson, R.M. (1986) 'Posttraumatic stress disorder as an insanity defense: Medicolegal quicksand', *American Journal of Psychiatry*, 143(5): 608–612.

Stuckenberg, C. (2016) 'Comparing legal approaches: Mental disorders as grounds for excluding criminal responsibility', *Bergen Journal of Criminal Law and Criminal Justice*, 4(1): 48–64.

Szmulker, G. (2009) 'Ethics in community psychiatry' in Bloch, S., Chodoff, P. and Green, S.A. (eds.) *Psychiatric ethics*, Oxford: Oxford University Press.

Timmermans, S. and Gabe, J. (2003) 'Introduction: Connecting criminology and the sociology of health and illness' in Timmermans, S. and Gabe, J. (eds.) *Partners in health, partners in crime*, Oxford: Blackwell Publishing.

Trebilcock, J. (2009) *Journeys through managing the unknowable: Making decisions about dangerous patients and prisoners with severe personality disorder*, PhD thesis, Keele University.

Trebilcock, J. and Weaver, T. (2012) '"Everybody knows the prisoner is going nowhere": Parole Board (PB) members' views about the conduct and outcome of PB reviews with Dangerous and Severe Personality Disorder (DSPD) prisoners', *International Journal of Criminology and Sociology*, 1: 141–150.

Trebilcock, J. and Worrall, A. (2018) 'The importance of throughcare and resettlement for working with violent and sexual offenders' in Ireland, J.L., Ireland, C.A. and Birch, P. (eds.) *Violent and sexual offenders: Assessment, treatment and management*, London: Routledge.

Turner, M., Payne, S. and Barbarachild, Z. (2011) 'Care or custody? An evaluation of palliative care in prisons in North West England', *Palliative Medicine*, 25(4): 370–377.

van Voren, R. (2014) 'Is there a resumption of political psychiatry in the former Soviet Union?', *International Psychiatry*, 11(3): 73–74.

Völlm, B.A., Clarke, M., Herrando, V.T., Seppänen, A.O., Gosek, P/. Heitzman, J. and Bulten, E. (2018) 'European Psychiatric Association (EPA) guidance on forensic psychiatry: Evidence based assessment and treatment of mentally disordered offenders', *European Psychiatry*, 51: 58–73.

Vossler, A., Havard, C., Pike, G., Barker, M. and Raabe, B. (2017) 'Introduction' in Vossler, A., Havard, C., Pike, G., Barker, M. and Raabe, B. (eds.) *Mad or bad? A critical approach to counselling and forensic psychology*, London: Sage.

Ward, T. (2013) 'Addressing the dual relationship problem in forensic and correctional practice', *Aggression and Behavior*, 18(1): 92–100.

Warner, J. and Gabe, J. (2004) 'Risk and liminality in mental health social work', *Health, Risk and Society*, 6(4): 387–399.

Webb, D. and Harris, R. (1999) 'Introduction' in Webb, D. and Harris, R. (eds.) *Mentally disordered offenders: Managing people nobody owns*, London: Routledge.

West, M., Alimo-Metcalfe, B., Dawson, J., El Ansari, W., Glasby, J., Hardy, G., Hartley, G., Lyubovnikova, J., Middleton, H. and Naylor, P. (2012) *Effectiveness of Multi-Professional Team Working (MPTW) in mental health care: Final report*, Southampton: NIHR Service Delivery and Organisation Programme, Southampton.

World Health Organization (WHO) (2009) *Women's health in prison: Correcting gender inequity in prison health*, Geneva, Switzerland: WHO.

Wright, N., Jordan, M. and Kane, E. (2014) 'Mental health/illness and prisons as place: Frontline clinicians' perspectives of mental health work in a penal setting', *Health and Place*, 29: 179–185.

Yamashita, M., Forchuk, C. and Mound, B. (2004) 'Nurse case management: Negotiating care together within a developing relationship', *Perspectives in Psychiatric Care*, 41(2): 62–70.

Zedner, L. (1991) *Women, crime and custody in Victorian England*, Oxford: Clarendon Press.

Zinger, I. and Forth, A. (1998) 'Psychopathy and Canadian criminal proceedings: The potential for human rights abuses' *Canadian Journal of Criminology*, 40(3): 237–276.

INDEX

Note: **Bold** page numbers refer to tables and page numbers followed by "n" denote endnotes.